THE CAMBRIDGE COMPANION TO AMERICAN LITERATURE OF THE 1930S

This *Companion* offers a compelling survey of American literature in the 1930s. These thirteen new essays by accomplished scholars in the field provide reexaminations of crucial trends in the decade: the rise of the proletarian novel; the intersection of radical politics and experimental aesthetics; the documentary turn; the rise of left-wing theaters; popular fictional genres; the impact of Marxist thought on African-American historical writing; and the relation of modernist prose to mass entertainment. Placing such issues in their political and economic contexts, this *Companion* constitutes an excellent introduction to a vital area of critical and scholarly inquiry. This collection also functions as a valuable reference guide to Depression-era cultural practice, furnishing readers with a chronology of important historical events in the decade and crucial publication dates, as well as a wide-ranging bibliography for those interested in reading further into the field.

WILLIAM SOLOMON is Professor of English at the University at Buffalo. He is the author of *Literature, Amusement and Technology in the Great Depression* (Cambridge, 2002) and *Slapstick Modernism: Chaplin to Kerouac to Iggy Pop* (2016). He has published numerous articles on the intersection of politics, American literature, popular culture, and film. These include "Politics and Rhetoric in the Novel in the 1930s" in *American Literature* (1996); "Wound Culture and James Agee" in *Arizona Quarterly* (2002); and "The Rhetoric of the Freak Show in Eudora Welty's *A Curtain of Green*" in *Mississippi Quarterly* (2015).

A complete list of books in the series is at the back of this book

THE CAMBRIDGE
COMPANION TO
AMERICAN LITERATURE OF THE 1930S

THE CAMBRIDGE
COMPANION TO

AMERICAN LITERATURE OF THE 1930S

EDITED BY
WILLIAM SOLOMON
University at Buffalo

CAMBRIDGE
UNIVERSITY PRESS

CAMBRIDGE
UNIVERSITY PRESS

University Printing House, Cambridge CB2 8BS, United Kingdom

One Liberty Plaza, 20th Floor, New York, NY 10006, USA

477 Williamstown Road, Port Melbourne, VIC 3207, Australia

314–321, 3rd Floor, Plot 3, Splendor Forum, Jasola District Centre, New Delhi – 110025, India

79 Anson Road, #06–04/06, Singapore 079906

Cambridge University Press is part of the University of Cambridge.

It furthers the University's mission by disseminating knowledge in the pursuit of education, learning, and research at the highest international levels of excellence.

www.cambridge.org
Information on this title: www.cambridge.org/9781108429184
DOI: 10.1017/9781108593892

© Cambridge University Press 2018

First published 2018

Printed in the United States of America by Sheridan Books, Inc.

A catalogue record for this publication is available from the British Library.

Library of Congress Cataloging-in-Publication Data
NAMES: Solomon, William, editor.
TITLE: The Cambridge companion to American literature of the 1930s / editor, William Solomon.
OTHER TITLES: American literature of the 1930s
DESCRIPTION: Cambridge, United Kingdom ; New York, NY : Cambridge University Press, [2018] | Includes bibliographical references.
IDENTIFIERS: LCCN 2018012046 | ISBN 9781108429184 (Hardback) | ISBN 9781108453226 (Paperback)
SUBJECTS: LCSH: American literature–20th century–History and criticism. | Literature and society–United States–History–20th century. | Popular literature–United States–History and criticism. | Depressions in literature.
CLASSIFICATION: LCC PS223 .C35 2018 | DDC 810.9/0052–dc23
LC record available at https://lccn.loc.gov/2018012046

ISBN 978-1-108-42918-4 Hardback
ISBN 978-1-108-45322-6 Paperback

CONTENTS

Table of Contents

ILLUSTRATIONS

CONTRIBUTORS

THOMAS J. FERRARO is Frances Hill Fox Professor of English at Duke University. He is the author of *Ethnic Passages: Literary Immigrants in America* (1993) and *Feeling Italian: The Art of Ethnicity in America* (2005). He is writing on transgression and redemption (the interplay of sex, violence, and sanctity) in the reconfigured canon (Hawthorne, Melville, Frederic, Chopin, James, Fitzgerald, and Cather).

LAURA HAPKE is an independent scholar. She has published extensively on the literary history of US labor and on the cultural production of the Great Depression. Her books include *Labor's Text: The Worker in American Fiction* (2001) and *Labor's Canvas: American Working-Class History and the WPA Art of the 1930s* (2008).

JENNIFER HAYTOCK is Professor of English at the College at Brockport, SUNY. She is the author of *At Home, At War: Domesticity and World War I in American Literature* (2003), *Edith Wharton and the Conversations of Literary Modernism* (2008), and *The Middle Class in the Great Depression: Popular Women's Novels of the 1930s* (2013).

CAREN IRR is Professor of English at Brandeis University. Her books include *The Suburb of Dissent: Cultural Politics in the United States and Canada during the 1930s* (1998) and *Toward the Geopolitical Novel: U.S. Fiction in the 21st Century* (2013). Current research interests include the environmental humanities, the history of childhood, ideology, and representations of capitalism.

RUTH JENNISON is Associate Professor of Modern and Contemporary American Poetry in the English Department at the University of Massachusetts Amherst. She is the author of *The Zukofsky Era: Modernity, Margins, and the Avant-Garde* (2012). Her current book project, "Figurative Capital: American Poetry and the World System," explores the relationship between poetry and uneven capitalist development.

List of Contributors

NATHANIEL MILLS is Assistant Professor of English at the University of Minnesota. He has published *Ragged Revolutionaries: The Lumpenproletariat and African American Marxism in Depression-Era Literature* (2017). His current project is the history of twentieth-century African-American writers' workshops.

CATHERINE MORLEY is Associate Professor of American literature at the University of Leicester. She has published *The Quest for Epic in Contemporary American Fiction* (2009) and *Modern American Literature* (2012). She has coedited *American Thought and Culture in the 21st Century* (2008) and *American Modernism: Cultural Transactions* (2009). In 2016 she published *9–11: Topics in North American Literature*.

PAULA RABINOWITZ is Professor Emerita of English, University of Minnesota, and serves as editor-in-chief of the *Oxford Research Encyclopedia of Literature*. Her most recent monograph is *American Pulp: How Paperbacks Brought Modernism to Main Street* (2014). Her earlier books include *They Must Be Represented: The Politics of Documentary* (1994) and *Black & White & Noir: America's Pulp Modernism* (2002).

ILKA SAAL is Professor of American Literature at the University of Erfurt. She is the author of *New Deal Theater: The Vernacular Tradition in American Political Theater* (2007). She is also the coauthor/editor of *Passionate Politics: The Cultural Work of American Melodrama from the Early Republic to the Present* (2008) and editor-in-chief of *Theatre Annual: A Journal of Theatre and Performance of the Americas*.

WILLIAM SOLOMON is Professor of English at the University at Buffalo. He is the author of *Literature, Amusement, and Technology in the Great Depression* (2002) and *Slapstick Modernism: Chaplin to Kerouac to Iggy Pop* (2014).

MATTHEW STRATTON is Associate Professor of English at the University of California, Davis and author of *The Politics of Irony in American Modernism* (2014). He is currently working on a book manuscript titled "Uncommon Sense: Dictatorship and the Political Imagination of Anglo-American Fiction."

CHRISTOPHER VIALS is Associate Professor of English and Director of American Studies at the University of Connecticut. He is the author of *Realism for the Masses: Aesthetics, Popular Front Pluralism, and U.S. Culture, 1935–1947* (2009) and *Haunted by Hitler: Liberals, the Left, and the Fight Against Fascism in the United States* (2014). He is also the editor of *American Literature in Transition, 1940–1950* (2017).

ALAN M. WALD is the H. Chandler Davis Collegiate Professor of English Literature and American Culture Emeritus at the University of Michigan. Among his eight books on literary radicalism are *The New York Intellectuals: The Rise and Decline of the Anti-Stalinist Left from the 1930s to the 1980s* (1987) and a trilogy: *Exiles from a Future Time: The Forging of the Mid-Twentieth-Century Literary Left* (2002), *Trinity of Passion: The Literary Left and the Antifascist Crusade* (2007), and *American Night: The Literary Left in the Era of the Cold War* (2012).

CHRONOLOGY

1929   Herbert Hoover sworn in as president
        "Happy Days are Here Again" copyrighted
        "Black Thursday" October 24, stock market crash
        William Faulkner, *The Sound and the Fury*
        Nella Larsen, *Passing*
        Thomas Wolfe, *Look Homeward Angel*
        Ernest Hemingway, *A Farewell to Arms*
        John Reed Clubs established
        Claude McKay, *Banjo*

1930   John Dos Passos, *42nd Parallel*
        Edward Dahlberg, *Bottom Dogs*
        Michael Gold, *Jews Without Money*
        Mary Heaton Vorse, *Strike!*
        Katherine Anne Porter, *Flowering Judas and Other Stories*
        Langston Hughes, *Not Without Laughter*
        William Faulkner, *As I Lay Dying*
        Twelve Southerners, *I'll Take My Stand: The South and
            the Agrarian Tradition*
        Hart Crane, *The Bridge*
        Archibald MacLeish, *New Found Land*
        Motion Picture Production Code Adopted
        Dashiell Hammett, *The Maltese Falcon*

1931   Nathanael West, *The Dream Life of Balso Snell*
        Kenneth Burke, *Counter-Statement*
        Scottsboro Boys Trial and Defense Campaign starts
        Pearl S. Buck, *The Good Earth*
        Hunger Marchers turned away at the White House
        Dashiell Hammett, *The Glass Key*
        George Schuyler, *Black No More*

City Lights, directed by Charlie Chaplin
Monkey Business, starring the Marx Brothers
Frankenstein, directed by James Whale
Public Enemy, starring James Cagney

1932   James T. Farrell, *Young Lonigan*
John Dos Passos, *1919*
Edward Dahlberg, *From Flushing to Calvary*
Grace Lumpkin, *To Make My Bread*
William Faulkner, *Light in August*
Erskine Caldwell, *Tobacco Road*
Louis Zukofsky (ed.), *An "Objectivist's" Anthology*
Culture and the Crisis, pamphlet-manifesto issued
Bonus Army camp in Hoovervilles attacked by troops under
    the command of General Douglas MacArthur
Scarface, directed by Howard Hawks
Horse Feathers, starring the Marx Brothers
Hitler appointed chancellor

1933   Jack Conroy, *The Disinherited*
Albert Halper, *Union Square*
Josephine Herbst, *Pity Is Not Enough*
Nathanael West, *Miss Lonelyhearts*
Hervey Allen, *Anthony Adverse*
Gertrude Stein, *The Autobiography of Alice B. Toklas*
Ezra Pound, *A Draft of XXX Cantos*
Prohibition Repealed
Judge Woolsey rules James Joyce's *Ulysses* is not obscene
Inauguration of Franklin Delano Roosevelt
National Industrial Recovery Act passed
Chicago World's Fair begins
Duck Soup, starring the Marx Brothers
King Kong, starring Fay Wray
Gold Diggers of 1933, directed by Busby Berkeley and
    Melvin LeRoy

1934   Robert Cantwell, *Land of Plenty*
James T. Farrell, *The Young Manhood of Studs Lonigan*
Waldo Frank, *The Death and Birth of David Markand*
Edwin Newhouse, *You Can't Sleep Here*
Henry Roth, *Call It Sleep*
Tess Schlesinger, *The Unpossessed*

Lauren Gilfillan, *I Went to Pit College*
Nathanael West, *A Cool Million*
William Rollins Jr., *The Shadow Before*
James M. Cain, *The Postman Always Rings Twice*
F. Scott Fitzgerald, *Tender Is the Night*
William Saroyan, *The Daring Young Man on the Flying Trapeze*
Henry Miller, *Tropic of Cancer*
George Oppen, *Discrete Series*
San Francisco Waterfront (and General) Strike

1935   First American Writers' Congress
Sherwood Anderson, *Puzzled America*
Kenneth Fearing, *Poems*
Nelson Algren, *Somebody in Boots*
Jack Conroy, *A World to Win*
James T. Farrell, *Judgement Day*
Clara Weatherwax, *Marching! Marching!*
Sinclair Lewis, *It Can't Happen Here*
Thomas Wolfe, *Of Time and the River*
Ellen Glasgow, *Vein of Iron*
Horace McCoy, *They Shoot Horses Don't They?*
Zora Neale Hurston, *Mules and Men*
Clifford Odets, *Waiting for Lefty*
Roosevelt signs National Labor Relations Act (NLRB) and forms Works Progress Administration
John L. Lewis establishes the Committee for Industrial Organization (CIO)

1936   Djuna Barnes, *Nightwood*
William Faulkner, *Absalom! Absalom!*
John Steinbeck, *In Dubious Battle*
Arna Bontemps, *Black Thunder*
John Dos Passos, *The Big Money*
Margaret Mitchell, *Gone with the Wind*
Wallace Stevens, *Ideas of Order* and *Owl's Clover*
Genevieve Taggard, *Calling Western Union*
Kenneth Patchen, *Before the Brave*
Spanish Civil War begins
Moscow Trials begin
Modern Times, directed by Charlie Chaplin
Sit-down strike at General Motors by United Autoworkers

Federal Theatre Project's Living Newspaper opens in New York
The Plow That Broke the Plains, directed by Pare Lorenz
You Can't Take It With You, by George S. Kaufman and Moss
    Hart, premiers on Broadway

1937   Erskine Caldwell and Margaret Bourke-White, *You Have Seen
    Their Faces*
Robert and Helen Lynd, *Middletown in Transition*
Louise Bogan, *The Sleeping Fury*
Zora Neale Hurston, *Their Eyes Were Watching God*
Ernest Hemingway, *To Have and Have Not*
Kenneth Roberts, *Northwest Passage*
The Cradle Will Rock, music by Mark Blitzstein
Wallace Stevens, *The Man with the Blue Guitar*
Dust Storm hits West, Midwest, and California
The Memorial Day Massacre in South Chicago
Archibald MacLeish, *The Fall of the City* (radio play)
The Spanish Earth, directed by Joris Ivens
A Star Is Born, directed by William A. Wellman

1938   John Crowe Ransom, *The World's Body*
Louis Adamic, *My America*
Walker Evans, *American Photographs*
Sol Funaroff, *The Spider and the Clock*
Muriel Rukeyser, *U.S. 1*
Kenneth Fearing, *Dead Reckoning*
Richard Wright, *Uncle Tom's Children*
Thornton Wilder, *Our Town*
Establishment of House on Un-American Activities
War of the Worlds, Mercury Theatre broadcast narrated by
    Orson Welles
The River, directed by Pare Lorentz
Germany Annexes Austria

1939   Ruth McKenney, *Industrial Valley*
Federal Writers' Project, *These Are Our Lives*
Nathanael West, *The Day of the Locust*
Kenneth Patchen, *First Will and Testament*
John Steinbeck, *The Grapes of Wrath*
Dalton Trumbo, *Johnny Got His Gun*
Pietro di Donato, *Christ in Concrete*
Henry Miller, *The Tropic of Capricorn*

Raymond Chandler, *The Big Sleep*
Katherine Anne Porter, *Pale Horse, Pale Rider*
Thomas Wolfe, *The Web and the Rock*
The Wizard of Oz, starring Judy Garland
Gone with the Wind, starring Vivien Leigh
The Second World War begins
Nazi-Soviet nonaggression pact signed
Mr. Smith Goes to Washington, starring Jimmy Stewart

1940   *The Great Dictator*, directed by Charlie Chaplin
Richard Wright, *Native Son*
Ernest Hemingway, *For Whom the Bell Tolls*
William Faulkner, *The Hamlet*
Thomas Wolfe, *You Can't Go Home Again*
The Grapes of Wrath, directed by John Ford
Germany begins building Auschwitz

1941   James Agee and Walker Evans, *Let Us Now Praise Famous Men*
Carson McCullers, *The Heart Is a Lonely Hunter*
Edmund Wilson, *To the Finland Station*
William Attaway, *Blood on the Forge*
Budd Schulberg, *What Makes Sammy Run?*
Kenneth Burke, *The Philosophy of Literary Form*
F. O. Matthiessen, *American Renaissance*
Citizen Kane, directed by Orson Welles
The Maltese Falcon, directed by John Huston
Sullivan's Travels, directed by Preston Sturges
The Last Tycoon, F. Scott Fitzgerald

WILLIAM SOLOMON

Introduction

In Thomas Wolfe's posthumously published novel *You Can't Go Home Again* (1940), his autobiographical protagonist, George Weber, reflects on the emotional devastation the recent economic catastrophe in the country has caused. To the character (as well as the novelist), the traumatic effect of the abrupt closing in 1930 of the Citizens Trust Company, a bank in Libya Hill – an imaginary version of the author's North Carolina hometown – and subsequent suicide of the town's mayor dealt a blow that destroyed all sense of happiness within the community. And in this regard it presaged a national calamity. The widespread despair of those who "had lost their life savings," and who now felt "that all hope was gone," constituted "a tragic spectacle the like of which had probably never before been seen in America. But it was a spectacle that was to be repeated over and over again, with local variations, in many another town and city within the next few years."[1] That the boom years during which the townspeople had become intoxicated with the promise of prosperity through "speculation and real estate" were over was indisputable. In the 1920s the "prospect of quick and easy money" had been thrilling, "the possibilities of wealth, luxury, and economic power hitherto undreamed of" seemingly "just lying around waiting for anyone bold enough to seize them." So confident at this time were people "of a golden future" that "no one gave a second thought to the reckless increase in public borrowing. Bond issues involving staggering sums were being constantly 'floated' until the credit structure of the town was built up into a teetering inverted pyramid." Indeed, the sudden end "of this complicated web of frenzied finance" left them "saddled with debts that they could never pay." "Yesterday they could count their paper riches by ten thousands and by millions; today they owned nothing and their wealth had vanished" (346). But for Wolfe the ruin was as much spiritual or existential as it was monetary:

> What happened ... has been described in the learned tomes of the overnight economists as a breakdown of 'the system, the capitalist system.' Yes, it was

that. But it was also … the total disintegration of what, in so many different ways, the lives of all these people had come to be. It went much deeper than the mere obliteration of bank accounts, the extinction of paper profits, and the loss of property. It was the ruin of men who found out, as soon as these symbols of their outward success had been destroyed, that they had nothing left – no inner equivalent from which they might now draw new strength. It was the ruin of men who, discovering not only that their values were false but that they had never had any substance whatsoever, now saw at last the emptiness and hollowness of their lives. (348)

Wolfe's fictive account of the onset of the Great Depression is notable in the emphasis it places on subjective responses to the socioeconomic crisis. Here the impact of the defining event of the era is to negate the convictions to which individuals had previously held. Like the risky financial schemes in which they had overenthusiastically invested, the belief of the town's inhabitants in the meaningfulness of their existence now stands revealed as baseless. Consequently, the task of the writer became to help the nation renew its sense of purpose, to begin again.

Indeed, creative artists and critical intellectuals accepted throughout the 1930s that one of their primary tasks was henceforth to participate in if not guide the ideological recovery of the nation. For many progressively oriented writers and thinkers this led to an active involvement during the first half of the decade in the rise of a proletarian literature. The eccentric stance Kenneth Burke staked out in "Revolutionary Symbolism in America," a paper he delivered at the first American Writers' Congress in 1935, is a related but distinctive case in point. In arguing for a rhetorical shift in radical discourse from the figure of the "worker" to that of the "people," he presciently recognized the power of industrialized entertainment and the mass media to sway their audiences by supplying them with images of what they wanted: a more luxurious lifestyle.[2] Filmmakers in particular know how "to create a maximum desire for commodities consumed under expensive conditions – and Hollywood appeals to the worker mainly by picturing the qualities of life in which this commercially stimulated desire is gratified" (314). To counteract this demand and win adherents to left-wing enterprises would require a degree of psychological insight that had heretofore not been sufficiently integrated into political "propaganda."

A comparable concern with the susceptibility of the masses to emotional manipulation by reactionary forces can be discerned in Richard Wright's work throughout the second half of the Depression era. For instance, in one of the opening scenes of "Cesspool," Jake Jackson, a black postal worker, sits down to breakfast and proceeds to express what we are clearly intended to take as a set of misguided and contradictory allegiances.[3] After reading in the daily newspaper a headline referring to Roosevelt's ambition to eliminate corruption in the financial sector, Jackson claims in opposition that "these old Democrats" are "crazy troublemakers" who simply envy rich and famous "robber barons": "who's going to tell old man Morgan and old man Rockefeller and old man Ford what to do?" [4] But worse than his idealization of such tycoons are the fictive entity's xenophobia and correlative respect for fascist dictators. Upon reading the following headline —"HITLER CALLS ON WORLD TO SMASH JEWS"– the book's confused protagonist reflects on the domestic situation: "That's what's wrong with this country, too many Jews, Dagos, Hunkies, and Mexicans. We colored people would be much better off if they had kept them rascals out" (32). That Wright hopes his readers will overcome such attitudes once they see them in print is obvious. Moreover, despite his inability to secure a publisher for this significantly experimental text, one that drew heavily on the formal innovations of modernist predecessors such as James Joyce and John Dos Passos, Wright maintained his critical focus on the affectively charged state of mind of poorly educated and disenfranchised minorities. Thus in "How Bigger Was Born" (1940), Wright's retrospective account of the genesis of his groundbreaking novel *Native Son* published earlier that year, he explained that the problem he wished to investigate was as much a psychological as a sociological topic. A "dispossessed and disinherited man," the character carries "within him the potentialities of either Communism or Fascism"; consequently, "in looking and feeling for a way out" of his predicament he might just as easily "follow some gaudy, hysterical leader who'll promise rashly to fill the void in him" as he might "come to an understanding with the millions of his kindred fellow workers under trade union or revolutionary guidance."[5] Only "the drift of events in America" will decide the fate of this type of individual, but given "the fear, the hate, the impatience, the sense of exclusion, the ache for violent action," it is certain that he will not become a "supporter of the *status quo*" (447).[6]

The American writer's commitment in the 1930s to registering widespread distress and dissatisfaction with contemporary conditions of existence was frequently presented as a cry coming directly from those in despair. A striking example is William Saroyan's use in the short story "Aspirin is a Member of the N.R.A." of the first person to express powerfully his dismay at the anguish he both personally endures and perceives around him in those struggling like him to survive in the aftermath of the stock market crash. "Everybody was in pain. I was studying the subway and I could see the pain in the faces of everybody." Yet the speaker remains resilient, voicing his determination to "laugh about" the fact that "all of us are riding to death," that "a low fire" "burning" in the soul "is eating its substance slowly."[7]

He then unexpectedly identifies aspirin as "the hero of the story" to the degree that it serves as a viable means of, if not curing, than at least dulling one's awareness of one's mortality: "all of us six million people in New York, swallowing it, day after day. All of us in pain, needing it. Aspirin is an evasion. But so is life. The way we live it. You take aspirin to keep going. It deadens pain. . . . It stifles remembrance, silences weeping" (137). Even more surprisingly, the speaker then seizes ironically upon a radio announcer's assertion that "Aspirin is a member of the N.R.A." For the speaker this is an unintentionally metaphorical formulation of a "truth" about contemporaneous methods of trying to alleviate collective suffering: the pharmaceutical product and the New Deal agency are alike in that both are half measures that do not address the underlying problem (presumably the contradiction of capitalist modes of production). They "make a pretty slick team" but all they do is help "everyone to evade fundamentals ... to keep people going to work." Aspirin is analogous to (and a near palindrome of) the N.R.A. in that both are designed to send "millions of half-dead people to their jobs." They may be "doing a great deal to keep the spirit of the nation from disintegrating"; yet neither is "preventing anything." All they accomplish is the "deadening [of] pain" (138). The shortcomings of the government's strategic intervention, figured as an effort to treat the symptoms rather than the cause of mass sickness, will soon become apparent. Thus, the speaker predicts that when the medicinal remedy stops working, violent uprisings will ensue. "That is when you begin to be mad about the way things are going in this country. . . . That is when, weak as you are, something old and savage and defiant in you comes up bitterly out of your illness and starts to smash things ... destroying cities" (139). Revolutionary rage will result in acts of destructive dissent once the State's method of pain management ceases to be effective.

The impulse to serve as a conduit for the emotive speech of sociopolitically disenfranchised persons informed a considerable portion of the literature produced in the 1930s. The respective titles of Benjamin Appel's *The People Talk: Voices from the Great Depression* (1940) and Richard Wright's *12 Million Black Voices Can't Be Wrong* (1941) indicate the degree to which an appeal to the intimate immediacy of oral discourse structured much of the non-fictional reportage carried out toward the end of the era. Earlier precedents for this approach can be found both in Whittaker Chamber's short story "You Can Make Out their Voices" – published in the March 1931 issue of *The New Masses* – as well as the Hallie Flanagan play based on the story, *You Have Heard Their Voices*, which opened later that same year. Equally telling is the prologue John Dos Passos composed in 1937 for a revised edition of *The 42nd Parallel* (1930) and subsequently attached to the *U.S.A.* trilogy as a whole. In this piece the author remarks that "it was speech that clung to the ears, the link that tingled in the blood" and that ultimately the nation "is the speech of the people."[8] Even more striking is the abrupt shift from third to first person that takes place in "A Country Letter," a section of James Agee's *Let Us Now Praise Famous Men* (1942). Here the author unexpectedly abandons his finely wrought descriptive prose and proceeds to ventriloquize the female members of the tenant farmer family with whom he has been staying in Alabama. It is as a plural (and then a singular) woman that he now tries to convey the confusion and agony of the impoverished subjects of his journalistic inquiry. "In what way were we trapped? where, our mistake? What, where, how, when, what way, might all these things have been different, if only we had done otherwise? If only we might have known."[9] Conversely, Tillie Olsen selected, as the epigraph to the Depression-era novel she was unable to complete at the time, lines from a Walt Whitman poem that in effect convey her sense of sorrow at not being heard. "A muffled sonorous sound, a wailing word is borne through the air for a moment, / Then blank and gone and still, and utterly lost."[10] Appropriately, the only piece of the original manuscript to appear in print in the 1930s did so in the form of a short story about a mining accident titled "The Iron Throat" (1934).[11]

Much has been written about the visually based cognitive imperatives of the vast number of documentary undertakings launched in the second half of the decade, due in large part to the Works Progress Administration's support of the Federal Writers Project. Indeed, at the end of *On Native Ground* (1942), after a chapter dealing with the achievement of William Faulkner and Wolfe, Alfred Kazin reproached what he called this "literature of empiricism" on the grounds that it marked "the failure of so many to discriminate between the pen and camera."[12] For him, books such as *You Have Seen Their Faces* (1937), a collaboration between Erskine Caldwell and the photographer Margaret Bourke-White, were naive due to their attempt to model their verbal component on the representational accuracy or "objective realism" of the mechanical device (387). Yet despite the epistemological limitations he discerned in such enterprises, they indicated to the young literary historian a morally admirable desire on the part of American writers "to assess what could be known and to establish a needed security in the American inheritance," in the hope of serving "the people" and thus coming "to grips with the subject that lay closest at hand – the country" (381). Moreover, from our present vantage point, it is evident that Kazin's canonical survey of the nation's literary past, completed at the end of the Depression era and written with great rhetorical panache, itself stands as one of the most distinguished realizations of the general aspiration on which he was remarking. The essays that make up this Cambridge Companion volume seek to live up to such previous examples of rigorous, thought-provoking critical scholarship. In so doing, they offer us an image of the 1930s as a period during which political and literary ambition combined to produce an enduringly meaningful set of cultural artifacts.

Alan M. Wald's opening chapter on the relevance of the decade for contemporary radicalism challenges us to comprehend it as a rich and variegated archive worth researching in depth. Consequently, he contests earlier interpretive approaches that sought to simplify the object of investigation, and in the process tended to minimize the creative contribution of those who affiliated themselves in heterogeneous ways with left-wing undertakings in the era. For him, attempts to reclaim the period as one that speaks to twenty-first-century concerns must recognize this earlier generation's lucid commitment to struggling in diverse manners against – at home and abroad – economic exploitation, racialized violence, fascist aggression, and colonial domination. The sense of ethical responsibility individuals felt in involving themselves in collective forms of protest should be studied in depth through historical research rather than caricatured as a passing fashion. He thus singles out participation in the Sacco-Vanzetti defense and the signing of the Culture and Crisis manifesto in 1932 as progressive actions that prefigured a sustained series of decisive efforts on the part of artists and intellectuals to intervene in world events. Of particular importance to Wald is the way in which otherwise impressively synthetic accounts of the period tend to overlook or distort the significance of Marxist literary debate at the time. Morris Dickstein's *Dancing in the Dark: A Cultural History of the Great Depression* (2009) is a case in point in that, despite its salutary move away from older approaches that emphasized "the melodrama of disaster and unresolved angry revolt," the recent study embraces a nostalgic tenor that in effect mutes academic inquiry into the contemporaneous pertinence of Depression-era militancy. Correlatively, in an assessment of Michael Denning's magisterial *The Cultural Front: The Laboring of American Culture in the Twentieth Century* (1997), Wald cautions against the writer's relatively indiscriminate utilization of the concept of "social democracy," for such a procedure homogenizes, and in so doing obscures, the disparate and often conflicting positions adopted in the era toward the USSR, toward Stalinism, as well as toward communism.

Matthew Stratton's essay situates theoretical reflection in the 1930s on the relation of aesthetics and politics against a philosophical background that reaches back to antiquity. Beginning with Plato's meditations on the danger of art as mimesis to the state and society, Stratton moves swiftly from Kant's emphasis on disinterest as a precondition for appreciating beauty through

Pater's aestheticism and the subsequent flowering of art for art's sake to fascist appropriations of the spectacle as a means of generating sensorially pleasing images of self destruction. The historical significance of reflection on this topic in the Depression era is a consequence of various critics' determination to elucidate the non-oppositional aspects of the aesthetics/politics nexus. Stratton maps out three areas of thought on this matter. First, conservatively-oriented thinkers such as Paul Elmer More, a leading figure in the rise of the New Humanists, sought to defend a classical aesthetic and traditional values as a bulwark against present-day confusion. Taking the poetry and criticism of T. S. Eliot as a touchstone, Southern Agrarians such as Allen Tate and John Crowe Ransom expressed comparable sentiments in their respective formulations of a reactionary modernism. In sharp contrast, on the Left, figures such as Joseph Freeman, James T. Farrell, and Michael Gold voiced powerful affirmations of the purposefulness of literature, declaring that the time had come for art to embrace its social functionality. In the middle was the liberal aesthetic endorsed by the various New Deal programs and epitomized by John Dewey's pragmatism. In retrospect, the latter's ideas on the embodiment of intellectual labor, his assertion of the need for educational reform through perceptual reorientation, and his valorization of aesthetic experience as representative of experience in general, offer a solid conceptual frame for comprehending the decade-long aspiration to reconcile art and life.

Recent critical scholarship on the 1930s has decisively moved beyond the stereotypical notion that the dominant aesthetic of the period was a "return to realism" and thus a "reaction against the modernist impulse."[13] Indeed, the rise to prominence in literary history of the category of late modernism has illuminated the ongoing investment in formal innovation throughout the interwar years. One of the most significant aspects of this sustained concern with creative originality (or the "new") was a turn within artistic endeavors away from the conventions of narrative fiction toward factual discourse and loose, episodic structures. In effect a rehabilitation of previously minor genres such as autobiography, travel writing, and documentary, this shift in method extended the remarkable achievement of a filmmaker such as Dziga Vertov into the 1930s, whose *Man With a Movie Camera* (1929) demonstrated the feasibility of correlating aesthetic experimentation with left-wing aspiration. Henry Miller's anarchic political inclinations were much different than the Soviet director's revolutionary enthusiasm, yet the 1934 publication (in Paris) of the American writer's *Tropic of Cancer*, and its successor, *Tropic of Capricorn* (1939), showed in striking fashion the value artistically inclined authors were in the process of discovering in a prose that approached everyday life without the mediation of standard novelistic devices such as character and plot. (Agee's *Let Us Now Praise Famous Men* is another example and several chapters below address aspects of his enduringly important accomplishment.) Thomas Wolfe's impulses were in this same autobiographical direction, and it was only Maxwell Perkins's immense editorial labors on Wolfe's massive and disorderly manuscripts that enabled the emerging writer to attain commercial success and critical recognition as a proper novelist.[14] Also relevant in this context are the works of young Jewish-American writers such as Edward Dahlberg (*Bottom Dogs* [1929] and *From Flushing to Calvary* [1932]) and Daniel Fuchs (*Williamsburg Trilogy* [1934–37]. *Summer in Williamsburg*, the first installment of the latter's trilogy, is especially telling, for it is simultaneously a sincere attempt to recreate the lived experience of being a member of a minority community at the time and an epistemologically reflexive meditation on the impossibility of completing this representational task. Instructed by his mentor to "make a laboratory out of" the neighborhood, and told that in order to "discover the reason for people's actions" he would have to "pick Williamsburg to pieces until you have them all spread out before you on your table, a dictionary" through which he must then "[p]ick and discard," "[c]ollect and analyze," the protagonist realizes in the end that the book he had hoped to complete would inevitably "be unfaithful to the whole" (376). "Literature was not reality. That was all there was to it. Writers who said otherwise were fakers, claiming more than they could do. A book was an artificial synthesis."[15]

It is from the perspective of all this that the genealogical link between Depression-era literary undertakings and the postwar intervention of the Beats comes sharply into focus, for the most salient feature of Jack Kerouac's overall output was his commitment to taking his actual experiences as raw material for his often ambitiously stylized prose. (The posthumously published *Visions of Cody* [1972] is a much better reference than *On the Road* [1957] for understanding the experimental energies informing Kerouac's still underappreciated late modernist accomplishment.) A poem such as Allen Ginsberg's "Manhattan Thirties Flash," from the collection *The Fall of America* (1972), helps confirm the memorable status of the decade in the imagination of the generation of American writers who grew up in the period. But E. L. Doctorow's *The Book of Daniel*, published in the preceding year, is even more revealing. Structured in part around the research of a young graduate student composing a dissertation on the trial and execution of his parents in the 1950s for treason, the novel also details the difficult struggle of the increasingly politicized protagonist to come to terms amidst the rise of the counterculture in the 1960s with the legacy of the Depression era. Most importantly, the novel has become a canonical touchstone for the ways in which radical aspiration, the desire to engage in sociopolitical protest, may manifest itself at the practical level of rhetorical technique. The next three chapters of this volume examine the pursuit in the 1930s of this kind of complementarity between progressive political aims and literary inventiveness.

In her essay, Catherine Morley attends to the complexity of the tensions structuring the literary field during the Depression era, exploring the degree to which a concern with formal innovation coexisted with a reliance on traditional narrative strategies in well-known and obscure works from the period. She begins her inquiry with a reassessment of John Steinbeck's *The Grapes of Wrath* (1939), acknowledging its sentimental strains without rejecting the novel as past commentators have on the grounds that it sacrificed aesthetic invention to political immediacy. After isolating the subtly experimental dimensions of Steinbeck's text, Morley shifts her discussion to one of the major proponents in the United States of proletarian realism: Mike Gold. His critical repudiation of avant-garde techniques and melodramatic depiction in *Jews Without Money* (1930) of his early life and eventual conversion to Communism serves as a foil to Pietro di Donato's more aesthetically ambitious handling of similar material in *Christ in Concrete* (1937). Although there is a shared religiosity in the two writers, who also had an immigrant background in common, di Donato's surrealist method of describing events such as a ghastly workplace accident at a construction site distinguish the novel as an expressively forceful instance of modernist artistry. Morley then examines the capacity of a canonical modernist like William Faulkner to assimilate the priorities of late-nineteenth-century regionalists or local colorists into a modernist enterprise. Thus, in *The Sound and the Fury (1929)* and *Absalom! Absalom!* (1936) a preoccupation with the specific temporality of Southern history occurs in conjunction with the use of multiple perspectives, nonlinear narration, and reflexive analyses of the limitations of language as a medium of communication. Lastly, Morley turns to Dos Passos' *U.S.A.* trilogy, which she deems a successful reconciliation of the opposition between modernism and radicalism due to the author's conviction that, as she phrases it, "experimental form *is* political ... experiment is protest."

Similarly, Ruth Jennison argues in her account of avant-garde poetry in the 1930s that literary invention and progressive politics converged throughout the decade. Her initial focus is on the Objectivists, a loosely coordinated movement predicated on among other things the artists' shared antipathy to the commodity form. In reading portions of Louis Zukofsky's long poem "*A*" and George Oppen's *Discrete Series* (1934), Jennison examines the way in which the poets deployed paratactic compositional methods to detail the specificity of contemporary existence in urban environments without ignoring the materiality of language. Lorine Niedecker's *Progression* (1933) then serves as a means of showing how the core principles of Objectivism laid the basis for a feminist intervention aimed at disrupting the reproduction of normative subjectivities. Correlatively, Charles Reznikoff's 1934 prose poem *Testimony* rearranges portions of the juridical record both to register the violently coercive forces that have been required to maintain oppressive regimes in this country and to clear a space for the voices, especially of working-class African Americans, to be heard. Although not officially aligned with the Objectivists, Muriel Rukeyser and Kay Boyle also incorporated documentary artifacts into their anticapitalist and antiracist literary undertakings. In "The Book of the Dead" (1938) and "A Communication to Nancy Cunard" (1937), respectively, the two poets extracted citations taken from legal archives to preserve the speech of victimized miners in West Virginia and the defendants in the "Scottsboro boys" case. Jennison concludes her inquiry with a discussion of Kenneth Fearing's communist inspired yet melancholic turn toward popular culture and Langston Hughes's reliance on African-American vernacular traditions to forge a collective voice. Whereas the former sought via the ironic juxtaposition of contradictory utterances to put readers on guard against the persuasive thrust of the manufactured verbiage swirling around them, the latter, in "Wait," drew on the format of the newspaper to encourage a reading process in which the intersecting determinations of seemingly disparate events could be comprehended.

As Paula Rabinowitz demonstrates, aesthetic experimentation also played a vital role in the plethora of documentary enterprises to which American artists committed themselves in the 1930s. Throughout the period, the impulse to show as powerfully as possible the effects of extreme poverty, and to locate its causes in the greed of the more fortunate, spread across the entire cultural field. It manifested itself in the murals of Diego Rivera, the songs of Woody Guthrie, the poetry of Archibald MacLeish and Muriel Rukeyser, gangster films and Busby Berkeley musicals, as well as plays such as Arthur Arent's *Ethopia* put on by the Living Newspaper of the Federal Theatre Project. Notably, in many such instances, avant-garde tactics of collage and montage served as a means of blurring "the boundaries of form, genre, and media." Still and moving images were particularly crucial in enterprises aimed at depicting the ravages of economic inequality. Rabinowitz surveys several of these, paying close attention to the interaction between writers and filmmakers or photographers in the Depression era. While the importance of the collaboration between James Agee and Walker Evans that produced *Let Us Now Praise Famous Men* is common knowledge, the comparable desire on the part of John Steinbeck to learn as much as he could from Pare Lorentz's cinematic ventures (like *The Fight for Life)* is a less well-established area of inquiry. Thus Rabinowitz traces the impact working with the director had not only on Steinbeck's vision of his task in *The Grapes of Wrath* but also examines in this light his subsequent involvement in the formation of a production team to shoot in Mexico *The Forgotten Village*, a fact-based film dealing with the potentially beneficial effects of integrating modern medicine into traditional modes of healing the sick. Ernest Hemingway's written praise of Luis Quintanilla, whose drawings rendered the devastation wrought by Franco's assault on the people of Spain, offers a final example of the politicized interplay between the visual and the verbal, image and word, in the Depression era.

Next, Ilka Saal's critical survey of Depression-era drama traces the growth and development of an artistically vital and socially relevant theater in this period. The swing to the left of the American stage was more gradual than elsewhere in the cultural field, and Broadway productions in particular resisted this trend, initially preferring to satisfy the carriage trade's taste for light-hearted romantic comedies such as George S. Kaufman and Moss Hart's *You Can't Take it With You* (1936). Meanwhile, amateur troupes like the Worker's Laboratory Theatre took agitation rather than entertainment as their primary goal, performing at rallies and meetings in support of the class struggle. The formation in 1932 of The League of Workers' Theatre provided valuable support to hundreds of such amateur organizations. The militant phase of radical workers' theaters yielded around mid-decade to more moderate approaches. Clifford Odet's *Waiting for Lefty* (1935) is a telling manifestation of the moment of transition in that it made numerous concessions to theatrical convention in order to broaden its appeal to middle-class audiences, employing devices associated with bourgeois realism to meet the demands of a public less predisposed to tolerate the shock aesthetics of the avant-garde. The subsequent establishment of the Federal Theatre Project proved that an experimental and politically engaged theater could flourish in this country – the Living Newspapers inventive address to contemporary topics a striking case in point. Other distinguished FTP productions include in 1936 an adaptation of Sinclair Lewis' *It Can't Happen Here* (1935); T. S. Eliot's *Murder in the Cathedral*; the New York Negro Theatre Unit's all black, "Voodoo" version of *Macbeth*, directed by Orson Welles; and a few years later Marc Blitzstein's musical drama *The Cradle Will Rock*. Saal brings her discussion to a close with an analysis of one of the most profitable shows of the decade, *Pins and Needles* (1939) – a play that began in the drama workshops of the International Ladies' Garments Workers' Union and ended with a command performance at the White House.

The most notorious literary phenomenon of the Depression was undoubtedly the proletarian novel, and condemnation of it and the purportedly naive intellectuals who produced it has frequently functioned as a means to dismiss cultural production in the decade as a whole. In "Literature and Labor," Laura Hapke contests this familiar perspective by demonstrating that at the level of theme, composition, and ideological outlook the texts in question were more unorthodox than previous interpreters have acknowledged. Her first topic is the "bottom dog" novels of writers such as Tom Kromer, Edward Dahlberg, Nelson Algren, and Edward Anderson. Focused on the lives of protagonists desperate to survive, these books do not make the attainment of a proper working-class consciousness the crux of their respective narratives. Rather, these picaresque works follow in episodic fashion the adventures of characters whose conditions of existence in the world are closer to that of the lumpenproletariat and who remain ambivalent about their relationship to the labor movement. Correlatively, Jack Conroy's *The Disinherited* (1932) and Robert Cantwell's *The Land of Plenty* (1934), in pragmatically attending to the myriad obstacles to revolutionary upheaval in the present, pushed back against the notion of the impassioned rebel worker as blindly devoted to a cause sure to succeed. Utopian aspirations are also necessarily set to the side in one of the few proletarian novels written by an African American: William Attaway's *Blood on the Forge*. Published in 1941, Attaway's novel exposes the way in which fostering racial animosity within the working class serves the interests of factory owners. Unrecognized by the union, the black characters end up caught in the middle of the violent clash between capital and labor. Next, Hapke turns to the effort of Meridel Le Sueur in her essays and short fiction to help overcome the organized Left's relative neglect at the time of the specificity of women's issues, especially with regard to institutionalized brutality directed at unwed mothers. Hapke completes her chapter with a reading of Ruth McKenney's *Industrial Valley* (1939), a generic hybrid that mixes factual and fictive, journalistic and imaginative discourse in telling the story of the triumphant rise of mass unionism during the Akron Rubber Strike of 1936.

In his memoir, Alfred Kazin asserts that more "than the age of the ideologue, of the literary revolutionary and the 'proletarian' novelist," the 1930s "were the age of the plebes – of writers from the working class, the lower class, the immigrant class."[16] Yet in taking up the rise of minority literatures in the decade, Thomas J. Ferraro deemphasizes the idea of a break or the emergence of the "new" in order to situate the work of Depression-era writers in a tradition of dissent and irony extending far back into the literary past. Coining (by way of Leslie Fiedler and Nina Baym) the term "melodramas of beset sexuality," Ferraro details the way in which in the period the "aesthetic force of religio-ethnic difference" governed the canonical problem in American literature of the dialectical relation of transgression and redemption. Thus, on the threshold of the period, Nella Larsen, Claude

McKay, and George Schuyler addressed from an expressly African-American perspective the entanglement of sex and race in this country, previously an issue of major importance to F. Scott Fitzgerald, Willa Cather, and Ernest Hemingway. Similarly, Henry Roth and Pietro di Donato put the mythic American thematics of love and death into "poorer and greasier" hands. Moreover, in the work of both authors, the modernist "stream of consciousness" technique was brought to bear on youthful experiences of familial and religious crises in ghetto surroundings. For Ferraro, Faulkner's *Absalom! Absalom!* (1936) and Zora Neale Hurston's *Their Eyes Were Watching God* (1937) confirm the centrality of martyr-tales of forbidden love in our literary heritage, while simultaneously relocating these affairs outside the realm of the Anglo-American upper classes.

The next two chapters address the specificity of minority writing in the period. To begin with, Christopher Vials delineates the historical and cultural sites from which ethnic/proletarian literature emerged. Deploying Jodi Melamed's concept of "race radical texts," Vials distinguishes between materials that pursue a "liberal multicultural" agenda and those that sought to expose interracial conflicts as a structural consequence of capitalist economics. Depression-era fiction as exemplified by the stories collected in Richard Wright's *Uncle Tom's Children* (1938), H. T. Tsiang's *And China Has Hands* (1937), and Gold's *Jews Without Money* tended to fall into the latter category. Indeed, throughout the decade, authors from particular ethnic groups told working-class tales in the hope of weaving a new class-conscious, national fabric out of the threads of personal experience. Complementing the legislative and organizational goals of the Popular Front, these writers struggled alongside many others to forge a working-class unity across ethnic and racial lines. Correlatively, Nathaniel Mills explains the profound influence of an emerging historical consciousness on black thought and expression during the Depression. As he shows, in the 1930s, critics, novelists, and historians became acutely aware of the role of the past in conditioning the present and as a potential resource for mass political action aimed at a better future. Drawing a parallel between the contemporaneous literary theory of Georg Lukács and the practice of figures such as Ralph Ellison, Margaret Walker, W. E. B. Du Bois and C. L. R. James, Mills describes the ways in which African Americans utilized Marxist ideas to reevaluate black history and produce new accounts of black political agency. Portraying fictive characters or real individuals as shaped by historical events and processes served as a means of contesting racial and economic oppression. Correlatively, black writers accepted the task of challenging the distortions of white historiographers with racist agendas. What was required in this regard was the production of experience-based narrative accounts of the way the transition from the feudal South to the capitalist North had been lived by African Americans. To illustrate his claim that the ethical and political priorities of black writers in the period led them to highlight the relevance of the past for the emancipatory needs of the present, Mills concludes his chapter with a close reading of two historical novels by Arna Bontemps: *Black Thunder* (1936) and *Drums at Dusk* (1939).

The following chapter shifts the object of critical scrutiny toward Depression-era popular culture. In the first half of this chapter, Jennifer Haytock explains the tasks popular realist fictions performed for their mass readership. Tracking the rise of marketing phenomena like Best Seller lists and the Book-of-the-Month club and the Literary Guild, Jennifer Haytock argues that such institutional tools and organizations guided consumers toward materials that provided them with valuable lessons applicable to their everyday lives, helping them to bond with others, to affirm their social status, and navigate a complex environment. Two products of the decade – Pearl S. Buck's *The Good Earth* (1931) and Margaret Mitchell's *Gone With the Wind* (1936) – are exemplary in this regard, their nostalgic depictions of the past appealing to utopian desires for escapism while simultaneously registering the importance of acquiring the skills necessary to survive in the contemporary world. Other equally commercially successful authors of the era include Josephine Lawrence, Margaret Ayers Barnes, Jessie Fauset, Edna Ferber, and Fannie Hurst, all of whom supplied their predominantly female readers with potentially meaningful and pleasurable narratives that reflected their own domestic and professional concerns with love, marriage, mother-hood, and entering the workforce. My contribution to the second half of this chapter investigates a comparably popular genre of fiction, yet one that sought to startle – rather than comfort – its audience with tales of violent cruelty. Occupying a cultural terrain between the proletarian novel and modernist experimentation, the major crime writers of the 1930s probed hellish realms in which the conventional morality governing everyday life ceased to operate. I argue that the detective stories of Dashiell Hammett and Raymond Chandler, as well as the victim narratives of James M. Cain and Horace McCoy, may be considered ethically-oriented ventures designed to reflect on the more disturbing aspects of subjective desire. Complementary to yet distinct from the typical left-wing author's concern with the sociopoli-tical benefits of forming collective bonds, the crime writers encouraged their respective readers to contemplate, if only at the level of fantasy, their own potential to engage in egregiously evil forms of conduct.

The penultimate chapter to this collection (also written by me), details the process whereby innovative writers looked to modes of collective fun for aesthetic inspiration and formal guidance. In the 1930s, modernists such as

Henry Miller, Djuna Barnes, William Saroyan, and James Agee turned to the realm of public amusements in order to develop a more performance-based compositional approach. Frequently rowdy modes of popular entertainment – Coney Island attractions, burlesque and vaudeville shows, the circus, and the display of human oddities – thus supplied experimental artists with an alternative to conventional representational methods. Neither the autobiographical priority to express actual experiences of the subject, nor the documentary concern to provide a reliably accurate depiction of objective reality vanished entirely from the work of those listed above; yet such generic demands were supplemented by an authorial desire to excite readers, to situate the latter as if they were members of an audience at an exhilarating, affectively-charged spectacle. The motivation for these kinds of literary enterprises was the hope that the generation of shocks would prove socially beneficial, that extreme pleasure would furnish a measure of relief for persons burdened by the pressures of everyday life. Appealing to the cathartic or therapeutic notion that emotional intensity and corporeal stimulation could alleviate mental illness and physical fatigue, certain avant-garde writers enthusiastically embraced elements of popular culture, especially its comic manifestations, as a cure or solution to the problems of existence in the world. Eudora Welty is a partial exception to this rule in that she modeled some of her most famous short fictions on the visual and verbal structures of the freak show while simultaneously cautioning at the level of theme against the duplicities and cognitive aberrance of racially inflected exhibitions of ostensibly anomalous beings.

In the concluding chapter of *The Cambridge Companion to American Literature of the 1930s*, Caren Irr examines how several twenty-first-century novelists have repurposed the story of the Great Depression in light of contemporary crises. Many prose writers of late have employed revisions of genres and styles common during the 1930s as a means of engaging current economic matters. These sometimes anachronistic fictions tend to modify the kinds of narratives of poverty, ethnicity, and childhood associated with the decade to address concerns pertinent to our own millennial moment. E. L. Doctorow's *Billy Bathgate* (1989) is one case in point in that it locates the origins of the insider trading and investment banker scandals of a subsequent era in the 1930s. Correlating criminality and legitimate business ventures, the novel encourages us to recognize the beginnings of post–New Deal deregulation and speculative risk taking in the behavior of Depression-era gangsters. Another example is Anita Shreve's *Sea Glass* (2002), which recasts the Gastonia strike novel in order to think through questions of gender and eroticism in a more present-day manner. Pete Hamill adopts a different yet related approach in *North River* (2007), reviving motifs from the 1930s to assuage contemporaneous anxieties about the stability of the capitalist system, in the process transforming the working-class ethnic *Bildungsroman* into a narrative of multicultural conviviality. Meanwhile, Alan Brennert's story of carnivals and high-diving in *Palisades Park* (2013) updates Depression-era skepticism about mass culture for a media-saturated digital age. Probably the most compelling post-Recession reimagining of the 1930s, though, can be found in Marilynne Robinson's *Lila* (2014). Gender-shifting the bottom dogs and drifter stories of the 1930s, Robinson's novel moves its orphaned and homeless heroine through a series of sacred and secular crises – directly confronting the experience of deprivation associated with a stagnant economy, as well as the theologically oriented responses to it. Thus, the circle closes, returning us from a fraught past to an equally precarious present as we once again strive to bring an uncertain future into existence.

NOTES

1 Thomas Wolfe, *You Can't Go Home Again* (New York: HarperCollins, 1998), 347.
2 Burke's essay appears in *The Strenuous Decade: A Social and Intellectual Record of the Nineteen-Thirties*, a still useful collection of primary materials from the period. Eds. Daniel Aaron and Robert Bendiner (New York: Anchor Books, 1970). Equally valuable are *The American Writer and the Great Depression* (1966), ed. Harvey Swados, and *Years of Protest: A Collection of American Writings of the 1930's* (1967), eds. Jack Salzman and Barry Wallenstein.
3 This was the title of the manuscript when he unsuccessfully circulated it to presses in 1936; it was published posthumously in the 1960s as *Lawd Today!*
4 Richard Wright, *Lawd Today!* (Boston: Northeastern UP, 1995), 29. Matthew Josephson's 1934 critical study, *The Robber Barons: The Great American Capitalists, 1861–1901* helped popularize the term.
5 Richard Wright, "How Bigger Was Born," *Native Son* (New York: Perennial Classics, 1993), 446–47.
6 The potential for a homegrown variant of fascism to come to power in this country received a good deal of attention around mid-decade. See for instance the satiric novels *A Cool Million: The Dismantling of Lemuel Pitkin* (1934) and *It Can't Happen Here* (1935), by Nathanael West and Sinclair Lewis, respectively. Also of interest is in this context is Edward Dahlberg's novel *For Those Who Perish* (1934). Dahlberg also delivered a talk at the American Writers Congress titled "Fascism and Writers." Other relevant materials include Kenneth Burke's "The Rhetoric of Hitler's 'Battle'," (1939) a brilliant critical analysis of *Mein Kampf* and two articles, "Portrait of American Fascism" (1935) and "Star-Spangled Fascists" (1939), by Lawrence Dennis and Stanley High; abridged versions of the latter two articles can be found in *Strenuous Decade*, 326–54. Burke's piece is reprinted in *The Philosophy of Literary Form: Studies in Symbolic Action* (1941), an indispensable collection of his Depression-era work.

7 William Saroyan, "Aspirin is a Member of the N.R.A.," *The Daring Young Man on the Flying Trapeze* (New York: New Directions, 1997), 133, 136. The acronym refers to the 1933 National Recovery Act, a phenomenon of the Roosevelt Administration's first term. The result of a congressional act (NIRA) designed to get labor, the government, and industry working together to regulate the economy, it was deemed unconstitutional by the Supreme Court in 1935 – though some of its aims resurfaced in the Wagner Act.

8 John Dos Passos, *The 42nd Parallel* (Boston and New York: Mariner Books, 2000), xiv. See also the materials gathered together in *First Person America* (1980). The editor, Ann Banks, explains that the myriad life histories recounted in the volume were the result of interviews conducted under the auspices of the FWP and were intended for anthologies that were left unfinished at the time. Interviewers included Ralph Ellison, Nelson Algren, and Jack Conroy. Equally pertinent is *Such as Us: Southern Voices of the Thirties*, a belatedly published companion volume to *These Are Our Lives* (1939). The first piece in *Such as Us* is aptly titled "Talking is My Life." Eds. Tom E. Terrill and Jerrold Hirsch (New York: W. W. Norton & Company, 1978).

9 James Agee, *Let Us Now Praise Famous Men* (Boston: Houghton Mifflin Company, 1988), 78.

10 Tillie Olsen, *Yonnondio: From the Thirties* (Delta: New York, 1974), np. For more on this topic, see Michael Staub, *Voices of Persuasion: Politics of Representation in 1930s America* (New York: Cambridge, 1994).

11 The imperative to speak in defense of the oppressed even impacted Charlie Chaplin in the late 1930s. Whereas the voice in *Modern Times* is primarily associated with cruelty and discipline (in the form of the factory owner who issues commands to speed up the production process), at the end of *The Great Dictator* (1940), the barber (disguised as the dictator Adenoid Hynkel) addresses "the audience directly ... hurling words against organized power, delivering an impassioned statement of political belief." Richard H. Pells, *Radical Visions & American Dreams: Culture and Social Thought in the Depression Years* (Middletown, CT: Wesleyan University Press, 1973), 182–83. Correlatively, Warren Sussman noted long ago the degree to which technologically mediated speech helped facilitate the performance of ideological tasks in the era. Referencing the "Fireside Chats," Sussman remarks that "Roosevelt was able to create a new kind of presidency and a new kind of political and social power partly through his brilliant use of the medium." His radio broadcasts thus served as a means to "create or reinforce uniform national values and beliefs." "The Thirties" (http://xroads.virginia.edu/~ma98/haven/susman.html).

12 Alfred Kazin, *On Native Grounds: An Interpretation of Modern American Prose Literature* (New York: Doubleday Anchor, 1956), 381.

13 Fredric Jameson, "The Synoptic Chandler," *Shades of Noir*, ed. Joan Copjec (New York: Verso, 1993), 36. Tyrus Miller's *Late Modernism: Politics, Fiction, and the Arts between the World Wars* (1999) played an important role in this shift in conceptual outlook on the period.

14 Wolfe recounts this process in "The Story of the Novel" (1936).

15 Daniel Fuchs, *Summer in Williamsburg* (New York: Carroll and Graf, 1983), 373–76. See also John Fante's *Ask the Dust* (1939).

16 Alfred Kazin, *Starting Out in the Thirties* (New York: Vintage, 1980), 12.

I

ALAN M. WALD

Marxist Literary Debates in the 1930s

Parts of the Truth

The traumatic onset of the 1930s retains its darkly mythic pull over any attempt to represent this complex and variegated period. The very notion of a "Thirties Culture" should invite skepticism, especially if the enterprise entails a retroactive search for a governing logic. Even the idea of a distinctive chronology can be deceptive inasmuch as the decisive events that made up the beginning of 1930s culture are still open to debate, and the continuing attentiveness to so many aspects of the decade up to the present show that there are ways in which it has never really ended. By economic class, region, gender, and color, the experience of the era was different for different kinds of cultural workers and audiences. Although there are various 1930s, the attraction to radicalism of so many of the best-known and respected writers of the time continues to compel the attention of abundant students, scholars, and political activists.

This engagement with radicalism was foreshadowed by the 1927 Sacco and Vanzetti Defense Committee, formed on behalf of the two anarchist Italian immigrants accused of murder. Writers such as John Dos Passos (1896–1970) and Edna St. Vincent Millay (1892–1950) took to the streets, and a remarkable amount of fiction, poetry, drama, and art was produced to commemorate their failed effort to obtain clemency. A more coherent kind of movement, with Marxism at center stage, was emphatically under way by the 1932 appearance of the "Culture and the Crisis" manifesto of the League of Professionals for Foster and Ford. This was issued under the names of Sherwood Anderson (1876–1941), Langston Hughes (1902–1967), Edmund Wilson (1895–1972), and fifty other intellectuals who proudly supported the Communist Party presidential election campaign. Ever since, decade after decade, young people have felt a sense of solidarity with the motivating point of this effort. That is, 1930s literary radicalism represents a still-unfinished exertion on the part of a new generation committed to creatively thinking its way through a recalcitrant universe of war, revolution, fascist aggression, colonial domination, brutal economic inequality, and violent racism.

Undeniably, there was a specificity to the context in which this occurred, which any attempt to discuss the 1930s needs to address. Against a background of probing and often documentary-like fiction, poetry, and drama customarily associated with the decade, one finds essays and declarations in which Marxists, radicals, and liberals of various types duke it out over the efficacies of the Communist policies of "social fascism," "proletarian literature," and the Popular Front, as well as the events in Spain, the Moscow Trials, and the fear of international war. For those who continue to work in the Marxist tradition, there are two overriding issues: (1) how to assess the experience of "Stalinism," the accepted term for Soviet rule after the 1920s and the kind of communism embraced by the official Communist parties; and (2) how to parse and develop the elements available in the 1930s for forging an independent revolutionary socialism reaching to our own times. (Note: Pro-Soviet Communism will be designated with a capital "C" and the broader ideology with a small "c.") These and related topics comprise the circumambient intellectual culture in which artistic discourse was situated, affecting even those at a distance from or opposed to the militant elements. A portion of scholarship on the 1930s episodically revisits this legacy in ways that can be rich, thought-provoking, and subtle.

In spite of many admirable studies of the topic, how to calibrate the actual weight and significance of any ideological presence, such as Marxism, remains in dispute. Dissimilar assessments are no doubt related to the difficulty of neutrally assembling data to determine impact and also to the kinds of definitions held by the research scholar. One must also consider the manner in which to think about examining and evaluating cultural importance itself. Does the scholar focus on epic successes in sales and reputation, such as *The Grapes of Wrath* (1939) and *Native Son* (1940)? Or on works later esteemed to be of high quality but with minimal readership at the time, such as *Towards the Understanding of Karl Marx* (1933) and *Call It Sleep* (1934)? Incomplete projects that may reveal elements of thought not fully appreciated then or even now, such as Tillie Olsen's fragment "The Iron Throat" (*Partisan Review*, 1934) and the aborted collaborative journal *Marxist Quarterly* (1937)? What about the vast amounts of correspondence, private diaries, and unpublished manuscripts by the famous and forgotten? To organize a clear and comprehensive narrative from so many competing voices and experiences may be less suitable to the task than assembling a story of stories ... or a puzzle of puzzles.

A judicious enquiry into the published record concerning the literature and art of the decade suggests some emerging patterns in the sequence of re-appropriations of the differing tempos and contested meanings generated by the long-ago events of the Great Depression. The upshot of such a review is not that it unmasks disastrous efforts to impose a single strong narrative; instead, one discovers step-by-step alterations in the manner in which the politico-cultural ethos and import are represented as singular components and also part of the big picture. In fact, by the new millennium we can discern a persistent trajectory of an expanding bandwidth accompanied by an eclipse of some one-time core concerns. In effect, there is a literary version of "uneven and combined development," the sociopolitical theory that progress does not necessarily come through a sequence of unilinear stages. Scholarship in one discipline never exists in isolation from neighboring disciplines and from changes in the larger intellectual climate; there are spillover effects that produce ruptures, regressions, and incomplete results. To reclaim the unity and diversity of the cultural upsurge of the 1930s for the twenty-first century will require a powerful interpretative synthesis to avoid diffusion and disarticulation of its constituents, including the place of Marxist literary debates. But how is this to be accomplished? Have we been progressing to a deeper and more insightful understanding of the Great Depression, or to multiple versions of a past that never was?

Paths Taken

What is *not* new in the paths we find taken by researchers and chroniclers is the marked interdisciplinary approach, the incorporation of a range of cultural practices. From the very first, the study of the 1930s was associated with the growth of the discipline of American Studies, itself a product of the Great Depression. This meant an engagement with fiction, poetry, drama, art, film, photography, radio, music, journalism, and architecture, along with a consciousness about social class, and racial and ethnic factors. This ensemble comprised the foundation for the elements most attractively pronounced in the evolution of scholarship about the culture of the 1930s.

On the one hand, the record shows a welcome increase in technical sophistication with which scholars address literary practice and varied cultural artifacts. This has culminated in inventive books over the last quarter of a century, such as Cary Nelson, *Repression and Recovery: Modern American Poetry and the Politics of Memory, 1910–45* (1989); James Bloom, *Left Letters: The Culture Wars of Mike Gold and Joseph Freeman* (1992); Carla Carpetti, *Writing Chicago: Modernism, Ethnography and the Novel* (1993); Barbary Foley, *Radical Representations: Politics and Form in U.S. Proletarian Fiction, 1929–41* (1993); Alan Filreis, *Modernism from Left to Right: Wallace Stevens, The Thirties, and Literary Radicalism*

(1994); Walter Kaladjian, *American Culture between the Wars: Revisionary Modernism and Postmodern Critique* (1994); Paula Rabinowitz, *They Must Be Represented: The Politics of Documentary* (1994); Rita Barnard, *The Great Depression and the Culture of Abundance: Kenneth Fearing, Nathaniel West, and Mass Culture in the 1930s* (1995); Robbie Lieberman, *My Song Is My Weapon: People's Songs, American Communism, and the Politics of Culture, 1930–50* (1995); Paul Sporn, *Against Itself: The Federal Theater and Writers' Projects in the Midwest* (1995); Michael Szalay, *New Deal Modernism: American Literature and the Intervention of the Welfare State* (2000); Michael Thurston, *Making Something Happen: American Political Poetry between the World Wars* (2001); William Solomon, *Literature, Amusement and Technology in the Great Depression* (2002); Andrew C. Yerkes, *"Twentieth-Century Americanism": Identity and Ideology in Depression-Era Leftist Fiction* (2005); Jani Scandura, *Down in the Dumps: Place, Modernity, American Depression* (2008); Chris Vials, *Realism for the Masses: Aesthetics, Popular Front Pluralism, and U.S. Culture, 1935–1947* (2009); Jeff Allred, *American Modernism and Depression Documentary* (2010); and Ichiro Takayoshi, *American Writers and the Approach of World War II: A Literary History* (2015).

Concurrently, there has been a steady stream of well-researched volumes treating a diversification of populations – mainly by color and gender – increasingly acknowledged to have produced "worthy" art: Bill Mullen, *Popular Fronts: Chicago and African American Cultural Politics, 1935–46* (1990); Paula Rabinowitz, *Labor and Desire: Women's Revolutionary Fiction in Depression America* (1991); Douglas Wixson, *Worker-Writer in America: Jack Conroy and the Tradition of Mid-Western Literary Radicalism, 1898–1990* (1994); Constance Coiner, *Better Red: The Writing and Resistance of Tillie Olsen and Meridel Le Sueur* (1995); Laura Hapke, *Daughters of the Great Depression: Women, Work and Fiction in the American 1930s* (1997); William J. Maxwell, *New Negro, Old Left: African American Writing and Communism between the Wars* (1999); James Edward Smethurst, *The New Red Negro: The Literary Left and African American Poetry, 1930–46* (1999); Rachel Rubin, *Jewish Gangsters of Modern Literature* (2000); Michael C. Steiner, ed., *Regionalists on the Left: Radical Voices from the American West* (2013); Erin Royston Battat, *Ain't Got No Home: America's Great Migrations and the Making of an Interracial Left* (2014); Steven S. Lee, *The Ethnic Avant-Garde: Minority Cultures and World Revolution* (2015); T. V. Reed, *Robert Cantwell and the Literary Left: A Northwest Writer Reworks American Fiction* (2015); and Benjamin Balthaser, *Anti-Imperialist Modernism: Race and Transnational Radical Culture from the Great Depression to the Cold War* (2016).

As one might anticipate, following the perspective of uneven and combined development, this often splendid expansion and enrichment has not been without some costs. For many different reasons, and in varying degrees, a number of these books present the political commitments of radical cultural workers as vague and simplified. Political identifications, when given, can be gutted of substance rather than be made more precise in light of new research and thinking. "Left" or "Progressive" has in some places replaced "Communism." Individuals who did not explicitly declare themselves Party members are from time to time described as non-Communist, even when there is abundant evidence that they shared the outlook of the broad Communist-led movement. In one worst-case scenario, the terms "anti-Stalinist," "anticommunist," and even "anti-Marxist" are presented unabashedly as "interchangeable."[1] This move obscures the historical fact that pro-Soviet politics can be opposed from widely different points on the political spectrum, from Leninist to liberal to fascist; even worse, it reinforces the conservative view that Stalinism is the essence of Marxism and communism. Finally, there seems to be a diminished attention to some of the critical intellectual and political history components – especially the actuality of the Russian Revolution. Progress in theory and research is being made, but on some topics it appears to go sideways more than forward.

In other words, various elements have combined to produce some stage-skipping and lateral movement that has been inconsistently productive. New research and a longer perspective on the politics of 1930s writers should have produced more well-rounded portraits of the web of desires, identifications, and practices of radical cultural workers; these are essential to cultural analysis to the extent that all works of art are crafted transmutations of personal experience and imaginings. Yet the drift is occasionally toward bypassing or playing down a creative rethinking of 1930s Marxist literary affiliations and contested ideas.

Some of these controversies of the Great Depression have actually increased in relevance. One of these is the recurrent weaponization of "authenticity" that began in the 1930s with declarations of writers and art that they were "proletarian" as a bid for literary value; starting in the late twentieth century, comparable claims of authenticity became mobilized on behalf of one's gender and ethnicity. Just recently, the 2016 campaign of Bernie Sanders for the presidential candidacy of the Democratic Party launched a discussion of the historical meaning of socialism and how it can be distinguished from the New Deal and Communism. To see the links between present and past requires a well-versed and fair-minded recapitulation of what was actually said in the debates of the literary Left. Many aspects, of course, involve the hot-button issue of Stalinism, which a number of critics viewed as a regression from the promise of the Bolshevik Revolution and others assessed to be the logical result of Leninism and even Marxism. Although particulars may still be in dispute, much of what was suspected by various Soviet detractors in the 1930s Marxist literary debates has since been confirmed, which presents inconvenient truths for anyone who likes their radical narratives untainted by major paradoxes. Even those of us who correctly hold dear the Communist achievements in industrial unionism, the struggle for civil rights, and the instilling of an antifascist consciousness in the general population, must seek stark truth before comfort when it comes to the discrepancy between the widespread pro-Soviet beliefs (hardly limited to Party members) and the bloody reality. When writers become part of a movement that adulates a dictatorial thug and a system that murders its own cultural luminaries, some kind of unequivocal accounting is needed beyond familiar exculpating talking points – that the writers' intentions were good, that the United States had its own record of violence, and that reliable knowledge was difficult to obtain.

What is not needed is a "Communist Confidential," inasmuch as anticommunists, mostly in political science, history, and popular journalism, have already inundated the field with endless tales of espionage, slavish devotion to a Party leadership, and even moral turpitude. Nevertheless, there is no way to bottle up what has already been unbottled, which is the ruthless record of the Soviet Union to which the Communist movement required allegiance. A few scholars may operate in an echo-chamber of like-minded colleagues where the erosion of credibility is not an issue, but anyone committed to abetting the active continuity of literary radicalism as a self-critical tradition has a responsibility to clarify what happened to earlier generations as a prerequisite to doing better in the future. One must therefore work in a territory equidistant from those who view pro-Communist cultural workers through the oversimplifying anticommunist gaze, and those who just fudge the question by offering a drive-by blur of political associations that leaves vital matters indistinct.

What is at stake here at the end of the day is the pursuit of a materialist approach to "commitment." I do not mean "commitment" as a formal statement of allegiance, which might lead simply to the excerpting of the texts of not-always-scintillating manifestos. What matters for cultural commitment is stressed by Raymond Williams in *Marxism and Literature*: a "conscious, active, and open … choice of position," which requires that scholars explore "its hard and total specificities."[2] In this instance, one is looking at choices made under the pressure of a precise social, political, and historical situation that shaped the landscape of the 1930s. One finds changes in "alignment" (Williams's term for the normal expression of a point of view merely through selected experience) that involve different considerations of the role of artist and critic; the relation of innovative aesthetic forms to tradition; the forging of a new culture; the reconciliation of dogmatic versions of Marxism with US political and cultural realities; the personal costs of joining a movement (to family, career, self); the challenge of a revolution betrayed; and the temptations and fear of apostasy. Where possible, this means an investigation into the palimpsests of the mind that produced the art, the mental resources of the literary imagination. What we should have in the end is a view of committed radicals as a network of fully-realized personalities. Yes, there was a shared horizon, but writers could be substantially at odds with each other even as they worked within it.

Some of the relevant debates and exchanges can be found within the framework of the communist movement itself. Oft-cited ones include the lively "Authors' Field Day: A Symposium on Marxist Criticism" in the July 3, 1934, *New Masses*; the rich and diverse "American Writers Congress Discussion Issue" that comprises the April–May 1935 *Partisan Review*; and the rebuttal to Horace Gregory (1898–1982) by Meridel Le Sueur (1900–1996), "The Fetish of Being Outside," in the February 26, 1935, *New Masses*. Many more can be found in literature responding to splits and breaks, for it was often the case that the shattering of relationships with the Party had the effect of producing even more interesting Marxisms and radicalisms. One can readily turn to the writings of Sidney Hook (1902–1989) on dialectics, social fascism, and the Popular Front, often in *Modern Monthly*; the debate between W. E. B. Du Bois (1868–1963) and James S. Allen (born Solomon Auerbach, 1906–1986) over *Black Reconstruction in America, 1860–1880* (1935); the response by various factions on the Left to *A Note on Literary Criticism* (1936) by James T. Farrell (1904–1979); the post-1937 *Partisan Review*; and the exchange between John Dewey (1859–1952) and Leon Trotsky (1879–1940) on "Ends and Means" in the June and August 1938 *New International*.

Nostalgia on Overdrive?

The current status of Marxist literary debates in light of uneven and combined development in the field may be explored by means of the recent publication of three high-quality books. All are exclusively devoted to an overview of Great Depression culture, although none could possibly live up to the sizable promise of their titles: David Eldridge, *American Culture in the 1930s* (2008); Peter Conn, *The American 1930s: A Literary History* (2009); and Morris Dickstein, *Dancing in the Dark: A Cultural History of the Great Depression* (2009). Collectively they include some of the Marxist literary debates, but in such a manner that both commitment and contemporary relevance recede to the margins as a strange and spectral presence. In Eldridge, the entire topic of Marxist radicalism is partitioned; mainly just a few pages in an introduction about "The Intellectual Context" and a half-dozen more in a subchapter called "Literature as Weapon." In Conn, there is a closing chapter about "the party line," although *Black Reconstruction* receives a few pages in a chapter on "Black Memory." In the work of Dickstein, who has always understood that the continuity between culture and politics is too thick to be compartmentalized, radicals and their commitment are omnipresent, albeit undeveloped, and in the end overwhelmed by nostalgia on overdrive.

The outcome is a downgrading of 1930s radical culture and its concomitant controversies to museum pieces. This is particularly vexing inasmuch as we live again in times when mainstream liberalism in the United States is facing predicaments to which it has no compelling response, when it has no solutions to the real pain experienced by large sectors of the population, and when a foreign policy leading to endless quagmires. Whatever their failings and disagreements, Marxist literary intellectuals of the 1930s tried hard to identify the actual causes of suffering and exploitation, and to formulate appropriate responses dramatically different from those producing the status quo. Although teleology is impermissible in historical scholarship, continuity is not. The problem of "the committed writer" that troubled the 1930s did not exist as an island in time. It once was quite clear that the Depression era stood out as an ideational crucible for the experiment of "engaged" literature in the United States, and a testing ground for the responsibilities of the intellectual and artist in the face of social crisis. The relationship between the writer and commitment is an emblematic paradox of modernity; no comprehensive overview can exist without creatively probing the tensions enacted. Is the interpretative frame about to be flipped? Not necessarily. If we place the current treatment of Marxist literary debates in a longer view, the present situation is explainable and – hopefully – rectifiable.

Starting after World War II, the study of the era was typically painted with a gloomy palette. The titles of the volumes launched to define the field seventy years ago mostly dramatized in shorthand the fear, angst, and efforts at rebellion generated by economic calamity and international uncertainty: *The Angry Decade: American Literature and Thought from 1929 to Pearl Harbor* (1947), by Leo Gurko; *The Anxious Years: America in the 1930s* (1963), edited by Louis Filler; *When Drama Was a Weapon: The Left-Wing Theater in New York, 1929–41* (1963), by Morgan Himmselstein; *Years of Protest: A Collection of American Writings of the 1930s* (1967), edited by Jack Salzman and Barry Wallenstein; *The Strenuous Decade: A Social and Intellectual*

Record of the 1930s (1970), edited by Daniel Aaron and Robert Bendiner; *Writers in Revolt: The Anvil Anthology* (1973), edited by Jack Conroy and Curt Johnson; and *Literature at the Barricades: The American Writer in the 1930s* (1982), edited by Fred R. Hobson and Ralph Bogardus. The cultural narrative that emerges from this catalog is rather rough and tumble.

What was being handed down to new readers in these earlier representations was neither stable nor finished. The first volumes to encapsulate the 1930s understood that its intellectual and cultural legacy was clearly a past, but had elements feeding into an ongoing quest by those not entirely comfortable with postwar society. To the extent that the tradition of the 1930s survived as something that might be usable, it was expected to undergo new fissures, thereby requiring much-needed research and theorization in years to come. For fledgling readers to come upon these accounts of Great Depression writing was a stimulus to immerse oneself in the many questions raised: Was the rise of this type of cultural radicalism an aberration or prefigurement, something of a prehistory of our intellectual present? To what extent did the 1930s tremors of change and volcanic eruptions produce a distinct break from previous influences and traditions? Could Marxism be "Americanized"? What does it mean, emotionally and in activism, to be a "committed" writer? How does one fashion revolutionary sensibilities in literary form? To what extent was the fascination with the Russian Revolution and Soviet Union a spur to hope or the route to disillusionment?

Fast-forward a few decades to the economic meltdown of 2008. The most popular of the three new syntheses from 2008 to 2009 is surely Dickstein's six-hundred-page doorstop narrative, showcasing his ability to weave many knotted-together tales into a colorful tapestry. The distinguished literary scholar aimed to make connections between the cultural events of the Depression and the recent crises that shook the new millennium. Nevertheless, the longingly pensive title he selected, *Dancing in the Dark: A Cultural History of the Great Depression* (2009), suggests a move away from the old approach of a melodrama of disaster and unresolved angry revolt. In seventeen chapters, grouped in four parts that go from "Discovering Poverty" to "The Search Towards Community," Dickstein provides a wistfully philosophical or meditative take on the 1930s as he touches the national culture in nearly every region of the creative and commercial arts. From a historiographical perspective, *Dancing in the Dark* is worth detailed attention; it registers, with a deft and generous balance, many of the broad tectonic shifts in academia occurring between the deluge of belligerent book titles, such as *Literature at the Barricades*, and the present.

Dickstein's tour-de-force skillfully transports the reader from grim tenements and the adversity of class and racial oppression to the dream-factories of Hollywood make-believe; the somber sensibility expressing the pain of hard times in much social-realist fiction often dissolves into a mass culture of buoyant fantasies offering more than simple escape and distraction. *Dancing in the Dark* was rightfully received as recreating the 1930s landscape as a source of new hope, proof of our nation's ability to persevere, and even a light for our own troubled times. The profoundly nostalgic appeal of the book is not entirely unique; Conn, too, is preoccupied with the intriguing effort to connect the 1930s to "earlier American pasts" (8) and Eldridge ends with a wonderful chapter on "The Cultural Legacy of the 1930s" that treats its reconstruction up through the films *The Legend of Bagger Vance* (2000), *Seabiscuit* (2003), and *Cinderella Man* (2005).

Dancing in the Dark also serves as a commanding exemplification of the late-twentieth-century celebration of accomplishments past with an accent on the positive, especially in matters of gender, race, ethnicity, and mass or popular culture. Nevertheless, the overriding "dancing in the dark" metaphor for the culture obscures the fractious Marxist debates of the 1930s as a vital feature; and this surely removes any need for the author to make sense of and recoup revolutionary hopes – embraced by a substantial number of cultural workers he treats – in a contemporary manner that is fully aware of their vulnerabilities. More survey than treatise, Dickstein's approach forgoes even the germ of a radical restatement of the politico-cultural challenge to build a new world. He essentially combines a hopeful picture of artistic achievement with a bleak picture of social breakdown, and he is particularly original about the cathartic role of the former. When it comes to the revolutionary views embraced by so many of the Left cultural workers of the time, Dickstein acknowledges in passing some political and organizational affiliations but never imparts to us anything of the mental and moral universe of writers attracted to movements such as Communism. Instead of ending, canonically, on the shock of the Hitler–Stalin Pact of 1939 or the violent note of Pearl Harbor in 1941 – both of which raised unresolved dilemmas for the radical tradition – he closes on the hopeful promises of the World's Fair of 1939–1940. His rather chipper summary reads: "Artists and performers rarely succeed in changing the world, but they can change our feelings about the world, our understanding of it, the way we live in it. ... Their work and serious play did much to ease the national trauma. They were dancing in the dark, moving in time to a music all their own, but the steps were magical."[3]

Cultural nostalgia, some of which is rooted in the happy personal associations to which Dickstein refers in autobiographical asides, seems to inflect the political template of the book when it comes to Communism, too. Certainly, he sees the Soviet-inspired hopes as an allure that crashed on the rocks of reality, but not much is said by way of explanation. The warmth and coping strategies provided by music, theater, film, dance, literature, and so forth are the main point. What we have are the conventional negative asides about Party hackery; this is perhaps overdone when he oddly declares the anti-intellectual Mike Gold (1894–1967) "the representative Communist intellectual of the twentieth century" (19), and then sums up Gold's later career with boilerplate invective as "a nasty propagandist who swallowed every shift and betrayal, every violent twist of policy the party sent his way" (21). But Dickstein's nostalgia successfully distances him from most liberal anticommunists and he is ultimately less censorious than quietly bemused. It is not merely that Communism, along with any other Far Left variants, is now a dead horse that there is no need to flog. Dickstein is writing as a mature and tolerant parent recalling a stage of wildness that his children have now – thankfully! – outgrown. His memories of their tantrums and acts of blatant disrespect and disobedience have mostly faded as he cheerfully attributes to them an achievement compatible with his current state of mind: "Like FDR himself they [the artists] boosted the people's morale, supplying a charge of social energy that also illuminated their works and days" (xxiii). If Dickstein succumbs more than Eldridge and Conn to the temptation to find dramatic unity through the imposition of a too-narrow theme, it is that 1930s culture serves as the analogue for New Deal politics and no further debate is necessary.

Dancing in the Dark, then, is a charming rendition of the 1930s as providing a kind of cultural Geritol to service the tired blood that comes with new anxieties. It is a sensible and credible book, but it promotes a connection to the 1930s distinct from what the Marxist literary debates of the 1930s can provide to the point of suggesting that his nostalgia works to mute a disconcerting relevance different from a warmth that facilitates coping. What is not communicated is a sense of shared belonging, across time, to a set of militant political and ethical values that still demand a conscious commitment to a redeeming future. The cultural power of the 1930s can be found in the cogency of articulation in the Marxist literary debates with regard to the concrete dilemmas of the period. These include a skeptical view of the New Deal liberalism, a passionate commitment to internationalism, and a belief that writers might create a new kind of literature for a new kind of audience. In its finest moments, these expressions of commitment transcend their own time. After all, the same old fight of property rights versus human rights vexes generation after generation, and now more than ever. For every student of the Great Depression whose reaction is to download CDs and DVDs of 1930s classic songs and films to assuage despair, there are others who come away inspired to set about the project of developing a new and improved "cultural front" to counter a world of Trumps, Clintons, Putins, al-Asaads, and worse.

Dickstein, however, is the most open of the three to the radical presence. He does not go to the extreme of Eldridge, who explains that "the notion of the years 1930–39 as the 'Red Decade' does not stand up to scrutiny ... [but] was a perception generated primarily by anti-Communists."[4] Nor of Conn, who says that he wrote the book "to argue against the currently, widely shared assumption that the 1930s were largely characterized in cultural terms by Left aesthetics and politics."[5] Both statements miss the point that the centrality of the role of "Reds" in the culture came not from their absolute numbers or sales figures. Rather, it was from the challenge that Red arguments presented to numerous others, and the fact that the matters addressed by Reds represent paradigmatic crises and conflicts of the modern era itself. A great deal of 1930s radical thinking exceeds this one decade; it is responsible for much of the longevity and current appeal of the 1930s. Moreover, there is also the literary quality of the writers drawn to the Red cause and the fact that much of their art is now regarded as fundamental to modern US culture. We still speak much of the language of the 1930s and political allegiances formed during the Great Depression and its aftermath are with us yet. *Dancing in the Dark* presents the indubitably rich topsoil of the 1930s cultural moment that includes a substantial radical presence; but we also require scholarship that reveals, from other angles, the personal choices and changes that actually powered the culture of the 1930s. Nostalgia is necessary but insufficient to explain why we are still affected by the ability of so many 1930s artists to recreate a specific landscape infused with decade-transcendent dreams. We must also drill to the bedrock of commitments that dare not speak their political names in a substantial portion of newer cultural histories of the subject.

Let Us Now Praise Famous Scholars

Between the earnest pioneering investigations of the 1930s, focusing on the agonies and antinomies of militant Marxist cultural commitment, and Dickstein's humane recreation of a sensibility of hope and perseverance, sits the long history of an uneven and combined development, both an enlargement and thinning of a beguiling field of study. The groundwork, however, was remarkably solid, based on primary research, interviews, and close reading of journals and newspapers; this occurred to a degree not always duplicated and to which it is always informative to return. As the Cold War era of McCarthyite demonization of the Left waned in the late 1950s, a cohort of Left-liberal scholars waged a struggle through academic books to establish the 1930s as the centerpiece in a lengthier tradition of literary radicalism, a fractious movement that addressed complex and near insoluble problems facing "engaged" cultural workers: Walter Rideout's *The Radical Novel in the U.S., 1900–1954: Some Interrelations of Literature and Society* (1956); Daniel Aaron's *Writers on the Left: Episodes in American Literary Communism* (1961); and James B. Gilbert, *Writers and Partisans: A History of Literary Radicalism in America* (1968). Whereas the anticommunist Right and a section of Cold War liberals saw the crudity and delusions of 1930s radicalism as a causal factor of W. H. Auden's 1939 "low dishonest decade" ("September 1, 1939," *New Republic*, 1939), the new scholarship explained why intellectuals turned Left as the consequence of the crisis of a social system.

The three authors lacked political unanimity, adhered to many now-dated ideas about what constitutes "literature," and displayed an astounding blind spot about the Jewish presence in the literary Left. But they grasped the significance of the 1930s from the point of view of the question of whether United States citizens continued to live in a social order that required radical solutions. Behind their books churned the same question that arose in the 1930s literary debates among Marxists: Should intellectuals fight for profound structural changes benefitting all, and what might be the significance for cultural creativity and analysis? Rideout concluded by reaffirming that literature was not an "independent category," but he also saw it as "distinct" from politics in a way that the Communist movement could not recognize; if there was to be a future for the radical novel, it would be "almost wholly with the independent radical."[6] Gilbert insisted that the elevation of "negativism" destroyed the radicalism of *Partisan Review* magazine by the early 1950s;[7] he called upon the New Left to "understand" what must be "rejected" in the Old Left and rediscover "the compatibility of Bohemianism and radicalism which is reminiscent of Greenwich Village before World War I" (7). Most arresting were the final thoughts of Aaron: "We who precariously survive in the 1960s can regret [the Communist writers'] inadequacies and failures, their romanticism, their capacity for self-deception, their shrillness, their self-righteousness. It is less easy to scorn their efforts, however blundering and effective, to change the world."[8]

What came after produced a truly a positive and stunning shift from which we now benefit: a near endless proliferation of well-crafted studies of literary and cultural radicalism, often extending the bookends of the 1930s. These perform the crucial work of reintroducing forgotten or misunderstood cultural works and provide narratives from perspectives that steadily enrich our understanding of what occurred in context and what it all means. Surprisingly, despite undying anticommunism among the general public, many studies appear to be characterized by politics suggestive of the Popular Front fellow travelers of the late 1930s combined with neo-Marxist critical terms. (Dickstein, Conn, and Eldridge are exceptions to the latter.) Whatever one thinks of that combination, this expansion was necessary and indispensable.

The earlier books by Aaron et al. must be faulted for a limited selection of cultural workers and cultural sites, too often white males and New York focused, and for failing to recognize the masculinized discourse of leading Left thinkers. Moreover, it was necessary for subsequent scholars to challenge, in general histories, any overfixation on Marxists running the 1930s; no one can seriously argue that the Left commitment of intellectuals and their debates about aesthetics, philosophy, and politics should be the only story if our concern is the culture consumed by the total population of the United States. Every year of the 1930s was crowded with immense political and intellectual change beyond the class, race, and international preoccupations of the urban intelligentsia; and when we expand a field, we invariably see new and potentially helpful patterns at work. Finally, the notion that the radical literary movement of the Great Depression was a failure, promoted primarily by Left critics of the Communists such as *Partisan Review* editor Philip Rahv (1908–1973), had to be displaced.

What appears to account for retarding the pursuit of the meaning of Marxist literary debates, the clarification of commitment, and the reclamation of the roots of an independent revolutionary socialism, is the mood that swept academia as the 1970s became the 1980s. Rideout, Aaron, and Gilbert were never directly challenged or refuted in any important way, but the decline of New Left social movements, the disappearance of radical political organizations, the growth of various types of "identity politics," the appearance of a new version of social democracy that embraced Popular Front culture, the triumph of literary theories that diminished the role of authors and placed structure above agency, combined to propel scholarship in new directions. Warren Susman's essays "Culture and Commitment" (1973) and "The Culture of the 1930s" (1983), powerfully introduced the notion that the Marxist Left was a lesser presence than had been thought. A brilliant disciple, Richard Pells, extended the concept in *Radical Visions and American Dreams: Culture and Social Thought in the Depression Years* (1973), where he managed to incorporate the debates of Marxists in his work while bending this material to a countervailing theme: "though their intentions were innovative and radical, it is possible to see (particularly in the years after 1935) an underlying conservatism in their outlook as well as in the implications of their ideas."[9]

Even more persuasive was Michael Denning's *The Cultural Front: The Laboring of American Culture in the Twentieth Century* (1996). With a

Jedi-like mastery, Denning incorporated a large number of discussions among the literary Left, although he excluded those explicitly about Stalinism and the Russian Revolution. In his boldest move, one that constituted a major advance for the field, 1930s radicalism was persuasively extended as an "historical bloc" (a union of social forces) into the 1950s. Then Denning swiveled to a surprising direction with the following claim: "the culture and politics of the Popular Front [historical bloc] were not simply New Deal Liberalism and populism. It was a social democratic culture, a culture of 'industrial democracy' and 'industrial unionism'."[10] With "Cultural Front," "Popular Front," and "The Age of the CIO" all coterminous with social democracy, Denning allied himself with the tendency to homogenize and marginalize the often specific varieties and experiences of commitment permeating the Left. That so many, perhaps the majority, of cultural figures claimed for social democratic culture actually despised social democracy is a problem Denning never satisfactorily clarifies.

In presenting the Cultural Front as a usable past, part of Denning's argument is that a scholar's identification of certain kinds of commitment as "Communist" likely leads to a core-periphery model, which is "commonly told as a morality tale of seduction and betrayal" (xvii) and "ultimately a search for Moscow gold" (xviii). Thus, an interpretative loophole was put in place that too easily allows scholars to take an easy way out. Why wrestle with all the paradoxes and contradictions of a committed writer's location when one can dismiss the research into their ideological and organizational choices as irrelevant, if not a Red-baiting concession to anticommunist conspiracy theorists? In fact, Denning's strategy never erased the problem of Stalinism, a permanent blot, but simply outsourced the subject to others with less sympathy and understanding of Left history.

Speaking of Communists

Although some works of the late twentieth century simply ignore the tradition of Marxist literary debates, books by Pells and Denning set out to manage them in various ways. Or perhaps it is more accurate to observe that these studies provided openings that could go in various directions, but that a frequent one was a tendency to embrace the less complicated themes. This explains the pattern that has coalesced: A celebration of simpler kinds of political commitment in which a writer's association with "The Left" is treated more often as a quick alignment than a thought-out choice; a view that an emergent independent Marxism in the 1930s was actually anticommunist or a necessary transit to Cold War liberalism and neoconservatism; and an understanding of the Communist presence that was vague and devoid of substance precisely at the time when new primary research – especially politically-revised biographies of Agnes Smedley (1892–1950), Jim Thompson (1906–1977), Arthur Miller (1915–2005), Ralph Ellison (1913–1994), and Langston Hughes – suggested that our notion of the Communist writer and the Communist presence needed to be broadened.

The notion that identifying writers as pro-Communist and pursuing the matter with any depth is a way of pigeonholing artists and narrowing 1930s culture is primarily a matter of what is in the eye of the beholder. As with any biographical or personal information about a cultural figure – including his or her sexual orientation, a childhood trauma, a grievous loss – the issue is what the scholar *does* with it. If one sees Communism reductively as a monotone, and Party members as wooden stereotypes, perhaps it is better to claim that most writers of the 1930s weren't really Communists and move to another subject. But there is abundant evidence to suggest that the communist cultural movement was vibrant and peopled with colorful characters. Moreover, it does violence to reality to ignore that the 1930s literary radical was primarily Soviet centered and the Communist Party was a determinant in the way that many literary radicals thought – far beyond the actual Party membership and even beyond fellow travelers.

The explanation for such devotion is not just the economic crisis but that the Soviet Union, from the time of the 1917 Revolution, was a genuine beacon for racial, ethnic, and national equality. Radical writers in the United States *wanted* to make the prestige of the USSR their own; they did not need to be duped or pressured into such loyalty, even if fear of persecution induced many to be cautious about public declarations. Communist militants were admired by literary radicals for the guiding role they played in social movements and trade unions, for fighting racism and anti-Semitism. As a result of Communist propaganda and activity there was a strong internationalist presence on the US Left; events and upheavals in remote corners of world received attention that would otherwise have gone unnoticed. Even when collaborating with liberalism in the Popular Front, Communists were in the vanguard of social transformation. For those mainly inspired by the Soviet Union as a working model of a future society, the Communist Party played a mediating role. Finally, despite dogmatism of many Party spokespersons in cultural matters, in creative practice the ideology of Communists could be fluid and flexible. This is especially critical to cultural production; none of the substantial cultural works of the era are reducible to the pro-Soviet version of communism.

Yet there is something more. The Marxist literary debates of the 1930s remain a potential source of encouragement for creative scholars as well as cultural activists inspired by a Marxism liberated from the past. This will only come through candid understanding of the older mixed record and the crafting of new forms of commitment; otherwise, we will be like amnesiacs, lost when we should have some knowledge of the terrain, and more helpless than ever if we wish to derail the train to disillusionment. Cultural issues raised in the 1930s are already in discussion, even if their earlier background is not fully appreciated. One concerns the technologies of representation – who does the cultural representing and how? The 1930s arguments about "the proletarian novel" suggest the need to differentiate between the creation of proletarian experience in a text – which long predated the 1930s – and a vanguard cultural tendency that can explore its own aesthetic, freely developing forms and language without the interference of political watch-dogs. Young people who today are launching new journals and experimenting with the promotion of social movements, can look back to these old disputes to learn how one might do effective work from the fringes. Above all, these 1930s literary debates are rich with regard to the whole complicated and still-unresolved matter of possible connections between social beliefs and literary aims; everything may be political, but the primacy of political experience has been a poor guide to understanding the principles of artistic creativity and aesthetic achievement.

Methodologies must also be refined; the scholar should be able to zoom in on personal lives and the implications for art, but also to zoom out and tell more about the place of 1930s radicalism in the greater culture. A superior unity of cultural history and intellectual history seems required as well. If Marxism continues to be the guide, it must be one that commands a dizzying array of approaches – historical, aesthetic, psychological, cultural, political, sociological. Finally, as we pass the one-hundredth anniversary of the Bolshevik Revolution, scholars in that field have been hard at work in the effort to understand what was positive about the event, what went wrong, and why. This research, often revealing new data that resists containment within inherited storylines, can be a critical counterpoint to some of the narrative myths about 1930s literary radicalism that reappear with deadening monotony. If one has no sense of what might have been "real" in this once-profound attraction of US writers to the communist cause, it's hard to know what to care about when estimating their legacy. One cannot expect that answers to such matters will be certain and beyond dispute, that all paradoxes will be settled; but to isolate the material of fact and experience from reconsiderations of literary radicalism is to absolve ourselves from thinking about the history that matters.

NOTES

1 Barbara Foley, *Radical Representations: Politics and Form in U.S. Proletarian Literature, 1929–1941* (Durham: Duke University Press, 1993), 7.

2 Raymond Williams, *Marxism and Literature* (New York: Oxford University Press, 1977), 200, 204.

3 Morris Dickstein, *Dancing in the Dark: A Cultural History of the Great Depression* (New York: W. W. Norton & Co., 2010), 530.

4 David Eldridge, *American Culture in the 1930s* (Edinburgh: Edinburgh University Press, 2008), 8.

5 Peter Conn, *The American 1930s: A Literary History* (New York: Cambridge University Press, 2009), 6.

6 Walter Rideout, *The Radical Novel in the United States, 1900–1954: Some Interrelations of Literature and Society* (Cambridge, MA: Harvard University Press, 1956), 290.

7 James Gilbert, *Writers and Partisans: A History of Radical America* (New York: Columbia University Press, 1967), 282.

8 Daniel Aaron, *Writers on the Left: Episodes in American Literary Communism* (New York: Farrar, Straus, and Giroux, 1974), 396.

9 Richard Pells, *Radical Visions and American Dreams: Culture and Social Thought in the Depression Years* (New York: Harper & Row, 1973), xii.

10 Michael Denning, *The Cultural Front: The Laboring of American Culture in the Twentieth Century* (New York: Verso, 1997), xvii.

2

MATTHEW STRATTON

Aesthetics and Politics of the Depression Era

Aesthetics were all right in your *day ... but this is war-time! We need ammunition, not poetry!*
        –Tess Slesinger, *The Unpossessed*

Aesthetics and Politics

Ever since Plato warned against the dangers that mimesis posed to the ideal Republic, art has lived in a vexed relationship with individuals collectively trying to improve states and societies. "Aesthetics" has been minimally understood to mean the study of beauty and beautiful representations on their own terms and through the experiences generated by those representations. Conversely, "politics" was most succinctly defined by American political scientist Harold Lasswell as *Who Gets What When How* (1936). In one view, then, aesthetics stands in opposition to active politics, whether articulated by earnest Marxist undergraduates in novels like *The Unpossessed* (1934) or by more recent accounts of activist critics in the 1930s, wherein "Politics was one thing, and aesthetics another."[1] In the contentious relationship between aesthetics and politics, however, arguments change and nothing is minimally succinct: "aesthetics" signifies more than reflections upon beauty, and politics must account for more than the distribution of goods. Nonoppositional relationships between aesthetics and politics thus pervade a thorny thicket of continuing debates that frequently distinguish both the politicized literary culture of the Depression era and the legacy of "The Thirties" as a distinct historical phenomenon.

The understanding of beauty as disengaged from practical public affairs conventionally finds its strongest articulation in Immanuel Kant's 1790 *Critique of the Power of Judgment*, which insisted that a perceiver's "disinterest" in a "purposeless" object was a precondition for judging its beauty. A century later, British critic Walter Pater transformed philosophical aesthetics into the loose artistic movement of Aestheticism by declaring that "art comes to you proposing frankly to give nothing but the highest quality to your moments as they pass, and simply for those moments' sake."[2] In the twentieth century, many literary critics and theorists, especially those on the Left, have taken German Marxist philosopher Walter Benjamin's cryptic 1936 riposte as conclusive: with the rise of mass cultural media technologies, "art for art's sake" led indirectly but ineluctably to cultures that generated and tolerated the genocidal mania of Axis totalitarianism. For Benjamin and the Frankfurt School after him, the "consummation of *l'art pour l'art* " was visible in the historical moment when the "self-alienation" of humanity had "reached the point where it can experience its own annihilation as a supreme aesthetic pleasure. *Such is the aestheticizing of politics, as practiced by fascism.*"[3] Here, the multiform forces of modernity had produced technologies of representation and modes of life that were quantitatively and qualitatively different from prior aesthetic experience; defeated was the capacity of individuals to experience and evaluate safely the representations they encountered, eagerly pursued, and even enjoyed. Thus, as historian Martin Jay writes, "Insofar as the aesthetic is identified with the seductive power of images, whose appeal to mute sensual pleasure seems to undercut rational deliberation, the aestheticization of politics ... means the victory of the spectacle over the public sphere."[4] Contrary to the way that Enlightenment thinkers idealized the public sphere as a space for the free exchange and evaluation of information and ideas among autonomous, rational individuals who wanted to know about and influence public affairs, "Aestheticized politics are said to be able to deceive people into accepting manufactured needs as real needs, simplifications as full pictures, and illusions as reality."[5] In sum, modernity had capitalized on a site of Kantian distrust – the ability of representations to generate merely "charming" representations at the expense of better judgment that would lead to an embodied experience of morality – and built an entire industry on the final inability of people to be rationally disinterested. Totalitarianism went even further by building entire political regimes upon modes of sensorial gratification, and the consequences were more disastrous than idealist philosophers could have imagined.

Today, when authoritarian tweets have supplanted both Franklin Delano Roosevelt's half-hour fireside chats and the anti-Semitic ravings of popular Michigan radio priest Father Coughlin, this critique warrants continued attention. For Benjamin also claimed that antifascist communism had "politicized art" (42). Indeed, a series of counter-statements about how aesthetics do and should affect nonauthoritarian politics can be traced back through the 1930s to the nineteenth century, when radical ideas made their way from Europe to England via Friedrich Schiller and the English Romantic poets. For a variety of thinkers before and after the 1930s, the conversation about how individual identities and behaviors should be politicized by art expanded to consider how individuals and collectivities were affected by aesthetics, more broadly understood as the delineation of affective experience by multiform phenomena. These investigations produced more than practical, empirical analyses of how legislation should be written, goods and services should be distributed within managed forms of political economy, or beauty should be created and appreciated. Rather, the relationships between aesthetics and politics served to elaborate the ways that different forms of representation define experience itself: how elites, masses, individuals, cultures, and perhaps even a universal "humanity" employ a variety of symbolic activities to understand and change the world they inhabit.

Far from relegating art to a discretely isolated realm of autonomous beauty and feeling, aesthetic speculation has moved well beyond the mere feelings inspired by representations, to "make insistent if necessarily indirect claims for their extra-aesthetic power (moral, religious, epistemological, political), asserting not just a specifically aesthetic agency but agency in realms extending far beyond art or culture."[6] Those realms include – perhaps have always included – politics, as the divorce ceremony elaborated by Kant and ratified by Pater was neither exhaustive nor conclusive. Indeed, for a different line of thinking inspired by Kant and running through the twentieth-century philosophy of Hannah Arendt to current political philosophy, the "link of aesthetics and politics is natural: both are the realms in which one must determine a relation between the private and the public, between the first-person singular and the first-person plural, between individual response and collective validity."[7]

In literature of the 1930s, this link between an active "I" and a social "We" is often implicit, familiar, and controversial: take, for example, John Steinbeck's *The Grapes of Wrath*'s narrative invitation to connect Tom Joad's defiant claim that "wherever they's a fight so hungry people can eat, I'll be there. Wherever they's a cop beatin' up a guy, I'll be there" with Ma Joad's reassurance that "we're the people – we go on."[8] Historically speaking, the California farmworkers who inspired Tom would have been largely Mexican and Filipino rather than the exclusively Anglo families iconically committed to page and screen; as with all of American history, defining qualities of the "I" and who could be included in the "We" is a contentiously, even violently unfinished project for politically committed artists and critics, debates among whom reached an unprecedented salience during the Great Depression.

In the years following the stock market crash of 1929, which saw rampant un- and underemployment, when by 1932 "perhaps a quarter of the entire population ... found itself without adequate means to buy shelter or food,"[9] it was widely understood that the "atmosphere of American literature became more political than at any time in its history."[10] This was true not only among coolly detached academic philosophers and wild-eyed activist poets, but among those wide masses whose faith in American exceptionalism was hungrily shaken even as the very future of civilization fell under the shadow of fascism. As attested in the 1935 proceedings of the first Congress of American Writers – a gathering of artists, theorists, and critics on the Left – "From 1930 on, more and more American writers – like their fellow-craftsmen in other countries – began to take sides in the world struggle between barbarism (deliberately cultivated by a handful of property owners) and the living interests of the mass of mankind."[11]

Many artists and critics were consumed by questions about what kind of art – especially literature – could forge desirable relationships between "individual response and collective validity": what that art would look like, what kind of responses could be expected, and what kind of society was required in order to produce that art and those responses without slipping into murderous unanimity. What remains is a complicated set of overlapping critiques and styles advocating dramatically different actions to achieve dramatically different social and political goals. On the one hand, these arguments can be viewed as distractions from the putatively "true" business of art and be sidelined as the "melodramas of orthodoxy and heresy,"[12] notorious quarrels to be derided as "finagling among literary politicians."[13] On the other hand, these arguments were symptomatic of the social, economic, and political crisis that affected the global population, and the arguments themselves changed perception: as some current philosophers describe how art and criticism effect ways of seeing and judging the world, Depression-era discourses on the aesthetic created "forms of community laid out by the very regime of identification in which we perceive art."[14]

Classifying political aesthetics and untangling the debates around them is both difficult and problematic: partially because theoretical assertions frequently masquerade as empirical observations and partially because "right," "left," and "liberal" are inherently relational positions. As anyone who has observed the last eight years of American electoral politics knows, the policies reasonably self-described by a Democratic president as "moderate Republican" can simultaneously (if incoherently) be described as "communist" and "fascist" by his right-wing detractors, and this is nothing new: as one editor of a 1937 anthology wrote, "The words Right and Left perhaps means more today than at any time in the history of American criticism – and they have been used so widely and indiscriminately that they are about to lose coherent meaning."[15] Nonetheless, writers then composed taxonomies of aesthetics and political positions. This is, for example, what Joseph Freeman did as the communist introducer of the anthology *Proletarian Literature in the United States* (1935):

> The Communist says frankly: art, an instrument in the class struggle, must be developed by the proletariat as one of its weapons. The fascist, with equal frankness, says: art must serve the aims of the capitalist state. The liberal, speaking for the middle class which vacillates between monopoly capital and the proletariat, between fascism and communism, poses as the 'impartial' arbiter in this, as in all other social disputes.[16]

Here, Pater's prescription for "art" speaking "frankly" has been transformed into metonymic political individuals "frankly" advocating for activist art, highlighting the social function of representation and rejecting disinterested art, artist, and audience as a falsely apolitical "pose."

Barrels of ink were emptied in subsequent debates over the details and practical implications of Freeman's tripartite taxonomy, further suggesting that any single relationship between aesthetics and politics in the 1930s would be grossly reductive. To delineate all of the stipulated relationships between aesthetics and politics *per se*, even within a single decade, would require a flow chart so convoluted it would itself become a sublime aesthetic object. Nonetheless, with the benefit of hindsight and expanded views of both aesthetics and politics, perhaps this basic tripartite structure is legibly useful through a position on which otherwise divergent thinkers could occasionally agree: "It is true," Freeman wrote in a line that obtained across party boundaries, "that the specific province of art, as distinguished from action or science, is the grasp and transmission of human experience" (10). Across the literary-political spectrum of the 1930s, the category of "experience" emerged as a central determining concept for understanding not only aesthetics and politics, but the evolution of how "The Thirties" came to be known as an object of cultural history: people in the moment and retrospectively attempting to make political sense of experience through narrative or visual form and content. Thus, before further questioning the wisdom of such simplified taxonomies, we should consider representative samples of more-or-less Right, Left, and Liberal assertions from the 1930s about what kind of society needs what kind of art and why.

Right

Is there actually any poetry capable of balancing a budget?
– H. L. Mencken, 1936

Canonically fascist aesthetics were but a sidenote in the United States; however, much of the iconic literature of the 1930s repudiates a conservatively oriented American aestheticism that culminated in the movement known as "New Humanism." Spearheaded by venerable critics Paul Elmer More and Irving Babbit, the anthology titled *Humanism and America: Essays on the Outlook of Modern Civilisation* (1930) articulated a variety of relatively reactionary viewpoints about art and society that was easily summarized: "our humanists are well agreed" More wrote. "[T]hey all perceive, and more or less explicitly declare, that the present confusion in letters is connected with a similar confusion in our ideas of life. They see that as we live, so shall we paint and write, or that, as Plato would put it, as we paint and write, so shall we come to live."[17] Drawing on classical and early modern philosophers and artists as well as more recent figures like Pater, they advocated a return to "traditional" aesthetic and social values of the past in order to revivify moribund American culture.

Like many other friends and foes, the New Humanists saw in their own present a fractured, dissolute culture of which social and economic collapse were only the most recent factors responsible for bad art (and vice versa). They positioned themselves against a century's rise of democratic norms and for preceding periods' aesthetic values of beauty and sublimity, which they promoted not as historical phenomena but as "the eternal values of life." Figures such as Leonardo Da Vinci and J. S. Bach were "great for various reasons, no doubt; but certainly among those reasons is the fact that they are not art at all as the modernists would have us believe."[18] What passed among "the moderns" and "the modernists" as artistic innovation and social progress – ranging from Cubist painting and avant-garde poetry to women, African Americans, and the landless being allowed to vote – was a grand and vicious illusion, for in modern art "there has been no true liberation, but a progressive descent in slavery" (62) that degraded elevated human minds and spirits, that left them conquered and oppressed by "the dictatorship of sensuality" (63).

By 1930, American society had decisively changed since the days when Jeffersonian ideals of liberty and beauty thrived alongside and upon the institution of chattel slavery, and for the New Humanists the root of many contemporary crises was the dissolution of core traditional values. In an era when bedrock economic, social, and political assumptions were ever more aggressively questioned, they asserted that "some set of assumptions as to the experiences most valuable and important for mankind ... is as necessary in the establishment or the maintenance of an aesthetic convention as in any purely social or political activity."[19] Whereas the advent of public education and the expanded franchise were greeted by many Americans as the progressive (though incomplete) fulfillment of the natural equality that was both declared and denied by founding documents of the American Revolution, New Humanists saw in change the promiscuous decline of aesthetic and moral standards. In language echoing the contemporary discourse of eugenics, they argued that social and aesthetic degeneration had started in the nineteenth century, when "the false glamour thrown about the artist life by romantic poets and novelists brought new hordes of the unfit to join the bewildered survivors from the old régime."[20] What could be expected of modern art, they asked, when anyone was allowed to create it, when an increasing sense of national identity and expanding democratic values were diluting a centuries-old "aristocratic vision of the good life" that had "always been the foundation on which great national art has been reared in the past" (121)?

The New Humanists found a kindred spirit in the later work of T.S. Eliot, whose poetry, plays, and critical essays (including one for *Humanism and America*) often echoed their sentiments. In the words of Donald Davidson – a member of the Southern Agrarians, the more shockingly reactionary Humanist fellow-travelers comprised of proudly white Southern men – Eliot believed that the "recovery of tradition demands a revived version of united Christendom, in which authoritative religion, conservative politics, and classic art can blend harmoniously" because "with no traditional society to support him, the artist can fix upon no single set of assumptions to animate his art, and hence is forced into a difficult reconcilement of scattered and conflicting phenomena."[21] While their manifesto *I'll Take My Stand: The South and the Agrarian Tradition* (1930) focused more on regional identity and history than on specific artworks, their subsequently elaborated views were inextricably associated with an attendant rejection and transformation of modernist aesthetic values. For prominent Agrarians such as poet-critics John Crowe Ransom and Allen Tate, economic organization was inextricable from the organization of experience more broadly. They defiantly valorized both deep history and the recent past before it was pockmarked by the Civil War and Reconstruction, advocating for a denationalized return of prelapsarian days when a "way of living ... 'feels' right, it has aesthetic quality" because based on local, pre-industrial values.[22] Writing in a journal that within a few years would endorse not only literary regionalism but also political fascism, Ransom held up the example of indigenous American cultures where "aesthetic values are as serious as the economic ones, and as governing" (293); against the pluralism of American modernity wherein "We now lack the unity of life," Agrarians pined for the days when "Men had won a great moral advantage of raw nature in achieving a coherent way of thinking about their experience. They called the general scheme of that experience *Christianity*, a unified conception of man in relation to God and nature – and the conception was upheld by belief."[23]

Ranging from genteel valorization of yeomanry to unapologetically virulent racism, Agrarian critics and artists proposed a devolutionary solution to fragmented culture: by promoting the aesthetic movement of "Regionalism" rather than a national literature, they sought to reintegrate experience by contesting the fact that we have been "delude[d] us into thinking that a novel about a ploughboy is only a regional curiosity, but a novel about a bellboy, a national masterpiece," and in so doing reclaiming a specific version of the Anglo-European-American tradition (Davidson 239). Regionalism – whether of the sort represented by Robert Penn Warren's poetry or by the paintings of Thomas Hart Benton – was by definition opposed to "non-regionalism," whether the latter was called "cosmopolitanism, progressivism, industrialism, free trade, interregionalism, internationalism, eclecticism, liberal education, the federation of the world, or simple rootlessness" (Ransom 294). For Tate and others, "A traditional society not only makes possible, but actually enjoins, the affirmation of a high code that permeates every implication of public and private experience. The economic process thus looked upon as a medium is, precisely as paint and canvas are to the artist, the medium of the moral conduct of man" (Tate 740). Tate's language of political and social production *as* artistic production indicated that the boundary between the two spheres was not only porous but that the spheres were mutually constitutive: "The traditionist attempts only what the sculptor attempts to do with his stone, to bring his experience to form and order" (743). Here, life itself is to be shaped along the lines of artistic creation, which was thus both analogous to and inseparable from political organization; both depended upon experience as a dynamic exchange through which subjects and objects could be produced in order to organize or reorganize society.

Of course, not all literary conservatives were openly racist, aristocratic, or associated with the Agrarians or New Humanists. Moreover, it is worth recalling that a scathing indictment of capitalism lay at the center of the Agrarian critique, and even the most aggressively reactionary members wanted the death of the "system which allows a relatively few men to control most of the nation's wealth and to regiment virtually the whole population under their anonymous holding companies and corporations, and to control government by bribery or intimidation."[24] Neither should literary formalism, nascent in the Agrarian milieu and eventually evolving into the American version of New Criticism, be equated with reactionary politics. By 1938, Cleanth Brooks, in a statement that would influence generations of readers, echoed "art for art's sake" by declaring that "the poem in itself, if literature is to be studied as literature, remains finally the object for study" and thereby openly rejected the "Inspirational and didactic interpretation" of literature – regardless of the political position a poem inspired or taught.[25] Nonetheless, when viewed in the context of more tenaciously enduring Left and liberal literary cultures, political aesthetics from the wrong side of history will often strike today's readers as fusty relics from a generation frequently out of touch with their time.

Left

Rocking with crisis, death of the old order, birth pangs of the new. You could almost see man, all of laboring humanity struggling back from a dreadful hell. Wasn't it true? Summoning courage to dare all. And in the andante *and* finale *movements he did find courage.*
— Myra Page, *Moscow Yankee*, 1935

It is possible to overstate the influence of conservative literary aesthetics in the 1930s, for their ideas and the work they promoted are little read today. A year after Hitler took power in Germany and a year before Ezra Pound published his pro-fascist *Jefferson and/or Mussolini* (1935), William Phillips forthrightly declared that "Only the blind would hesitate to call Eliot a fascist."[26] By 1937, he and Philip Rahv plausibly claimed that Allen Tate "found a favorable reception only among the formalist critics, who closed their eyes to his fantastic social ideas for the sake of his aesthetic mystifications" ("Literature in a Political Decade" 173). That same year, Edmund Wilson would shed a crocodile tear over the fact that "the literary Right, it hardly exists any more. Irving Babbitt is dead, and Paul Elmer More writes little. It is unfortunate that there is nobody nowadays to uphold the conservative point of view."[27] Indeed, artists and critics on the Left – largely though not exclusively affiliated with various factions of socialism and communism – drew upon an entirely different "set of assumptions" from Davidson and Chase to fight against all that "defends the status quo, argues against democratic principles, condemns strikes, views the issues in the modern world as a clear-cut fight between Christianity and Communism, and is unqualifiedly repugnant and reactionary."[28] They opposed the New Humanist and Agrarian positions as one part of a broader struggle against grotesque inequality and the multiform fascism that they saw as an especially weaponized form of capitalism. This was true before the 1930s, but even in the earliest days of the decade the idea that "There are signs ... of a new interest in social problems on the part of writers who were formerly preoccupied with esthetics" seemed like the literary understatement of the century.[29] Rather than a monolithic program being externally imposed by artists and critics, writers like Joseph Freeman saw taste itself changing in the crisis, and thus as an opportunity for the convictions of the literary Left to be newly legible and appealing to expanding audiences: "The experience of the mass of humanity today," Freeman wrote in a piece appearing alongside Richard Wright's anti-lynching poem "Between the World and Me," "is such that social and political themes are more interesting, more significant, more 'normal' than the personal themes of the previous decade."[30]

In a pamphlet titled *Culture and the Crisis*, fifty-two "American writers, painters, teachers, and other professional workers" – including poets and novelists who still tower over us, such as Countee Cullen, John Dos Passos, and Langston Hughes – declared their support for Communist Party candidates in the 1932 presidential election. In language that echoed across the decade, they argued that "The struggle for the emancipation of society from the blight of capitalism is not only an economic question, it is a cultural question as well," for "a truly human society in which all forms of exploitation have been abolished" would both facilitate and depend upon "a new cultural renaissance which will produce integrated, creative personalities."[31] In the Democratic landslide that brought Roosevelt the first of his four terms as president, that Communist ticket garnered only .26 percent of the popular vote, but that fact belied how widely and influentially the cultural critique of capitalism was shared among major figures in the arts and humanities. This was especially true after 1935, when the Communist International declared the Popular Front strategy – identifying fascism specifically rather than capitalism generally as the immediate enemy – to encourage alliances among communists, socialists, and progressive liberals. What emerged was a "cultural front" of artists that "embodied a politics of form, an aesthetic ideology" wherein "the critical controversies and debates that surrounded [their poetry, fiction, film, painting, and drama] established ways of seeing and judging, canons of value" (Denning xx) far beyond the electoral milieu.

While Left writing of the period is often dismissively associated with mechanistic "proletarian literature" and the kind of propagandistic Social Realism enforced by Soviet authorities, the American experience was far more varied. As the leader of the Communist Party USA remarked in 1935, "the method of our work in this field cannot be one of Party resolutions giving judgment upon artistic, aesthetic questions."[32] Indeed, traditional aesthetic language never fully disappeared as prominent literary theorists of the Left focused on the present and the future to call for a literature of "beautiful youthful clarity."[33] While Mike Gold "gagged at" American Romanticism and viciously punned on Eliot's "The Waste Land" by proclaiming in verse that "Poetry is the cruelest bunk / A trade union is better than all your dreams,"[34] he could also muster Romantic sentiments by declaring that "Art is the expression of the soul of a people, and the artist is the channel through which that soul pours."[35] Focusing on the silenced voice of alienated laborers rather than the rarified effusions of a singular poetic genius, proletarian writers railed against the aristocratic musings of the "official mandarins and play-actor iconoclasts and psalm-singing Humanists of the moribund bourgeois culture" ("Proletarian Realism" 204) while often emphasizing aesthetic "feeling" in the experience of art. In doing so, Gold exhorted proletarian writers to "write with the courage of our own experience" (205) and blasted through the presumed autonomy of the aesthetic object to proclaim that "life itself is the supreme melodrama. Feel this intensely, and everything becomes poetry – the new poetry of materials, of the so-called 'common man', the Worker molding his real world" (Gold "Proletarian Realism" 208). If a New Human-ist could champion the music of Bach as exemplifying truly beautiful art, the Detroit protagonist of proletarian bildungsroman *Moscow Yankee* could equally be moved to proto-communist "courage" upon hearing a Soviet orchestra perform Beethoven's symphonies.

More than a century earlier, William Wordsworth had recommended a poetry composed of "language really spoken by men" to produce "excite-ment and pleasure" in the reader.[36] Yet Wordsworth was no worker. Relocating the site of authorial genius in the collective consciousness of the dispossessed laboring classes was itself a bold attempt to end economic exploitation, which had created proletarian experiences in the first place. It was a move to revolutionize both art and experience, and thus to serve as the articulating joint between artistic creation and political action, even as both "writing" and "doing" retained associations with emotion and beauty. "Art for its own sake is doomed to suffocation and extinction, but art auxiliary to higher life expands and ever widens the bounds of human experience" wrote the painter Max Weber in 1936;[37] or, as novelist and critic Waldo Frank asserted, "The part of consciousness, or if you prefer of *experience*, in historic evolution is important for us because it leads straight to the social function of art." Far more than simply representing, let alone idealizing, the material world to provide a particular set of feelings in viewer or reader, for radical writers "The work of art is a means ... for extending, deepening, our experience of relationship with life as this organic whole."[38]

While "Aestheticism" is the term for art produced and experienced purely for heightened, self-contained passion where "experience itself, is the end" (Pater 197), "propaganda" is the term for aesthetic representations trying to generate intensely directed feelings in order to mobilize audiences for a particular political action. Yet many theorists on the Left rejected the oppos-ition of "art" and "propaganda" as a conceptual mistake. As Georg Lukács wrote in the New York journal *Partisan Review* in 1934, Marxist writers needed urgently to progress "beyond the Kant-Schiller statement of the underlying problem [of aesthetics and politics] or beyond bourgeois esthetics in general" and thus reject "the dilemma of 'pure art' versus 'propaganda art'."[39] Rather than orienting audiences toward a particular course of action by means of specific representations, one should seek the reintegration of human experience fragmented by industrial capitalism, speculative finance, and the cultures that lionized them. "Propaganda" versus "poetry" was finally a false dilemma, novelist-critic James Farrell wrote, for "when experience is harmonious and coordinated, there is no split between the functional or objective and the aesthetic or subjective" (5) and thus "literature does not perform an aesthetic function alone, nor an extra-aesthetic function alone; it performs *both*" (154).

Exploded boundaries between "world" and "word" included not only poetry and fiction but philosophy and political economy, because art wasn't merely a byproduct of rational, historical analysis. Indeed, Marxist political theory itself could be encountered as an aesthetic representation, described by Richard Wright as "a picture which, when placed before the eyes of the writer, should unify his personality, organize his emotions, buttress him with a tense and obdurate will to change the world" and bolster "his ability to fuse and make articulate the experiences of men."[40] As visual artist Hugo Gellert explained in his illustrated selections from Karl Marx's magnum opus, "The translation into graphic form of the revolutionary concepts of *Das Kapital*" could transmit more than pleasure or pain, and were more than visual adjuncts to the ideas expressed in prose: "with the aid of the drawings the necessary material for the understanding of the fundamentals of Marxism is included." This strain of Left "understanding" included both reason and feeling in a world where "the dichotomy between poetry and politics had vanished, and art and life were fused" (Freeman "Introduction" 28).

Given actually existing economic and social conditions, however, a unifying art wasn't yet possible: "For a totally universalized art, if established in America to-day," a key theorist of the cultural front wrote in 1935, "would simply be the spiritual denial of an underlying economic disunity (the aesthetic of fascism)."[41] For many on the Left, it was an article of faith and reason that "In a communist society, social control of the processes of production will enable us to break down the false separation between aesthetic significance and utility, between artificial museum art and the natural life of the people."[42] Yet, as history would have it, it was a popularly elected liberal president rather than communist revolution that produced and distributed vast amounts of actionable art in the American 1930s, serving as a key part of "the most assertive and thoroughgoing American attempt to restructure the economy under democratic auspices."[43]

Matthew Stratton

Liberal

Over the course of Franklin Delano Roosevelt's "New Deal" for Americans, the US government employed tens of thousands of writers, painters, filmmakers, musicians, composers, dancers, actors, and directors under the auspices of federal agencies: the Federal Writers Project, the Federal Art Project, the Federal Music Project, the Federal Theatre Project, and others. From post office murals to grand mountain hotels, from fiction to travel guides, from neighborhood art classes for children to theatrical productions and LaGuardia Airport, legions of workers engaged in a gigantic national project to restore hope, income, and a vision of national unity to a socially and economically battered populace. "The president-patron had no interest in art for its own sake or in history that had no message for present action" (Kennedy 61) and the "action" at hand was filling bellies, rebuilding confidence and infrastructure, fighting fascism, and rendering the prospect of communist revolution less attractive by harnessing capitalism for public wellbeing.[44] Indeed, Roosevelt himself was known to direct the form and content of specific aesthetic objects – from selecting muralists and building materials for post offices to approving the script for the Hollywood movie *Gabriel Over the White House* (1933) – not from general aristocratic love for beauty but because the daily experience of the country was understood to be both aesthetic and tied to the political reforms he sought.

For many people, the crash of 1929 inaugurated no new crisis: as one historian notes, the "fear, insecurity, and shame" that continues to define our vision of the Great Depression "had been the common, lifelong condition of perhaps half, and certainly a third, of the American people." What was novel, however, was that the "New Deal served to politicize such private nightmares, giving to them a visibility and legitimacy unknown since the heyday of urban Progressivism."[45] Novels such as *The Grapes of Wrath* (1939) deploy a variety of modernist and realist narrative techniques implicitly to advocate for liberal institutions (safe housing and adequate food for farm workers, unemployment insurance, legal protections for labor unions, etc.). They neither call for wholesale revolution nor formally resemble canonical reform novels like Upton Sinclair's *The Jungle* (1906), proletarian memoirs such as Mike Gold's *Jews Without Money* (1930), or proletarian factory novels such as Mary Heaton Vorse's *Strike!* (1930). Given that free-indirect discourse and formal fragmentation are just as central to canonical Left novels such as Josephine Herbst's *Pity is Not Enough* (1933) and poetry such as Muriel Rukeyser's *U.S.1* (1938), how then does one identify a specifically "liberal" aesthetics?

The first logical step might be to work by definition and categorize as "liberal" the art that was officially produced under and approved by a liberal Democratic administration. Yet federal agencies were themselves heavily populated by writers and artists with expressly Left convictions and occasionally administered by appointees who shared them. Literary historian Peter Conn has argued that "tensions between political aspirations and the constraints imposed by imaginative conventions pervaded most of the radical writing of the thirties decade," ultimately to reveal "the limits of the radical imagination."[46] Yet it was precisely that radical imagination that was often employed and deployed to liberal ends, that was materialized and publicized through liberal institutions. Whereas it might thus be inadvisable to categorize any particular set of aesthetic objects as liberal perforce, it still makes sense to consider the most influential philosopher of New Deal art.

John Dewey was a key proponent of the philosophy called "pragmatism," and historians have argued that agencies such as the Federal Art Project were "essentially an implementation of Dewey's ideas on art and education."[47] His theories about action, perception, education, and politics appeared from the 1880s into the 1950s, and remain influential, admired, and contested. His interest in how human perception affected beliefs and action (and vice versa) often invoked creative literature but weren't fully elaborated as an aesthetic theory until the publication of *Art as Experience* (1934). There, he contended that human experience was a form of embodied social intelligence that should be viewed as fundamentally aesthetic. Despite his occasionally dense prose style, his works were popularly read, steeped in the philosophical tradition, and democratically oriented; as one historian writes, "Taking a lead from Schiller, Dewey identified all active citizens as creative artists. This was radical in the eighteenth century and again in the 1930s."[48] Exploding the conventional boundaries between private and public, between art and life, Dewey produced a "radically democratized notion of aesthetic experience"[49] that rested on two central tenets: "ART is a quality of doing and of what is done" and "esthetic experience is experience in its integrity."[50]

Taken in isolation, these claims are perhaps mystifyingly epigrammatic; yet in the context of his larger project and of European aesthetics as a whole, they were groundbreaking. In arguing that barriers between representations and individuals, between individuals and social groups, are constructed and porous rather than natural, Dewey doesn't completely remove pleasure from the equation, stipulating instead that "[t]o be truly artistic, a work must also be esthetic – that is, framed for enjoyed receptive perception" (49). This is more than a banality stretching back to Kant, for Dewey goes much further to define aesthetic experience specifically as representative of experience itself. Far more than an individualist means of retreating into inspired interiority, "art" by definition describes an interpersonal exchange across social hurdles, a particular subspecies of "communication in its pure and undefiled form. Art breaks through barriers that divide human beings, which are impermeable in ordinary association" (254). Schiller's account of aesthetic education, seeing political promise in the shared feeling of a universal human joy, is famous as a poem set to music in Beethoven's Ninth Symphony, and Dewey identifies creative writing as a particular case of the aesthetic in general, for "[t]his force of art, common to all the arts, is most fully manifested in literature" (254). The lack of unified, integrated experience lamented from Communists to Agrarians could be remedied, Dewey thought, by face-to-face communication among different people and by reorienting perceptive faculties through imaginative engagement with aesthetic representations. This was no one-way street from active author to standardized text to passive audience, however, because the active qualities of embodied intellect were already required to experience the world in which artworks were a special component: dialectically predicting the similar language of Joseph Freeman, Richard Wright, and others, Dewey claimed that "To some degree we become artists ourselves as we undertake this integration, and, by bringing it to pass, our own experience is reoriented. Barriers are dissolved, limiting prejudices melt away" (348).

Despite strong allies on the Left (such as his former student, philosopher Sidney Hook), Dewey and the New Deal artistic programs he helped to inspire frequently came under fire as both theory and practice. To many critics, *Art as Experience* damnably exemplified Dewey's "political liberalism, his educational theories, his metaphysics, his esthetics, [which] are all tantalizingly suggestive of a revolutionary outlook, while they finally manage to repose snugly in the arms of the *status quo*."[51] From the Left, some of the most enduring iconography of the New Deal (such as Dorothea Lange's photograph called "Migrant Mother") generated popular sympathy for the plight of some disenfranchised workers by "using [problematically] gendered symbols ... to elicit public support for New Deal programs that would alleviate their need, rather than overturn the structural conditions that produced it."[52] In considering the aesthetic values of New Deal liberalism, however, the view from the Right ironically could strike the same note of critique: "The liberals are busy collecting the pieces of Humpty Dumpty," conservative historian Herbert Agar wrote in 1934, "and trying to fit them into a less gruesome shape."[53] To those for whom revolution was either required or anathema, aesthetics that generated support for political reform fell short by producing analgesics rather than curing what ailed the body politic.

Outside the heated moment of the 1930s, however, Dewey's aesthetic-political theory is more plainly radical than Left or Right would concede. As Dewey argued for aesthetic experience to serve as the model for all experience, he also stoutly opposed anything resembling Aestheticism. If New Deal art inspired people to vaccinate their children and support unions, Dewey also knew that "The labor and employment problem of which we are so acutely aware cannot be solved by mere changes in wage, hours of work, and sanitary conditions. No permanent solution is possible save in a radical social alteration."[54] Of course, he was not arguing against the eight-hour work day or clean milk publicly distributed to hungry children, but Dewey did publicly denounce New Deal programs for not going far enough: they all were "compromised, prejudiced, yes, nullified, by private monopolization of opportunity" ("Socialization" 256) when the United States should rather "go to the root of the matter and give the unemployed an opportunity to work by socialization of the land" ("Socialization" 257). Just as architecture would remain stunted so long as buildings were designed for private property, human experience had to be changed before the beauty of objects could improve. Experience was a dialectical process of engagement between individuals, social groups, and objects, so of course it was useless to imagine that art, society, or its members could improve without a reciprocal revolution in both subjective and material conditions: after all, "[t]he psychological conditions resulting from private control of the labor of other men for the sake of private gain ... are the forces that suppress and limit esthetic quality in the experience that accompanies processes of production" (357) Dewey argued. Oh, for such "impartial" liberals today.

Untidy Unities: A Conclusion

Things were strange and unrelated and made no pattern that a person could trace easily.
— Josephine Johnson, *Now in November*

It is a selection, and therefore a reduction, to let Mike Gold speak for "The Left," Allen Tate for "The Right," or John Dewey for "The Liberal." Yet an exhaustively coherent, reasonable account of a decade's political aesthetics would be lucid and coherent in all the ways that the 1930s were not. History is not composed of neutral facts and objects but is the result of a selection designed to serve the wants and needs of particular historical moments; indeed, as early as 1932, history could be understood as "an imaginative creation, a personal possession which each one of us ... fashions out of his individual experience, adapts to his practical or emotional needs, and adopts as well as may be to suit his aesthetic tastes."[55] Perhaps my history overemphasizes anti-fascist cooperation after 1935, when "the borders between Communism and New Deal liberalism became blurred," in order to highlight ideas in concert when they were often in conflict. [56] Perhaps I have done so intentionally to serve a historical moment when *It Can't Happen Here* (1935), Sinclair Lewis's dystopian tale of fascism coming to the United States, strikes new audiences as hauntingly prescient and dangerously relevant from Charlottesville to Sacramento and beyond. With gratitude for decades of work that have recovered and revivified lost or suppressed literary voices from the Depression, perhaps I imagine a successfully woven consensus where generations of literary historians have found a disappointingly tangled aesthetic of disagreement.

NOTES

1 Vincent Leitch, "Marxist Criticism in the 1930s," *American Literary Criticism Since the 1930s*, 2nd ed., (New York: Routledge, 2010), 13.
2 Walter Pater, *The Renaissance* (New York: The Modern Library [dedication 1873]. [n.d.]), 199.
3 Walter Benjamin, "The Work of Art in the Age of Its Technological Reproducibility: Second Version," trans. Edmund Jephcott and Harry Zohn. *The Work of Art in the Age of Its Technological Reproducibility, and Other Writings on Media*, ed. Michael W. Jennings et al. (Cambridge, MA: Belknap Press of Harvard University Press, 2008), 42.
4 Martin Jay, "Aesthetic Ideology; Or, What Does It Mean to Aestheticize Politics?" *Cultural Critique* 21 (Spring 1992): 45.
5 Jon Simons, "Democratic Aesthetics," *Culture, Theory and Critique* 50:1 (2009): 1.
6 Sianne Ngai, *Our Aesthetic Categories* (Cambridge, MA: Harvard University Press, 2012), 22.
7 Tracy Strong, *Politics Without Vision: Thinking without a Banister in the Twentieth Century* (Chicago: University of Chicago Press, 2012), 50.
8 John Steinbeck, *The Grapes of Wrath* (1939; New York: Penguin Classics, 2006), 419, 280.
9 Eric Rauchway, *The Great Depression & The New Deal: A Very Short Introduction* (New York: Oxford University Press, 2008), 40.
10 Philip Rahv and Williams Phillips, "Literature in a Political Decade," *New Letters in America* 1, eds. Horace Gregory and Eleanor Clark (New York: Norton, 1937), 170.
11 Henry Hart, "Introduction," *American Writers' Congress*, ed. Henry Hart (New York: International Publishers, 1935), 14.
12 Michael Denning, *The Cultural Front: The Laboring of American Culture in the Twentieth Century* (New York: Verso, 1997), 45.
13 Kenneth Burke, "Letter to Malcolm Cowley," 12/01/1940, *The Selected Correspondence of Kenneth Burke and Malcolm Cowley, 1915–1981*, ed. Paul Jay (New York: Viking Penguin, 1988), 232.
14 Jacques Ranciére, *The Politics of Aesthetics: The Distribution of the Sensible*, trans. Gabriel Rockhill (New York: Continuum, 2006), 60.
15 Horace Gregory, "Introduction," *New Letters in America* 1, eds. Horace Gregory and Eleanor Clark (New York: Norton, 1937), 15.

16 Joseph Freeman, "Introduction," *Proletarian Literature in the United States* (New York: International Publishers, 1935), 9.

17 Paul Elmer More, "A Revival of Humanism," *The Bookman; a Review of Books and Life* 71 (March 1930): 2.

18 Paul Elmer More, "The Humility of Common Sense," *Humanism and America: Essays on the Outlook of Modern Civilisatio,* ed. Norman Foerster (New York: Farrar and Rinehart, 1930), 58.

19 Stanley P. Chase, "Dionysus in Dismay," *Humanism and America: Essays on the Outlook of Modern Civilisation,* ed. Norman Foerster (New York: Farrar and Rinehart, 1930), 218.

20 Frank Jewett Jr. Mather, "The Plight of Our Arts," *Humanism and America: Essays on the Outlook of Modern Civilisation,* ed. Norman Foerster (New York: Farrar and Rinehart, 1930), 118.

21 Donald Davidson, *The Attack on Leviathan: Regionalism and Nationalism in the United States,* Orig. University of North Carolina Press, 1938 (Reprint. Gloucester, MA: Peter Smith, 1962), 85.

22 John Crowe Ransom, "The Aesthetic of Regionalism," *The American Review* 2:3 (January 1934): 291.

23 John Crowe Ransom, "The Aesthetic of Regionalism," *The American Review* 2:3 (January 1934): 291.

24 Frank L. Owsley, "The Pillars of Agrarianism," *American Review* 4 (February 1935): 520.

25 Cleanth Brooks and Robert Penn Warren, "Letter to the Teacher," *Understanding Poetry: An Anthology for College Students* (New York: H. Holt, 1938), iv.

26 William Phillips [pseud. Wallace Phelps], "Eliot Takes His Stand," *Partisan Review* 1 (April–May 1934): 52.

27 Edmund Wilson, "American Critics, Left and Right," *The Shores of Light: A Literary Chronicle of the 1920s and 1930* (1937; New York: Farrar, Straus and Giroux, 1952), 650.

28 James Farrell, *A Note On Literary Criticism* (1936; The Vanguard Press. New York: Columbia University Press, 1992), 20, n 3.

29 C. Hartley Grattan, "Editor's Note," *The Critique of Humanism: A Symposium* (New York: Brewer and Warren, 1930), n.p.

30 Joseph Freeman, "Mask, Image, and Truth," *Partisan Review* 2:8 (July–August 1935): 16.

31 League of Professional Groups for Foster and Ford, *Culture and the Crisis: An Open Letter to the Writers * Artists * Teachers * Physicians * Engineers * Scientists * and Other Professional Workers of America* (New York: Workers Library Publishers, 1932), 29–30.

32 Earl Browder, "Communism and Literature," *The American Writers Congress,* ed. Henry Hart (New York: International Publishers, 1935), 68.

33 Mike Gold, "Proletarian Realism," *Mike Gold: A Literary Anthology,* ed. Michael Folsom. Orig. *New Masses* (September 1930) (New York: International Publishers, 1972), 208.

34 Mike Gold, "Ode to Walt Whitman," *New Masses* (November 5, 1935): 21.

35 Mike Gold, "No More Nudes, No More Fish!" *New Masses* (December 14, 1937): 18.

36 William Wordsworth, "Preface to *Lyrical Ballads." The Norton Anthology of Theory & Criticism,* 2nd ed., ed. Vincent Leitch (New York: W.W. Norton, 2010), 566, 571.

37 Max Weber, "The Artist, His Audience, and Outlook," *Artists Against War and Fascism: Papers of the First American Artists' Congress* (New Brunswick, NJ: Rutgers University Press, 1986), 126.

38 Waldo Frank, "Values of the Revolutionary Writer" *American Writers' Congress*, 71–72.

39 Georg Lukács, "Propaganda or Partisanship?" trans. Leonard F. Mins, *Partisan Review* 1:2 (April–May 1934): 40, 44.

40 Richard Wright, "Blueprint for Negro Writing" (1937), *Within the Circle: An Anthology of African American Criticism from the Harlem Renaissance to the Present*, ed. Angelyn Miller (Duke University Press, 1994), 102.

41 Kenneth Burke, "Revolutionary Symbolism in America," *American Writers Congress*, 92.

42 Sidney Hook, "Communism without Dogmas: A Reply," *The Meaning of Marx: A Symposium* (New York: Farrar & Rinehart, 1934), 115.

43 Ira Katznelson, *Fear Itself: The New Deal and the Origins of Our Time* (New York: Liveright Publishing, 2013), 245.

44 Roger G. Kennedy and David Larkin, *When Art Worked: The New Deal, Art, and Democracy* (New York: Rissoli International Publications, 2009), 61.

45 Nelson Lichtenstein, *State of the Union: A Century of American Labor* (Princeton, NJ: Princeton University Press, 2002), 26.

46 Peter Conn, *The American 1930s: A Literary History* (Cambridge: Cambridge University Press, 2009), 225, 237.

47 Andrew Hemingway, *Artists on the Left: American Artists and the Communist Movement 1926–1956* (New Haven, CT: Yale University Press, 2002), 152.

48 Doris Summer, *The Work of Art in the World: Civic Agency and Public Humanities* (Durham, NC: Duke University Press, 2014), 10

49 Martin Jay, *Songs of Experience: Modern American and European Variations on a Universal Theme* (Berkeley, CA: University of California Press, 2005), 166.

50 John Dewey, *Art as Experience* (1934; New York: Perigee Publishing Group, 1980), 222, 285.

51 Wallace Phelps, "Dewey's Esthetics," review of John Dewey, *Art as Experience*, *Minton, Balch and Co. New Masses* (June 19, 1934): 27

52 Erin Royston Battat, *Ain't Got No Home: America's Great Migrations and the Making of an Interracial Left* (Chapel Hill, NC: University of North Carolina Press, 2014), 95.

53 Herbert Agar, "The Task for Conservatism," *The American Review* 3:1 (April 1934): 11.

54 John Dewey, "Socialization of Ground Rent," *The Collected Works of John Dewey, 1882–1953. Later Works, 1924–1953*, vol. 11, ed. Jo Ann Boydstun (Carbondale, IL: Southern Illinois University Press, 1967–1991), 256–257.

55 Carl Becker, "Everyman His Own Historian," (Presidential Address delivered before the American Historical Association at Minneapolis, December 29, 1931), *The American Historical Review* 37:2 (January 1932): 228.

56 Alan M. Wald, *Exiles from a Future Time: The Forging of the Mid-Twentieth-Century Literary Left* (Chapel Hill, NC: University of North Carolina Press, 2002), 123.

3

CATHERINE MORLEY

Architects of History

Politics and Experimentalism in American Writing of the 1930s

What do you write for then? To convince people of something? That's preaching, and is part of the business of everybody who deals with words; not to admit that is to play with a gun and then blubber that you didn't know it was loaded. But outside of preaching I think there is such a thing as straight writing.

John Dos Passos, introduction to the Modern Library edition of
Three Soldiers (1932)

In February 1924, seeking respite from the cold Northern weather, the young John Dos Passos visited New Orleans. At first, he felt overwhelmed, alienated even, by the decaying old city's exoticism, its streets 'full of inconceivable old geezers in decrepit frockcoats, of tall negresses with green and magenta bandannas on their heads, of whores and racingmen and South Americans and Central Americans of all colours and shapes'. Yet soon Dos Passos came to love New Orleans, its architecture and its waterfront, 'the streets of scaling crumbling houses with broad wrought iron verandahs painted in Caribbean blues and greens'. And before long he found himself part of a small literary coterie which included writers such as Sherwood Anderson, Lyle Saxon and William Faulkner.[1] This oddly incongruous group – the local colourist, the New Orleans journalist, the Southern regionalist, and the least glamorous member of the Lost Generation writers – met at the Original Tivoli, on Chartres Street, a restaurant run by an Italian American couple, and which would later find its way into Dos Passos's novel *The 42nd Parallel* (1930). As a group they could hardly have been more diverse. Yet in many ways their little gatherings perfectly captured the trends and preoccupations of American writing of the 1930s. This was the decade in which each of them produced arguably his best work. But it was also a decade defined, in the eyes of many, by a fiercely political and sometimes overtly Marxist literature of protest. It was the decade that marked the high point of the documentary element in American writing. And it was, perhaps above all, the decade in which the high modernist experimentalism of the

1920s found its way into the regional writing which had, until that point, been described and even dismissed as mere local-colour naturalism.

If there is one writer who, in the public mind at least, has come to define the American experience in the 1930s, it is not Dos Passos, Anderson or even Faulkner, but John Steinbeck. Few novels of the decade are better known than Steinbeck's saga of Dustbowl migrants *The Grapes of Wrath* (1939), which was awarded the Pulitzer Prize a year later, and is typically held up as both an epic of human resilience and an elegy for populist agrarianism. Yet Steinbeck's novel, though a staple of high school and undergraduate courses, has never been universally popular. At the time, Father Arthur D. Spearman spoke for many on the right when they attacked the book as 'communist propaganda', while there were always plenty of critics who dismissed it as a tub-thumping middlebrow distraction.[2] Leslie Fiedler, for instance, described it as mere 'sentimental entertainment (hoked up with heavy-handed symbolism)', which, while harsh, is not, perhaps, entirely unwarranted.[3] Yet at the time, there were also critics who saw something deeper in Steinbeck's vision. Writing for the *New York Times* in April 1939, for example, Peter Monro Jack even suggested that in terms of his style, Steinbeck ranked alongside Dos Passos, Faulkner and Ernest Hemingway. For Jack, Steinbeck seemed a modernist, at least of a kind – a verdict that few critics today would wholeheartedly endorse.[4] Indeed, if Steinbeck appears radical to modern readers, it is because of his left-wing politics – and specifically his anger at the Californian agricultural companies' exploitation of Oklahoman migrant labourers – rather than any inclination towards formal experimentation or desire to overturn the literary conventions of his day. Yet this is easily overstated. Steinbeck's novel is more than merely politically inspired naturalism in the mode of earlier European writers such as Emile Zola or Arnold Bennett. He intersperses longer fictional chapters documenting the travails of the Joads with shorter, documentary-style intercalary chapters detailing the socio-economic factors and natural forces which had forced so many families onto the roads. His book is not just the story of a single fictional family; it is simultaneously a work of documentary journalism, exploring, say, the effects of drought on sharecroppers, the dilapidation of abandoned homesteads, or the consequences of bank foreclosures for the individuals who depended on them.

So while *The Grapes of Wrath* is, of course, irrevocably political in its heartrending story and its unashamed message of shared humanity, it is also much more formally surprising – experimental, even – than is often recognised. And in that respect, Steinbeck's bestseller, rather like that little gang of writers who met at the Old Tivoli in New Orleans, absolutely captures the spirit that defines the literary 1930s. This was a decade suffused with tension: not just the political and economic tensions born of the Depression, but the literary tension between directly political works by Jewish American and African American intellectuals such as Mike Gold, Carl Sandburg and Richard Wright and the more indirect rhetorical methods employed by figures like Djuna Barnes and Henry Miller. A related conflict can be observed as well in the difference between the work of Italian anarchist writers such as Emanuel Carnevali, Pietro di Donato or Arturo Giovannitti, on the one hand, and the experimental modernism pioneered by writers such as Hemingway, Faulkner and Wallace Stevens, on the other. And it is this sense of tension that I want to explore in this chapter, beginning with an appraisal of Gold's semi-autobiographical novel *Jews Without Money* (1930) and an examination of di Donato's *Christ in Concrete* (1939), before moving towards the regional experimentalism of Faulkner's companion novels *The Sound and the Fury* (1929) and *Absalom, Absalom!* (1936). In the final pages of the chapter, meanwhile, I will return to Dos Passos, making the case that it is in his *U.S.A.* trilogy (1930–1936) that the Chicago-born writer, a curious mixture of left-wing radical and defiant libertarian, found a way to reconcile the political and experimental strands that dominated American writing in the 1930s.

As the founder of the radical magazine *The New Masses*, Mike Gold was nothing if not controversial. Nobody, however, better personified the reaction in some quarters against the experimentalism of modernist writing. In one of his most infamous essays (which even now remains a hilarious read), he once called Gertrude Stein an idiot whose works 'read like the literature of students in padded cells in Matteawan', and described her experimental efforts as 'the monotonous gibberings of paranoiacs in the private wards of asylums'. To Gold, Stein's writing was one of the supreme examples 'of the most extreme subjectivism of the contemporary bourgeois artist, and a reflection of the ideological anarchy into which the whole of bourgeois literature has fallen'.[5] By Gold's standards this was actually relatively restrained: he once described Marcel Proust, for example, as the 'master-masturbator of the bourgeois literature'.[6] For Gold, experimentalism of any kind was pointless, indulgent and impractical, a distraction from the real business of socialist transformation. Like so many radical writers in the inter-war years, he looked for inspiration not inwards, to the workings of the unconscious, or even in the kaleidoscopic potential of literature itself (its ability to present multiple perspectives at once), but in the utopian possibilities of the new Soviet Union. In one early essay for *The Liberator*, 'The Jesus Thinkers' (1922), for example, he explicitly saw Lenin as the prophet of a new age. 'The legend of Lenin', he wrote, 'is more beautiful to me than the legend of Jesus. A strong, practical man with a heart as pure as that of Jesus leads great masses to emancipation, steels himself against the bloody sacrifices that must be made, and wins to a tentative victory'.[7]

It is only against this background that we can really make sense of Gold's sole novel, the semi-autobiographical *Jews Without Money* (1930). Written in the second half of the previous decade, the book charts the life of an impoverished Jewish family in Lower East Side Manhattan at the turn of the century. Not unlike Anzia Yezierska's *Bread Givers*, which was published five years earlier, the novel depicts the squalor and the destitution of the Jewish community with an exaggerated and often melodramatic realism. But unlike Yezierska's scholarly Sara Smolinsky, who is bent on improving herself through assimilation with mainstream American culture, Gold's young hero, the bright, high-school valedictorian Michael, sees salvation only in the workers' revolution. In the novel's rousing final lines, which have become a famous example of literary Marxist millenarianism, young Michael waxes lyrical about the hope he has found in a 'world movement ... born to abolish poverty':

> O workers' Revolution, you brought hope to me, a lonely, suicidal boy. You are the true Messiah. You will destroy the East Side when you come, and build there a garden for the human spirit.
> O Revolution, that forced me to think, to struggle, and to live.
> O great Beginning![8]

For Michael, it is his conversion to communism that represents the novel's crucial epiphany, tearing him from the ethnic past and identity that have hitherto defined him and dominated his recollections. It is worth remembering that the novel is composed as a series of dreamlike vignettes, memories which not only document the harshness of life in the tenements, but suggest how much it has been his family's Jewishness, the everyday experience of their faith, that has provided them with solace, community and identity. For Michael, however, true solace is found not in Judaism but in communism. And of course this is precisely what lends so much power to his invocation of the Messiah – the personification of the workers' revolution – in the passage quoted earlier.

The crucial awakening in *Jews Without Money* is the birth of a radical political consciousness within an individual who has, until now, been predominantly passive. Like Sara Smolinsky in *Bread Givers*, who is pushed on to the streets to sell herring, young Michael only finds his voice when he is forced outside, into a public space, to work. In this instance, the young child provides the peddler's yell for a father embarrassed and ashamed to be selling bananas on the street. Indeed, the entire novel is preoccupied with an economics of exchange, with the notion of buying and selling space, bodies, lives and labour. As a good Marxist, Gold saw the principle of the market in very negative terms indeed. Indeed, in his essay 'Proletarian Realism', published in the same year (1930) as his novel, Gold laid out a kind of literary Marxist manifesto, recalling the manifestos of the Imagists, Vorticists or Futurists, but arguing for a new kind of literature, based not on formal experiment but on the principle of proletarian utility:

> Proletarian realism deals with the real conflicts of men and women who work for a living. It has nothing to do with the sickly mental states of the idle Bohemians, their subtleties, their sentimentalities, their fine-spun affairs ...
>
> Proletarian literature is never pointless. It does not believe in literature for its own sake but in literature that is useful, has a social function ...
>
> As few words as possible. We are not interested in the verbal acrobats – this is only another form for bourgeois idleness.[9]

It has to be said that Gold's aggressive rejection of literary experimentation ('verbal acrobats'), his disregard even for psychological complexity ('sickly mental states'), often gave his own work a disconcerting flatness. In many ways Gold's subject could hardly have been more dramatic. Young women and girls are assaulted, gang-raped and sometimes killed; mothers are bereft of their children; young men are brutalised by thugs, bullies and bosses; and all the time, the community is exploited almost to nothingness by the capitalist machine. Yet despite the intensity of his characters' experiences at the level of content, Gold sees no point in literary/stylistic pyrotechnics. The prose in *Jews Without Money,* for instance, is deliberately colourless, the sentences stripped of ornament and even beauty. These are tough, unromantic, fatalistic characters condemned to grinding, difficult lives devoid of pleasure; for the reader, at least, the writing itself offers no consolation.

Similar realities to those described by Gold are evident in the work of the American-born, trade unionist and bricklayer Pietro di Donato, who became a life-long supporter of the Communist cause following the executions of Nicola Sacco and Bartolomeo Vanzetti in 1927. Ten years later, di Donato published his religiously allusive and largely autobiographical short story 'Christ in Concrete' in *Esquire* magazine, and the story formed the first chapter of the expanded novel of the same name, published two years later, in 1939. Set in the Lower East Side shortly before the Great Depression, *Christ in Concrete* opens with the dramatic Good Friday collapse of a building under construction, which impales and buries alive in concrete a worker called Geremio. The dead man's oldest son Paul, just twelve years old, assumes his father's role within the family and on the building site. Divided into five sections, the novel is bookended by the twin pillars of his two parents – Geremio and Annunziata – each of whom is crucial in the formation of Paul's consciousness. It is his father who allows him to discover his labouring self; from his mother, he learns about his religious (and subsequently atheistic) self. Perhaps most remarkable, though, is di Donato's personification of 'Job' (the second title of the five sections), by which he means first Geremio's job and then Paul's job after his father's death. Indeed, shortly after he is embraced by his father's co-worker, we learn that 'Paul clung to Job. ... [he felt] the first fleshly sense of Job, Job who would give living to mother Annunziata and the little ones'.[10] For Paul, and indeed for his family, 'Job' represents both prosperity and alienation. It is 'Job' that offers comfort, but it is also 'Job' that robs them of their vital and spiritual meaning. In a sense, the real story of the novel is Paul's attempt to come to terms with this reality.

As this personification of 'Job' might suggest, di Donato's novel is fundamentally concerned with the meaning, the price and the effects of labour. When Paul starts to lose his religious faith, for example, he places his hope in salvation through 'Job'. For while God is unknowable and ethereal, 'Job' is present and tangible: 'a great mass of interwinding stone foundation walls lay waiting to bear building upon its rubble shoulders. ... [Job is] an expanding organism-banging, thudding, groaning and pushing UP' (135–136). But just as religion lets Paul down, so does the almighty 'Job', when the Depression sets in and work dries up. Indeed, the book's most compelling single scene – Geremio's death – is ultimately a blistering indictment of the devastating impact of the forces of labour upon the individual. It comes shortly after the novel's opening, which brims with the optimism of Geremio's new family home, his anticipation of a new arrival, and his cheerful sexual banter with his friends, who joke about their reproductive prowess. Yet within moments all this is brutally undermined, as the ground seems to 'vomit upwards' (13) and 'Job tore upon them madly' (13). Because of cost-cutting measures, a floor gives way and Geremio falls downward, impaled by and trapped between the building's steel and wooden support beams. Pinned with his arms outstretched, like a ghastly parody of Christ, he has become a human sacrifice to the demands of capital. The melding of his body with the wood and the steel girders, and later the concrete, literally nails him to his labour: in death, he has been consumed by, and made one, with 'Job'. Indeed, the image of consumption runs right through the novel: as the critic Michele Fazio points out, Geremio's workmates, Nick the Lean, Giacomo, Tomas and Snoutnose, are all 'edible commodities ... sacrificed for capitalist consumption and profit'.[11] So it is that after his accident, Geremio is forced literally to ingest the materials of his labour, while his cries for help are choked by the pieces of wood in his mouth and the concrete pouring through the cavities of his head. In this savagely memorable scene, di Donato renders the battle between the immigrant and the products of capitalism in unsparing, unflinching detail:

> He had bitten halfway through when his teeth snapped off to the gums in the uneven conflict. The pressure of the concrete was such, and its effectiveness so thorough, that the wooden splinters, stumps of teeth, and blood never left the choking mouth. (15)

Here, through a series of extended metaphors and images, di Donato demonstrates the imbalanced working relations between the labourer and corporate America. For Geremio and his fellow workers are not merely destroyed by the city, they are literally *consumed* by it, eaten alive by the great icon of modernity, the supreme symbol of American capitalism, which promised such a shining future, but delivered only death.

Yet although di Donato's work very clearly shares common ground with Gold's novel – notably in its combination of intense religiosity and utopian Marxism – its approach is very different. Through a combination of linguistic and rhetorical innovation, di Donato constructs an alternative modernist? aesthetic, occasionally surreal, occasionally naturalistic. In practice, he employs this expressive form as a means of representing the violent demise of working-class labourers, not least the death of Paul's father Geremio. For many critics, di Donato's focus on the economic inequalities suffered by working-class immigrants places him in the revolutionary socialist tradition of the *sovversivi*, although he was never directly connected to the movement.[12] Like the poetry of writers such as Arturo Giovannitti and Emanuel Carnevali, his work suggests a willingness to accommodate a tension between oratory and subjectivity in order to textualise radical imperatives such as the conditions faced by the labourers of the text.

Yet it is the novel's political mission, rather than its formal innovations, that has most interested critics. In 1939, E. B. Garside heralded di Donato as a 'shining figure to add to the proletarian gallery of artists' and soon afterwards Halford Luccock described the book as a proletarian novel written by 'a workman resembling more nearly the much heralded actual "proletarian" author than any other'.[13] That said, not all readers have interpreted the book in such exclusively 'proletarian' terms. Writing in 1939, the Slovene-American socialist Louis Adamic even applauded the book's refusal to 'conform to the notion of synthetic Marxians ... there is nothing twisted to fit an intellectual hypothesis. There is no ideology, no simplification of life ... there is no sentimentality or subservience. There is always a sense of the dignity of man and the worker'.[14] This seem pretty fair: while Gold's book *Jews Without Money* often reads like a manifesto, di Donato's *Christ in Concrete* has a much greater sense of vitality and freedom. That is not to say, of course, that there is no obvious political message: indeed, di Donato is clearly keen to expose the exploitation of immigrants and children, as well as the effects of this exploitation upon family life, communities and individual consciousness. And although Paul's awakening is less overtly political than that of Gold's Mike, the novels are similar insofar as they explore the way the consciousness of the worker can be liberated, whether from the shackles of the labour market or the fetters of religion. In *Jews Without Money*, Mike's prayer-like incantation of the hope offered by the coming of the worker's revolution speaks of a new beginning. By contrast, it is the death of Paul's God-fearing mother at the end of *Christ in Concrete* that offers him a new beginning, freed from the conservative doctrines of Italian Catholicism – a faith which promised that 'Jesus Never Fails' (106), but which, like Geremio's faith in the capitalist city, ultimately disappoints.

Where di Donato most obviously departs from Gold is, of course, in his style. *Christ in Concrete* is laden with evocative, poetic language, heavy with symbolism and allusion, but it is also remarkable for its unswerving commitment to representing the Italian American voice in all its rich vernacular tang and grammatical idiosyncrasies. Running right through the novel, therefore, is a deep tension between the implied homogeneity of the modernist city and the kaleidoscopic diversity of the individual experience. And in this respect, di Donato is perhaps not so different from one of the most obviously experimental of American writers of the day, the Nobel Prize–winning William Faulkner. Although Faulkner published his first story in 1919 and continued writing until his death in 1962, it was the 1930s that marked his apogee. Between the Wall Street Crash and the Japanese attack on Pearl Harbor he published no fewer than ten novels, among them landmark works such as *The Sound and the Fury* (1929), *As I Lay Dying* (1930), *Light in August* (1932) and *Absalom, Absalom!* (1936). With his meticulous attention to the vocal cadences of all Southerners, from slaves to aristocrats, and his sense of the overlapping histories of individuals and families, he produced a rich, almost Dickensian tapestry of ancestral and geographical interconnection. Nothing captures that better than his Yoknapatawpha stories, or the characters who appear and reappear throughout the cycle. One such character is Quentin Compson, through whom sections of Faulkner's novels, *The Sound and the Fury* and *Absalom, Absalom!* are filtered. Both novels chart the decline of important Southern families unable to deal with the shock of modernisation, both play with the temporal structure of the novel, offering a nonlinear chronology and a fragmented consciousness, and both stretch language and grammar itself, questioning its ability adequately to represent the tangibly lived and psychological realities of individuals locked within their contemporary moment.

In the second section of *The Sound and the Fury* (1929), which takes its title from Shakespeare's *Macbeth*, Quentin Compson twists the hands from the face of a wristwatch given to him by his father. This symbolic act represents the manipulation of time, which occurs throughout Faulkner's technically challenging novel. Chronological time breaks down completely, and the reader is shuttled forwards and backwards through the thoughts and memories of a series of characters, notably the Compson brothers, Benjy, Quentin and Jason, and latterly their African American servant Dilsey Gibson. In temporally mapping the novel, we can detect four important timeframes: the period around 1900 when the four Compson children, the brothers and their sister Caddy, are very young; 1910, with Quentin's suicide and Caddy's ill-fated marriage; 1913, when Benjy is sterilised having frightened a schoolgirl he mistakes for his absent sister; and 1928, the novel's present, in which Caddy's nineteen-year-old daughter, Quentin, hatches her escape from the family home with a man from a nearby visiting carnival. Thus, Quentin's removal of the hands from the watch is a moment heavy with significance; indeed, perhaps even more than Benjy, it is Quentin whose grip on temporal reality is most skewed. Critics and readers often find Benjy's narrative the most complex and confusing section of the novel, and while the youngest brother's narrative is undoubtedly challenging, Quentin's lost grip on time is perhaps the most startling. Benjy's cognitive and linguistic disabilities clearly hinder his grasp of contemporary reality; for him, the past lives and breathes within the present. The past *is* the present in Benjy's interior world, which is why the narrative slips from 1928 to the early 1900s without the debilitating sense of loss or self-consciousness which the reader encounters in Quentin's narrative. In Benjy's section the shift in the temporal setting is accompanied by a switch to italics in the typeface, or induced by particular images (for instance, the word 'caddie' called by the golfers in the adjacent plot of land sets Benjy off into the past and his life with Caddy), or evident from the change in his African American companion: Versh and T.P. in the past, but Luster in the present.

By contrast, the temporal slippages in Quentin's narrative are more disquieting, filtered as they are through what initially seems the lucid and rational mind of a Harvard undergraduate. Indeed, Quentin's narrative, set in the past and being *about* the past, opens with a deliberate and considered meditation on the nature of time:

> When the shadow of the sash appeared on the curtains it was between seven and eight o'clock and then I was in time again, hearing the watch. It was Grandfather's and when Father gave it to me he said, Quentin, I give you the mausoleum of all hope and desire … I give it to you not that you may

remember time but that you may forget it now and then for a moment and not
spend all your breath trying to conquer it.[15]

In fact, the rather pompous and ponderous words of Jason Compson III are
some of the most important in the entire novel. Reflecting the tomb-like
nature of marked clock time, these words haunt Quentin's narrative; they
torture his consciousness in the hours before his death, as he struggles with
his memories of his sister's sexual awakening and his own imminent suicide.
And whereas Benjy is seemingly untroubled by the overlapping of time,
Quentin is haunted by the past and unable to reconcile it with the present –
which is why he elects to lie down in the mausoleum of time altogether. In
short, he is unable to conquer time, and it is precisely his struggle to come to
terms with this failure which creates the fitful, analeptic narrative of a mind
consciously hurtling toward disintegration.

The novel's preoccupation with time is, of course, also a regional, distinctly *Southern* matter. The story charts the decline of the South through the
fortunes of the Compsons, whose land is eventually eroded to a thin plot and
whose control over their African American servants becomes increasingly
feeble.[16] For Faulkner, the decline of the South was a frequent concern, and
the imaginary Yoknapatawpha County, in which *The Sound and the Fury* is
set, is part of this impulse to create a mythical South.[17] Indeed, in Faulkner's
later novel *Go Down, Moses* (1942), the narrator describes the ledgers of the
McCaslin plantation, which record the 'slow trickle of molasses and meal
and meat, of shoes and straw hats and overalls, of plowlines and collars and
heelbolts and clevises, which returned each year as cotton ... that chronicle
which was a whole land in miniature, which multiplied and compounded as
the entire South'.[18] Faulkner's own writing, with its portrayal of fields,
farms, small business holdings and family fortunes, can be seen as a 'whole
land in miniature'. Indeed, the desire of various characters to return to the
past is a marker of a wider regional impulse to reinvent a Southern past. For
Faulkner, identity, whether personal or cultural, is indelibly marked by
history. And just as all his characters are haunted by their pasts, so too is
the South of his fictions.

Faulkner's commitment to the South, with its peculiar history and institutions, was real and undeniable. Yet he was nevertheless one of the most
important American modernists of his generation. As a young man he was
enormously influenced by French Symbolism, and modelled his own poetry
on that of Mallarmé and Verlaine. Like Hemingway and Fitzgerald, he took
the mandatory trip to Paris, albeit with less success than his contemporaries,
returning to Mississippi after just a few months. Nonetheless, in France he
encountered Gertrude Stein and Ezra Pound, from whom he learned the

economy of language. (Clearly, then, he did not share Mike Gold's views on 'monotonous gibberings'.) The most obvious modernist influence upon his work, though, was undoubtedly James Joyce's novel *Ulysses* (1922), from which he learned the art of the interior monologue, the stream of consciousness, the collapse of linear time and the importance of preserving oral tone and dialect, as we see most convincingly in the voice of Dilsey. In the character of Stephen Dedalus, meanwhile, he found a model for an intellectual young hero simultaneously repelled by and yet drawn back to his homeland. Like Stephen, Quentin Compson is a solipsistic young man, preoccupied by his role in life, by the arbitrary nature of language, and by the fleeting yet circular nature of time. For both Stephen and Quentin, history is 'the nightmare from which [they] are trying to awake'.[19]

Moreover, both men are haunted by guilt. Stephen believes himself to be responsible for the death of his mother, while Quentin holds himself culpable for the banishment of his sister. For both, however, language seems an insufficient vehicle to explore the dense history and unpeel the emotional layers of family, consciousness and nation (or region). Stephen Dedalus can only '*forge* the conscience' of his race', the linguistic tools at his disposal rendering the truth of that native conscience at best ambiguous.[20] And in *The Sound and the Fury*, Faulkner's narrators attempt to tell the same story four times – and fail every time. In Benjy's narrative, for example, language lets him down when he attempts to communicate with the passing schoolgirls: 'They looked at me, walking fast, with their heads turned. I tried to say, but they went on' (42). Similarly, Quentin's language disintegrates completely as his narrative comes to a close, losing all sensible grammar and meaning before 'the last note sounded' (151). Words fail Jason, too: he moves in circles around the sentence 'Once a bitch always a bitch' (224) when considering his inability to control his niece or come to terms with his sister. Even Dilsey, whose rich, colloquial and biblical intonations make the final chapter of the novel the most immediately readable, is tempted to give up on language in approaching the history of the Compsons. Softly weeping, she makes 'no sound' but the sad refrain, 'I've seed de first and en de last' (252). But the failure of words to express the ambiguous history of the South is best encapsulated by the final paragraph of the novel. As Luster drives left instead of right around the square in which 'the Confederate soldier gazed with empty eyes beneath his marble hand into wind and weather', Benjy roars in 'astonishment ... horror; shock; agony eyeless; tongueless; just sound' (271). In this final image, sound, history and sterility come together to provide an affectively charged portrait, beyond the compass of words, evoking the fury of the title, of a region going the wrong way.

Faulkner returns to this non-chronological approach to revealing the history of the South in *Absalom, Absalom!*, in which first Rosa Coldfield tells the pre–Civil War story of her ancestry, focusing specifically on Thomas Sutpen, to Quentin Compson – who, as we know from the previous novel, is preparing to kill himself. Latterly, Quentin's father and his grandfather offer him insights into the story of Sutpen, his origins and immersion into the community. Finally, Quentin, the ghostly consciousness which binds the novel, recounts the tale to his roommate at Harvard. The various frames of narration, of course, destabilise the historical tale of the South held within them, rendering it multiple, ambiguous and ultimately unknowable. As the critic Eric Casero puts it, Faulkner's multiple narrators and their stories trace 'direct lines of causality between the conscious contents of different characters' minds across historical eras', allowing him to 'depict consciousness as a historically and socially determined *system* of events and processes, not as the production of an individual mind or a set of individual minds'.[21]

This sense of a specifically Southern consciousness, engaged in constant dialogue with the past, works to upset the notion of chronological time or narrative linearity; if the consciousness through which the novel is filtered is shot through by the past, then it seems that the past lives on in the contemporary moment, becoming literally ever present. This idea not only informs the shape of the novel, it *becomes* the story. So *Absalom, Absalom!*, which lays almost its entire plot before the reader in the opening chapter, is not so much the story of Thomas Sutpen's brutal past, but a story about the stories of Thomas Sutpen. As in *The Sound and the Fury*, none of these stories is complete. Each is characterised less by wholeness but by gaps and omissions. Indeed, Chapter 8 formally demonstrates the notion of a gap freighted with significance in the relationships between Henry Sutpen and Charles Bon and Compson and Shreve, as each becomes enmeshed in the lives and narratives of the other:

> ... the old Sabine –"
> They stared – glared – at one another. It was Shreve speaking, though save for the slight difference which the intervening degrees of latitude had inculcated in them (differences not in tone or pitch but in turns of phrase and usage of words), it might have been either of them and as in a sense both: both thinking as one ... "the old Sabine ..."[22]

Various phrases here are repeated across the chapter, as is the structure of the 'stared – glared – at one another' sentence; the words locked within the dashes are, of course, the most significant. Here, the overlapping identities and stories, some real, some imagined (those by Shreve can only be imagined as much of what he knows is second-, third-, or even fourth-hand), powerfully demonstrate the interconnectivity of past and present. Indeed, for Faulkner it is in those gaps and the omissions that the true, untellable story lies. Here is a space that language cannot penetrate; here is the definitive proof that language cannot adequately reveal the lived histories of a South marked by racial hatred and violence, by acquisition and territorialisation, by generation after generation scarred by racism and resentment.

If the tortured abstractions and self-conscious difficulty of novels like *The Sound and the Fury* and *Absalom, Absalom!* could hardly make for a starker contrast with the strident political radicalism of books like *The Grapes of Wrath* or *Jews Without Money*, then this is a useful reminder that the literature of a given moment cannot easily be reduced to a neat formula or set of stereotypes. How, then, to bridge the gap between, say, Faulkner's experimentalism and Gold's radicalism? Perhaps the answer lies in the works of the former's New Orleans dinner companion John Dos Passos, whose trilogy *U.S.A.* effectively combines both political protest and formal innovation. Dos Passos, for example, had been intimately concerned in the Sacco and Vanzetti case, the same case that helped to radicalise Pietro di Donato. Throughout 1926 he had researched the case and talked to the accused men, and a year later he published a 127-page pamphlet entitled *Facing the Chair: Story of the Americanization of Two Foreign-born Workmen*. The case affected Dos Passos profoundly. Indeed, in an open letter to Lawrence Lowell, published in the *New York Times*, he wrote:

> The Sacco-Vanzetti case has become part of the world struggle between the capitalist class and the working class, between those who have power and those who are struggling to get it. In a man in high office ignorance of the new sprouting forces that are remaking society, whether he is with them or against them, is little short of criminal. ... It is upon men of your class and position that will rest the inevitable decision as to whether the coming struggle for the reorganisation of society shall be bloodless and fertile or inconceivably bloody and destructive.[23]

Dos Passos's sense of an imminent struggle was fuelled by his association with various members of the Communist Party, his involvement as treasurer with the Emergency Committee for Southern Political Prisoners in New York City (set up under the direction of Theodore Dreiser), his chairmanship of the National Committee to Aid Striking Miners Fighting Starvation, and his sense of the possible Americanization of Marx. Yet Dos Passos himself always remained ambivalent about Soviet communism, and was never a member of the party. Indeed, throughout the 1930s he was involved in a long-running political feud with Mike Gold, who printed a number of negative appraisals of Dos Passos's work and even referred to him as a 'bourgeois intellectual'.[24]

Dos Passos once described *U.S.A.* as 'a slice of the continent', and certainly it is designed to evoke the tones and textures of twentieth-century American life.[25] Amidst a rich tapestry of characters, Dos Passos interweaves semi-fictional biographies of historical personages such as Henry Ford, J. P. Morgan, Thorstein Veblen and Frank Lloyd Wright, among many others. Interspersed throughout the book are *Newsreel* sections punctuated with bold headlines and the famous stream-of-consciousness *Camera Eye* sections, devices both of which were undoubtedly influenced by his familiarity with the pioneering film editing work of D. W. Griffiths and the Russian Constructivist director Sergei Eisenstein.[26] In the midst of this innovative portrait of the nation, in the final book of the trilogy, Dos Passos interweaves Sacco and Vanzetti's story with that of Mary French, a labour activist and journalist for the *Freeman*. At a rally outside Charlestown jail, Mary is beaten by the police, whereupon she merges with the crowd, raising her voice in song in support of the prisoners. Dos Passos gives three versions of this occasion: first in the standard narrative recounting Mary's experience, then in the *Newsreel* section which follows, and finally in *The Camera Eye*:

> Mary was terribly scared. A big truck was bearing down on her. She jumped to one side out of the way behind one of the girder supports. Two cops had hold of her. She clung to the grimy girder. A cop was cracking her on the hand with his club. . . .

Newsreel LXVI
SACCO AND VANZETTI MUST DIE

. . .

The Camera Eye (50)

they have clubbed us off the streets they are stronger they are rich they hire and fire the politicians . . .
there is nothing left to do we are beaten . . .[27]

The tripartite account of the demonstration, the subsequent execution of the anarchist immigrants, and the all-seeing camera eye, offers an excellent example of Dos Passos's experimental modernist proclivities as a writer. One might interpret these scenes as cinemascopic, as cubistic or as fragmented; indeed, Dos Passos scholars have read the book in all three ways. Others, meanwhile, have read the novel as a powerful machine, with its intricate structure reflecting the sophisticated and diverse cultures and socio-political dynamics of the nation.[28] For Dos Passos, *form itself* – the constant motion, the to-ing and fro-ing of the narrative in a dynamic swirl of characters amidst the paraphernalia of modernity – is the message. It is the form that represents the mechanisms whereby human beings are consumed, absorbed by national and political structures against which they are power-less. For Dos Passos, in other words, experimental form *is* political, for experiment is protest.

Perhaps, then, it was Dos Passos, more than any other writer of the day, who best captured the spirit of American letters in the years of the Depression. 'The mind of a generation is its speech', he wrote in 1932. 'A writer makes aspects of that speech enduring by putting them in print. He whittles at the words and phrases of today and makes of them forms to set the mind of tomorrow's generation. That's history. A writer who writes straight is the architect of history.' Whether Dos Passos himself wrote straight is probably a matter of opinion. But few writers of his generation, I think, have a better claim to stand as an architect of history.[29]

NOTES

1 Letter to Rumsey Marvin, cited in Virginia Spencer Carr, *Dos Passos: A Life* (Evanston, IL: Northwestern University Press, 2004), 200.

2 See Jeffrey Schultz and Luchen Li, *John Steinbeck: A Literary Reference to His Life and Work* (New York: Facts on File Books, 2005), 100.

3 Michael Denning, *The Cultural Front: The Laboring of American Culture in the Twentieth Century* (New York: Verso, 1997), 259.

4 Peter Monro Jack, 'John Steinbeck's New Novel Brims with Anger and Pity', *New York Times* (16 April 1939): www.nytimes.com/books/97/07/06/home/history-grapes.html

5 Mike Gold, 'Gertrude Stein: A Literary Idiot' in *Change the World!* (1934); reprinted in *The Critical Response to Gertrude Stein*, ed. Kirk Curnett (Westport: Greenwood Press, 2000), 209.

6 Mike Gold, 'Proletarian Realism', *The New Masses* (September 1930), 5.

7 Mike Gold, 'The Jesus Thinkers', *The Liberator* (September 1922), 12.

8 Mike Gold, *Jews Without Money* (1930; New York: Carroll and Graf, 1996), 309.

9 Mike Gold, 'Proletarian Realism', *The New Masses* (September 1930), 5.

10 Pietro di Donato, *Christ in Concrete* (1939; New York: New American Library, 2004), 69. All subsequent references will appear in the text.

11 Michele Fazio, 'Vomit Your Poison": Violence, Hunger, and Symbolism in Pietro do Donato's *Christ in Concrete*', *MELUS* 32.4 (Winter 2007), 117.

12 Marcella Bencevenni, *Italian Immigrant Radical Culture - The Idealism of the Sovversivi in the United States, 1890–1940* (New York: New York University Press, 2011). Sovversivi is a term that refers to an organic movement of Italian American dissidents from across the full spectrum of revolutionary socialism.

13 Cited in Fred L. Gardaphe, *Leaving Little Italy: Essaying Italian American Culture* (New York: State University of New York Press, 2004), 61–62.

14 Cited in Louise Napolitano, *An American Story: Pietro di Donato's Christ in Concrete* (New York: Peter Lang, 1995), 70.

15 William Faulkner, *The Sound and the Fury* (1929; London: Vintage, 1995), 63. All subsequent references will appear in the text.

16 Malcolm Cowley, in compiling *The Portable Faulkner*, asked Faulkner to compile a brief introduction to explain the relation of the characters in the novel. Faulkner complied but eventually sent Cowley a much longer piece which included a genealogy of the Compsons from their first arrival in America (dating back to 1745) and through to 1943 when Jason has sold the family mansion. See Cowley, *The Portable Faulkner* (London: Penguin, 2003).

17 See, for instance, Walter Taylor, *Faulkner's Search for a South* (Urbana: University of Illinois Press, 1983); Arnold Goldman, 'Faulkner and the Revision of Yoknapatawpha History' in *The American Novel and the Nineteen Twenties*, ed. Malcolm Bradbury (London: Edward Arnold, 1971), 165–195; Cowley, 'Faulkner: The Yoknapatawpha Story', in *A Second Flowering: Works and Days of the Lost Generation* (London: Andre Deutsche, 1956), 130–155; and see Richard Gray, *The Life of William Faulkner* (Oxford: Blackwell, 1994).

18 William Faulkner, *Go Down, Moses* (1940; New York: Vintage, 1990), 280.

19 James Joyce, *Ulysses* (1922; London: Penguin, 1992), 42.

20 James Joyce, *A Portrait of the Artist as a Young Man* (1916; London: Penguin, 1965), 276.

21 Eric Casero, 'Designing Sutpen: Narrative and Its Relationship to Historical Consciousness in Faulkner's *Absalom, Absalom!*', *The Southern Literary Journal* 44.1 (Fall 2011), 87.

22 William Faulkner, *Absalom, Absalom!* (1936; London: Vintage, 2005), 303.

23 Cited in Virginia Spencer Carr, *Dos Passos: A Life* (Evanston, IL: Northwestern University Press, 2004), 226. Lowell was the president of Harvard who had been appointed by the governor of Massachusetts to serve on the advisory committee of the case.

24 See '*The New Masses* I'd Like', *The New Masses* (June 1926), 81; Virginia Spencer Carr, *Dos Passos: A Life* (Evanston, IL: Northwestern University Press, 2004), 306. As the latter shows, for Dos Passos, the association between the Party line and Soviet orthodoxy was rather too close for his liking and he feared that governments born in revolution were inevitably autocratic and potentially dictatorial. Later, in 1957, Dos Passos reflected on the rationale of voting for the Communist ticket in 1932: 'It was somewhere during the years of the New Deal that I rejoined the United States. I had seceded privately the night Sacco and Vanzetti were executed. It was not that I had joined the communists. The more I saw of the Party the more I felt that the kind of world they wanted had nothing in common with the kind of world I wanted. I wasn't joining anybody. I had seceded into my private conscience like Thoreau in Concord jail. That protest vote in 1932 was already a step back into the American way of doing things. It indicated a certain scepticism about the Marxist millennium. So far as I can remember I hadn't quite recovered from the plague on both your houses attitude toward the two conflicting systems'.

25 John Dos Passos, '*Prologue to U.S.A.*' (*1936*; New York: The Library of America, 1996), 2.

26 For an extended discussion of the filmic aspects of Dos Passos's work see Lisa Nanney, *John Dos Passos Revisited* (London: Twayne, 1998), 152–169.

27 John Dos Passos, *The Big Money* in *U.S.A.* (1936; New York: The Library of America, 1996), 1155–1156.
28 See Cecilia Tichi, *Shifting Gears: Technology, Literature, Culture in Modernist America* (Chapel Hill: University of North Carolina Press, 1987).
29 John Dos Passos, introduction to *Three Soldiers* (1921; New York: Modern Library, 1932), vii–viii.

4

RUTH JENNISON

Radical Politics and Experimental Poetics in the 1930s

Left American poets from the 1930s offer the reader a unique and spectacular formal transcoding of revolutionary, anticapitalist popular consciousness. Their projects shared the goals of the European avant-garde, articulated famously by Peter Bürger as a negation of "art as an institution that is unassociated with the life praxis of men [*sic*]," while their involvement in social movements was in many cases much more robust than their European counterparts.[1] Radical American poets sought to suture art and life, art and politics, and in many cases, art and revolution. The forms these poets endeavored to create forged new modes of expression, and marked signature breaks with the lyric and with poetic conventions of the nineteenth century, breaks that continue to set the rules of engagement for the poetry of the present day. These pathbreaking forms of American anticapitalist poetry mediate, in complex and sometimes contradictory ways, the presence of revolutionary consciousness within broad layers of the national population, and the working class in particular. The avant-garde, as its name would suggest, positions itself in what it considers the most politically developed and forward moving sectors of revolutionary movements. However, the rapid advancement of political consciousness in the broader population in the 1930s not only created new social and organizational forms but also at times outpaced the formal strategies of even the most left poets of the day. To this end, American experimental poets aimed to create texts adequate to the fore of mass political movements, but they also were often scribes of larger movements which they travelled alongside or followed.

In focusing on the contact points between poetry and the intensification of class and antiracist struggle of the 1930s, we can learn more about the ways in which poetry intervenes in and is in turned shaped by the social world. For reasons of space, readers requiring a historical background of the political terrain of the period should seek out the master texts in the footnotes.[2] However, in the interests of waymarking the politics ambient to our poets, some statistics convey the depth of immiseration caused by the Great

Depression, as well as the struggles of both employed and unemployed workers. The 1930s marks a high-water point for working-class militancy in the United States. In 1933, the unemployment rate was 25 percent. Amid these conditions, workers organized and participated in 1,856 work stoppages. When they could find work, women workers entered the workforce at twice the rate of men, and often led labor struggles in their gender-segregated employment sectors, especially textile. Corollary to this militancy was an increased sense of confidence on the part of the class as a whole, and just as new forms arose in poetry, so too did they in forms of struggle: workers invented, further developed, and/or refined the flying picket, the sit-in, the factory occupation and myriad forms of mutual aid. Interracial solidarity did inform many of these struggles, although very unevenly. Black workers experienced greater economic immiseration, and the Roosevelt government's relief programs, like the National Recovery Act, often exercised racist exclusionary hiring practices. The Communist Party and other revolutionary and left political activists, with some important and tragic exceptions, did provide leadership in important struggles to form the multiracial Congress of Industrial Organizations, to attempt to organize Black sharecroppers, and to resist the systemic legal lynching practiced under Jim Crow laws.

It was in a triangulation of contexts – the escalation of class and antiracist struggle, the uneven effects of capitalist crisis on land, region and sectors of the population, and a great expansion of left press and letters, including novels, poems, and plays – that American avant-garde poets crafted their forms and found their contexts. It is worth noting here that poetry in particular achieved popular status. It was a regular feature in the liberal, left, and far left press, workers' dailies, strike bulletins and broadsheets, social movement pamphlets and flyers, and progressive magazines. This provided openings for writers on multiple cultural levels: many poets would write poems for both the popular and left press, as well as for their own coterie communities and the usual petty bourgeois consumers of avant-garde letters.

In what follows, we explore both individual poets and constellations of poets; each elaborates a unique intersection between formal innovation and radical politics. Our sites of inquiry include: Louis Zukofsky, George Oppen, Lorine Niedecker, and Charles Reznikoff, who constellated around practices Zukofsky described as "Objectivism"; the documentary approaches of Muriel Rukeyser's word-photographs in "The Book of the Dead;" Kay Boyle's antiracist juridical assemblages; Kenneth Fearing's pop-cultured communist melancholy; and Langston Hughes's merging of African American vernacular traditions with experiments in collective voice. This list is far from exhaustive, and is meant rather to give the reader a sense of the multiple modes of engagement and practice of experimental poets, and also to explore the diverse contact points between poetic form, capitalism's Depression-era crisis of legitimacy, and insurgencies of working-class people, African Americans, and women.

"Objectivism"

In 1931, Louis Zukofsky edited a special issue of *Poetry* magazine, in which he inaugurated a current he would call "Objectivism."[3] The "Objectivist" poets contained in the issue convened loosely around the principles of (1) language as a material signifier that mediates our relationship to the world, (2) a fidelity to "historic particulars," and (3) a shared progressive politics. Poets associated with "Objectivism" include George Oppen, Carl Rakosi, Lorine Niedecker, Basil Bunting, and Charles Reznikoff. Defining "Object-ivism" (scare quotes in the original signal the poet's warning against calcifying the fluid poetic movement) in his program for the loose movement, Zukofsky writes:

> An Objective: (Optics) – The lens bringing the rays from an object to a focus. (Military use) –That which is aimed at. (Use extended to poetry) –Desire for what is objectively perfect, inextricably the direction of historic and contemporary particulars.[4]

In concert with the increasing confidence and activity of social movements in the 1930s, the program aligns militancy and art. The "Program" appears not to ratify the desirability of being "in advance of" history during a period of uprisings and mass transformations in political consciousness. Instead, the Objectivist's desire moves "in the direction of historical and contemporary particulars"; the act of detecting and moving within the stream of populated, social time becomes the key task of the vanguard, which is no longer the spear of history but within it. This is, I want to argue, an important moment of maturation for avant-garde experimental poetry, in which it transforms itself by submitting itself to the revolutionary energies that surround it.

Both the Depression and the global revolutionary response to the crisis provided the materials and the theater for the Objectivist experiment. As I describe in *The Zukofsky Era*, Objectivism was not aligned with any particular radical tendency, yet its practitioners were embedded in many left currents of the 1930s:

> Objectivism ... occupies a complex position amongst these Depression-era left cultural tendencies. Indeed, the WPA employed Zukofsky as a contributor to *The American Index of Design*; he and other Objectivists wrote occasional

poems for *New Masses* and other radical print organs; Oppen organized for the Communist party; and Niedecker was a research editor for the WPA guide to Wisconsin. The political sophistication of the works produced under Objectivism's mast offer an index of the degree to which the texts and discourses of revolutionary Marxism penetrated the consciousness of American poets, regardless of their organizational affiliation and/or stated political commitments. For some Objectivists, like Zukofsky and to a lesser extent, Oppen, the pursuit and mastery of Marxist theory is central to the poetics they elaborate; for others, like Niedecker, Marxism and the cultures of radicalism arrive mediated by epistolary contact with a broader literary community, little journals, mass news organs, occasional urban expeditions, coterie contact, and, of course, the enduring left populist cultures of the American periphery. (6)

Throughout the 1930s Zukofsky worked on the fifth through ninth sections of *"A"* (his masterwork of over eight hundred pages composed between the 1920s and the 1970s) and wrote material that would later appear in the important collections *55 Poems* and *Anew*. The 1930s also saw Zukofsky's most sustained engagements with Marxism; the first half of *"A"*-9 takes the form of a canzone voiced by commodities, who lament their separation from their laborers who made them. They sing: "But see our centers do not show the changes/ Of human labor our value estranges" and "Hands, heart, not value made us, and of any/ desired perfection the projection solely,/ Lives worked us slowly to delight the senses,/Of their fire shall you find us ..."[5]

Other sections of *"A"* are comprised of vast assemblages of historical and cultural particulars; these range impossibly widely, and their surprising adjacencies often suggest the possibility of international solidarity as well as the global contours of both capitalism and anticapitalism; "roving Red bands of South China" share textual space with antiworker tirades by Henry Ford, the "steel works of Gary" Indiana, and Siberia's "great metallurgical plants" (35, 25, 32, 32). Critical narratives of experimental poetries have tended to read their forms as fragmented indices of the experiential dissonances of a war-marked modernity. By some contrast, in Zukofsky's poetry we find particulars that at first appear unrelated, assembled in a radical parataxis that encodes the interdependence of capitalism's vexing asymmetries into provisional and fluctuating totalities.

Such parataxis is likewise a feature of George Oppen's 1934 Objectivist book of poems *Discrete Series*. Oppen wrote *Discrete Series* in part, as a formal parallel to his experience of riding the New York City subway; the poem's form approximates the experience of "serially" surfacing to survey in "discrete" scenes and images the contradictory spatial landscapes of 1930s

New York and its surroundings. For example, in "White, From the," the poem moves its cinematic eye from beneath the sidewalks to an exploration of the "limited alternatives" of up and down offered by a skyscraper's elevator.[6] Such urban poems nestle jarringly alongside seascapes, meditations on the historical qualities of art, and portraits of "city ladies," whose bodies are inseparable from urban commodity culture. (28)

The spaces of crisis and unevenness explored by Objectivism were not limited to the urban core. Lorine Niedecker, writing largely from Wisconsin, at once draws on the practices of Objectivism and on the transatlantic surrealist feminist movement flourishing in the 1920s and 1930s. Major works of this period include *Progression* (1933) and *Next Year or I Fly My Rounds Tempestuous* (1935). In two important triptychs within *Progression*, Niedecker progresses from "subconscious" to "wakeful" to full consciousness" and also from "subconscious" to "toward monologue" to "social-banal." In these movements, Niedecker arranges exterior particulars alongside the contours of subjectification itself. In textual geographies riven by capital accumulation and populated by a vast diversity of social particulars, the subject strives to position herself ("I was born on a farm") as the war economy's "soldier dead" haunt rural and factory spaces alike "over the factories and hills of our country."[7] *Next Year* is composed of small rectangles of papers carefully pasted over the middle of twenty-seven pages of a 1935 devotional calendar. Drawing on the countertemporalities of "folktime," by the end of the poem, Niedecker arrives at a bodily freedom not tied to the rhythms of the calendar: "Jesus, I'm / going out / and throw / my arms / around" (57, 67). Niedecker's treatment of the interior elaborates core Objectivist principles, most prominently, the materiality of language and a fidelity to the materials of history; these commitments lay the basis for a feminist inquiry into, and disruption of, the reproduction of normative subjectivities.

Charles Reznikoff, Muriel Rukeyser, Kay Boyle: Poetry, Solidarity, and the Document

Objectivists constelled loosely around a shared anticapitalist vision and the deployment of materialist poetic practices that transcoded capitalist crisis and the increasing tyranny of the commodity form. In some contrast to the Objectivist formation, our next poets did not align with one another under a shared banner, nor commingle in publications curated by any one of them. Their commonality is of neither coterie nor manifesto, but rather their shared use of documentary materials as a central formal feature and structuring device. These poets excerpted data from the juridical and legislative apparatuses of bourgeois power in an effort to create a transformed social theater in which oppressed voices, in particular working-class African American voices, could testify. The first of these poets who we will examine, Charles Reznikoff, was indeed a central figure in Objectivism, although other Objectivists did not adopt his robust commitment to the record of the document; his liminal status in this regard offers a useful transition from Objectivism to the documentary poets.

Reznikoff's 1934 prose poem *Testimony* takes both its form and content from the juridical record. Published by the Objectivist Press and dedicated to Zukofsky, *Testimony* evinces a key Objectivist ideal; its emphasis on the arrangement of objective, historical particulars convokes a poetic sincerity measured by history itself, as its contents are arranged into a rhythmic, lineated totality. However, in contrast to other Objectivists' forms, Reznik-off's poem follows a loose narrative trajectory. The prose poems are redacted, compressed and occasionally rather radically altered versions of testimony and proceedings from the *Federal Reporter*, a compendium of American legal cases that Reznikoff began reading in the 1930s during his time as an employee of the American Law Book Company. This small book would form the basis of a decades-long much longer project with an expanded name, *Testimony: the United States (1885–1915): recitative.* As Reznikoff's gloss to the 1934 book explains: "I glanced through several hundred volumes of old cases – not a great many as law reports go – and found almost all that follows."[8]

The text is organized along lines both spatial and temporal, sometimes eliding the two; the three major sections, "Southerners and Slaves," "Sailing-Ships and Steamers," and "East and West" also contain subcat-egories related to historical periods ("Depression"), manner of death ("Gunshot Wounds"), means of production and circulation ("Machinery" and "Rivers and Seas, Harbors and Ports), and social categories ("Mis-tress"). The text at times documents resistance, from slaves who poison the families of their masters, to interracial defiance of the recapture of a man under the fugitive slave law. But the majority of Reznikoff's redacted cases testify to the violent coercion that underwrites the reproduction of racial and class regimes in the United States. The following is a typical passage, addressing a typical scene: the violence visited upon both enslaved and "free" labor by masters:

> ... The master had him lashed to a rigging, his trousers stripped down, and lashed him with a cat upon the naked buttocks until Ryan could not help letting his dung fall. At this Captain Cush-man had Ryan cut down and told him to get a shovel to clean it away. But he did not find a shovel as quickly as

> Captain Cushman thought he might and he cut Ryan across the legs and arms
> with the cat and ordered him to the masthead. There he was kept for nearly
> four hours in the cold and rain until he was so benumbed with cold he could
> hardly keep himself from falling. (561)

In addition to such scenes of extreme violence, we also find nigh imagistic
excerpts:

> GUNSHOT WOUNDS
>
> I
>
> In gunshot wounds the edges are sunken; in wounds made with a knife
> the edges are smooth and the lips of the wounds stick out. (574)

And still other parts of the text, such as "RIVERS AND SEAS, HARBORS
AND PORTS" unspool into catalogues of ships, cargo and commodities,
workers, ports of call in the global south, and detailed, recursive and lengthy
descriptions of the weather at sea. In their adjacencies to sketches of cyclical
and brutal forms of domination, such natural imagery functions as the long
historical shadow of literary naturalism on the text. Also throughout, we
find descriptive contents in the realist mode, with its debt to juridical
"truth." In its leveraging of naturalism's disavowel of historical explanations
for the violence of class society, *Testimony* deprives its realist elements of
descriptive historical context. This tempering of realism's contextualizing
drive provides the basis for an experimental poetic practice that insists on the
ongoing violence of class society that cannot be contained, explained or
justified by liberal historicism.

Reznikoff's extraction method, and his willingness to offer only the barest
of geographical or historical coordinates, thusly has a triple effect, providing: (1) an immanent critique of a bourgeois legality that brackets inequality,
immiseration and social background in general in the examination of testimony, even as it marks testifiers as raced, classed, and gendered speakers; (2)
a formal manifestation of the persistence of violent injustice, where dateless,
ongoing trauma remains unresolved by the inadequate resolutions of criminal punishment and governmental adjudication; and (3) a supersession of
the category of "the character" by that of "the subject," the former of which
is a feature of the realist novel, and enjoys a bed of contextualizing narrative,
and the latter, which is an effect of discipline and insertion into the
juridical scene.

Muriel Rukeyser's "The Book of the Dead," published in 1938 in her
collection *U.S. 1*, is undoubtedly one of the most famous examples of an
American documentary poetics. Rukeyser's life-long commitment to social
justice is well established; her activities of the 1930s reveal involvement in

the signature political events for revolutionaries as well as the broader left united front: she covered the Scottsboro case as a reporter, wrote for the *Daily Worker* and many other publications of the international left press. And, as if transported by the wind of history itself, she endeavored to write in the not-yet-created genre of Marxist sports reporting by covering the antifascist People's Olympiad in Catalonia, an event still-birthed when the Spanish Civil War erupted in 1936.

"The Book of the Dead" is a record of, and protest against, what is historically referred to as the Hawk's Nest Tunnel Mining "disaster" or "tragedy," although both words naturalize what was a deliberate massacre on the part of capitalists in their project of superprofit extraction. A Union Carbide subsidiary employed workers in West Virginia to dig a tunnel for a hydroelectric project; when the excavation revealed silica, owners saw the opportunity to mine the mineral. Workers were provided with no respiratory protection, and hundreds, perhaps thousands, (estimates vary widely) perished from silicosis of the lungs. African Americans constituted a large portion of the workforce. Rukeyser's poem hosts a number of formal experiments, including lyrical addresses, redacted testimonies to legislative bodies charged with investigating the "disaster," pastoral reveries, futurist, angular portraits of fixed capital and power generators, perspectives from documentary cameras, blues song structures, citations from statements by reformers, victims and survivors, and doctors both independent and in the service of the company. Rukeyser's long poem begins with a journey from the city to the country; a photographer "unpacks camera and case ... viewing on ground-glass an inverted image."[9] The poem frequently invokes images seen through glass, which, not coincidentally, is made of silica, to point up the ways in which even the most seemingly transparent representation is mediated in ways that may not be perceivable. The poem draws on the left traditions that devoted themselves to unveiling suffering and inequality in photographic evidence, dating back to nineteenth-century American reformers such as photographer Jacob Riis and continued by contemporaries of Rukeyser such as Dorothea Lange.

"The Book of the Dead" suggests that ideological unveiling is an ongoing task. The poem includes much congressional testimony regarding the lung x-rays of the victims; objective interpretation by independent doctors is juxtaposed with medical diagnoses by corporate doctors. Rukeyser's emphasis on the x-ray reveals her commitment to *exposure*, at the same time as it suggests the poet's frustrations with any representational strategies that find their limits in presentation of the data alone. The sophistication of this position requires the poem to do two kinds of work at once: to document what is often imperceptible and to encourage in the reader a restlessness that resists the notion that the image will confess the truth on its own. In this way, "The Book of the Dead" reveals a complex understanding of the relationship of the visual field to ideology and power.

"The Book of the Dead" – as we will find soon in the work of Kay Boyle – frequently deploys direct citation. For these poets, it is no longer sufficient to represent the voices of those directly affected by the grinding illogics of capitalist violence; they must be allowed to represent themselves. Surely this is the kind of impulse Cold War narratives about the supposedly dogmatic artistic production of the Communist left has hidden from view; these poets' commitment to citation in an arrangement pointing to justice is the fruit of a vision of discourses and practices of direct democracy and self-emancipation increasingly widespread in the social upheavals of the 1930s. Yet, like the x-rays, these citations are in themselves not enough, and the poet intervenes not infrequently; the poem braids together direct quotation and other materials, including chemical symbols of silica, stock reports, and interludes of what is clearly Rukeyser's own poetic voice. In this way, the poem works to construct a constellation of possible contexts, prisms through which the voices of suffering might be heard.

It is important to note here Rukeyser's political work for racial justice, as well as that of broader sections of the left, which began to understand antiracism and class struggle as dialectically imbricated. More specifically, cases like that of the defense of the "Scottsboro boys," where activists merged legal strategies with public campaigns, political education and mass propaganda, revealed, often newly, to white activists, that bourgeois juridical and legislative institutions were not only not neutral, but mechanisms of discipline, control and suppression. The testimony of defendants who were members of oppressed classes, like the Scottsboro nine or before them Nicola Sacco and Bartolomeo Vanzetti, if allowed at all, were ripped from the context of larger structures of domination, and weighed unequally in the scales of justice. If we have characterized the 1930s as a decade in which capitalism suffered a crisis of legitimacy, so too did its chief ruling institutions and their attendant ideologies of blind justice based on an impartial assessment of testimony.

At times Rukeyser heavily edits the voices she cites. Notably this takes place in a section entitled "George Robinson: Blues," in which Rukeyser experiments with the structure and tone of blues music in her representation of the voice of George Robison, whose surname's spelling she altered. Robison was a miner who testified at congressional hearings along with others whom the poem cites directly with little or no intervention. Rukeyser creates a poetic voice for Robison, in Blues form. Rukeyser spoke of her formal decisions: "George Robinson was a real man to me. He speaks for a great many things – not only the dust – much more for the men, and women and children behind them. It seems to me that social justice comes in here as a matter of what is happening to lives – the way in which horizons are opened up, the way in which they are thrown away." (606) The George Robinson section of "The Book of the Dead" contains some of the most heavily transformed citations in the whole poem; where there is direct citation, it is reshaped through line breaks and enjambments that tease out an inner rhyme scheme. The lines quoted here are redacted in particularly interesting ways:

> As dark as I am, when I came out at morning after
>   the tunnel at night,
> with a white man, nobody could have told which man was
>   white.
> The dust covered us both, and the dust was white (88)

Critic David Kadlec provides the original testimony:

> As dark as I am, when I came out of that tunnel in the mornings, if you had been in the tunnel too and come out at my side, nobody could have told which was the white man. The white man was just as black as the colored man.[10]

Rukeyser's poem offers a clear political-pedagogical message, in which the deadly dust eliminates racial differences, leaving only the uniformity of a collectively doomed class. Rukeyser has altered the text to remedy Robison's original "mistake" that the dust is black, and not white. We can identify in these lines a recognizable moment in certain prominent strands of left discourse, in which the universal of social class subsumes the difference of race. For Rukeyser, Robinson, and the blues form, occasions a politics and poetics where "horizons are opened up." The Robinson section suggests through its form that Blackness is the vanishing mediator between the present and the future histories pried open by a universal and united working class. Yet, as Kadlec points out: "written out of Rukeyser's brilliant exposure of corporate and state mechanisms of erasure are the less-than-superficial racial dimensions of Gauley tunnel" (38). Even as the poem often prefers invention to direct citation in much of the George Robinson section, Rukeyser insists that it is the quasi-fictional Robinson who "speaks for" the "men, and women and children behind them." The answers to the political questions about what it means for a white, middle-class radical to represent the voices of working-class Black people under the threat of death lie, for Rukeyser, in the production of a hybrid of citation and her own poetic intervention. Rukeyser's poem uses a rich array of formal strategies to engage with the social movements in which she was embedded, and it does so while seeking, if not finding, a political and artistic solution to the problematics of representing the voices of others, especially those of the victims of racial capitalism.

Kay Boyle's 1937 "A Communication to Nancy Cunard" also attempts to combine cross-racial representations with an equally diverse array of formal strategies. Boyle was a prolific author, who, like Rukeyser, was also a journalist. Although she was the object of McCarthyite witch hunts later in life, she was not a communist but rather a fellow traveler and sympathizer with the signature left campaigns of the 1930s. While our focus here is less on biographical detail or particular histories of literary dissemination, some details offer a window onto the kind of interartistic force fields that obtained in the 1930s, as well as the fairly spectacular porousness in this era between the poet, the left liberal and far left presses, and perhaps most importantly, the oppressed themselves. Boyle's poem is addressed to Nancy Cunard, whose *Negro Anthology Made by Nancy Cunard* contained extensive documentary materials related to the "Scottsboro boys" case. Boyle drew on reporting on the trial in *The Nation*. She also was in direct epistolary communication with Scottsboro defendant Haywood Patterson, whom she remunerated for his contribution to the poem. The poem is separated into four sections, loosely grouped around different moments in the trial; these include three separate embedded titles: "The Testimony," "The Spiritual for Nine Voices," and "The Sentence."

Like "The Book of the Dead," "A Communication to Nancy Cunard" engages in a sustained effort to represent the voices of African Americans. The poem opens with explicit concern about audience: "These are not words set down for the rejected."[11] These poetic meditations on who the poem is "for" introduce direct citation from the trial itself; in these combinations, the poem presents multiple modes of political speech. Present day readers, largely familiar with left discourse that is often defensive in nature, will find themselves perhaps surprised by the positional and affective diversity of the 1930s left. Their rhetorical menu included, at minimum, appeals to reason, propaganda for an alternative moral compass, for a revolutionary transformation of existing social relations, for solidarity with revolutionary movements abroad, agitational slogans, calls directly addressing oppressed communities, as well as for solidarity from beyond those communities, and militant, confrontational speech directed at racists, capitalists, and patriarchs.

Within this vast range of discourse, there existed a sophisticated distinction between calls for solidarity and requests for sympathy, and "A Communication to Nancy Cunard" reflects this. The poem is "for" the white supremacists presiding over the legal system, and as such it is a poem that does not seek sympathy, but rather the solidarity of a broader readership in the struggle to defeat those it addresses. Through strategic citation of court-room proceedings, the poem exposes the racism that structured the trial. It is difficult to tell when and where citations are entirely fabricated, although when we leave the scene of the trial altogether to listen in on a private boxcar conversation between the white female accusers, in which the women talk of their own transient lives of casual labor and sex work, we can be fairly confident the poem is "inventing citation" to thicken the fabric of class relations. Other experiments in representing the injustices of the trial include a text in two columns, in which Haywood Patterson's testimony appears across from the testimony of Victoria Price, one of the accusers. Patterson's testimony is self-reflexive and anxiously peripatetic, as he explains his search for language appropriate to the obscure discursive laws of the proceedings. Price's testimony, by contrast, hangs spare amidst white space, and is com-prised of two utterances of "I cain't remember" (67). Even in her silence, Price's testimony bears more weight.

Other sections of the poem abandon citation altogether for the by turns utopian dreams and lamentations of an African American spiritual, and a final poetic meditation on "The Sentence," which closes the poem with the words of defendant Ozie Powell: ""It sure don't seem to me like were/ getting anywheres./ It don't seem to me like we're getting anywhere at all (69). These final lines reflect a mood of abjection, one which underwrites not only the situation of the defendants, and prospects for racial justice more broadly; in closing the poem they also point up the exhaustion of the poem's own formal strategies. As in "The Book of the Dead," Blackness marks the conditions, and limits, of the representational possibility of documentary poetics.

Popular Forms, Revolutionary Politics: Kenneth Fearing

Many American poets of the early twentieth century mixed what are com-monly known as "high" and "low," or mass, culture. Obvious examples include T. S. Eliot's *The Waste Land*, which incorporated portraits of working-class life (generally in the service of a negative lesson about the declining values of modernity's cultural life), or, on the other side of the political spectrum, the work of W. C. Williams, which wove threads of popular life in American capitalist society into progressive lyrics and longer experimental poems. Kenneth Fearing was one of those poets from the 1930s most engaged with the incorporation of popular life into poetry; interestingly the vigorousness of his experiments, coupled with the radical nature of his political commitments has not made him a poet that is easy to categorize, or, it seems, to install into the canon of modernism, despite the sophistication of his poetics, breadth of reference, and a filigreed figurative language that often encodes a deep revolutionary enthusiasm. Fearing's incorporation of popular forms and working-class cultures was a natural extension of his own writerly engagement with a broad set of popular forms. He wrote across many genres: hard-boiled detective fiction, advertising, pornography, editorials, mystery, reportage (he was a founding editor of *The Partisan Review*), and poetry.

Fearing's poetry addresses concerns and deploys forms by now familiar: rebellion against the tyranny of the commodity form; the incorporation of everyday speech and popular culture; a blending of the raw data of history with poetics; and paratactically assembled totalities designed to reveal the relation between events and persons whose connections within a capitalist regime are fractured and obscured by, individuated, alienated modes of perception that suppress any historical fact that does not ratify the ideological position of the always already victorious ruling class. Fearing's "1933" and "Denouement" conjures an ironic fidelity to the tones and forms of mass culture news reporting. This fidelity informs poetic compositions of recognizable, and jarring, popular images, often presented in cinematic style. "1933" presents us with a puzzle: like some others of Fearing's poems from this period, it is addressed to "you"; a "you" that experiences contradiction:

> You heard the gentleman, with automatic precision, speak the
> truth.
> Cheers. Triumph.
> And then mechanically it followed the gentleman lied.
> Deafening applause. Flashlights, cameras, microphones. Floral
> Tribute. Cheers.[12]

The poem's "you" is a consumer of propaganda, in the form of "news," spectacles, fabrications, and tabloid impossibilities. Occasionally the experience of the "you" brushes with the realities of Depression-era America and the threat of fascism abroad. These moments are quickly absorbed into ludic and fantastical reportage:

> Evicted again, you went
> downtown, slept at the movies, stood in the breadline,
> voted yourself a limousine.   (94)

"1933"'s address to its complex "you" presents a challenge to the Depression-era reader, whose training in the languages and forms of popular culture is surely deeper than in the reading of experimental poetics. In order to resist absolute capture by the direct address, the reader must sift through data which is usually presented with neutrality by capitalist organs and cultural apparatuses. Even time is branded ("the Lucky Strike Hour") and daily stock reports are blended with collective calls that protest war profits ("... steel five points up, rails rise/ du Pont up, disarm, disarm and heard again") (95). "You" witness the lies of leaders, and impossible reversals of the consequences of the imperial war machine ("ten million dead returned to life"). Fearing's method is one of immanent critique, which teases out contradictions from within the object itself. In this way, it is distinct from a liberal aesthetic which seeks to *unveil injustice to the light of reason*. "1933" assumes that its readerly subject is in possession of an internal world of contradictory viewpoints; the poem does not cohere intentionally because "you" cannot totalize amid a vast mediatized world of popular discourse that shears its consumers of a grounding perspective, class or otherwise.

Fearing's poem "Denouement" amplifies the stakes of "1933"; it also suggests a détournement, where the very forms of capitalist mass culture are repurposed for a revolutionary vision. Like "1933" it employs direct address to a "you," and assembles together historical debris, popular discourse, and vast figurations of nature, torture, and class war. Hortative calls and political slogans anchor the text throughout. "Denouement" is essentially a letter to the future; while it predicts and chronicles the defeat of its present-day revolutionary movements, the poem is bookended by passages that present ecstatic utopian content. In the opening stanzas, "Denouement" calls for nothing less than the transformation of nature itself by perception made new in the fires of revolutionary consciousness, and for the dialectical superseding of the opposition between nature and humans, and even between life and death: "Sky, be blue, and more than blue; wind be flesh and blood; / flesh and blood be deathless" (115). This joyful reconnoitering of human and nature results from a historical unfolding of struggle that produces new forms of human thinking and action capable of exceeding the limits of bourgeois knowledge:

> Truth, be known, be kept forever, let the letters, letters,
>   souvenirs, documents, snapshots, bills be found at last,
>   be torn away from a world of lies, be kept as final
>   evidence, transformed forever into more than truth
>
> Change, change, rows and rows of rows of figures, spindles,
>   furrows, desks, change into paid-up rent and let the
>   paid-up rent become South Sea music;
>
> Magic film, unwind, unroll unfold in silver on that million
>   mile screen, take us all, bear us again to the perfect
>   denouement –   (115)

In these stanzas, we find the interpenetration of popular forms ("magic film" and "South Sea music"), the scraps of data that the defeat of revolutionary movements scatters and unbinds from one another into an illegible fragmented network of "evidence," and the everyday instruments of labor: "spindles / furrows, desks." The future is bodied forth by a voice which calls for the triumph of something in excess of bourgeois juridical "truth": in its call to find "more than truth," we might locate a point at which Fearing's poetry presses against the ideological limits of a documentary aesthetic. The poem alternates between searching, Socratic questions to a future reader ("Who are these people and what do they want, why do they / walk back and forth with signs that say 'Bread Not / Bullets...'") with cinematic vignettes of state repression of the labor movement, the cadaver of a suicide victim, and compressed figurations of a sooty, enflamed world of war and famine (119). "Denouement" closes with a cosmic vision of what will be required to defend against the eradication of radical movements from the historical record altogether. To prevent this requires a revolutionary project extended far beyond the traditional categories of time available under class society: generations, ages, decades, centuries, periods. Instead, the poet suggests we think of struggle as unfolding over a vast, universe-wide or cosmic space and time: no less than a figure of the light of a dead star which is synaesthetically "... heard only in the words, as millions of voices / become one voice ..." embodies the survival of revolutionary histories against the efforts of the powerful to extinguish them (119). In "1933," the media's reversals of death were grossly impossible lies; "Denouement" achieves a deathlessnesss of revolutionary memory.

Langston Hughes in the 1930s

Langston Hughes's poetry is embedded in radical political currents, possesses a revolutionary, internationalist perspective, a commitment to the vernacular voice, and formal experimentation whose intention is to provide form to emergent modes of protest. In a political and aesthetic extension of the aims of the poets above, Hughes's poems contest the legitimacy of the state itself, establish a provisional vocabulary for an international, racialized proletariat, and supersede the opposition between the vernacular-voiced individual and the unified, universal chorus that previous poetry struggles to overcome.

Hughes's lifework cultivated a broad range of forms, and a shifting set of political orientations and concerns. His poetry from the 1930s evinces a twinned focus on resistance to capitalism and white supremacy, with special attention to developing aesthetic and cultural practices that supplant religion as an organizing model for social life (see "Goodbye Christ"). Hughes travelled to Haiti, China, Japan, the USSR, and Mexico in this period, collaborating with an international web of leftist writers and artists. His poetry reflects both his internationalism as well as addresses important struggles within the United States such as the aforementioned movement to exonerate the Scottsboro defendants ("Ballad of Ozie Powell") as well as demands to end the widespread practices of legal and extralegal lynching. Hughes's poems from the period crest forward in relentless critique, refusing at every turn the containment of revolutionary energies by reformist legislation (see "Ballad of Roosevelt"), statist iconography of dead revolutionaries, or seemingly progressive movements which truck in conciliatory language.[13] On his way to treating these concerns, Hughes takes a moment to incorporate and sublate the experimental poetics that preceded his own:

> Poem
> Strange,
> Distorted blades of grass,
> Strange,
> Distorted trees,
> Strange,
> Distorted tulips on their knees.[14]

The poem incorporates the Whitmanian tradition (*Blades of Grass*) and unfurls into a critique of Imagism's inhumanism, insisting that figurations of nature are mediations of social domination. The alternation of a refusal and embrace of end-rhymes elaborates a porous and flexible relation to the musically-driven, popular form of the rhyming couplet. "Poem" eschews the lyric altogether; other poems deploy the chant form (see "Chant for May Day"), direct address, and librettos for chorales. Witness here Hughes uprooting the barriers between poetics and political discourse:

> History
> The past has been
> A mint of blood and sorrow –
> That must not be
> True of tomorrow.   (140)

The enjambment of lines 4 and 5 initiates a pause between the negation and the superseding of histories of violence and profit, and line 5 politicizes the genitive form, where "tomorrow" is in possession of nothing but the truth. Still other poems propel forward in a negation not just of capitalist immiseration, but of any revolutionary movement that threatens to mark the end of history with the entombment of former leaders. "Ballad of Lenin" features the voices of "Ivan, the peasant," "Chico, the Negro," and "Chang from the foundaries / On strike in the streets of Shanghai," addressing Lenin's tomb:

> Comrade Lenin of Russia,
> High in a marble tomb,
> Move over, Comrade Lenin,
> And give me room. (140)

Hughes writes into a future where individual and collective voices are no longer separated by the membrane of alienation. In "Open Letter to the South" we find the heady convergence of a catalogue of occupation and geography that reminds one of Reznikoff, a post-lyric in which the Black speaker, via the typographical assertion of agitprop, is at once the subject and object of history:

> White workers of the South
>   Miners,
>   Farmers,
>   Mechanics,
>   Mill hands,
>   Shop girls,
>   Railway men,
>   Servants,
>   Tobacco workers,
>   Sharecroppers,
>   Greetings
> I am the black worker,
>   Listen:
> That the land might be ours,
> And the mines and the factories and the office towers
> At Harlan, Richmond, Gastonia, Atlanta, New Orleans,
> That the plants and the roads and the tools of power
> Be ours ... (147)

The poem's turn after "listen" is instructive; if the reader provides the elided subjunctive, such that "so" precedes "that," it turns out that "listening" to the Black worker is both the necessary and sufficient condition for the expropriation of the entire means of production. The poem restlessly undermines the divisions that separate people, and even forms of thought; the abstraction of "power" achieves concretion and materiality as it appears in serial fashion alongside the architecture of production ("plants" and "tools") and circulation ("roads"). Geographical distance is subtracted in the proximity of the pulse points of class struggles, and the space of the United States is mapped not by borders, but by internal struggles, both urban and rural, moving easterly and southerly.

We close our investigation with a concluding passage from Hughes's poem "Wait," which features a planetary assemblage of political actors, commodities, revolutionary history, and proletarian occupations. "Wait" convenes this expansive cast of subjects, objects, and terrains of history using three columns of text and an all-capitalized envoi. This draws on the format of the newspaper; unlike the capitalist press, however, Hughes's poem encourages a reading process in which disparate social elements and geographies of struggle are arranged in a totality of intersecting determinations.

AFRICA	I, silently,	HAITI
	And without a single learned word	
GRAPE	Shall begin the slaughter	BONUS
	That will end my hunger	
JAPANESE	And your bullets	KOREA
	And the gas of capitalism	
CONSCRIPTS	And make the world	HAITI
	My own,	
JOHANNESBURG	When that is done	SUGAR
MINERS	I shall find words to speak	MEERUT
	Wait!	

HAITI UNEMPLOYED MILLION CALIFORNIA CHERRY PICKERS STRIKING MINERS ALABAMA SUGAR BEET WORKERS INDIAN MASSES SCOTTSBORO SHANGHAI COOLIES PATTERSON SUGAR BEET WORKERS COLONIAL ASIA FRICK'S MINERS CUBA POOR FARMERS JAPANESE CONSCRIPTS WORKERS JOHANNESBURG MINERS CHAPEI ALABAMA NEGROES OXNARD SUGAR BEET WORKERS INDIAN MASSES BONUS MARCHERS FORD STRIKERS HAITI   (235)

There is a great deal to say about the complex political economy of this poem; its tour de force fusion of point-of-production struggle in both agricultural and machine sectors with an interconnected series of anticolonial movements provides an unparalleled insight into the robust internationalist communism of sections of the 1930s left. Hughes, like many experimental poets of the 1930s, composes his poetry around the problematic of representation of the voices of the oppressed. And his answer to that question here is to create an impossible text: the poem is a record of silence, of a revolutionary subject not in possession of "words to speak," even as the poem is a record of that very speech. The unsilent-silent speaker is buttressed by columns of exploitation and of struggle. The typographic exertions demand the reader's attention, and blur the distinctions between poetry, placard, chant, newspaper and urgent telegraph communique. The practice of capitalizing every letter forecloses recognition of the "proper" noun, and the products of labor ("BEET") and collective categories ("MINERS," "CON-SCRIPTS," "MASSES," etc.) bear equal weight as the geographic designations. The poem demurs narrative hypotaxis; there are no deictics or linking verbs to suggest the manner of interconnection. The effect is twofold: the contents are permitted to emanate their significance from within, and yet such significance depends entirely on their position within a fabric of solidarity.

Hughes brings together the many threads of Depression-era experimentalism: the Objectivists' paratactical arrangements of particulars in totalities structured by unevenness, as well as their protests against commodities shorn of their origins in labor; Rukeyser's investigations into the aesthetics and politics of representing the voices of suffering and resistance; Boyle's innovative typographic compositions transcoding asymmetries of power; Reznikoff's Whitmanian poetics of gathering and collating; and Fearing's use of popular forms to create a brave, melancholic representation of revolution deferred. "WAIT" offers form to a suspended future, when its voice, retroactively installed, will find language adequate to the poem's revolutionary present.

NOTES

1 Peter Bürger, trans. Michael Shaw, *Theory of the Avant-Garde* (Minneapolis: University of Minnesota Press, 1984), 49.

2 See Michael Denning, *The Cultural Front: The Laboring of American Culture in the Twentieth Century* (London: Verso,1996); Philip Foner, *Organized Labor and the Black Worker, 1619–1981* (New York: International Publishers,1982); Chris Harman, "The Crisis Last Time," *International Socialism* 2.13 (1981): 1–28; Mark Naison, *Communists in Harlem during the Depression* (Urbana: University of Illinois Press,1983); Sharon Smith, *Subterranean Fire: A History of Working-Class Radicalism in the United States* (Chicago, IL: Haymarket Books, 2005), chapters 3 and 4; Howard Zinn, *A People's History of the United States* (New York: Harper Collins Publishers, 2015); and Robin D. G. Kelley *Hammer and Hoe: Alabama Communists during the Great Depression* (Chapel Hill: University of North Carolina Press,1990).

3 For fuller treatments of Objectivism and Objectivists, see Mark Scroggins, *Upper Limit Music: The Writing of Louis Zukofsky* (Tuscaloosa: University of Alabama Press, 1997) and *Louis Zukofsky and the Poetry of Knowledge* (Tuscaloosa: University of Alabama Press, 1998); Rachel Blau DuPlessis and Peter

Quartermain, eds. *The Objectivist Nexus: Essays in Cultural Poetics* (Tuscaloosa: University of Alabama Press, 1999); and Ruth Jennison, *The Zukofsky Era: Modernity, Margins, and the Avant-Garde* (Baltimore, MD: Johns Hopkins University Press, 2012).

4 Louis Zukofsky, *Prepositions +: The Collected Critical Essays*, ed. Mark Scroggins (Hanover, NH: Wesleyan University Press, 2000), 12.

5 Louis Zukofsky, *"A"* (Berkeley: University of California Press, 1978), 106–107.

6 George Oppen and Michael Davidson, *New Collected Poems* (New York: New Directions, 2002), 6.

7 Lorine Niedecker, *Lorine Niedecker: Collected Works*, ed. Jenny Penberthy (Berkeley: University of California Press, 2002), 34.

8 Charles Reznikoff, *Testimony: the United States (1885–1915): recitative* (Boston: Black Sparrow, 2015), 526. For a useful history of Reznikoff's shorter 1934 text, restored to print in New Directions' 2015 republication of the larger work, see introductory notes by Justin Parks, 519–525.

9 Muriel Rukeyser, *The Collected Poems of Muriel Rukeyser*, eds. Janet E. Kaufman and Anne F. Herzog (Pittsburgh: University of Pittsburgh Press, 2006), 73.

10 David Kadlec,"X-Ray Testimonials in Muriel Rukeyser," *Modernism/Modernity* 5.1 (2013): 23.

11 Kay Boyle, *Collected Poems of Kay Boyle* (Port Townsend, WA: Copper Canyon Press, 1991), 66.

12 Kenneth Fearing, *Complete Poems*, ed. Robert M. Ryley (Orono, ME: The National Poetry Foundation, 1994), 94.

13 See Arnold Rampersad's authoritative biography *The Life of Langston Hughes* (New York: Oxford University Press,1986).

14 Langston Hughes, *The Collected Works of Langston Hughes: The Poems 1921–1940*. Vol. 1 (Columbia: University of Missouri Press, 2001), 124–125.

5

PAULA RABINOWITZ

"I plan to send you some pictures"

Documenting the 1930s in Cold Blood

The documentary impulse, then, is to seek to know in such a way that the telling really works, connects others to an observed situation. It is the impulse to reconnoiter, to scout successfully, and report back, to send signals (and more) about what has been spotted or surveyed.[1]

Robert Coles

If I could do it, I'd do no writing at all here. It would be photographs; the rest would be fragments of cloth, bits of cotton, lumps of earth, records of speech, pieces of wood and iron, phials of odors, plates of food and of excrement . . . A piece of the body torn out by the roots might be more to the point.[2]

James Agee

Just to write the words "documentary" and "factual" gives me a headache . . .[3]

Pare Lorentz

Seeing

The "it" to which James Agee refers may or may not be a manifestation of the documentary impulse charted so eloquently sixty years after he and Walker Evans encountered the three tenant families with whom they lived in 1936 by psychoanalyst Robert Coles. For Coles, this impulse is really a pulse, an effort on the part of the one who sees to be the one who tells, like the beating of a heart. For Agee, this shift from seeing to telling is fundamentally a translation process, vision into language, a process at which he agonizingly excels but which is fraught with the problems of misrepresentation, of lying or sentimentalizing, an impossible task that will always miss the point: the tactile and sensuous encounter with what "*exists* " (LUNPFM, 12). And what exists, at least for those engaged in this "curious" (as he calls it) practice of documentary – government agents, artists, publishers, journalists – is a collaborative striving to pry open the lives of others and examine how these lives are lived. To see what is going on around these lives and perhaps effect some kind of changes in them or for them – ideally in the world, "to make a difference in a neighborhood, a nation" (Coles 252) – this, for Agee, is precisely the central problem of documentary itself, its self-affirming mission to ameliorate, to make the world over in an "obscene" vision of progress. The resulting headache, according to filmmaker Pare Lorentz, happens because of both the collective labor required to do the work and the troubling overexposure of the form, as well as its failed competition with Hollywood movies. He detailed the difficulties shooting on location footage at the source of the Mississippi for *The River*:

> We tried to take the shots ourselves last fall [1936] but when we arrived at Lake Itasca a peat fire made shooting impossible, a mink chased us off a raft where we were shooting, we nearly froze to death in tourist cabins, smoke from a Manitoba forest fire choked us and then the temperature dropped to 12 below and the snow began to fall.[4]

The almost slapstick physical calamities of making a documentary are matched by the poignancy of human encounter with disasters and poverty. What happens when making a documentary, whether filmed, photographed or reported, cannot be controlled; serendipity reigns over its technical requirements and its emotional effects.

Agee's book, begun in the heady days of the New Deal, when even an organ of the capitalist class, *Fortune* magazine, thought to send writers and photographers (in this case one on the payroll of the US government's Farm Security Administration) into the depths of impoverished Alabama and report back, morphed into the great work of American modernist analysis and methodology. It was published just days before Pearl Harbor was bombed. By then, poverty or in the case of Lorentz's film about maternal death rates, *The Fight for Life*, healthcare, which had both been deep concerns of the federal government during the Depression (each project supported in part by the Roosevelt administration), were subsumed by the declaration of war. The focus had shifted although the practices of documentary, its forms and media, continued to entwine government and art. In the words of film historian Haidee Wasson: "politically radical, aesthetically conservative, and unrelentingly governmental forces have long shaped film culture" and more broadly all documentary expression.[5] Documentary is a fugue playing variations on these terms: politics, radicalism, aesthetics, government, force. Its impulse thrived in the volatile interwar years, as theories about social realism and the avant garde collided with new mass media – radio, movies, magazines – and the specters of poverty and fascism materialized.

The documentary impulse of the Depression era emerged from a conflu-ence of technology and ideology. Photography was a century old and had, by the 1930s, with the advent of Kodak, on the one hand, and inexpensive phototextual rotogravure printing (used by Henry Luce's *Life* magazine, for instance), on the other, entered everyday life; cinema was institutionalized within national or corporate studio systems, with talkies vanquishing silent film and by the decades' end color hailing the end of black and white. As director Mike Nichols notes black-and-white cinematography reinforces the metaphoric aspect of film, an effect – much as voice-over narration – that counterintuitively enhances its conveyance of reality.[6] This effect of heightened realism through metaphor was crucial to ideological forces shaping documentary as well. The new mass media, especially radio and film, enabled the widespread dissemination of various political ideas: communism within Stalin's Soviet Union, as the great 1920s film architects of montage and kino-eye (Sergei Eisenstein and Dziga Vertov) had developed new means of reflecting and even reconstructing life; fascism in Nazi Ger-many, as Joseph Goebbels and Leni Riefenstal deployed radio and film technologies to aestheticize the mass appeal of Adolph Hitler. In the United States, Franklin Delano Roosevelt also took full advantage of his access to radio to speak directly to the American public through his weekly fireside chats and fostered film and photography within various departments of the New Deal.[7] The balance among the various pressures on documentary shifted throughout the decade, but not necessarily in ways that were predict-able. Film historian Alice Lovejoy demonstrates, for instance, that the Army Films of Czechoslovakia (made before and after World War II) were instru-mental in fostering the experimental films that fed into and then grew out of the 1968 Prague Spring; Jonathan Kahana argues that citizenship in Depres-sion America was invoked not only through federally-sanctioned documen-tary work, such as that of the FSA, but also by the bold documentary forms of the left-wing Film and Photo League, even though the group was associ-ated with the CPUSA.[8] Documentary allowed those not present to see what was being observed by those who had ventured to the source and thus to become part of a political body.

Observing

"I plan to send you some pictures of the Salinas and Stockton strike where people were murdered in cold blood," wrote novelist John Steinbeck to his friend Pare Lorentz of the violent lettuce strike of 1936. In this 1939 letter, Steinbeck explains that he is doing a series on agriculture for *Life* magazine, travelling along with a photographer, though, he muses, it may be "too tough for Life." He continues: "Words and generalities don't mean anything anymore, but I hope with these pictures to pin a badge of shame on the greedy sons of bitches who are causing this condition, and it is caused, make no mistake about that" (FDR's Moviemaker 123). Like Agee, Steinbeck, despite being a writer, demurs about the usefulness of words; what counts is the image, pictures. Unlike Agee, who was racked with shame at his complicity in the project of social persuasion and amelioration, which by the time *Let Us Now Praise Famous Men* was published seemed doomed to sink into sentimentalism and condescension, Steinbeck, on the verge of publishing a novel full of "anger and pity," *The Grapes of Wrath*, feels compelled to use any means necessary to combat the efforts of the Associated Farmers to destroy farm workers' organizing. No one could escape the power of the image – best exemplified by Hollywood: Agee wrote film criticism and eventually screenplays; Steinbeck, whose novels were appearing on the screen, was planning a number of film projects in Mexico. He wanted to assist Lorentz on location: "If I could be of any service in your work, I'd like to be. I am quite selfish about this. I want to learn the medium or something about it and I want to study it under you ... If in return I can do dialogue or anything I'll be glad" (FDR, 122). Ultimately, Steinbeck did provide "service" to Lorentz on both the unmade film *Ecce Homo* and the completed documentary *The Fight for Life*, by writing, assisting with bureaucracy and even filming and editing.

This desire "to learn the medium or something" connect Steinbeck's project to that of Agee and Evans. But, despite their joint belief in the power of the image – the documentary image – as crucial to the work of modernist representations of poverty and labor, and their invocations – however different – of emotion, the similarities between the two writers are tenuous. For Agee: "the camera seems...next to unassisted and weaponless consciousness, the central instrument of our time; and is why in turn I feel such rage at its misuse" (11). Writing should take a backseat – as it does in the layout of "the book," as he referred to *Let Us Now Praise Famous Men* – because he intended the sixty or so photographs made by Evans to overshadow the impact of hundreds of pages of prose. Those whose "corruption of sight" had destroyed its power included *Life* magazine's photographer Margaret Bourke-White (and presumably Steinbeck's unnamed *Life* photographer as well). This radical disjuncture – between Agee's violent rejection of sensationalism and sentimentality (albeit written in the context of one of the great works of sensation and sentiment) and Steinbeck's effort to shame "the greedy sons of bitches" through anger and pity – was expressed within the prevailing documentary aesthetics of the camera: the central instrument of its time. Walker Evans's photographs were presented by Agee as having the force of raw vision; yet we know that Evans rearranged furniture and posed his subjects; moreover, his streetscapes and images of vernacular architecture and landscapes were deeply indebted to the aesthetics of picture postcards gleaned from his extensive collection of these artifacts of local boosterism.[9] Steinbeck's Joad family came to be seen through the images of Dorothea Lange's photographs and Pare Lorentz's films of Dust Bowl migrants.

In his review of *The Grapes of Wrath*, Peter Monro Jack felt the novel "reads as if it had been composed in a flash, ripped off the typewriter and delivered to the public as an ultimatum." While it scans like the news and comes to "no conclusion," its "ending on a minor and sentimental note" betrays its commitment to social amelioration through representation. This sense of immediacy, "a curious and sudden intensity," was in the air, a general mode of expression among American novelists:

> it is most interesting to note how very much alike they are all writing: Hemingway, Caldwell, Faulkner, Dos Passos in the novel, and MacLeish in poetry are those whom we easily think of in their similarity of theme and style. Each is writing stories and scenarios of America with a curious and sudden intensity, almost as if they had never seen or understood it before. They are looking at it again with revolutionary eyes. Stirred like every other man in the street with news of foreign persecution, they turn to their own land to find seeds of the same destructive hatred. Their themes of pity and anger, their styles of sentimental elegy and scarifying denunciation may come to seem representative of our time.[10]

In "our time," as this reviewer recognizes, writers could not help but respond to the news abroad by looking closely at what was going on at home and keening an elegiac lamentation full of sentimentality and denunciation. The documentary impulse elicited feeling in both artists and audiences.

In the papers of Pare Lorentz at Columbia University is a note he wrote in response to queries by one of a number of biographers and critics of John Steinbeck seeking insights about the novelist after he was awarded the 1962 Nobel Prize for Literature. In it, he reports that while yes, he and Steinbeck had spent time together in the late 1930s when Steinbeck was writing his novel about migrants in California (given the title *The Grapes of Wrath* after Lorentz had sent the Steinbecks a record of the soundtrack, which featured "The Battle Hymn of the Republic," to his radio broadcast of the screenplay for *Ecce Homo*); but no, he had no influence on Steinbeck's use of "documentary" effects in the novel.[11]

Despite his refusal to claim any influence on Steinbeck's vision, the novelist had worked as an "assistant director" with Lorentz during the shoot of *The Fight for Life*. Steinbeck apprenticed behind the camera and alongside an editor and Lorentz had put him to work revising the scripts of *Ecce Homo* and *Fight*. Like so many phototextual writers, Steinbeck had already been accompanying a photographer as he travelled up and down the Salinas Valley observing and reporting on the misery of migrant farmworkers and their families, collecting the source material for *The Grapes of Wrath*. As Steinbeck wrote to Lorentz on March 6 of 1938 or 39 (no year) in the middle of writing his novel, which came out of his series of articles for the *San Francisco News* and was also based on the fieldwork of Sanora Babb (done for Tom Collins of the FSA and manager of the migrant camp at Arvin, California, in 1936):

> I just got back from another week in the field where the starvation and illness have been driven to a fine logical conclusion by the wet and flood. It might interest you to know but not to repeat just now that a nice revolutionary feeling is the concomitant of this suffering. I mean it is something that I hoped but was not sure of, that a certain amount of suffering is deadening but a quick increase such as this storm shakes off the apathy. The thing is very dangerous now. (Lorentz 122–123)

Presenting the thing – revolutionary feeling and its concomitant suffering – bringing the news – whether in the Living Newspapers of the Federal Theater Project or in the form of a novel – was an overpowering aesthetic commitment during the 1930s. Hollywood studios, Warner Brothers most spectacularly, produced films ripped from the headlines: *I Was a Fugitive from a Chain Gang*, *The Public Enemy*, even the fluff of Busby Berkeley's *Golddiggers of 1933* cannot escape the "wailing, wailing" of a bereft streetwalker bemoaning her "forgotten man" during the hard times of the Depression.[12] William Stott calls this aesthetic "a documentary motive" (as in both leitmotif and raison d'être) found in "the rhetoric of the New Deal and the WPA arts projects; in painting, dance, fiction, and theater; in the new media of radio and picture magazines; in popular thought, education, and advertising," in short "throughout the culture of the time."[13] These very American works reverberated with the dynamic political and aesthetic movements in Europe, from Futurism to Dada to Surrealism, each gleaning a central practice of cinema: cut and paste. "Authentic montage is based on the document," according to Walter Benjamin's comments on Alfred Döblin's 1929 novel *Berlin Alexanderplatz*: "the stylistic principle governing this book is that of montage." He catalogues the elements comprising this narrative montage, eliding character and place; the subtitle being, "The

Story of Franz Biberkopf": "Petty-bourgeois printed matter, scandalmonger-ing, stories of accidents, the sensational incidents of 1928, folk songs, and advertisements rain down in this text."[14] A similar litany of vernacular documents was common as well to many American novels after John Dos Passos's *42nd Parallel*: Clara Weatherwax's *Marching! Marching!* pastes articles and leaflets from strikers and company goons side by side in two columns on the same page for entire chapters to convey the dialectics of a labor struggle in the Northwest; Ruth McKenney's *Industrial Valley* inserts various newspaper accounts of the rubber workers' strike in Akron, Ohio, into its fictional tale. Lauren Gilfillan's *I Went to Pit College* blurred the borders between fiction and journalism by developing an insider's view through reportage, which brought more than an eyewitness sensibility to account for what can be understood to occur during a strike or on the dole. Reportage implied the engagement of the writer in the events she recounted; not only was she there to see, she was there to act. In Caroline Slade's *Sterile Sun*, there is no narrator; instead readers walk the streets with teenaged prostitutes as verbatim accounts by the girls she administered as a social worker in upstate New York fill the book's pages. Steinbeck's approach was akin to human-interest journalism, from which *The Grapes of Wrath* emerged; but readers recognized the connection to the news – articles and books were appearing about the violent tactics of the Associated Farmers and the photographs and films of those displaced by the Dust Bowl could be found in newspapers, posters, theaters and magazines.

Telling

Shortly after the success of *The Grapes of Wrath*, and especially of the John Ford film with a screenplay by former journalist Nunnally Johnson, Stein-beck formed a production company, Pan-American Films, Inc., with the editor of the journal *New Theatre and Film*, Herbert Kline, and others, to shoot a documentary film in Mexico, *The Forgotten Village*. In the preface to the volume, based on the film, published by Steinbeck's publisher, Viking, in 1941, Steinbeck described it as a "curious and true and dramatic film."[15] Its "method" of storytelling reveals Steinbeck's attempt to create a "voice which interpolated dialogue without trying to imitate it, a very quiet voice [nar-rated by Burgess Meredith] to carry the story only when the picture [shot by Alexander Hackensmid, later Hammid] and the music [composed by Hanns Eisler] could not." The story recounts the tensions within a traditional Aztec Indian village between the old ways of healing practiced by the *curandera* Trini and the new science of germs, vaccinations and water purification brought to the village from the city by a teacher and doctors summoned by a village boy, Juan Diego. His efforts save his sister from dying of enteric bacillus (perhaps what is known now as anthrax) but he is cast out of his village, and subsequently travels with the doctor to an urban school where he will study medicine and bring it back to his people – as many others will do too. The final words of the film: "'The change will come, is coming, as surely as there are thousands of Juan Diegos in the villages of Mexico.' And the boy said, 'I am Juan Diego'" (142–143).

In posing the triumph of Western medicine over the tradition of a Wise Woman – and in doing so in the context of seeing the exploitation of peasants by landowners and the promise of education through schooling to free the villagers from rituals that at once predate Spanish colonialism and reenact its long ago and far away battles with Moorish conquerors – the film appears enmeshed in the classic narrative of Western progress: science will vanquish superstition; youth will surpass elders; with modernity, life will improve. But the tale is a bit more complicated. Named Juan Diego, for the peasant whose vision of the Virgen de Guadalupe is a foundational myth of modern Mexican nationalism, the film suggests there need not be conflicts between the old ways and the new in post-revolutionary Mexico. This boy is, after all, the people. With the help of the village teacher, whose connections to the outside world are cemented by his access to various technologies: books and microscopes and the cinema (he shows a film about disease to the villagers but first warms the audience up with cartoons – shades of Preston Sturges's *Sullivan's Travels*), Juan Diego works to convince his family that his brother died of contaminated well water, which has also sickened his sister, not bad "airs" as the *curandera* insists. But they refuse to believe him, and his father strikes him then banishes him from home. On his first venture from his village to seek medical help in the terrifying city, Juan Diego meets a soldier, a former village boy like him, who calls on Juan Diego to perform (as he does) "'the true people's work ... saving, not killing; growing, not dying. That is the people's work, yours and mine'" (99). In classic allegorical fashion, this peasant boy is at once himself and a type, representative of the people whose story serves as emblematic of the nation's. Past and present coincide. He will work to improve healthcare through science; the villagers will continue to seek aid from Trini, who also serves a midwife, bringing children (and thus citizens) into the world.

Like many books appearing the late 1930s, *The Forgotten Village* took the sense of "documentary" effect latent in the "sentimental elegy" expounded by Steinbeck and other 1930s novelists, poets and playwrights and literalized it by placing images and texts in direct conversation – exactly as a film would (and in this case, did) through an extra-diegetic voiceover speaking along with the flow of images. The book version presents stills from the "story documentary," which originated with Steinbeck's "elastic story," as he called his script.[16] To some extent, images followed text (which was true for some photo-textual books, Richard Wright's *12 Million Black Voices* [1941] among them), in that the words preceded the selection of images, though the shape of the final product was often interactive. In other documentary books, text and images are coequals, imagined simultaneously, as in *Let Us Now Praise Famous Men* (1941); and in still others, the text responded to the images, as did Archibald Macleish's *Land of the Free* (1938). Other examples of collaboration, Margaret Bourke-White and novelist Erskine Caldwell's *You Have Seen Their Faces* (1937) and Dorothea Lange and sociologist Paul Shuster Taylor's *American Exodus: A Record of Human Erosion* (1939), were made by husband-and-wife teams travelling together with camera and typewriter (as had James Agee and Walker Evans, but they had then gone separate ways after their three weeks together in Alabama) who then worked on the final product together.

Even with these differences, all photo-textual documents, as John Puckett called them,[17] including *Let Us Now Praise Famous Men*, foreground visualization, the depiction of documenting reality, in the work of socially engaged literature. Telling (and of course showing) demanded looking – by the artist and the audience. Nowhere would this be more apparent than in Lynd Ward's *Vertigo*, his graphic novel made entirely of woodcuts recounting the early years of the Depression. Here the only text consists of the advertisements, newspaper headlines, leaflets or posters, such as the "NOTICE: ALL MEN ON NIGHT SHIFT LAID OFF UNTILL (sic) FURTHER NOTICE" found in "April" of the "1935" section.[18] Documentary blurred the boundaries of form, genre and media. After Lorentz had published a "lyrical version" of the script for his film *The River* in *McCall's* magazine, it was brought out as a pamphlet with film stills. This booklet was nominated for the Pulitzer Prize in poetry (a fact conveyed to Lorentz by Roosevelt himself),[19] suggesting a further breakdown of the boundaries among genre and media, text and image, both still and moving. These works – some wordless, others lyrical – shift among genres; as Steinbeck notes of *The Forgotten Village*, they were "elastic," accommodating various bits and pieces of reality and ideology to pose "a question."

While critics assume Steinbeck gleaned the idea of documentary from Lorentz, the filmmaker himself had been dismissed as violating documentary practice for using professional actors in his adaption of Paul de Kruif's book on the Chicago Maternity Center, *The Fight for Life* (*FDR's Moviemaker*, 127). But the documentary motive itself was "elastic." Lorentz's photo album for *Ecce Homo*, which was originally to have been a follow-up film to the two he made for the Resettlement Administration (*The Plow that*

Figure 5.1 Arthur Rothstein, *Sign, Birmingham, Alabama*, 1937, black-and-white photograph. Library of Congress Prints and Photograph Division, Washington, DC. Source Collection: Farm Security Administration, Office of War Information Photograph Collection.

Broke the Plains and *The River*), is full of images that resonate with those taken by Walker Evans, Dorothea Lange and other FSA photographers – images of depleted land, barren industrial landscapes, and ironic signage on billboards and storefronts advertising the good life. In the documentary aesthetic, image was textual and text was visual, especially in this moment of depression and fascism.[20] (See Figure 5.1.) Political rhetoric and propaganda were part of the ambient elements of national identities. The pervasive Burma Shave billboards along the highways, as Gertrude Stein noted when she toured the United States in the 1930s, became the new literary form of vernacular America.[21] "There on the roads I read Buy your flour meal and meat in Georgia."[22] Succinct phrases captured in motion, they told an ironic story of possession and loss.

Documentary expression by 1930s artists, spurred by pressing international crises and the sense that history must be not merely recorded but reordered, even remade, by art, could not be separated from the avant garde and experimentalism. This radical interventionism – into form and politics – was the impetus behind the Living Newspapers. For instance, the censored Living Newspaper play by Arthur Arent, *Ethiopia*, contained scenes proclaiming themselves as news, with script directions presented as if they were teletypes from the front:

TELETYPE: "BETRAYED!" CRIES BRITISH PUBLIC.
TELETYPE: SHEFFIELD SHEFFIELD SHEFFIELD SHEFFIELD
SHEFFIELD
(Light up on street scene. Man, soap box, etc.)
SPEAKER: ... and what do you think everybody else is going to say about this – all the little countries like Romania. Greece, Turkey, Jugoslavia, Poland, and the rest of them. What are they going to think of British diplomacy and the League of Nations now? [23]

The direct use of conventions of news reporting and the pointed reference to international events conveyed the topicality of the Living Newspaper as a documentary form.

The controversy sparked by the suppression of the Federal Theater Project's performance of *Ethiopia* caused Elmer Rice, head of its New York Unit, to resign his post. The US government had censored the play for its intervention into government policy, despite it being "a carefully documented factual presentation of public events." Rice's statement challenged the federal government, thus making the case that the play could affect "international relations," especially when the government's "growth of fascism, which uses censorship as one of its most effective weapons" was being put to use by "the Democratic party to be reelected at all costs."[24] If facts – or at least factual presentations – could be interpreted as dangerous to global politics (a precursor to the charges against Daniel Ellsberg, Chelsea Manning, and Edward Snowden), then these were important elements to be mobilized in art and particularly in the novel, which has always toggled between support for the status quo (as the bourgeois form par excellence) and subversion of it (as a means of expressing dissenting views through its inherent heteroglossia). This ambivalent connection between propaganda (or advertisement) and critique was part of the urge to cross generic, formal and media boundaries, as if a photograph might serve as a corrective to slippery language; or a dramatic performance might challenge the theater of politics and war.

For example, as early as 1930, despite finding *Berlin Alexanderplatz* exemplary as a new form of epic, with "Biblical verses, statistics, and texts from hit songs ... to confer authenticity" (301), Benjamin was skeptical of its literary mode of mining the news through "the fashionable appeal to 'facts'." In Germany, this was known as the *Neue Sachlichkeit*, the New Objectivity, and was both celebrated (as being "hostile to fictions removed from reality') and derided (because "it attacks theory").[25] Its aesthetic practice filtered into contemporary culture, not just left-wing writing, because, as Benjamin noted, New Objectivity was a two-edged sword useful only when, as in Bertolt Brecht's Epic Theater, the artist was committed to changing the world, not merely revealing its apparatus.[26] Otherwise, the left-wing writer, proclaiming his allegiance to socialism but shying away from revolution, became a "hack" (as Benjamin claimed of Döblin), whose work served no other purpose "than to wring from the political situation a continuous stream of novel effects for the entertainment of the public" (774). For Benjamin, the "popularity" of "the technology of publication: radio and the illustrated press" pushed the "photographic form" and with it literature, in the direction of the "modern," so that, in his famous words, a photograph "can no longer record a tenement block or a refuse heap without transfiguring it ... into an object of enjoyment" (774–775). The dilemma for the revolutionary artist hinged on how to use the apparatus (of documentary, of the state, of the economy) to reveal the workings of capitalism and fascism, but resist the fashion of simply presenting it via the new (and increasingly entertaining) technical media. A tricky move for any artist, almost an impossibility when it was the federal government funding the work (as in the FTP or FSA or RA) or worse, a Hollywood studio or Henry Luce's magazine empire. The decision by Lorentz to screen his 1936 film *The Plow that Broke the Plains* along with Walt Disney's first full-length feature, *Snow White*, best exemplified this conundrum. While neither Lorentz nor Disney controlled movie exhibition and were thus united in opposition to Hollywood's monopoly on viewing venues, the imbrication of popular culture (animation) with governmental agencies (instructional cinema) defused the power of documentary critique. The force of its oppositional aesthetic appeared diminished by its connection with a commercialized mode of supplying pleasurable fun. (Though again, *Sullivan's Travels*, with its final screening in an African-American church of a Mickey Mouse cartoon for white Southern prisoners on a chain gang convulsed in laughter, suggests that of the two forms, pleasure might be the more subversive.)[27]

While the FTP's Living Newspapers were meant to bring the news into the theater as its performative style translated headlines into gesture, the news travelled through all media: topical songs (by Woody Guthrie), collages (by John Heartfield), poems (by Muriel Rukeyser ["The Book of the Dead"]), murals (by José Clemente Orozco) among them.[28] Mexican painter Diego Rivera, commissioned to decorate the Great Hall of the RCA Building in Rockefeller Center with a mural depicting current events – the rise of Benito Mussolini and Adolf Hitler among them – was "barred" from working after the artist refused to paint over the image he included of Vladimir Lenin. In this collective space created by capital, Rivera claimed he "painted the naked and objective truth about the essential factors of social strife ... because Rockefeller Center is a group of public buildings open to all the inhabitants of the city and containing theaters, lecture halls, offices, radio and television studios, laboratories, and even a subway station!"[29] The mural was "relevant" now and would still be in the future (16). The news that "Rockefellers Ban Lenin in RCA Mural and Dismiss Rivera," appeared on the front page of the *New York Times* a few columns away from another item, headlined "Nazis Pile Books for Bonfires Today," revealing that Berlin students had collected "twenty-five thousand 'un-German' books" and "consigned [them] to the flames."[30] How could fiction compete with reality? It didn't; rather, fiction and reality co-conspired in the New Objectivity, in the new world of now, our modern times: *In Our Time* as Ernest Hemingway had named it in 1925 and what Charles Chaplin would call *Modern Times* in 1936.

When Eugene Jolas translated *Berlin Alexanderplatz* into English in 1931, its method would have been immediately clear to American audiences. John Dos Passos's *Manhattan Transfer* (1925) and the first volume of the *U.S.A* trilogy, *The 42nd Parallel* (1930) convey a similar sense of the fast-paced urban spaces where newspaper headlines, popular songs and advertising jingles mesh with interior monologues and commentary to produce a sense of the time/space of modern life. Ian Buruma contextualizes the technique of Döblin's 1929 novel:

> Creating a collage of fleeting, fragmented impressions as a way to describe the modern metropolis is not unique to Döblin, of course. Walter Ruttman's experimental documentary film *Berlin: Die Sinfonie der Großstadt*, made in 1927, did exactly that, through a montage of images as fast and cacophonous as the city itself. So did George Grosz, in his drawings of Berlin, which don't simply break up the view of metropolitan life into a jumble of impressions, but make the city dwellers look transparent, as though one could see through them to their most private desires, often of a violent sexual nature. And in their different ways, Picasso, Braque, and others were doing the same, fragmenting perspective in Synthetic Cubism.

Döblin adds his own all-seeing authorial voice to the patchwork of speech, songs, police reports, private thoughts, commercials, and other big-city noises. His voice is as complex as those of his characters. Sometimes it is didactic, like Brecht's theatrical texts, or drily analytical like a doctor's analysis of his patients. Döblin was in fact a doctor, and practiced as a psychiatrist in Berlin, where he heard many crime stories firsthand. Sometimes the voice is ironic, even sarcastic, and often it is given to metaphysical musings, quoting from the Bible, especially the stories of Job and Abraham's sacrifice of Isaac.[31] Buruma crystallizes the complex ways modernist forms – cinematic, literary, painterly – responded to, while at the same time they represented, the internalized felt immediacy of the sights and sounds of

Figure 5.2 John Vachon, *Billboard in Transition, Minneapolis, Minnesota, 1939*, black-and-white photograph. Library of Congress Prints and Photograph Division, Washington, DC. Source Collection: Farm Security Administration, Office of War Information Photograph Collection.

urban, working-class life. (See Figure 5.2.) It required a "patchwork of speech, songs, police reports, private thoughts, commercials, and other big-city noises," a "synthetic cubism."

Witnessing

Even an attempt, like Steinbeck's *Forgotten Village,* to depict the lives of illiterate and impoverished indigenous Aztec peasants in rural Mexico required movement into the terrain of the urban. As Herbert Kline described it, in order to fake the reality of reality for the "story documentary," he and Steinbeck and Alexander Hackensmid were filming, they resorted to hiring villagers who had migrated from "the forgotten village" to the market towns where they had encountered Gringos and where their reality was already subject to the conventions of commerce and its social and economic exchanges. The film was premised on an argument for urban modernity: that traditional medicine was lethal, especially to women in childbirth and children, so villagers needed to welcome, and the Mexican government needed to provide, professional medical caregivers – doctors, nurses, trained midwives – rather than, or at least in supplement to, the local *curandera*. This was the content to be conveyed cinematically; as Kline explains, "documentary scenes are 'directed' in a way that resemble studio location work ... And despite the fact that your people are 'non-actors,' you can rehearse them" (Kline in Jacobs 152). A documentary film is conceived and constructed through scenes that are at once scripted and shot; text and camera cooperate because, as Kline explains, "you seldom find real-life ... the way you want to film it" (152). Documentary, even when it films what occurs, is fundamentally fictional in the literary ways of the novel; both forms are responses to reality, committed to reshaping that reality in order to fully convey its meaning as truth.

This commitment to using fictional forms – or metaphorical ones, forms that both efface and foreground the working of an artist's hand, eye, language, etc., through the manipulation of camera lens, pencil, paint, typewriter keys – to peel back the layers of real life extended beyond film or photography to other visual arts. Artists used the means available to them to disclose what they saw. For Spanish Loyalist commander Luis Quintanilla, drawing became a means to record the devastation of Francisco Franco's assault on the people of Spain. In 1939, Modern Age Books published a collection of Quintanilla's drawings prefaced by Ernest Hemingway and with a text by Elliot Paul and Jay Allen, who in 1938 had translated photographer Robert Capa's documentary book, with Gerda Taro's photographs and Capa's prose, about the Spanish Civil War, *Death in the Making*. During the 1930s, Modern Age Books published cheap paperbound volumes (perhaps at the urging of the Comintern, if one believed Whittaker Chambers),[32] often with topical themes. Titles from 1937 include: Leo Huberman's *Labor Spy Racket*, William Burnett's *Little Caesar*, Andre Gide's *Travels in the Congo* as well as stories by William Saroyan, mysteries by Dorothy Sayers and E. M. Forster's *Passage to India*. In 1938, in addition to Quintanilla's *All the Brave*, the press brought out an edition of Margaret Bourke-White and Erskine Caldwell's *You Have Seen Their Faces*, the WPA Guidebook, *U.S. 1*, a kind of documentary Baedeker of the states from Maine to Florida, as well as a Steinbeck novel.

Publisher Louis P. Birks was in correspondence with Hemingway to bring out a volume, similar to the one Viking would publish of stills from *The Forgotten Village* for the Joris Ivens' film, *Spanish Earth*, but Hemingway opted to have his prose and the stills appear in *Life* magazine for greater impact.[33] Nevertheless, Hemingway was convinced to contribute a few paragraphs, "a thousand words or less," to help publicize the volume.[34] These became "Three Prefaces" penned over the course of a season, each with a dateline reminiscent of news reports: the first dated March 10, 1938, is from Key West (just a week before he left for Spain); the second and third are dated April 18 and May, 1938, from the midst of war, "somewhere in Spain." In the first iteration, Hemingway recalls a meeting with Quintanilla the previous year when he learned that "a bomb had gutted" the artist's studio and that his frescoes in University City and Casa del Pueblo were, as the artist told him: "Finished." "These paintings that were destroyed by the bomb, and those frescoes that were smashed by artillery fire and chipped away by machine gun bullets were great Spanish works of art ... When the Republic that he loved and believed in was attacked by the fascists, he led the attack on the Montaña Barracks and saved Madrid for the government." Hemingway continues: "The drawings are of war. They are to be looked at; not written about in an introduction ... the drawings say all they need to say themselves" (7). His rage at the destruction of the Spanish Republic, of a Spanish artist's work, and of Spain itself, turns into disgust with the inadequacy of language in the face of war's horrors. He shudders at what war does to people and their language – it "cauterize[s] itself" just as those "seeing very much of it" become "brutalized" or "frightened" if not "killed" (11). What therefore matters are the images; in this case, sketched on the frontlines of battle, they track bombings, sieges, troop transports and the civilian and military casualties that inevitably result to provide a record of what Quintanilla had witnessed. Speaking of the artist-turned-military man now sent by his government to depict the battlefield, Hemingway concludes: "I envy Quintanilla very much that he has his drawings made. For now I have to try to write my stories" (11). The anger motivating these documents of barbarity produces radical citizens, forged through affect into political subjects.

Writing documentary in the 1930s was an act twice removed – from the action and from the visual images of action. This modernist-influenced practice of witnessing called forth the sort of loathing and self-loathing found in Steinbeck's letters from the frontlines of the lettuce fields of California and the Ebro River front in Spain where Hemingway was embattled against fascism along with the International Brigades and Spanish loyalist troops; it runs as a constant leitmotif through Agee's bitter yet sweet prose poem to the Gudgers and their extended families and the elegant photographs by his picture postcard-collecting collaborator Walker Evans. The documentary impulse found expression in a lyrical rendering of plain English – the vernacular English Gertrude Stein found so profound because so simple. A language that attempts to bring the world inside the self alters the self fundamentally in the process;and if one is really a "genius," according to Stein *and* the left-wing documentarists, it changes the world as well: "All this makes anything written interesting to any one interested in it the number of ways any one tells anything theatre novels history poetry biography autobiography newspapers letter-writing and conversations ... this thing at one and the same time listening and telling really listening and really telling."[35] This is the thing to see.

NOTES

This essay was completed while I was 2016 resident fellow at the United States Studies Centre at the University of Sydney.

1 Robert Coles, *Doing Documentary Work* (New York: Oxford University Press, 1997), 250–251.

2 James Agee, *Let Us Now Praise Famous Men* (Boston: Houghton Mifflin, 1941), 13.

3 Pare Lorentz, *Lorentz on Film: Movies 1927–1941* (Norman: University of Oklahoma Press, 1986), 170.

4 "Movies for Education Impractical, Declares Producer of 'The River'," *Minnesota Daily* November 5, 1937. The University of Minnesota's Visual Education Service eventually provided the shots.

5 Haidee Wasson, *Museum Movies: The Museum of Modern Art and the Birth of Art Cinema* (Berkeley and Los Angeles: University of California Press, 2005), 191

6 In *Becoming Mike Nichols* ([d. Douglas McGrath, 2016] HBO), the director explains why he filmed *Who's Afraid of Virginia Woolf* in black and white. By this time, its use called attention to the medium's removal from reality, even as it gestured to the highlighted reality of black-and-white documentary. Thus, paradoxically, it pushed metaphor to the forefront of representation.

7 See Paula Rabinowitz, "March 1933: FDR's First Fireside Chat" in Greil Marcus and Werner Sollors, eds. *A New Literary History of America* (Cambridge, MA: Harvard University Press, 2009).

8 Alice Lovejoy, *Army Film and the Avant Garde: Cinema and Experiment in the Czechoslovak Military* (Bloomington: Indiana University Press, 2014) and Jonathan Kahana, *Intelligence Work: The Politics of American Documentary* (New York: Columbia University Press, 2008).

9 See Jeff Rosenheim, *Walker Evans and the Picture Postcard* (Göttingen: Steidl and Partners, 2009).

10 Peter Monro Jack, "Steinbeck's New Novel Brims with Anger and Pity," *New York Times* (April 16, 1939). www.nytimes.com/books/97/07/06/home/history-grapes.html.

11 See Pare Lorentz to Robert Wallstein, Typescript, Box 171. Pare Lorentz Papers 1914–1992 (1932–1960), Rare Book & Manuscript Library, Columbia University in the City of New York.

12 For a fuller elaboration on the documentary codes within *Golddiggers of 1933*, see Paula Rabinowitz, *They Must Be Represented: The Politics of Documentary* (New York and London: Verso, 1994), 64–83 passim.

13 William Stott, *Documentary Expression and Thirties America* (Chicago: University of Chicago Press, 1986), 4.

14 Walter Benjamin, "The Crisis of the Novel," in Ed. Michael W. Jennings, Howard Eiland and Gary Smith, Trans. Rodney Livingston *Selected Writings Volume 2* (Cambridge, MA: Belknap Press of Harvard University, 1999), 299–304, 301.

15 *The Forgotten Village* (With 136 Photographs from the Film of the Same Name by Rosa Harvan Kline and Alexander Hackensmid). Story by John Steinbeck (New York: The Viking Press, 1941).

16 Herbert Kline, "Films Without Make-Believe," in Lewis Jacobs, ed. *The Documentary Tradition* 2nd ed. (New York and London: W. W. Norton, 1979), pp. 148–157, 152.

17 John Puckett, *Five Photo-Textual Documentaries from the Great Depression* (Ann Arbor: UMI Press, 1984). See also James Curtis, *Mind's Eye, Mind's Truth: FSA Photographs Reconsidered* (Philadelphia: Temple University Press, 1991).

18 Lynd Ward, *Vertigo: A Novel in Woodcuts* (1937) (Mineola, NY: Dover Publications, Inc., 2009), np.

19 *FDR's Moviemaker: Memoirs and Scripts* (Reno and Las Vegas: University of Nevada Press, 1992), 78, 81.

20 Scrapbook for Ecce Homo, Series I: Ecce Homo, 1938–1942, MS# 1461 Box 17, Pare Lorentz Papers 1914–1992 (1932–1960), Rare Book & Manuscript Library, Columbia University in the City of New York.

21 For more on Stein's fascination with advertising, see Mike Chasar, *Everyday Reading: Poetry and Popular Culture in Modern America* (New York: Columbia University Press, 2012).

22 Gertrude Stein, *Everybody's Autobiography* [1937] (New York: Vintage Books, 1973), 254.

23 Arthur Arent, "A Scene from the Censored Play," in Herbert Kline, ed., *New Theater and Film, 1934–1937: An Anthology* (New York: Harcourt Brace Jovanovich, 1985), 103–104.

24 "A Statement by Elmer Rice," in Kline, 102–103.

25 Walter Benjamin, "Critique of the New Objectivity," in *Selected Writings* Volume 2, 417.

26 Walter Benjamin, "The Author as Producer," in *Selected Writings*, Volume 2, 777

27 See Paula Rabinowitz, *They Must Be Represented*, 85–86.

28 See Robbie Lieberman, *"My Song Is My Weapon": People's Songs, American Communism, and the Politics of Culture, 1930–1950* (Champaign-Urbana: University of Illinois Press, 1995) for topical song movement. On muralismo, see Anthony W. Lee, *Painting on the Left: Diego Rivera, Radical Politics and San Francisco's Public Murals* (Berkeley and Los Angeles: University of California Press, 1999). James Smethurst, "Remembering Nat Turner: Black Artists, Radical History and Radical Historiography, 1930–1955," in Howard Brick, Robbie Lieberman and Paula Rabinowitz, eds. *Lineages of the Literary Left: Essays in Honor of Alan M. Wald* (Ann Arbor, MI: Maize Books, 2015) argues that for African-American artists, including muralists and printmakers – such as Elizabeth Catlett – this work provided a counter-history to the standard racist 1930s historiography about slavery.

29 Diego Rivera, *Portrait of America* (With an explanatory text by Bertram D. Wolfe) (New York: Covici, Friede, Publishers, 1934), 15–16. This book includes some photographs (including of Lenin) from the destroyed mural.

30 Both articles appeared on page one of the *New York Times* (May 10, 1933) and are reprinted in Irene Herner de Larrea, *Diego Rivera's Mural at the Rockefeller Center* (Mexico City: EDICUPES SA. 1990).

31 Ian Buruma, "The Genius of Berlin" *New York Review of Books* January 17, 2008. He wrote this review on the occasion of the release of Fassbinder's film. www.nybooks.com/articles/2008/01/17/the-genius-of-berlin/.

32 See Herbert Romerstein and Eric Breindel, *The Venona Secrets: Exposing Soviet Espionage and America's Traitors* (Washington, DC: Regnery Books, 2000), 123–134.

33 See Christopher P. Stephens, *Modern Age Books: A Checklist* (Hastings-On-Hudson, NY: Ultramarine Publishing Co., Inc., 1991) for the complete offerings of the 1930s press. See also, David Welky, *Everything Was Better in America: Print Culture in the Great Depression* (Champaign-Urbana: University of Illinois Press, 2008). On this last point, see, Alex Vernon, *Hemingway's Second War: Bearing Witness to the Spanish Civil War* (Iowa City: University of Iowa Press, 2011), 124.

34 Ernest Hemingway, "Three Prefaces," in Luis Quintanilla, *All the Brave: Drawings of the Spanish War*. Text by Elliot Paul and Jay Allen (New York: Modern Age Books, 1939), 7.

35 Gertrude Stein, "Narration: Lecture 3" (1935) in *Gertrude Stein, Writings, 1932–1946* (New York: The Library of America 1998), 342.

6

ILKA SAAL

Songs of Social Significance

Theater of the Depression Era

When the stock market crashed in the fall of 1929 and the Great Depression began to wash over the country, Broadway was slow to respond. It watched the number of productions go down, theaters close, and audiences dwindle as fewer and fewer people could afford ticket prices and wandered off to the mushrooming movie theaters. To those audiences that remained, Broadway pretty much continued to offer its regular fare of society comedies, revues and musicals, folk dramas, and theater classics. Even as the ensuing decade proved to be a fruitful one for American drama, with production of plays by Maxwell Anderson, S. N. Behrman, Paul Green Lillian Hellman, Langston Hughes, John Howard Lawson, Eugene O'Neill, Irvin Shaw, Robert Sherwood, and Thornton Wilder,[1] few plays tended to address the social issues of the economic crisis at hand. Broadway remained, as theater critic Barrett H. Clark put it at the time, "a somewhat remote institution, patronized by the wealthy and idle."[2] Not surprisingly then, of all the Pulitzer Prize–winning plays of the 1930s, the longest running (and, hence, by Broadway standards most successful one) was not Maxwell Anderson's acerbic political satire *Both Your Houses* (1933) but the light-hearted, middle-class social comedy *You Can't Take it With You* (1936) by George S. Kaufman and Moss Hart.[3]

Kaufman and Hart's romantic depression comedy is in a way exemplary for Broadway's response to mass unemployment and poverty, the demise of the middle class, and ever-greater inequality between the upper and lower echelons of society. While ostensibly dealing with class conflict by pitching the Wall Street company-owning Kirby family against the seemingly impoverished Sycamore-Vanderhof clan and while sprinkling its dialogues with references to topical issues such as unemployment relief and the widespread leftist fervor of the decade (Paul is reading Trotsky, Penny is writing plays about class, war, and sex), *You Can't Take It With You* steers clear of dealing with the concrete social and economic issues of the depression. What is at stake is not class tensions but the conflict between conformism and individualism. The Sycamores' life style (cheap but comfortable living) turns out to be a choice rather than necessity, enabled by a lush annual income from grandfather Vanderhof's real estate assets.[4] Any lingering tensions between the moneyed and the less-moneyed, the conservative and the radical are sublimated in the romantic union of their sensible and moderate off-springs, Tony Kirby and Alice Sycamore. Moreover, the fast-paced verbal sparing between Kirby Sr. and Grandpa Vanderhof, the characters' eccentric personalities and bizarre hobbies, and the accumulation of absurd occurrences (including an explosion of illegally produced fireworks and a blintzes dinner prepared by a visiting Russian Grand Duchess) provide a light-hearted comedic, even farcical outlet for any social frustration the audience might hold. These comic devices work together to expose the hubris of the mighty Kirbys, to take them down a peg, and to teach them a valuable lesson in humanity according to the popular motto of many a Broadway show of the time: "For what is a man profited, if he shall gain the whole world, and lose his own soul?"[5] Displaying wit, energy, determination, and self-confidence the ostensibly radical Sycamore-Vanderhofs, by contrast, have managed to carve out for themselves a more "soulful" existence not against but within the existing capitalist system. Their quirky but rugged individualism is presented as an Ur-American ideology, far more efficient than collective action in the pursuit of happiness. Kaufman and Hart's solution to the calamity of capitalism – the assertion of ingenuity, freedom of choice, and individualism against the hardships of depression – was the culture industry's favored answer to the economic and social crisis.

In the early 1930s, however, as leftist sympathies were high among workers, bohemians, and intellectuals, great parts of the public were clamoring for a more radical analysis of the depression. Leftist theater designer Mordecai Gorelik quipped, "lower middle class audiences scarcely need the advice not to gain the whole world. Most of the audience is concerned with holding on to jobs or meager professional clienteles or keeping their small businesses from going bankrupt."[6] That this audience of petit bourgeois and workers was eager to see their experience of the crisis represented on stage became clear during the short run of Claire and Paul Sifton's unemployment drama *1931-* in December 1931.[7] The play was a rather crude exercise in expressionism but startled its viewers for its sheer nerve of topicality: "Seldom has a bad play stunned an audience quite so completely," Brooks Atkinson remarked.[8] In the figure of a modern-day everyman, Adam, the Siftons compellingly traced how long-term unemployment affected the American people emotionally, psychologically, and socially. Disconcerted by this analysis, one theater critic felt prompted to reassure himself that certainly life was not as bleak and cruel as portrayed on stage. Looking at the men and women standing in line at the nearby movie theaters, Percy Hammond concluded that "none of them was cold or hungry. They were warmly clothed and had the price of admission. No symptoms of destitution were present."[9] Little did he take note of the over half million unemployed in New York City alone, standing in line for bread and shelter in various parts of the city, not so very far from Broadway.[10] In the end, the Siftons' play was quickly dismissed by critics like Hammond from the attention of the carriage trade. It ran for only twelve performances – during each of which, however, a different kind of audience made itself heard: the lower-middle and working-class spectators in the galleries who enthusiastically applauded each night's performance and appealed to the producing Group Theatre not to close the play.[11] As Harold Clurman of the Group Theatre observed, "The production of *1931-* had made us aware, for the first time of a new audience. It was an audience to whom such a play as *1931-* was more valuable than the successful *Reunion in Vienna*. It was an audience that later kept the Theatre Union going for a few seasons, helped sustain the Federal Theatre Project [...]. It was potentially the audience for a national theatre."[12]

This audience was "new" only to Broadway producers. It had long been fostered by various amateur and professional theater groups, as, for instance, by the numerous immigrant theaters who cultivated within their ethnic communities both the classic humanist tradition of the European People's Theatre (e.g., the Ukrainian Dramatic Circle, the Yiddish Art Theatre, the Hungarian Dramatic Circle) and the avant-garde aesthetics of German agitprop and Russian constructivism (e.g., the German Prolet-Bühne, the Jewish Artef).[13] In addition, various professional leftist theaters emerged in the 1920s as more and more intellectuals rallied to the support of the workers' movement.[14] Foremost among them were the Workers' Drama League (1926) and its successor, the New Playwrights' Theatre (1927–1929).[15] Although only short-lived, these experimental theaters stirred up considerable attention with regard to the revolutionary fervor of their plays as well as their efforts in implementing European avant-garde aesthetics on the American stage.[16] In the early 1930s, it was then, above all, workers' amateur theater troupes, supported by the labor movement, who addressed the economic and social issues of their time and provided a forum for discussion. Leading among them were the German-speaking Prolet-Bühne (1925)[17] and the English-speaking Workers' Laboratory Theatre (WLT, 1928) – both militant street theater troupes performing at rallies and meetings. With agitation to class struggle as their primary goal, they drew on the agitprop techniques of German and Russian modernist political theater: alienation effects, montage, mass recitation, and biomechanics. In the sketch *Scottsboro* (1931), for instance, players of the Prolet-Bühne attempt to mobilize audience support for the nine African American teenagers arrested on false charges of rape in Alabama by encircling spectators from all sides and reciting their lines in a half-whisper and fast-paced staccato rhythm, so as to convey the horror of their situation: "In Scottsboro / In Scottsboro / Murder stalks the streets / In Scottsboro / In Scottsboro / Death haunts the cells."[18] The WLT Shock Troupe similarly relies in their twelve-minute sketch *Newsboy* (1933) on fast-paced, stylized action, on the extreme economy and precise timing of word and gestures. The sketch demonstrates how a young newsboy, hawking the daily tabloid papers to passers-by, is converted to political awareness when he begins to notice the incongruity between the sensational headlines of sex, wealth, and murder propagated by the papers he sells and the reality of deprivation and racism experienced by the people in the streets. Both *Scottsboro* and *Newsboy* were extremely popular at their time, frequently performed by amateur troupes across the country.[19]

In April 1932 several proletarian theater troupes joined in a national umbrella organization, the League of Workers Theatres (LOWT). Over the course of the decade LOWT established itself as the backbone of the American workers' theater movement. With the help of its monthly magazine *Workers' Theatre* (renamed *New Theatre* in 1935), it managed to reach out to hundreds of amateur organizations, providing them with dramatic scripts and theoretical insights, helping them to organize and share their ideas. By 1934 LOWT supported over four hundred amateur troupes across the country – a third of them foreign-language speaking. Its magazine achieved a circulation of eighteen thousand copies by 1938. Moreover, with the Theatre Union (1933), it set up the first stationary, English-speaking professional workers' theater. In short, the workers' theater movement played an eminent role in redefining the function of theater in American society, reaching out to broad sections of the population and insisting on the social relevance of artistic productions. "The theatre being born in America today is a theatre of workers," Hallie Flanagan commented in 1931. "Admittedly a weapon in the class struggle, this theatre is being forged in the factories and mines."[20] The stimuli sent out by this energetic theater extended far beyond the labor movement, influencing the emergence of a dynamic leftist culture in the United States, both amateur and professional. They extended as far as the government. In the mid-1930s, Washington set up among its various Works Progress Administration (WPA) programs the Federal Theatre Project, which in its effort to reach out to a broad American public also drew on the talent of the workers' theaters.

Given these combined efforts by amateurs and professionals, workers and bohemians, labor, intellectuals, and government alike, by mid-decade the American theater of the depression era proved to be vital, experimental, and politically engaged – a "living theater," to borrow Elmer Rice's phrase,[21] for a broad and heterogeneous audience. In 1935 *The New York Times* conceded, "the commercial theatre's custodians have lifted their eyes from the ledgers and discovered pretty close to their doorstep a lustily kicking youngster, well shed of its swaddling clothes."[22] This realization along with significant political changes in the mid-1930s also brought about a general opening of the Broadway stage to socially committed drama, leading to a number of collaborations between the established commercial and leftist theaters.

The general swing to the left in American theater in the 1930s can be parsed into two distinct phases. The early years of the decade are marked by the militant phase of the radical workers' theaters, insisting on a sectarian stance in terms of politics and poetics. This is, as Ira A. Levine writes, the time of agitprop, abstract and stylized stagecraft, of mobile theater groups seeking out audiences of workers in their work environments (*Scottsboro* and *Newsboy* are products of this phase).[23] Strongly inspired by Marxist doctrine, the main goal of this "proletarianism" was to reveal capitalist exploitation and to incite collective, insurrectional action to overcome this condition. By mid-decade, however, in the face of rising fascism abroad and antidemocratic tendencies inside the United States as well as a growing disillusionment with Soviet-style Communism, leftist theater workers agreed that a broader audience needed to be reached and that a more moderate political and aesthetic approach was expedient to do so.[24] The second phase, hence, saw the rapprochement between proletarian avant-garde aesthetics and the realism favored by established "bourgeois" theaters and the general reaching out to nonproletarian and nonradical audiences. Professional, stationary workers' theaters, like the Theatre Union in New York, resorted to Broadway aesthetics (full-length realist plays) and promotional methods (benefit theater parties, subscription systems) to attract large audiences. This opening up of the workers' theater movement now enabled the collaboration of a wide spectrum of cultural workers, regardless of class differences and ideological sympathies, in a broad and heterogeneous cultural front against fascism and war, in the struggle against racism and labor repression, and in the defense of civil liberties and support of democratic reforms. According to Michael Denning, the emerging collaboration between labor movement, the established culture industries, and the government resulted in "the extraordinary flowering of arts, entertainment and thought based on the broad social movement that came to be known as the Popular Front."[25]

The transition from the militant to the moderate phase, from an exclusive focus on working-class audiences to a broader, heterogeneous public is compellingly illustrated in Clifford Odets's play *Waiting for Lefty*. Odets, a then unknown actor with the Group Theatre, wrote the play at the end of 1934 in response to the New York taxi strike earlier that year and went on to stage it with the help of a few of his acting colleagues from the Group at a fund-raising event for the New Theatre League (successor to LOWT). At its opening night on 5 February 1935 at the Civic Repertory Theatre on 14th Street it brought down the house. There was roaring applause, stomping of feet, and some twenty-eight curtain calls.[26] Even more striking was the reaction of the press: both leftist and conservative critics were enthused, hailing the play for its revolutionary fervor and its verisimilitude.[27] *Waiting for Lefty* was quickly picked up by workers' theaters across the country and abroad, and by March it was playing on Broadway as a production of the Group Theatre.[28] Thanks to its fervent rhetoric, Odets's play was and still is considered a prime example of proletarian, socialist, even Marxist theater.[29] Its politics, however, are far from radical. In fusing agitprop with realist drama, it reaches out to working- and middle-class audiences, inciting them not so much to actual strike and rebellion as to political awareness and commitment.

Waiting for Lefty is a minimalist play of six brief scenes. On a bare stage a handful of members of a taxi drivers' committee are assembled to debate whether or not to go on strike, while waiting for their leader Lefty. In agitprop fashion the audience is drawn into this debate through direct address and the placement of actors in the auditorium, suggesting that they are part of a cabbies' assembly. As the corrupt union secretary Harry Fatt harangues the audience that "the times ain't ripe for strike,"[30] the drivers on stage step forth one by one and recount in flashback episodes (indicated by a change of lighting) how they arrived at their decision to go on strike. Joe tells of his losing struggle to provide for his family, and Sid explains how he was forced to break off with his fiancée unable to afford marriage on his small income. Lab assistant Miller, medical doctor Benjamin, and actor Philips, moreover, recount how they ended up as cab drivers after losing their professions to coercion, ethnic prejudice, and business interests. These individual episodes essentially repeat versions of the same argument: Each cab driver, cornered by an adverse situation and hostile sentiment, eventually comes to the realization that it is up to him, and only him, to bring about change. Thus, Joe rushes off to organize his buddies, Miller knocks out his boss, Philips accepts a copy of the *Communist Manifesto*, and Benjamin resolves to fight for social change in his country. Through such repetition of scenes of individual conversion, Odets builds up dramatic suspense, which is then harnessed in a final speech to rally everyone on and off-stage to collective action: "What are we waiting for … Don't wait for Lefty! He might never come. [...] Hello America! Hello. We're the stormbirds of the working class! [...] Well, what's the answer?"[31] At the opening night (as well as on many successive nights), the audience spontaneously joined the actors in a boisterous call for "Strike, Strike, Strike!!!"[32] All these are familiar techniques of agitprop theater. What is new is how Odets weds them to established aesthetic principles of bourgeois realism. Dramatic conflict is articulated through issues of family life and romance, work ethics, professional ambitions, and defiance of ethnic prejudice. Moreover, with the notable exception of Fatt (described as "a fat man of porcine appearance"), Odets presents us with individuals, rather than sociological types or political caricatures (as typical for agitprop), rendering with each episode a miniature psychological portrait of its protagonists. His adroit use of the East Side vernacular further enhances this impression of verisimilitude. In short, Odets's characters and dialogues come across as utterly believable, inviting identification and empathy – two key requirements of the realist stage and one of the reasons the bourgeois public responded so enthusiastically to the play.

The fusion of techniques also raises the question of Odets's targeted audience. After all, as John Howard Lawson points out, half the strike committee is composed of actors, doctors, technicians – former members of the middle class, whom one "cannot reasonably call [...] 'stormbirds of the working class'."[33] Indeed, *Waiting for Lefty* is neither written exclusively for a workers' audience, nor does it entail a call for unionization. In half of its episodes it speaks precisely to those members of the fallen middle class, whose presence in an ostensibly proletarian play Lawson so sharply criticizes. This is the group most derailed by the depression, suffering from growing pauperization and degradation of their living standards. And yet, as cultural critic Lewis Corey asserts, it is also the group most reluctant to rethink its alliance to an economic system to whose formation and rise it has been influential.[34] In his subsequent plays *Awake and Sing* (1935), *Paradise Lost* (1935), and *Golden Boy* (1937), Odets was to articulate the economic and psychological malaise of this lost middle class more fully.[35] In *Waiting for Lefty* he attempts to arouse this class from bewilderment and apathy and to generate a broad emotional alliance with the working class. The final call to "Strike!" is crucial in this regard. It remains amorphous enough to serve as a symbolic rather than actual call to arms. Eberhard Brüning reminds us that while strike proved to be a popular motif in plays of the 1930s, it was rarely understood as an appeal to concrete intervention but primarily as a metaphor for conversion and personal decision making.[36] And many critics of the time understood it along those lines. "It was a call to join the good fight for a greater measure of life in a world free of economic fear, falsehood and craven servitude to stupidity and greed," Clurman observed.[37] Seen from this angle, *Waiting for Lefty* is perhaps not all that different from Kaufman and Hart's plea for a more soulful capitalism in *You Can't Take it With You*.[38] But it articulates its agenda in a refreshing dramatic form embodying the vigor and energy of a young and vibrant workers' culture, which was increasingly asserting itself in the cultural mainstream, including on Broadway. Odets's play thus also illustrates the extent to which the "new" audiences and their "new" drama were capable of affecting public culture at large.

The mid-1930s saw the high point of socially aware drama. Uptown the Group Theatre (1931–1941) produced Sidney Kingsley's Pulitzer-winning social drama *Men in White* (1933–1934) and Odets's plays about the middle-class depression crisis *Awake and Sing!*, *Paradise Lost*, and *Golden Boy*, while the conservative Theatre Guild put on John Wexley's Scottsboro court-room drama *They Shall Not Die* (1934) and the Gershwin/Heyward opera *Porgy and Bess* (1935). Downtown Theatre Union (1933–1937), the first professional leftist theater, had a successful run with the proletarian melodramas *Peace on Earth* (1933) by Albert Maltz and George Sklar and *Stevedore* (1934) by Paul Peters and George Sklar as well as the naturalist dramas *Black Pit* (1935) by Albert Maltz and *Let Freedom Ring* (1935) by Albert Bein. Similar to Odets and in accordance with the general reorientation of leftist theaters in mid-decade, Theatre Union believed that issues of class struggle were most effectively addressed in terms of family and domestic life.[39] *Stevedore*, the most popular of its plays, integrates the theme of racial persecution with class struggle. When the African American stevedore and labor activist Lonnie Thompson is framed for the rape of a white woman and when the town's black community is terrorized by a white mob stirred up by industry bosses, police, and media, a group of white, unionized stevedores rallies to their defense and support. Together they mount the barricades to fight back the racist and anti-unionist mob, and the play closes with a grand tableau of racial solidarity and joint class struggle. "Black and white workers unite, for the first time on an American stage, to beat off their common enemy," an ecstatic Michael Gold applauded.[40] Yet, despite the suggestive visual allegory of the final tableau, invoking the armed struggle of the French Revolution as well as of African Americans against slavery, the play refrains from advocating militancy. As Lonnie puts in his final speech, just before being killed: "We hyar to defend our homes. We hyar to fight fo' our lives. And we hyar to show'em dat we ain't gwine be kicked around, and starved and stepped on no mo.' We hyar to show 'em we men and we gwine be treated like men."[41] The final scene hence comes across not as a call for armed class struggle but as a rallying cry for the defense of home and family, for the recognition of human rights and human dignity.

In October 1935 the government stepped onto the stage with the Federal Theatre Project. In the four years of its activity, FTP put, according to its mandate, thousands of theater workers back to work and provided with hundreds of productions entertainment to millions of low-income Americans across the country.[42] In this manner, it created something akin to a national theater. Its repertoire included classic drama, new works, and experimental theater, children's theater, musical revues, dance shows, even circus programs. Although FTP eventually was to come under attack for its allegedly leftist agenda, director Hallie Flanagan insisted from the start and throughout the project's short-lived career, that this was not a political theater, that it was "neither adapting nor assuming any viewpoint beyond presenting a new and vital drama of our times, emerging from the social and economic forces of the day."[43] At the same time, FTP did not shy away from engaging these social and economic forces of the day head on and quite critically. In 1936 Flanagan accomplished the feat of opening simultaneously in seventeen cities nationwide an adaptation of Sinclair Lewis's timely anti-fascist satire *It Can't Happen Here* (1935). The play demonstrates how a self-confident democratic nation can be seduced by a populist demagogue promising to restore the country to political greatness and economic prosperity. Other Federal Theatre landmark productions included T. S. Eliot's *Murder in the Cathedral* (1936), the New York Negro Theatre Unit's all-black production of "Voodoo" *Macbeth* under the direction of Orson Welles (1936), as well as various issues of the Living Newspaper, such as *Triple-A Plowed Under* (1936), *Power* (1937), and *One Third of a Nation* (1938).

The Living Newspaper presents one of the most original contributions to American drama in the period. Taking its inspiration from modernist experiments in agitprop and epic theater, it examined with each of its editions in a series of highly theatrical sketches a controversial topic of the time, such as agricultural politics, public ownership of electricity, and housing shortage. Its goal was to provide the average citizen with information on current issues, on the basis of which he or she could then form an opinion and act accordingly.[44] *One Third of a Nation*, by far the most successful of all the Living Newspapers, for instance, takes its cue from Franklin D. Roosevelt's second inaugural address, in which he drew attention to the fact that one third of the nation was "ill-housed, ill-clad, and ill-nourished." With the help of a narrative voice-over (the Loudspeaker), a series of enacted flashback scenes, and projections of original documents, the paper proceeds to unravel to a representative Little Man the history of New York real estate speculation leading up to the current crisis and to detail the various but limited administrative initiatives that have so far failed to amend the situation. This, however, does not dishearten Little Man, who determines that government intervention is the way to go. Prompted by his wife, he decides to "holler" until his voice is heard: "We want a decent place to live in! I want a place that's fit for a man and a woman and kids. Can you hear me – you in Washington or Albany or wherever you are? Give me a decent place to live in! Give me a home! A home!"[45] Such assertion of the belief that change is possible through the electoral process was typical for the Living Newspapers. Underlying all of them is the ardent conviction that American capitalism can be made to work on behalf of the common people. It is perhaps in this regard that Flanagan considered the Living Newspaper "as American as Walt Disney."[46] Such "Americanism" and widespread public support notwithstanding, the Living Newspaper along with the entire Federal Theatre Project was discontinued by act of Congress in June 1939, for its alleged Communist sympathies. One of its productions, however, managed to dodge such censorship: Marc Blitzstein's musical drama *The Cradle Will Rock* (1937) about corporate greed, middle class corruption, and the power of labor unionism. When threatened by budgetary cuts, director Orson Welles and producer John Houseman (both working for FTP's Project #891) hijacked the show and turned it into a private venture. The spectacular case of the "runaway opera" became one of the finest examples of Popular Front activism and, incidentally, also one of the most applauded examples of epic theater in the United States.[47]

One of the most successful shows of the end of the Depression era was *Pins and Needles* (1937–1940), an amateur musical revue that originated in the drama workshops of the International Ladies' Garment Workers' Union at the Labor Stage Theatre, ended up giving a White House command performance, and finally became one of the longest running and most profitable Broadway shows of the decade.[48] The makers of the show (among them well-known artists of the time, such as Harold Rome, Marc Blitzstein, and Arthur Arent) conceived of it in the manner of the grand musical revues of the 1910s and 1920s, the *Ziegfeld* and the *Grand Street Follies*. Combining political satires and sketches of urban work life with catchy songs and clever dance routines, *Pins and Needles* was to provide entertainment to workers and to thematize issues relevant to workers' lives. The revue opens with a women's chorus claiming that they are "tired of moon songs, / Of star and of June songs," demanding of their beaux to woo them instead with "a song of social significance."[49] Notably, however, the show ends up establishing its social significance neither with its witty spoofs of Hitler and Stalin, nor of the American right, or of American labor union squabbles. Rather, it is with such seemingly apolitical tunes as "Sunday in the Park," "Nobody Makes a Pass at Me, "and "I've Got the Nerve to Fall in Love" that *Pins and Needles* asserts its labor politics. As Denning points out, with these romantic and ironic songs in the popular Tin Pan Alley music style of the time, the young garment workers reclaim leisure and romance from the affluent class and assert themselves as savvy and critical participants in modern consumer culture.[50] In establishing labor as an integral part of mainstream culture, as a force to be reckoned with, *Pins and Needles* effectively contributed to what Denning calls the overall "laboring of American culture," which according to him sustained the social movement of the Popular Front and generated support for Roosevelt's New Deal.[51] And yet, with public success also came the increasing commodification of the show for commercial purposes: the revue was moved to the larger Windsor Theatre uptown, amateur actors were replaced with professional ones, and the ethnic markers that connected the show with the Jewish and Italian immigrant communities downtown, were erased.[52] Soon the union revue was playing almost exclusively to the Broadway carriage trade. Offering up a youthful spectacle of energy, wit, optimism, and abundance, *Pins and Needles*, in the end, like many another show of the time, affirmed the regenerative potential of capitalism. With its final chorus "We've Only Just Begun," it however also made clear, that labor intended to have a voice in the country's future.

In sum then, in the 1930s there was a keen public interest that the arts speak to the various economic, social, and political issues of the decade, and many theater companies and playwrights (though certainly not all of them) were up to the challenge. The answers offered were diverse but ultimately not that dissimilar: change was needed and could be brought about by individual conversion and various forms of collective action (working-class solidarity, government intervention, electoral pressure, or the consolidation of a broad cultural front). Regardless whether the plays ended with the stuck-up capitalist sitting down for dinner with the free-spirited liberals (*You Can't Take It With You*) or with black and white workers joining in battle on the barricades in defense of their homes and families (*Stevedore*), whether they called out for "Strike!" (*Waiting for Lefty*) or "hollered" for government intervention (*One Third of a Nation*), the vast majority of the dramas and theatrical productions of the depression era shared the ardent belief that by affirming the nation's democratic legacy, capitalism could be made moral, humane, and soulful again. In 1933 Elmer Rice formulated the appeal in his play *We, the People* thus, "We are the people, ladies and gentlemen, we – you and I and everyone of us. It is our house: this America. Let us cleanse it and put it in order and make it a decent place for decent people to live in!"[53] Toward the end of the decade, the garment workers of *Pins and Needles* similarly asserted, "There are millions of us. / Yes, we'll have something to say!"

NOTES

1 For commentary on these playwrights' works see Anne Fletcher, "Reading across the 1930s," in *A Companion to Twentieth Century American Drama*, ed. David Krasner (Hoboken, NJ: Wiley-Blackwell, 2007), 106–126.
2 Barrett H. Clark, "Foreword," in Albert Bein, *Little Ol' Boy: A Play in Three Acts* (New York: Samuel French, 1935), vii–xii, xi.
3 *You Can't Take It With You* ran from December 1936 to December 1938 for a total of 838 performances and in 1938 was turned into a successful movie under the direction of Frank Capra. Anderson's play, by contrast, ran from March to May 1933 for a total of seventy-two performances, followed by another forty-eight performances the same spring at another Broadway theater. The Pulitzer Prize–winning musical comedy *Of Thee I Sing* by George and Ira Gershwin, George Kaufman and Morrie Ryskind – a light-hearted send-up of the American political system – fared better with 441 performances from December 1931 to January 1933. A search of the Internet Broadway Database for productions with over 100 performances in the initial depression years of 1930 to 1932, furthermore, reveals that at the time musicals, musical revues, and comedies by far outnumbered other productions.
4 Compare grandfather's income of $3,000–$4,000 per year with the average annual middle-class income of $1,745. Cf. Ann Fletcher, "The Theatre Union's 1935 Production of Brecht's *Mother*: Renegade on Broadway," in *Brecht, Broadway, and United States Theatre*, ed. J. Chris Westgate (Newcastle upon Tyne: Cambridge Scholars Press, 2007), 2–22, 6.
5 According to Mordecai Gorelik, the biblical proverb (Matthew 16:26) provided the motto for much of the Group Theatre's work and, so we might add, for a number of Broadway shows advocating a more humane form of capitalism. Cf. Mordecai Gorelik, *New Theatres for Old* (London: Dennis Dobson, 1947 [1949]), 243.
6 Gorelik, *New Theatres for Old*, 243.
7 *1931-* by Claire and Paul Sifton was the second production of the newly founded Group Theatre (1931). It ran for twelve performances in December 1931.
8 Brooks Atkinson, "The Play," *New York Times*, December 11, 1931.
9 Percy Hammond, "The Theaters," *New York Herald Tribune*, December 11, 1931.
10 By December 1930, 585,000 people were unemployed in New York City. See Edna Lonigan, *Unemployment in New York City: An Estimate of the Number of Unemployed in December 1930s* (New York: Research Bureau Welfare Council

of New York City, 1931), http://quod.lib.umich.edu/m/moa/aebo813.0001.001/
1?page=root;size=100;view=image. By 1933 unemployment nationwide peeked at
ca. twelve million, respectively at 25 percent of the working population.

11 Cf. Manuel Gomez, "A Proletarian Play on Broadway," *New Masses*,
January 1932.

12 Harold Clurman, *The Fervent Years: The Group Theatre & the 30's* (New York:
Da Capo Press, 1983 [1945]), 72. *Reunion in Vienna* is a romantic comedy by
Robert E. Sherwood, running from November 1931 to July 1932 for a total of
264 performances. Cf. Gerald Bordman, *American Theatre: A Chronicle of
Comedy and Drama, 1930–1969* (New York: Oxford University Press, 1996), 40.

13 On the role of immigrant workers' theaters see Bruce McConachie and Daniel
Friedman (eds.), *Theatre for Working Class Audiences in the United States,
1830–1980* (Westport, CT: Greenwood Press, 1985) and Maxine S. Seller (ed.),
Ethnic Theatre in the United States (Westport, CT: Greenwood Press, 1983).

14 See Daniel Friedman, "A Brief Description of the Workers' Theatre Movement of
the Thirties," *Theatre for Working Class Audiences in the United States,
1830–1980*, eds. Bruce McConachie and Daniel Friedman (Westport, CT: Greenwood Press, 1985), 111–120 and Stuart Cosgrove, "From Shock Troupe to
Group Theater," in *Theaters of the Left 1880–1935*, eds. Raphael Samuel, Ewan
MacColl, and Stuart Cosgrove (London: Routledge & Kegan Paul, 1985),
259–279.

15 John Howard Lawson, "The Crisis in Theater," *New Masses*, December 15,
1936. Workers' Drama League was founded by John Howard Lawson, Michael
Gold, Jasper Deeter, and Ida Rauh; its most important production was Gold's
mass recitation *Strike!* (1926). The New Playwrights was founded by Lawson,
Gold, Francis Farragoh, Em Jo Basshe, and John Dos Passos; its productions
include Lawson's *Loud Speaker* (1927) and *The International* (1928), Basshe's
The Centuries (1927) and *Earth* (1927), Upton Sinclair's *Singing Jailbirds* (1928),
Gold's *Hoboken Blues* (1927), Paul Sifton's *The Belt* (1927), and Dos Passos's
Airways, Inc. (1929).

16 Cf. Barnaby Haran, *Watching the Red Dawn: The American Avant-Garde and
the Soviet Union* (Manchester: Manchester University Press, 2016).

17 Prolet-Bühne was founded in 1925 as a drama circle of the German ethnic
community. It became politicized with the arrival of John Bonn (Hans Bohn)
from Germany in 1928 and broke away from its umbrella organization the
Arbeiterbund in 1929. See Stuart Cosgrove, "Prolet Buehne: Agitprop in America," *Performance and Politics in Popular Drama*, eds. David Brady, Louis James,
and Bernard Sharratt (Cambridge: Cambridge University Press, 1980), 201–212.

18 Ben Blake, *The Awakening of the American Theatre* (New York: Tomorrow
Publishers, 1935), 16. The Scottsboro trial was also addressed in Langston
Hughes's *Scottsboro, Limited* (1932) and John Wexley's courtroom drama *They
Shall Not Die* (1934).

19 Cf. Cosgrove, "From Shock Troupe to Group Theatre," 274.

20 Hallie Flanagan, "A Theater is Born," *Theater Arts Monthly* 15 (1931): 908.

21 Elmer Rice, *The Living Theatre* (New York: Harper, 1959).

22 Bosley Crowther, "Theater on the Left," *New York Times*, April 14, 1935.

23 Ira A. Levine, *Left-Wing Dramatic Theory in the American Theatre* (Ann Arbor:
University of Michigan Press, 1980), 86–99.

Ilka Saal

24 What form this new approach was to take was hotly debated in leftist newspapers and magazines and also became the central issue of the American Writers' Congress of 1935. Cf. Levine, *Left-Wing Dramatic Theory* as well as Ilka Saal, *New Deal Theater: The Vernacular Tradition in American Political Theater* (New York: Palgrave, 2007), 101–109.

25 Michael Denning, *The Cultural Front: The Laboring of American Culture in the Twentieth Century* (London: Verso, 1998 [1997]), xvi.

26 For eyewitness accounts of the opening night see Clurman, *Fervent Years*, 148 and cast member Ruth Nelson's account in David Barbour and Lori Seward, "Waiting for Lefty," *TDR* 28.4 (Winter 1984): 40.

27 For press reactions see Saal, *New Deal Theater*, 63–75.

28 *Waiting for Lefty* ran for 136 performances at the Longacre Theatre in a double bill with Odets's antifascist one-act *Till the Day I Die* from March to July 1935. It was then moved to the Belasco Theatre, where it ran together with *Awake and Sing!* for another twenty-eight performances in September that year. For information on its run in the workers' theater as well as attempts at state censorship, see Stuart Cosgrove, "Waiting for Lefty: Introductory Note," *Theaters of the Left 1880–1935*, eds. Raphael Samuel, Ewan MacColl, and Stuart Cosgrove (London: Routledge & Kegan Paul, 1985), 323–325.

29 Cf. John McCarten, "Revolution's Number One Boy," *New Yorker*, January 22, 1938; Fletcher, "Reading across the 1930s," 114; Christoph Herr, "American Political Drama, 1910–45," *Oxford Handbook of American Drama*, ed. Jeffrey H. Richards and Heather S. Nathans (Oxford: Oxford University Press, 2014), 280–295, 287.

30 Clifford Odets, "Waiting for Lefty," *Theaters of the Left 1880–1935*, eds. Raphael Samuel, Ewan MacColl, and Stuart Cosgrove (London: Routledge & Kegan Paul, 1985), 326–352, 326.

31 Odets, "Waiting for Lefty," 350–351.

32 Odets, "Waiting for Lefty," 351.

33 John Howard Lawson, "History Making Plays," *New Masses*, July 2, 1935.

34 Lewis Corey, *The Crisis of the Middle Class* (New York: Covici, Friede Inc., 1935).

35 Gerald Rabkin, *Drama and Commitment: Politics in the American Theatre of the Thirties* (Bloomington: Indiana University Press, 1964), 171–183.

36 Eberhard Brüning, *Das amerikanische Drama der dreißiger Jahre* (Berlin: Rütten & Loening, 1966), 139.

37 Clurman, *Fervent Years*, 148. Gerald Weales argues that the emotional and political climax of the final call for strike exhausts itself in the theater, providing, similar to Aristotelian catharsis, a spontaneous "fulfilling of the audience, a moment of community that substitutes for direct action and makes it unnecessary." Gerald Weales, "Waiting for Lefty," *Critical Essays on Clifford Odets*, ed. Gabriel Miller (Boston: G.K. Hall & Co. 1991), 141–152. 147.

38 The more America's Marxist sympathies faded, the more *Waiting for Lefty* was praised for its non-militant stance and hailed as a realist middle class play. The reference to the *Communist Manifesto* was removed with the excision of the "Young Actor's Episode" by the time the play moved to Broadway in March 1935. And while in 1935 conservative theater critics still compared the play to a "dramatic machine gun," attacking its audience "with emotional arguments, grim humor and sheer theatrical forcefulness," a few years later Random House

editor William Kozlenko, who selected *Lefty* for his 1939 anthology of *Best Short Plays of the Social Theatre*, established its social significance in the presentation of "living human values." Forty years later, Clurman who had once hailed the play as "the birth cry of the thirties," located the play's political value in its empathetic depiction of the metaphysical longing of the middle class. See Richard Watts, "Sight and Sound," *New York Herald Tribune*, March 31, 1935; John Mason Brown, "The Play," *New York Evening Post*, March 27, 1935; William Kozlenko, "Introduction," to *The Best Short Plays of the Social Theater*, ed. W. Kozlenko (New York: Random House, 1939), x; and Harold Clurman, "Introduction," to Clifford Odets, *Waiting for Lefty and Other Plays* (New York: Grove Press, 1979), ix.

39 The success of Theatre Union inspired the establishment of similar professional, stationary workers' theaters in Philadelphia, Chicago, Davenport, New Orleans, Los Angeles, and San Francisco. For more information on Theatre Union, its background, policy, and aesthetics, see Saal, *New Deal Theater*, 77–101.

40 Michael Gold, "Stevedore," *New Masses*, May 1, 1934.

41 Paul Peters and George Sklar, *Stevedore* (New York: Covici, Friede Inc., 1934), 137.

42 Admission to FTP productions was often free or available at the low cost of 10, 25, or 50 cents. It was not to exceed $1. See Hallie Flanagan, *Arena: The History of the Federal Theatre* (New York: Duell, Sloan and Pearce, 1940), 30. Compare this to Broadway prices starting at $3.50.

43 Flanagan, *Arena*, 112.

44 For more information, see Douglas McDermott, "The Living Newspaper as a Dramatic Form," *Modern Drama* 8.1 (May 1965): 82–94 and Saal, *New Deal Theater*, 123–135.

45 Arthur Arent, "One Third of a Nation: A Living Newspaper," *Federal Theatre Plays*, vol. 1 (New York: Random House, 1938), 3–121, 120.

46 Hallie Flanagan, "Introduction" to *Federal Theater Plays*, vol. 2, ed. Pierre de Rohan (New York: Random House, 1938), xi.

47 *Cradle* was originally conceived as a lavish musical revue. It was to open on 16 June 1937 at the Maxine Elliott Theatre in New York. Four days before the premiere, Washington decreed that no new FTP productions were to open before July, due to pending budgetary approval. Fearful that the opening of the show would be postponed indefinitely, Welles and Houseman decided to open the show as planned. Since they were barred from the Elliott, cast and audience walked up twenty blocks to the spontaneously hired Venice Theatre. Here the show opened without props and sets, with only a piano on the stage, which Blitzstein played, while the cast members sang their lines, due to union regulations, from their seats in the audience. When later staged at their own Mercury Theater, respectively on Broadway, this minimalist staging practice was maintained. See, e.g., Virgil Thomson, "In the Theatre," *Modern Music* (Jan.–Feb. 1938), 112–114, Marc Blitzstein, "Out of the Cradle," *Opera News*, February 13, 1960, 10–11, and J.E. Vacha, "The Case of the Runaway Opera: The Federal Theatre and Marc Blitzstein's *The Cradle Will Rock*," *New York History* 62.2 (April 1981): 133–152.

48 *Pins and Needles* had 1,108 performances, making it the most successful musical show, if not the most successful show in general of the decade. In the course of its

three-year run, sketches were constantly updated according to a changing political situation at home and abroad. It played in $1.5 million in clear profits. See
Saal, *New Deal Theater*, 136–149.

49 Lyrics are taken from unpublished song sheets at the Music Archive of the New
York Public Library of the Performing Arts at Lincoln Center.

50 Denning, *Cultural Front*, 299–306.

51 Ibid., xvi.

52 Performers with thick Jewish or Italian accents were replaced, actress Nettie
Harary was asked to get a nose job and other Jewish performers to change their
names. African American actress Olive Pearman was, moreover, barred from
performing at the White House. See Harry Goldman, "When Social Significance
Hit Broadway," *Theatre Quarterly* 7.28 (Winter 1977–78): 36.

53 Elmer Rice, *Seven Plays* (New York: Viking, 1950), 253. *We, the People* ran on
Broadway in early 1933 for only forty-nine performances.

7

LAURA HAPKE

Literature and Labor

With the coming of the Great Depression, literary radicals were convinced that the official truths about its causes and duration were false. Their lack of faith in capitalist solutions inspired the proletarian novel. The editor of the storied leftist journal the *New Masses*, Mike Gold, is credited with its first American mention.[1] The contentiousness surrounding the definition and leading characteristics warrants an essay of its own. What is clear is that it was a subgenre rooted in a myriad of authorial practices. Images of precarity dominated work experiences. Workers were at its mercy, in a future of hand-to-mouth jobs. To represent these socioeconomic conditions of existence, authors dismantled reigning prejudices about labor. In their imaginative fictions they defended marginalized groups such as the (white, male) unemployed, factory organizers, women toiling outside the home, and blacks in industry.

However, on the cusp of the Great Crash, even those devoted to a changed world could not apply preestablished aesthetic models to their own representational projects. Although a large majority of those involved in what Michael Denning called the "cultural front" respected the revolutionary precepts of the Communist Party (CPUSA), their literature did not reflect this allegiance. Thus, Jack Conroy, at least in the majority view of today's experts, rejected invincible toilers storming the centers of industrial might. "Conroy's views on proletarian literature," explains his chief biographer, "were not consistent with [any] literary practice, except ... the centrality of the [American] worker."[2] So too did his maverick colleagues disrupt the essentializing vision of the CPUSA. These pioneers on the cultural front in the field of literature were political advocates of multivocality, layers of meaning, and other experimental devices. They recast the monolithic people's plot. In a number of representative authors' story arcs, they also reflected the range of working-class politics and lifeworlds. Their texts even include many characters who detest labor organizers' rhetoric of collective action.

Laura Hapke

Among numerous examples were the roving "bottom dogs" in *Hungry Men* (1935), by Edward Anderson; the 1934 thwarted lumber-factory strike of Robert Cantwell, *The Land of Plenty*; Conroy's labor-picaresque *The Disinherited* (1933); and the female laboring body in the stories of Meridel Le Sueur, such as "Sequel to Love," published in Conroy's left periodical *Anvil* in January 1935. Black peonage before World War I symbolized 1930s murderous racism in works like that of the African American writer William Attaway's *Blood on the Forge* (1941). Ruth McKenney mixed the avalanche of documents on the first Congress of Industrial Organizations (CIO) union strike with on-the-ground reportage, fabricated news, historical actors and imagined characters in her classic, *Industrial Valley* (1939).

Since the Cold War, many analysts have consistently rejected working class literature, saying it is primitive, robotic; the characters are flat and the prose amateurish. More recent commentators argue instead that rediscovered labor authors repurposed traditional representations, forming a core of outlaw texts. Squarely in the period in their embrace of an aesthetic of resistance, left-wing novelists challenged orthodoxies such as the requisite revolutionary ending.

Over the past two decades, a bevy of critics have re-envisioned the best of Depression-era leftist cultural production. These critics have demonstrated that laborers were never depicted in progressive fictions as a faceless rank and file who simply seek or achieve class consciousness. Correlatively, this essay contends that on the formal level literary proletarianism employed a diverse set of compositional tactics. To understand the extent of such representational innovations is to chart the variety of ways in which radicalized American writers in the 1930s revised and enriched serious American literature.

Swept up in the difficulties of the pre–Franklin Roosevelt era, many accomplished writers were only subsisting by the early 1930s. Loosely termed the Bottom Dogs school, these men targeted President Herbert Hoover. Responding in customary fashion to the one-quarter of people left without work and the equal number of underemployed, Hoover decreed that joblessness was the (moral) responsibility of those who experienced it. Homelessness he equated with a failure of character. When indigent World War I veterans formed a "Bonus Army" in 1932 to march on Washington and demand back pay, the president simply called them hobos and communists and directed the military to run them out of the capitol.[3]

Voting with their feet, the bottom dog authors soon discovered that no longer were even the dirtiest jobs readily available. The protagonist of Tom Kromer's *Waiting for Nothing* exists among a corps of wretchedly paid laborers supplemented by charity. As much as anything, this text set the tone for the Going Nowhere plot. A variant is Nelson Algren's *Somebody in Boots* (1936). He rouses young men from somnolence to depict their petty thefts and readiness to skip town. Both novels ring changes on the deadbeat plot; Kromer's and Algren's young (white) men are as closed to hopes for the future as the subcultures in which they dwell.[4]

Edward Anderson's *Hungry Men* addresses the crushing effect of this life as well, and his novel is certainly downbeat. But he also interrogates spiritual nothingness. He positions his subjects' job hunt in the unstable nature of Depression-era work. Writing against the grain, he upends the common stereotypes of alienation: hatred of society, self-destructiveness, and the pathology of panhandling. Whether finding or losing waged jobs, his cast of characters acts out their own labor beliefs. Hence the title's double meaning. Hunger is so biting that there is always danger of deathly passivity. But hungriness is active as much as passive; it propels men to fight starvation. In the spirit of the familiar street-corner handheld signs reading "Will Work for Food," men thus saw their labor as a means to alleviate hunger. Those hired on for just a day's work are ravenous. One character talks about a daylong wood-yard ordeal: "They feed you [very little] twice, and I'm always hungry as hell an hour after breakfast."[5] Another recalls bartering dishwashing for a meager breakfast.

These wanderers, however, are just as wary of "Reds." In one scene, the sole organizer, Boats, exhorts his apolitical friends. As he gestures toward sleeping forms in front of buildings or along alleyways, he points out that, historically, even galley slaves were taken care of. In modern society, Americans are worse off than Russians. Despite Anderson's official interest in CPUSA doctrine, Boats's exhortations are futile. One voice speaks for all: "I do not intend to be like this for the rest of my life" (24). There are others too drunk or drugged to embrace this resolve, but the majority sustain a pragmatic will to endure amidst such brutal circumstances.

Anderson's association of hobos with workers was, ironically, stronger than in somewhat better times. His floating population had imprinted on their minds and bodies that being unemployed or homeless required a tremendous amount of effort to stay alive.[6] Thus, his novel is a speaking picture of the resourcefulness central to survival. Indeed, the desire to escape the derelict's life obsessed an array of personae from the footloose to the determined. But the real strength of *Hungry Men* is to fuse "work" with "worklessness." Both require proactivity. In this formulation, a stint on workhouse gangs after an arrest for vagrancy is brutally exhausting labor. Outside the forced work camps, there is a corollary outpouring of energy in riding the rails or seeking a night's rest. But the very effort of staying safe – and sane – in the flophouses or the windowless railroad cars strengthens rather than dashes their resolve.

Whatever the day's activity, paid or not, the night sees exhaustion. Whether panhandlers or not, they must draw on their emotional strength. Zigzagging from Standard to vernacular English, salt-of-the-earth characters nicknamed Sweat Shirt; the industrial victim, One Eye; and the most common, Mac, recount rough work experiences. At the same time, they counsel fellow migrants about which towns or farms may be hiring. In lieu of a formal workplace culture, they offer each other reassurance and support – or, as is also true to life, resentment and enmity. In any case, there is a grapevine of information and a wary reliance on others not to betray them to the authorities. Among this default brotherhood, one-night lodgings can be shared by those with little or no panhandling money or the slim proceeds from sweated work.

Complaint fuels communication rather than blocks it. And remembrance always includes past work. Thoughts filtered through the consciousness of Anderson's hard-luck musician Acel Stecker, reveal both an identification with and a resentment of his lot:

> How long have I been running around the country now?
> Two years. Damn near two years. It has been two years
> Since I played in that Juarez [cafe]. Godamighty.
> Two years I been on the bum … and [as a musician]
> I was a lot better than the rest of them. (9)

The passage, a poetic lament, reflects in its repetition the dulling effect of the road. But inscribed in the quotation is a professionalism that might be revived, for a hard-luck life, in Anderson's plot twist, is not his alter ego's fate.

Stecker is both participant and witness. Like his creator, he is a "class passer," a WASP from the dominant culture who gathers information as he picks fruit or stays in hobo jungles. Proof of his class status is that at novel's end he is reinstalled in the lucrative entertainment industry. Road traveling now has a new meaning, especially as he is Hollywood bound, having secured a film contract for his band. Previewing this mythic ending, Stecker's companions find their own opportunities beyond roving the countryside. Only at novel's end are they revealed as Able-Bodied seamen. Preferring their working-class jobs to the tramp's highway, they return to their maritime union and shipping jobs.

Despite these tacked-on conclusions, the subaltern transients of Anderson's sociologically oriented fiction reveal a key aspect of 1930s labor. Migrant jobholding can reduce men to starving animals, but a day's pay elsewhere redresses the balance. Whether drained or energized by the hunt for sustenance, the ragtag actors usually avoid the fall to penury. By the same token, upward mobility has no part in the constant movement of the One Eyes and the Macs. They have little use for a pre-1930s stability, despite their few statements to the contrary. They never stay in one place to compete for the few good factory, mining, or steel jobs. In their adaptive self-forging, they do not trade vagrant independence for contingent security.

The representative labor fiction of the time cast workers as strikers. In this standard model of the proletarian novel, the main characters were what Bottom Dog transitories called the "home guard," those whose full-time jobs kept them at the wheel or on the waterfront. Venues ranged from industrial hubs to mining-town coal pits. It was at such sites that this stationary, if restive, mass roused itself to direct action, occupying the contested labor space while seeking to cordon it off from strikebreakers.

The more triumphant of such works, like Bell's *Out of This Furnace* and McKenney's *Industrial Valley*, praised the fighting spirit of mass unions in heavy industry. McKenney's account even privileged the actual events week by week. In a similar vein a majority of period novels, whether documentary in aim or composites of watershed labor events, express a utopian optimism directed toward the future. As Melvyn Dubofsky informs us, the majority of 1930s strikes failed.[7] Thus, despite the crusading spirit of their various authors, most strike novels reflected widespread conditions. Whether defeat or Pyrrhic victory, in which gains were quickly undone by business interests, the agitational element inscribed in their subtext was often belied by dramatized setbacks.

Barbara Foley argues convincingly that the canon of storm-the-barricades fiction, rather than blindly adopt an apparatchik *Proletkult*, characteristically contained a shadow plot of ceaseless revolt.[8] Yet in my view the actual plotting most often told of thwarted rebellion. An exemplary book from this perspective include *Marching! Marching!* by Clara Weatherwax (1934), on Filipino fishermen's martyrdom. Similarly, Mary Heaton Vorse's *Strike!* (1930) recounted the Gastonia, North Carolina, strike of 1929, in which the CPUSA tried with transient success to recruit millworkers. Organizers also try to animate factory workers in James Steele's *Conveyor: A Novel* (1935). Other works ring changes on the motif in novels of union-busting agribusinesses such as John Steinbeck's *In Dubious Battle* (1936), which lays defeat at the door of CP leaders who subsume workers to a Red organizing agenda.

In true strike novel form, Robert Cantwell's *The Land of Plenty* particularizes conditions on the ground. This factory fiction springs from memories of his time in a Washington State wood-processing industry. He knew well the labor defiance familiar to the Pacific Northwest lumber industry. These wild logrollers were famous for everything from disseminating radical pamphlets in the bunkhouses to quitting angrily in midseason to speeches on the Red literature of an Americanized Marxism.

Cantwell, a veteran participant in the power politics of industry, places his story in a thinly veiled historical location. The setting is a circumscribed environment: a company town; a job-segregated work area, albeit with overcrowding on the factory floor itself. In its array of scenarios, his image of the tamed proletariat defies easy categorization. *The Land of Plenty* does experiment with the pro-marching imperative itself yet ambivalence rules a cowed factory force reluctant to enter the fray. Rather than limn the era's struggle between labor and management, the author illustrates a group resenting discipline but fearful of resistance. As such, the trope of the bewildered toiler portrayed the uncertainties of a hard-pressed proletariat.

Though no 1930s Plato, in his allegory of the cave Cantwell employs the darkness of the factoryscape as a symbol of its unenlightened workers. Reframing the myth, he opens with "Suddenly the lights went out."[9] Production stops. Ironically, the very power failure that shuts down the factory is a step toward clarity. Sharing a workplace culture developed out of the years they have spent together on the job, workers habitually complain about the bosses, but always with an undercurrent of apprehension. Fear of reprisal, not determined resistance, is the fugue-like motif of a lengthy section in *The Land of Plenty*. Already worried that by talking raucously or making fun of the boss they will lose "their card" and be fired – they act as if they are responsible for the power failure and are thus paralyzed when this event occurs. Soon they rouse themselves but still can't decide what to do. If they stay on the work floor, they will be censured as "lazy." If they try to release the sprinklers and power the machines, they may fail and the foreman will blame them for incompetence. One worried worker states, "If I stay in the shop he'll say I was loafing. If I don't, he'll say he couldn't find me" (43). Another echoes the fear: "Suppose the sprinklers [in the shop] blow. If they do, [the boss] will pin it on me" (44). In a group trance, they imagine punishment when the foreman enters their part of the factory. The very darkness is as much a mental as a physical condition they must overcome.

Slowly the work floor becomes a contested space. A rebellious spirit emerges as the novelty of the dark enables them to complain. As they listen to one another's anecdotes of injustice, they are emboldened. Soon fear of reprisal becomes a deliberate work stoppage, and a plan emerges. Some will stay behind, in a sit-down act of protest. Others will find their way out and make a stand in public.

This break with authority is telescoped into one night. In the dominant though obvious image, men gradually see through the darkness. They stream out into the light, in this case July Fourth. Cantwell swerves toward epiphany: without a plan or regional union support, they can only hide nearby, behind cars and forest camouflage. Inside, a few others stay – to no avail – as guardians of the law and the owners storm the factory. Scabs, protected by the owners, enter to man the machines. Outside fights ensue; a "rioter" dies; police bear down and occupy the site. Soon it is business as usual. As a final indignity, the employer, in the mode of Herbert Hoover, seeing protesters as communists, condescendingly rehires only the loyalists.

Paralleling the sociopsychological turmoil caused by a thwarted action, Cantwell provides many twists to the plot. At times the reader cannot follow the progress out of the darkened factory. At others, it is unclear which workers stumble and which lead the way. In Cantwell's appropriation of the cave myth, clarity vanishes no sooner than it emerges. Labor is coded as caught between subjugation and revolt. Neither lumpenproletarian nor empowered factory employee, the plywood hands return to the factory as confused about their labor's exchange value as they were the day before, and thus more defeated than ever.

Conroy was in the vanguard of those who admired the manifestoes appearing in *The Daily Worker* and the worker-writer clubs sponsored by Party regulars. Like Anderson and Cantwell, though, he did not encode this allegiance in his novels, published by centrist, well-known presses. Rather, his novels pushed back against the metanarrative of the rebel-worker. He bundled those like Anderson's hobo-survivalists and Cantwell's sometime factory strikers into his characterizations. Moreover, he utilized a formal structure that so multiplied the actors the sheer number of misadventures subverted the predictability of the proletarian format.

Conroy himself possessed a proletarian vita so full that he already had the material he needed to draw on for a rambling fictional account. To cull a few autobiographical facts: railroad shipman and unionist, autoworker, odd-job builder, itinerant. Old beyond his years when he published his first novel, *The Disinherited*, he had a sure hand in depicting a brew of rough-hewn labor veterans and vulnerable seekers for jobs subject to the deceptions of employment agency cheats called "sharks."

This college of hard knocks allowed him to limn a figure very much like himself – the traumatized coal miner's kid – who suffered from the shock of eating rotten food, wearing tattered clothing, and hanging around with cynical companions and crazed workmates. While migratory men usually mapped out their journeys to avoid bad weather, vagrancy arrests, and a number of other hazards, the "bottom dogs" fictions that depicted their life experiences maintained an aesthetic investment in surprise: it is for this reason that so many of the texts are picaresque or episodic, lacking transitions between chapters, scenes, seasons, time periods, and locales. On the macro level, the three sections of *The Disinherited* are disconnected thematically. The first carries the place name of Larry's early Missouri life. As a miner's son, he extricates himself from the dangers of this workplace. The second section shifts to an ironic use of "Bull Market" but has little to do with the financial wildness of the Great Crash. The title of the third section is a seasonal metaphor alluding to the widespread suffering of the time spent in urban environments: "Hard Winter." Thus, over the course of the narrative, a mining camp childhood bleeds into an acolyte's introduction to big-city manual labor. Along the way, World War I comes and goes, yet Larry has little emotional energy to react to this watershed event in US history.

Such a rhetorical style fractures the continuity of his daily life to reflect the rootless conditions of existence in general during the era. The constant presentism that breaks a chain of events is a commentary on the conditions of the time. In such a world, working-class authenticity means to keep moving and expect little.

The Disinherited garnered much praise when it first appeared for its convincing depictions. As the rare worker-writer with genuine, first-hand experience of life as a member of the proletariat, Conroy was able to give fictive energy to the contingency of lived experience in an unpredictable economy. He was praised by left and liberal establishment critics alike for his departure from the conventional narrative strictures of the proletarian novel. Declaring himself in touch with the people, he was favored by the cosmopolitan editor of the *New Masses*. Mike Gold opined that Conroy was now a major force in American proletarian literature.[10]

The unsophisticated autodidact found acceptance for a time. Important liberal voices in the New *Yorker* joined centrist ones in Philadelphia and Los Angeles book reviews in finding his approach honest and even refreshing (Wixson 328).Yet with the preponderance of radical fiction favoring the urban rank and file, Conroy had to defend himself against the charge that his focus on Larry's Midwestern trek across many open spaces was politically limited. Political assessments of *The Disinherited* were linked in other quarters with similar preconceptions of social protest fiction. Conroy was censured by *New York Times* reviewer John Chamberlain for an inability to give form to events (97).[11] Many found in his work sloppiness, backwardness, incoherence. In a similar assessment thirty years later, Walter Rideout is no more flattering: "Conroy probably committed every error known to the self-taught novelist." Rideout did defend the energy of portraiture of "the undirected life" of laborers. But he still found the author's "rambling ... distasteful."[12]

Looked at as an important addition to the inventiveness of leftwing fiction, Conroy's maverick contribution gives shape to radical belief in an unconventional way. The controlling narrative of *The Disinherited* was not teleological preaching but reflected the randomness of political involvement and fervent radicalism. Nowhere is the tension between theoretical prescription and authorial inclination more prominent than in the closing page. There Larry briefly abandons his picaro identity for a left-missionary one. He vows to "rise with my class, the disinherited: the brick setters, the flivver tramps, boomers [freight-catching hobos], and outcasts pounding their ears [sleeping on floors] in flophouses."[13] If critics agreed on little else, it was the abruptness of an ending that neither Larry nor his creator had prepared for. Explicating *The Disinherited* from the distance of decades, perhaps as a kind of sop to left critics, Conroy declared that he was simply trying to end on a politically correct note. A stronger explanation is that Larry is optimistically fantasizing a new adventure rather than naively anticipating a predictable future. Thus, in a swift return to his poverty-stricken childhood home in Missouri to visit his mother and girlfriend, he leaves some money, acknowledging it is less than they need. In any case, his view is that they must lean on each other for support. Counting on their understanding, or at least passivity, he emends his vow. He needs "to be free" of the burden of supporting his loved ones by staying in one place (283). He is a blue-collar Huck Finn, an updated boy-hero who wishes, in Mark Twain's phrase, to "light out for the territory."

Larry's rationale issues from a romance of the road best described by fellow author John Dos Passos, whose *The 42nd Parallel* (1930) gives a panoramic view of American history and contains interchapters on Mac, a 1910s radical, who gets caught up with the Industrial Workers of the World. Like Larry, Mac receives lessons on train-hopping, random jobholding, and the importance of radicalism. Despite a history of left-wing activity, Mac's real view of liberty is not walking the organizer's path. His real freedom is to "go on the bum" (qtd. Depastino 172). He leaves a wife and children for uncertain goals. So, too, in Conroy's descriptions of left-wing vagrancy. Regardless of his vow, Larry probably continues on a path that diverges from the programmatic march to the barricades. In sum, in its planlessness, *The Disinherited* creates a discourse of uncertainty with regard to the fate of the individual in an economy on its knees. The left-picaresque approach unmoors the proletarian novel from traditional realist narrative paradigms. In them the growth and development of a working-class subject inexorably results in class consciousness and politicized commitment.

As part of their resistance to American race-baiting, Anderson, Cantwell, and Conroy acknowledged the color line in passing. In theory, they sympathized with impoverished blacks relegated to second class status. Yet the figure was not in their writing a tragic one and too often functioned as a kind of human object in their representational landscapes. The wage earners whose aimless travels were variations on their labor identities possessed the privilege of whiteness. They had no need to seek encounters with those suffering from race and gender alterity. It was for other social-protest writers to imagine these marginalized groups into literature.

However desperate or despised as members of the lower or underclass, those who could lay claim to American manhood could still benefit from what David Roediger calls "white privilege" (*The Wages of Whiteness*). Nor was the term ironic. The freight-hopping tramps for the most part excluded black men from boxcars. At the other end of the working-class spectrum, black "regulars" in the extractive industries were menials. Exceptions certainly existed, but they were rarely reflected in proletarian cultural production.

Richard Wright's seminal work of fiction, *Native Son* (1941), countered this literary neglect. A migrant to Chicago, Wright soon attained membership in the Works Progress Administration writers' group, a forum that enabled his saga of a brutal protagonist, Bigger Thomas. Surprisingly given the Depression-era setting, Thomas is apathetic about looking for work in Chicago's vast labor market. An antitype of black proletarianism, he does not seek typical black men's jobs such as disposing of offal on the meatpacking cutting floor. An unlikely opportunity enables him to work as a chauffeur instead of the cleaning work typically available in job-segregated Chicago. While he is a servant, he certainly is not the prototypical ghetto laborer.

Native Son was a commercial blockbuster, but not as an account of a black man who understands the causes of racial bias too late. Rather Denning contends, in his study of leftist best sellers of the late 1930s through the wartime 1940s, that it drew an audience due to the interplay of leftism and popular fiction.[14] Whatever Wright's own left agenda, the thrilling police search for a black killer helped forge *Native Son*'s international reputation.

In a diametrically opposed way, the unjustly forgotten *Blood on the Forge*, by fellow Chicago author William Attaway presented black man's work as doomed in its search for decent pay. In the telos of the novel, blacks are killed or maimed by whites in the 1919 steel strike sweeping Pennsylvania and other states. Attaway's very title, *Blood on the Forge*, invokes the cruel fate of unwitting African American strikebreakers recruited by corrupt agents of the owner. The trio of characters who meet their doom are the Moss siblings, Big Mat, Melody, and Chinatown. Mat has a history of violence against whites and joins his half-brothers in seeing the North as a fresh start. In addition to their semi-fraternity, they are comrades in an oppressed labor force. Reflecting the labor practices of the owners, the novel's tragedy derives not only from a vicious white working class but also from the successful employer scheme to keep workmen racially divided.

From their train ride in a cattle car to their early encounters with steel workers, every page is searing. Their incipient entry into the world of extractive industry is from the first accompanied by images of doom. They can hear the clank of the mills as they walk to an unexpected human barricade. Chinatown complains to his brothers:

> "All this smoke and stuff in the air!
> How a man gonna breathe?"
> The drizzle stopped. Thin clouds rolled. Melody looked up.
> "Sun liable to break through soon."
> "Won't make no difference to us if the sun don't shine" ...
> "Sun make you feel better."[15]

The unbreathable air prefigures their treatment by workers who want to choke the life out of them. Equally proleptic is the fact that as they walk toward the mill, they see "in the eyes of all the Slavs a hatred ... different from anything they had ever experienced in Kentucky" (68–69). Beneath this hate is fear: these are the lowliest of the forge workers, who are nevertheless striving for whiteness.

Worse is to come. These raw recruits have no path to recognition. Inevitably, Mat and his brothers are pitted against the strikers. Attaway knew that blacks distrusted unions, rightly fearing segregated treatment. Instead Mat's status as scab lands him a job as the owner's enforcer, using his strength to defeat the strike. He is killed, ironically, by a swarthy Slav who fears a linkage with blacks. Without their brother's protection, Melody and Chinatown, wounded in body and soul, flee.

Attaway thus offers a brilliant counternarrative to white proletarian literature. John Oliver Killens lauds him for producing a crucial text in the literature of the US labor movement (7).[16] Echoing other commentators, Killens alleges that the subtext is the hope of racial unity (10); yet the morally grotesque whites belie the claim. The black man's labor is doomed. In that sense his work is no work at all.

Attaway's tragic elucidation of racially determined tensions in working class struggle does not confront the equally though distinctively conflicted situation of women as paid laborers. Misogyny produced widespread bitterness at the time about women's alleged job stealing. There were myriad claims. Among them was the belief that a working woman took a job from a male head of family. On the social and psychological level, a masculine labor venue was perceived to be unfeminine.

Proletarian literature reinforced such an outlook in three ways. First, proletarian literature rarely attended to the claims of women to be treated fairly in industrialized settings. Secondly, allusions to the female poor often were sympathetic but were only so in passing. Third, radical writers customarily foregrounded cultural production by or about men. Even female journalists such as Tillie Lerner Olsen had little time for woman-centered issues. What saw print were her publications on San Francisco's resistant dockworkers and their teamster comrades in Minneapolis; in a powerful 1934 essay simply titled "The Strike" she described the arrest in the name of law and order of a group of male protestors. She was also able to publish "The Iron Throat," a short story in which she drew on her experiences of "women's jobs" in the meat factory cutting pig ears; but significantly the book-length manuscript (*Yonnondio*) in which it was intended to serve as the first chapter was not published until 1974.

However, Agnes Smedley's semi-autobiographical *Daughter of Earth* (1929) reacted against the Party's masculinist emphasis. Her coming-of-age novel privileged Marie Rogers's early life in a filthy mining camp. Many later chapters depicted her rage at sweated labor and a series of debasing jobs. This education in injustice inspires Marie's subsequent break with the Red ideology of help-meet, never revolutionary. The novel sold well. But by 1935 it was reissued in a redacted edition. The influential Malcolm Cowley had erased all the concluding sections on female sexual freedom and political activism. Smedley herself, always an internationalist, moved on. In dispatches to Germany, England, and Cowley's *New Republic*, she famously covered the Chinese communist revolution from 1928 through World War II.

Among the other female authors determined to unseat hegemonic masculinity was Meridel Le Sueur. After a comfortable socialist girlhood, she refused to place gendered limits on her activities. Gathering material through life experience, she experimented with Bohemianism and an assortment of daring activities, including a stint as a Hollywood actor. Always judgmental of the bourgeoisie, she joined radical circles in proletarian authors' centers, Chicago and New York City. She was a friend and colleague of Conroy's, who supported her new career; his journal *The Anvil* as well as the *New Masses* published her early work.

Despite such female accomplishments, as Paula Rabinowitz argues in her introduction to an anthology of women's authorship, male writers typically allied the proletariat with manhood.[17] That view explains the logic of Le Sueur's autobiographical essays, such as "I Was Marching" (1934). In this piece, the male protesters are in front, women in the rear. Whether consciously or not, Le Sueur built literary capital by tacit acceptance of this hierarchy. This left-conventional approach, however, was a way of hiding in plain sight.

Other essays highlighted women neglected by the labor movement. Containing lengthy conversations with her toil-worn subjects, she defended such data gathering. Her interviews were not anecdotal but emblematic: "there must be as many women out of jobs in cities and suffering extreme poverty as there are men ... I needed to find out "what happens to them ... Where do they go?"[18] One classic example of reportage is her classic 1932 *New Masses* sketch, "Women on the Breadlines." She set it in an employment bureau where there were no job openings. She used the venue to explain her mission to give voice to the bottom-dog women interviewed. Reporting in 1932 for liberal journals as well, she employed a case history approach. She learned from shop girls that they received near-starvation wages. Jobless slum dwellers lived on one meal a day ("Women are Hungry"). All of her subjects were, she argued, statistically invisible.

Grounding her fiction in such proletarian reportage, she created documentary-like monologues in which unnamed protagonists complain about their problems and express feelings of defeat. Key titles, published in the left press, criticized unwed mothers' shelters ("Salvation Home," 1939) and New Deal surveillance of "wayward" women ("They Follow Us Girls," 1935). Among doctrinaire commentators, these examples attracted criticism for their woman-centered approach, politically incorrect subjectivity, and ideological pessimism. Le Sueur's own highly figurative style of writing also belied the masculinist emphasis on literal description.

Le Sueur demonstrated that the women's stories she had heard at a Minneapolis workers' center could be shaped and intensified by the rhetorical use of first-person point of view.[19] Presented as if they were exact tales, the sketches incorporate a given speaking subject's crude and associational style of conversing. The grammar is often poor, the English halting. Yet such seemingly verbatim transcription is undercut in many ways. The tales are structurally unified; there is no change in tone. The vernacular repetition and grammatical mistakes are curiously similar in all of the reshaped speeches.

Such is the case in "Sequel to Love," which appeared in the Midwestern radical journal *Anvil* in 1935. The irony of the title is soon revealed. As women seek solace and pleasure in the sex act, they risk entrapment in compulsory shelters if they are impregnated. Eugenics is shown to rule social attitudes toward women whose transient lovers routinely desert them. In these places, often approved by local authorities, promiscuity was viewed as synonymous with low intelligence. These husbandless women were sent, even by the New Deal Administration, to Salvation Army homes until their babies were born and taken from them. Some were sterilized, a practice enduring well past the Depression. The speaker in "Sequel" laments after she is placed in an unwed mother's shelter: "Workers ain't supposed to have any pleasure and now they're takin' that away because ... they're afraid I'll have another baby."[20] Shut away or thrown onto the streets after they give birth, they still challenged the patriarchal notion that men's struggles for the dignity of labor obliterated women's. Rather she introduced a new definition of the era's laborer. Being working class in this environment meant enduring the standard practices of eliding unwed motherhood and promiscuity. Worse, the only alternatives the government provided were sterilization or humiliating examinations of one's suitability for charity.

Attending in her imaginative literature to the realm of female labor, Le Sueur problematized male literary production through an aesthetic of bodily suffering and a discourse of entrapment. For her, storytelling itself was a way of witnessing the exploitation of child bearers, of unpaid workers who knew the "blow of oppression upon their bodies" ("Introduction," 1991: 1). The pain of labor thus refers in her fiction both to manufacturing commodities and birthing children.

The actual dangers of childbirth for poor women were legion. Subpar medical help combined with their partner-less state prevented them from supporting their new babies. A final irony was the state-sponsored relief agencies, including the New Deal's Aid to Dependent Children program, which required that single mothers could only qualify for payments if they did not work. The New Deal Cult of Motherhood thus reinforced the fact that only women who chose family over work would be protected.

In the lifeworld of Le Sueur's other manless characters, only commodified sexuality enabled some kind of wage earning. The prostitute is a key figure in this discourse of female exploitation. Angela Marie Smith finds the prostitute a universal symbol in a class-based society.[21] Yet Le Sueur's rhetoric of bodily imprisonment interrogated that generalization. Compounding the biological perils for women of casual sex, men hired impoverished prostitutes to satisfy their own (the men's) desires. Observed Le Sueur, this was a time when "you couldn't get a quarter or a meal for your body" (1991: 1).

Redefining the terms of male sweated labor, Le Sueur created a discourse of the body as the "register of proletarian consciousness."[22] She created fissures in the male labor imaginary of forgotten manhood. Le Sueur's emphasis on birthing as no less real or productive work than men's was not in the proletarian grain. After years of revising, she offered a manuscript of a novel in progress, *The Girl*, which included much of the material discussed earlier. No publisher would accept it, either then or some years later, when she submitted the final version. However, the very year Le Sueur began a rewrite and expansion of her manuscript, another professional journalist, Ruth McKenney, published a proletarian novel detailing a crucial Midwest triumph of union manhood. It was an enormous success in quarters sympathetic to labor. Not one critic caviled at the fact that it was by a woman author.

In 1939, the Ohio native Ruth McKenney published her proletarian novel, *Industrial Valley*. Central to the book's popularity was its meticulous chronology of the nation's "first CIO strike,"[23] the Akron Rubber Strike of 1936. This umbrella organization for mass unionism was founded in a breakaway spirit from the venerable but snobbish craft unionism of previous decades (the AFL). The CIO tribune, John L. Lewis, wasted no time in exhorting members of the Akron United Rubber Workers local to force management to the negotiating table. With CIO backing, the strike became a symbol of the drive for workplace democracy.

Industrial Valley was immediately ranked as a rare strike novel for two crucial reasons: it built on actual reportorial coverage, and it chronicled an actual working-class victory, in this case, over rubber-manufacturing czars like Goodyear, Goodrich, and Litchfield.

McKenney had worked hard for these accolades. She had laid the groundwork in the years prior to the victory, when she wrote for the paper of record, the *Akron Beacon Journal*. Visiting Akron during the heady days of struggle, she gathered more material. As she reinvented her research for a lengthy novel, she used the same readymade structure and immersive technique as in her voluminous dispatches for the *Journal* over the years. Rosters of business names joined income statistics, figures of bank profits, sites of protests, and records of visits from luminaries. Her diary format hewed to the original chronology of the daily or biweekly dispatches. From a January 19, 1936, Lewis oration, she selected key lines: "The record of a corporation in the rubber industry," he stormed, "is that it had made millions while it is a constant struggle for workers to live at all."[24] She also relied on the same deadpan satire that had bolstered her original pieces in skewering the callousness of the tire company owners. A September 30, 1932, squib was titled "Award." It read: "Harvey Firestone was presented with an honorary certificate for founding polo in Akron" (35).

The lengthy sections on class division bled into interchapters containing recognizable radical novel fare in accounts of the daily existence of workers like Job Hendricks, his name rightly suggesting a labor-biblical struggle against gods of the monolith. To intensify the force of this approach, actual speeches intersect with imagined responses. As further manipulation of a barrage of voices, she combined repetitive economic discourses with accounts of the ploys of both union and management to win the public to their respective sides: "Good news, maybe," December 1, 1933 (125); "I Say It's a Sellout," March 21, 1934 (141); and "The Same Sit-down," February 3, 1936 (238).

Faced with this labyrinth of data and stories, some critics explained it (away) as what one called a "compost of fact and fiction."[25] That stance begged aesthetic and discursive questions. Given the dizzying processions of real and imagined proletarians, another view was that the proletarian novel encompassed the entirety of the book. For, as Malcolm Cowley (who revised Smedley's novel by excising feminist sections) opined, though based on fact, it was the finest example of the kind of radical fiction that had been appearing in this country since the onset of the Great Depression (ctd. Nelson x). As soon as it appeared, a *New York Times* critic praised it, as would later twenty-first-century one[26] (Brown 8, Scott 4). An important modern historian of the strike concurs: "it is about real people and events but organized in *the form of the radical novel* and written from the perspective of the activist and social critic" (my italics; Nelson xi).

From its genesis, however, there was no ur-radical novel even at its most doctrinal. Like the terms "work," "worker," and "labor," the radical novel was hydra-headed. As the era's last incarnation of the literary phenomenon, *Industrial Valley* signaled the end of a progressive labor aesthetic. (Even the CPUSA's Popular Front proclaimed, "Communism is 20th century Americanism," subverting its own *Proletkult* credo.) The dream from Anderson to Le Sueur of a collectivist society proved apparitional, to be the product of a utopian hope that would not be fulfilled. Most cultural workers accepted or at least recognized this change. In 1939, as Amy Gentry explains, Philip Rahv, an eminent proponent of true class-based literature, tolled the bell for the "death of proletarian literature."[27] The new paradigm was to be broadly antifascist. In a sense, the enemy was no longer factory owners or capitalists inside the country; rather it was reactionary forces in other nations that needed to be fought.

NOTES

1 James D. Bloom, *Left Letters: The Culture Wars of Mike Gold and Joseph Freeman* (Columbia University Press, 1992) 71.
2 Douglas Wixson, *Worker-Writer in America: Jack Conroy and the Tradition of Midwestern Literary Radicalism, 1898–1990* (University of Illinois Press, 1994), 261.
3 Todd Depastino, *Citizen Hobo: How a Century of Homelessness Shaped America* (University of Chicago Press, 2003), 5. See also Lynne M. Adrian, "'The

World We Shall Win for Labor': Early Twentieth-Century Hobo Self-Publication," *Print Culture in a Diverse America*, edited by James P. Danky and Wayne A. Wiegand (University of Illinois Press, 1998); Frank Tobias Higbie, *Indispensable Outcasts: Hobo Workers and Community in the American Midwest, 1800–1930* (University of Illinois Press, 2003).

4 John D. Seelye, "The American Tramp: A Version of the Picaresque," *American Quarterly*, vol. 15, no. 4 Winter 1963): 335–353.

5 Edward Anderson, *Hungry Men* (Penguin, 1985), 10.

6 Mark Pittenger, *Class Unknown: Undercover Investigations of American Work and Poverty from the Progressive Era to the Present* (New York University Press, 2012), 85.

7 See David Wellman, *The Union Makes Us Strong: Radical Unionism on the San Francisco Waterfront* (Cambridge University Press, 1995).

8 Barbara Foley, *Radical Representations: Politics and Form in U.S. Proletarian Fiction, 1929–1941* (Duke University Press, 1993), 55.

9 Robert Cantwell, *The Land of Plenty* (Pharaos Editions/Dark Coast, 2013), 1.

10 Mike Gold, "A Letter to the Author of a First Book," *New Masses,* 4 January 1934: 15.

11 John Chamberlain, "Books of the Times." [Review of *The Disinherited*] *New York Times*, 22 November 1933: 97.

12 Walter B. Rideout, *The Radical Novel in the United States, 1900–1954* (Columbia University Press, 1956), 184–185.

13 Jack Conroy, *The Disinherited* (University of Missouri Press, 1991), 265.

14 Michael Denning, *The Cultural Front: The Laboring of American Culture in the Twentieth Century* (Verso, 1990), 225–226.

15 William Attaway, *Blood on the Forge* (New York: Monthly Review Press, 1987), 68.

16 John Oliver Killens, "Foreword," Attaway, 7–10.

17 Paula Rabinowitz, "Women and U.S. Literary Radicalism," *Writing Red: An Anthology of American Women Writers, 1930–1940*, edited by Charlotte Nekola and Paula Rabinowitz (Feminist Press, 1987), 3.

18 Meridel Le Sueur, "Women on the Breadlines," *Women on the Breadlines* (West End Press, 1991), 7. See also "Salvation Home," and "They Follow Us Girls," 18–21, 8–12.

19 See John Crawford, "Essay on the Book's Progress: The Making of *The Girl*." Le Sueur, *The Girl* (West End Press, 1987), 139.

20 Le Sueur, "Sequel to Love," *Women on the Breadlines*, 13.

21 Angela Marie Smith, "'Shriveled Breasts and Dollar Signs': The Gendered Rhetoric of Myra Page's *Moscow Yankee*," *The Novel and the American Left: Critical Essays on Depression-Era Fiction*, ed. Janet Galligani Casey (University of Iowa Press, 2004), 46.

22 Erin V. Obermueller, "Reading the Body in Meridel Le Sueur's *The Girl*," *Legacy*, vol. 22, no. 1, 2005, 47.

23 Gilbert J. Gall, "Rubber Workers Strike of 1936," *Labor Conflict in the United States: An Encyclopedia*, edited by Ronald L. Filippelli (Garland Publishing, 1990), 449.

24 Ruth McKenney, *Industrial Valley* (ILR Press, 1992), 248.

25 Quoted in Daniel Nelson, "Introduction," McKenney, x.

26 Francis Brown, "Workers of Akron," *New York Times Book Review*, 5 March 1939: 8. William Scott, *Power, Representation, and the Fiction of the Mass Worker* (Rutgers University Press, 2012), 4.
27 Amy Gentry,"Hungry Realism: Style and Subjecthood in Meridel Le Sueur's *The Girl*," *Reconstruction: Studies in Contemporary Culture*, vol. 8, no. 1 (2008). www.reconstruction.erserver.org/Issues/081/gentry.shtml.
Klitzman, Robert. "To the Editor," *New York Times*, 9 November 1986. www.nytimes.com.

8

THOMAS J. FERRARO

Transgression and Redemption in the 1930s

When it comes to matters of literary difference, particularly those hailed under the category of "minority literature," the 1930s is usually understood in terms of the impulses to ethnographic testimonial and socioeconomic redress. Fair enough: the 1930s was an era of anthologized voices, both literally (dozens of actual anthologies) and figuratively (a genre of left-leaning inclusiveness). And yet emphasis on documentary protest can take us back only so far. In this contribution, it is not the genre of ethnographic fiction per se that I am after but rather the aesthetic force of difference (especially religioethnic difference) as it emerged in the 1930s from the tradition of the American novel. I want to identify the sharp, often intimate interplay between our majority and minority literatures: to deexoticise and thus deghettoize ethnic novels, which pursue much more than autoethnography and sectarian protest, and to reclaim the differential workings of our mainstream texts, which enact much more than anxious liberal pluralism or unwitting caste-retrenchment. My ultimate goal would be to delineate how such novels take their place not only as unique revelations of Depression-era existence but also as crowning and ironizing and dissenting versions of long-standing American obsessions.

Critic Nina Baym once copped the keeper phrase "melodramas of beset manhood" to characterize Leslie A. Fiedler's characterization of the classic American novel of transgressive homosociality ("love") and redemptive sacrifice ("death").[1] She meant to use the term in double contempt, to lay siege both to the white male canon and to Leslie Fiedler's gothic reading of it, but the phrase itself is much more rehabilitative than destructive. With only a modest tweaking, "melodramas of beset manhood" becomes "melodramas of beset sexuality," and a gender-inclusive, indeed a race- and ethnicity-inclusive trajectory of the American imagination, especially the modern American novel, comes into view. The interpretative agenda of this chapter is to register the interplay of sex, violence, and sanctity in the novels of the 1930s writ large that plays across the minority/majority divide, where the creative tension between transgression and redemption captivates our most compelling protagonists and a fair number of writers, too.

On the threshold of the 1930s lie three black-themed, African American–scripted short novels, that, except for the racial identity of the writer and the racial inflection of its concerns, represent markedly different narrative projects: the middle-class angst-drama of Nella Larsen's *Passing* (1929), the episodic down-and-out port town sensationalism of Claude McKay's *Banjo* (1929), and the Swiftian fantasy satire of George Schuyler's *Black No More* (1931).[2] Starting with this para-canonical threesome will remind us that the category of "minority literature" – indeed, that of "the African-American novel" – may designate authorial identity, ethnographic content, and a political address to the reader but not, in fact, a genre, if by genre we mean a tight-knit set of story-telling conventions. But constellating the three novels is also constructive. It reveals what such otherwise disparate novels have in common besides race, how racialized culture is nonetheless implicated in that commonality, and to what ends race-conscious commonality reflects and, indeed, reinflects the canonical tradition preceding it. In doing so, the triptych throws crucial prismatic light onto what happens next – the commanding novels of the 1930s.

Nella Larsen's *Passing* is a melodrama of beset sexuality if ever there were one, in a sociologically acute, race-conscious register. *Passing* is a narrative exploration of the making of the black upper-middle class, at the time of "the new negro" movement, as it settled a lovely, broad-avenued, expansively optimistic Harlem, particularly the neighborhood deemed Sugar Hill. Up close, the novel reveals the haunting primacy of the self-disciplinary regime that Candice Jenkins calls the salvific wish – the felt need to out-Victorianize the WASP upper-middle classes – as both a formative tool for securing middle-class status and an ongoing public-relations plan for keeping it secure. The novel is told over the shoulder, in very tightly focalized third person, of Irene Redfield, whose childhood friend, Clare Kendry, has been passing so successfully that even her intensely bigoted husband does not know. The novel opens with a chance reencounter between the two women, after which Clare confesses that she wants to spend more time among "my people" than uptown Saturday night, thereby – to Irene's sense – risking everything. Irene's bodily discomfort and disdain for sex, unconfessed by her but dramatized recurrently and named as such by her husband Brian, is intimately tied to a professed fear of interracial tension, especially fear of racial exposure. Driving the story are several interrelated transgressive acts: Clare's libidinous appetite for disguised "miscegenation" (including her duet with her racist husband, who suspects Clare but remains blind to his own desire); the suppressed eroticism of Irene's response to Clare, whose convention-defying appetites hold Irene in thrall, her protests notwithstanding; and Irene's accusation that Brian is having an affair with Clare. (Brian for his own part wants to relocate to physician-needy, racially polymorphous, sex-affirming Brazil.) In rendering all this Larsen exposes the racial gaze-work of her protagonists, especially Irene, whom she subtly implicates in various ways, including an apparent obliviousness to the history of cross-racial congress in her own family (we know the origins of Clare's skin tone, but Irene keeps the secret of her own lightly toned descent-line from everyone, including herself); and she sets the reader up for analogous self-exposure, on the model – it would seem – of Melville's diabolically manipulative *Billy Budd* (published posthumously in 1924).

Irene tells herself that the safety of self, friend, and tribe are at stake, and to a significant extent they are. *Passing* is about the itch to mix, the sexiness of racial risk, and the dangers of raced sex among the lighter-skinned middle classes, who are its product as well as its producer. For Irene is, first to last, a border-control freak: an anxiety of border crossings, a suppression of the desire for same, and an absolute – indeed, deadly horror – at the instant of its emergence. That makes her a latter-day Puritan, in how she thinks and how we are supposed to see her: possessed by the logic and spirit of a persisting, reemerging Protestantism, the innocent whose subconscious same-sex desire is ultimately murderous of she-who-stirs it, in the grand proto-Freudian tradition of Billy Budd's self-denial. And her projection onto Clare – who tumbles out of a window to the street below, as Irene responds intuitively and ambiguously to the vociferous outing of Clare by Clare's husband – kills Clare. Clare is thus sacrificed – not so much to her own racially charged wanderlust, although there still is that, as to its emerging hold over Irene's imagination, Irene's libido. Clare dies so Irene may continue to deny.

In the end, *Passing* is a martyr-tale of escalating forbidden love with a psycho-social double twist, a black female reinflection of the centerpieces of 1920s American narrative – F. Scott Fitzgerald's *The Great Gatsby*, Ernest Hemingway's *The Sun Also Rises*, and Willa Cather's *The Professor's House* – each of which, we should remember, is a good ol' hetero-love story with homosocial intimations, violent consequences, and metaphysical resonances. In contrast, indeed in explicit dissent, Claude McKay's *Banjo* is an outright celebration of intimate mixing, and mixing it up, within the rich limits of the many-colored, many-nationed, multilinguistic dockside of Marseilles in the late 1920s, where mobility is no more desired – at least not understood to be desired – than it is possible and where, in its stead, immersion in the sociability of the senses is the holy pursuit.

Banjo calls itself "a story without a plot" – the story drifts episodically without going very far (in contradistinction to, say, the multiply-sited pilgrimage narratives, including Larsen's earlier *Quicksand*, 1928): which is to say, that the locus and focus stay, more or less, among the darker skinned, variously black-identified denizens of the industrial port of Marseilles, especially in the neighborhood informally called "The Ditch" – which is stuffed full of rough-and-tumble restaurants, bars, and "love-shops." The men hail mainly from the African west coast ("Senegalese"), the Caribbean, and the United States, including the two most important of the men, Banjo ("a child of the cotton Belt [who had] wandered all over America") and Ray, plus their crew. These men make music, cavort with women and each other, tell jokes and stories, get into and out of fights, render observations and pronouncements, and pick up intermittent day work, only then to make more music, make more love, and keep on thinking and talking. The novel ends as the two men drift off to sea together, in the time-honored fashion of America's homosocial (here, surely homosexual) bonding myth, now fully African-Americanized. Clearly, we're not in anxious, upscale Harlem anymore, as the down low has gone on high.

Banjo is not the first American fiction to feature flight, be it literal or figurative, from the master regimes of US capitalism, so perhaps the most relevant interlocutor text for *Banjo* is not *Passing* but a canonical one published several years earlier that also takes place in France – and the Spanish mountains that border it. *Banjo* is not only a riposte to the salvific wish and homosexual panic and border-patrolling of *Passing* but also – as befits a text that is ultimately about anglophone expats who are both male and black – a restaging of *The Sun Also Rises*, which is (Jake's not quite believable Catholicism notwithstanding) arguably the whitest of the white-boy texts of the 1920s. McKay's revisionism is profoundly formal, too. Several years before Henry Miller's *Tropic of Cancer* (1934) challenged the representational repertoire of European high modernism (Joyce, Eliot, Beckett), *Banjo* countered the subtle but no less sophisticated representational practices of the American 1920s. McKay's prose style refuses Hemingway's clipped and elliptical dialogue, Fitzgerald's populist symbolism and his cross-cutting of lyric testament with brutal insinuation, Cather's fractured plays of memory and craftily indexed histories of violence – all of which inform Larsen to the max. What *Banjo* gives instead are prose rhythms that step, hip, and dive to the music of Jelly Roll Morton, Louis Armstrong, and Ethel Waters, or strum along in linguistic manifestation and earthy collective self-exhortation. In *Banjo* there are long litanies, both analytically descriptive and sensorially evocative, that bear Whitmanian witness to the people and goods, the material conditions and work pasts, the activities and refusal of activity characterizing Ditch, docks, and dago rivals, yielding sociological acumen with liturgical force. Oft times, a character's internal meditations (not only the character Banjo but his best new bud, Ray the Philosopher) are quite sustained, and they often issue into excited debate, on almost anything that touches upon race, but especially music (the banjo as the instrument of slavery), other arts (midtown "ofay" entertainment like *Carmen*), the sad whiteness of blue cinema, successive forms of ethnic scapegoating, prejudicial operations in different nations (Jim Crow vs. French policing), labor conditions and, of course, the sporting life. Indeed, the combination of monologue and dialogue yield more ideas per square inch of prose than any other American novel of the modernist period. Its reception hung, of course, mostly on its out-sized insistence (politically incorrect even then) on a primal African diasporic sensuality at play at every turn in the novel and, indeed, named as such, as if McKay were tempting readers to the very stereotype he means to correct: "Negroes were freer and simpler in their sex urge, and as white people on the whole were not, they naturally attributed over-sexed emotions to Negroes" (252). I wonder if he ever consulted Zora Neale Hurston, who risked alienation by being notoriously forthright on this very issue, too.

George Schuyler's *Black No More* (1931) is a serio-comic fantasy that generates formidable sociological insight from a single, singular conceit: a medical process, perfected in Germany (eugenics, here we come!) and brought to market, that will change a person's skin tone from dark to light, Negroid to Caucasian. Thus, an individual becomes, in the nomenclature of hair straightening products, "black no more" – at least to casual, unperceptive (a.k.a. ofay) observers, and they are the ones who patrol access to dominant, exclusive institutions. Dr. Crookman's method of "processing" the whole body offers the allure of freedom from economic exploitation, political manipulation, and psychosocial diminution. A mass flight into whiteness instigates a dark comedy of revelations and reversals, parsing out the operations of American racism, chapter by chapter, verse by verse, beginning with white nativist panic and the hidden injuries of internalized racism. On the vile side of the ledger, Schuyler calls out the union-busting techniques of the white Southern corporate elite and their big-bank allies; on the merely slimy side, the self-interested leveraging of caste-anger and ethnic pride by a motley crew of fictionalized versions of W. E. B. DuBois, Marcus Garvey, and whatever ex-gangster is the head this week of Black Masonry. Unlike those of Larsen and McKay, or those of Fitzgerald, Hemingway, and Cather for that matter, Schuyler's narrative voice is neither first person nor its first cousin, that of third-person-limited indirect, but what we might call "third-person super-knowledgeable deadpan." The more American history and vernacular lingo the reader knows, the wittier the parody and the more trenchant its faux hyperbole.

The plot of the novel are the things we do for love, black-folks division, or rather, the "formerly black" folks division. For of course it is the American transgressive love of all transgressive loves – between the Southern black male and the Southern white female – that gets the story going, keeps its social insights and mythological resonances coming, and renders the final verdict on the American condition both insidious and wise. This in the heyday of Jim Crow. The comic fantasy that is vessel to the seriousness of Schuyler's sociology turns on the illicit intercourse between white and black – miscegenation was against the law in most states in 1930 – with its stubborn history (rape under slavery, prostitution and forbidden fruit thereafter) and borderline-oxymoronic form of border-patrol law: the asymmetric "one drop rule" of assigned blackness. The novel first makes light and then dark comedy of interracial reproduction, which given the loveliness of otherness and the imp of taboo-defiance, then as now, is *the* fact of life in these United States. "For the first time the prevalence of sexual promiscuity was brought home to the thinking people of America" (88). Our man-on-the-make, Max Disher, now the Anglo-apparent Matthew Fisher, a ranking member of the Nordica Knights and son of the Republican VP candidate, frets about the blackness of his first born, in the time-honored fashion of "recidivism" anxiety, á la *Passing*. Reversing expectations, Helen is delighted by their "very, very dark" boy – that's the rom-com uplift, undercut a bit by the fact that Helen is not the brightest bulb on the circuit. In the last event of the novel, with mulatto chic in ascendance, Nordicists Mr. Snobbcraft and Dr. Buggerie (yes, Buggerie) go on the lam together only to be hoisted by their own petard: in this case, another bad pun, given that they are lynched by the denizens of Happy Hill, Mississippi, whose Christ-struck preacher knows an evangelizing opportunity when he sees it. Dark comedy, indeed.

Larsen, McKay, and Schuyler can be said to stand on the threshold of the 1930s not only chronologically but thematically. Each of them revisits the white (that is, always already racially entailed) canonical issue of beset sexuality from an expressly African American perspective. Taken together, they establish the sex-race entanglement of the transgression-redemption dialectic as a major issue of the 1930s novel – not of all 1930s novels, of course, but of the corpus writ large, including its two most resplendent accomplishments: William Faulkner's *Absalom, Absalom!* (1936) and Zora Neale Hurston's *Their Eyes Were Watching God* (1937).[3]

Absalom, Absalom! is an epic of imploding dynastic ambition set in plantation Mississippi before, during, and well after the Civil War. The novel is centered on the impact of one Thomas Sutpen, a mysterious outsider who arrived in 1833 hell bent on inserting himself and thus his progeny-to-be into the upper echelon of the slavocracy. *Absalom, Absalom!* is, at the same time, a psycho-historical mystery thriller, not a whodunit it but a why-did-he-do-it, concerning the murder at the war's end of Sutpen's son Henry by Henry's best friend, Charles Bon. The event in question is understood and reconstructed, fifty years later, through partial witness, much hearsay, strenuous deduction, and invested projection, entailing a plethora of perspectives that converge upon a young Harvard student, Quentin Compson. And *Absalom, Absalom!* is a theatrical exposé of the barbaric, caste-making and caste-manipulative system of bound labor that was chattel slavery and its peonage aftermath. The melodramatic self-destruction of Thomas Sutpen's vaunted "design" stages the ideological self-deconstruction of its local and most peculiar – not only racialized but heavily gendered and fanatically spiritualized – institutional creation, chattel slavery. All this, even the murder, which hinges on a double, all-too-overdetermined revelation of race (maternity) and relation (paternity) – would seem to set *Absalom, Absalom!* wildly apart from both contemporary fiction and canonical tradition.

But *Absalom, Absalom!* is also, at the core of its staged violence and layered mystery, something much simpler and much more familiar: yet another martyr-tale of forbidden love. So much so that, this time around, the reader does not need the classic criticism of D. H. Lawrence, William Carlos Williams, or Leslie A. Fiedler; does not need the queer theory of Eve Sedgwick nor the critical race theory of Patricia A. Williams nor the deconstructive religious hermeneutics of Tracy Fessenden, because Faulkner does the work himself, through the mouths of the Compsons especially, issuing through the onslaught of thick and contrary memory explanatory schematics worthy of us all.

Henry Sutpen is his mother's son, a country Methodist, virginal and squeamish. Charles Bon is a New Orleans decadent, almost a decade older and a global port-city wiser, whose radiance is palpable to all. It is Henry who brokers Bon's engagement to his sister Judith, as an unconscious way of "having" Bon. And it is Henry who defies his father and goes with Bon to New Orleans, where he meets Henry's octoroon mistress (thereupon insisting that Bon wait four years before marrying Judith). "Yes, [Henry] loved Bon, who seduced him as surely as he seduced Judith" (76). As Henry is an Irene-Redfield type, "a puritan," anxious at all turns about boundary maintenance, so Bon is cast as a permeable, permeating voluptuary, "a Catholic of sorts," whose trespasses against the Calvinist Mississippi way of things ultimately goad Henry, his best friend and platoon-mate, into killing him. What we know for sure – the absolute *donné* of the novel – is that at the end of the war Charles comes to claim Judith, which somehow prompts Henry to shoot and kill him – at the symbolically fraught front gates of the Sutpen plantation. In short, the issue of how Charles Bon comes

Thomas J. Ferraro

to be martyred and the role played therein by his – and Judith's, and especially Henry's polymorphous sexuality – is *the* issue at play.

The trip to New Orleans is no digression. Charles Bon may be New Orleans incarnate, but the habits and habillement of the New World's most Mediterranean city prove a more profound challenge to Henry's plantation Protestantism than Bon's voluptuous persona alone, which, out of context heretofore, has been all seduction. To a young man with Henry's "background," the fact of Bon's mistress is nearly unfathomable – given that "the other sex is separated into three sharp divisions, separated [two of them] by a chasm that could be crossed but one time and in but one direction – ladies, women, females – the virgins whom gentlemen someday married, the courtesans to whom they went while on sabbaticals to the cities, the slave girls and women upon whom that first caste rested and to whom in certain cases it doubtless owed the very fact of its virginity" (87). Nineteenth-century Scots-Irish Calvinism was nothing if not boundary fixated, and in New Orleans the rich man's system of elevated concubinage comes to the inland South of Henry as a category-buster: Bon's mistress is educated and housed and addressed like a member of the upper crust, but her reputation is at least as compromised as that of a high-end prostitute, and she is in fact owned, sexually most of all, to the point where Bon is free to sell her son – their collective progeny, but *his* property alone – should he so choose. Lady/woman/female: the mistress is all three, a sentient being of refined sensibility who commands neither her body nor its issue – so that what offends Henry the puritanical boundary-freak is, in effect, the flaunting of the tripartite categorization of the female gender, which serves in the short term to rationalize the race system and, in the long term, pressing Mississippi towards New Orleans, to undermine it.

As a mystery, *Absalom, Absalom!* masks and then reveals the most peculiar – arguably, the most inhumane – dimension of American chattel slavery: namely, the common practice by the master class of disavowing paternity, such that a mixed-race child is taken from its enslaved mother and, nameless, sold off the plantation, to disappear, as it were, into an anonymous gene pool. Over generations, then, the racial ideology of the plantation south risks incest in order to deny blood-relation. To implicate the system's self-immolation, Faulkner devises the most overdetermined backstory in American fiction, a single-generation potboiler of double-trouble. Spoiler alert: the mysterious Charles Bon is actually Thomas Sutpen's son, conceived in the Caribbean with his aristocratic first wife, who turned out to have a trace of Negro blood. What is at stake in *that* buried fact, Sutpen's attempt to repudiate his reproductive past as guarantor of a racially secured future, prompts Bon's murder, as Quentin Compson and his

152

roommate at Harvard persuasively reconstruct it: " – *You are my brother. – No I'm not. I'm the nigger that is going to sleep with your sister. Unless you stop me, Henry* " (286). As goeth the Sutpen boys, so goeth their father's dynastic ambition and with it the genealogical denials upon which its vicious sexual exploitation of race depends. At stake in the love mess from the very start is the symbolic order of the inland Cotton Belt – which, as Faulkner slowly and insidiously reveals, operates as a race-class-gender system of a most inhumane, ultimately self-destructive un-humanity. The denial of fatherhood passed along into a refusal of brotherhood: fratricide, in the house divided.

Zora Neale Hurston's *Their Eyes Were Watching God* is structured as a three-marriage pilgrimage novel with the hagiographic pacing and aura of a Biblical parable, told at one degree of modernist removal from Janie Killicks-Crawford-Wood's vernacular recounting. The novel is set mainly in the interior of Jim Crow Florida, in and around the all-black town where Hurston grew up, near Big Lake Okeechobee. When Janie hits menses, her grandmother, who grew into adulthood under slavery and lost her daughter – Janie's mother – to the psychological scars of Jim-Crow tolerated rape, lays a heavy warning upon her: "'Ah can't die easy thinkin' maybe de menfolks white or black is makin' a spit cup out of you'" (19): the metaphor is a graphic reminder of male sexual exploitation, be the violence literal or psychosocial. For Janie's grandmother, called "Nanny" (after all those years of serving as Mammy), enslavement meant that the master commanded sexual compliance at will, the plantation mistress had you whipped in jealousy, and the issued child could be sold away. Searing pain, searing pain, searing pain. The first-order dream of emancipation for enslaved women was the freedom to choose with whom to have sex and with what consequences: no rape, a strong hand to protect, and keeping your child. By the 1930s, this was not enough for Hurston. Nanny wants self-determining security for Janie, with the promise of slow mobility and the dignity thereof; the idea of the novel is that Janie is haunted from her sixteenth year by her sensual intuitions. The sine-qua-non of the novel is that no matter whom Janie sleeps with nor how many times she sleeps with him she is not going to get pregnant – otherwise, under the conditions of black peonage in the agricultural South, story over.

Nanny arranges Janie's marriage to no nonsense, hard-drivin', and downright ugly Logan Killicks, who owns sixty acres and a piano and a mule, and whose plan for petit-bourgeois uplift is to put Janie to muling, too. So, poof! Janie runs away from the first marriage. In Nanny's terms, Janie's first transgression is to want to "love" her lover, period. The text plays first for comedy and then for tragedy. Logan is ditched, and Janie takes up with Jody

Crawford, who is gathering forces to make himself the big man in an all-black town. Jody installs Janie as a trophy wife, only to be forced out of the bedroom by his cruel insecurities seven years in, and then fourteen years later to die (Hurston works in Biblical stretches of time), after being figuratively emasculated in front of all. Jody deserved it of course, but Janie is still the symbolic murderer on the way to being, once again, an ex-post-facto adulterer. For black female romantic self-determination entails fundamental transgressions, with one male martyr down and a better one still to come.

In the introductory scene, the townsfolk remind each other that Tea Cake (Janie's third husband) is poor, young, and quite dark of skin. Later we learn that he crushes "aromatic herbs with every step," looks like the love-thoughts of women, and is "a glance from God" (102). The darker the berry, the sweeter the juice, and that's only half of the attraction. For what the novel understands yet Janie only partially recognizes is that Tea Cake's radiant force is not only that he talks with her and invites her to play checkers and strums the guitar. He is also a fighting gambler – good with his fists, a knife, and a gun. In Hurston's radical reimagining of the forest scene in *The Scarlet Letter*, the migrant farm utopia of the swamp, where "blues are made and used on the spot" (one of the great clauses in global literature), depends on violence, above all competitive violence among men (125). In season one, the violence of gambling and fighting and down-and-dirty jooking, is centered on Janie and Tea Cake's front porch, where, carefully contained, it serves Janie as intensely erotic spectacle. But in the second season, as Tea Cake feels the internalized racisms of poverty and skin, he beats Janie to assert possession before the masses (she has light skin; she doesn't fight back), who melt in envy. What the contrast between seasons is meant to indicate, parable-like, is simple. The violence of the muck is a sexual recourse of the highest order, but the companionate romance that it intensely sponsors can not, in fact, be domesticated over the long term – which means, one way or another, some dimension of Janie's otherwise soul-enhancing love has got to give.

The novel raises the hurricane, which serves many purposes. At the least it shows how dangerous Tea Cake's gambling is, as he bets their lives against the better judgment of the animals and, indeed, the Native Americans. If the opening irony that Janie's self-determination is dependent on a kind of neo-knight in shining armor – a guitar-totin' knife-hidin' migrant farm worker who is deft of tongue and sweet of walk – the closing irony is that, in order to preserve the spirit of their marriage, it has to end, and Tea Cake's refusal to seek higher ground allows him to go out a hero, throwing himself in front of a rabid dog to protect Janie. The figurative overload lies in the fact that it is Janie who kills Tea Cake, with the very gun that Tea Cake, as love-object but also coauthor of her romantic self-determination, gave her. Indeed, the first thing he taught her after they were married was how to use it: you never know, do you, when your lover has to be made gone? As the luminous love of Tea Cake for Janie has now been "infected" in year two by the caste distinctions of internal racism, so Tea Cake, infected by rabies, turns insanely against Janie, who must shoot him in order to avoid an equally horrible fate. The memory of Tea Cake ends up on Janie's mantelpiece as the young black lover who made the ultimate sacrifice, in the very fashion that Hurston famously announces in the second paragraph, that is, perfectly laundered, one might even say black-washed, of its oncoming, inevitable trespasses. In the sardonic knowing of Hurston's figurative regime, Tea Cake turns out to be the very man Janie needs not only to get to the horizon but to make it back because he is just the kind of "good" bad-boy who *forces* her to kill him, guilt-free and heroism-full, when his utility – for women, it's all about the memory – is used up.

In the mid-1920s our melodramas of beset sexuality, especially of beset manhood, were located in predominantly Anglo-American upper classes, moneyed or not. *The Great Gatsby* is ultimately set among the willed alliance between old (the Buchanans) and older (the Caraways) money, with the mobbed-up mystery man Gatsby (a Jew from the East Side? A Catholic cracker from the Louisiana swamps?) giving the crashed crass parties; *The Sun Also Rises* gathers fallen English aristocracy and self-made, white-washed Princetonians in postwar Paris, where they police each other with performance codes so haute-Protestant no wonder Jake considers himself a "bad" Catholic; and even Cather's *The Professor's House*, whose central character has French Canadian ancestry that he has resolutely never honored or even understood, presumes the small-town norms of an old Midwestern liberal arts college. In each novel, the assiduously WASPy circle experiences the social incursions and thus ethical pressures of an outsized Jewish masculinity (Meyer Wolfsheim, Robert Cohn, and Louis Marsellus, respectively), as we have been well instructed to apprehend. And yet each also feels the metaphysical temptations of a wayward Marian Catholic sacramentality (which descends through Harold Frederic, Kate Chopin, Theodore Dreiser, and Henry James from the first-and-still-most canonical novel of them all, *The Scarlet Letter*), in ways we are still working out. What happens, I wish to ask, in the next decade, when Jewish and Catholic novelists leave the precincts of the established American classes, to put the mythic American thematics of love and death into more ordinary – poorer and greasier – hands?

Henry Roth's *Call It Sleep* (1934) is a sophisticated Freudian tale set against the backdrop of the East Side of New York, in which filial anxiety and Jewish male identity constitute each other in escalating ways.[4] Focalized over a boy who is barely eight years old by novel's end, with a plot that turns on a somewhat phantasmagoric cuckolding charge directed by the boy at his father, *Call It Sleep* is a melodrama of beset masculinity, precocious-juvenile division. Recurrently celebrated since its republication in 1964 as the most "Jewish" of all American texts, I would call it one of the most Judaic as well. I say Judaic, not just socially or culturally "Jewish," because Judaism is by the very nature of Chosenness an orthopraxis of separateness – of ethnic boundedness – especially when it comes to marital intimacy, which is policed by the G-d of the Torah with a jealous vengeance. In *Call It Sleep*, goyish temptations – especially Catholics, their signifiers, and their material culture – are just about everywhere outside the home proper, almost everywhere David Schearl goes – except Cheder (what the next generation would call "Hebrew School") – and everywhere attached to one or another manifestation of besieged sexuality, especially David's.

David Schearl is one frightened little boy, though with certain cause, including an abusive father and too-early exposure to sex. Although his exact age is the source of contrary evidence and evident contestation, he is about six years old and still living in the relatively milder Brownsville when he is propositioned to "play bad" by a neighborhood girl, who is as explicit in nomenclature as she is clear in her directions. David is immediately, absolutely revolted. But the scene of instruction effects less suppression than the sharpening of an already nosey antenna. For the rest of the novel, he eavesdrops and pokes around and otherwise pursues half-understood recognitions of sexual, especially "adulterous" relations; that is, carnal knowledge in its figurative sense. By Book II of the novel, David is charting his mother's unduly excited response to his father's best friend, who does indeed mean to give his father the horns, and who in turn intuits David's sense that he – Albert, the father – has somehow been unmanned, "tampered with" as Melville might say.

The novel climaxes in the felt convergence of several trajectories of betrayal, both real and imagined, in which David leverages what he (thinks he) has learned about Christian threats to Jewish integrity. David supplies his Polish Catholic buddy Leo protected access to his adventurous female step cousin in exchange for the mystical promises of a broken rosary. Learning of his mother's premarital affair with a Church organist (oi, Freud!) back in Austria, he leaps to the conclusion that he was sired by a Christian. Although by Judaic law he would still be Jewish, he sees himself through his Cheder teacher's eyes as a Deuteronomic "abomination," the fruit of a mother's polluting denial of Jewish endogamy and proof positive of his father's connubial and thus paternal impotence. Beset relations, indeed!

David grabs a milk ladle (a Freudian collapse of female nurturance into male assertion) from his father's work tools and flees in a hallucinogenic fit (vocalizing to himself all the while) in pursuit of the electrified third rail of the East Side train tracks. Paradoxically, it is the combination of an uncertain electric shock (sexual therapy cum Pagan mystery) and the convergence of concerned city folk that returns David to the nuclear family unit, his father somewhat calmed and restored, and by extension to a less troubled Jewish identity in urban America – which may be an analog for the assimilationist threat more generally. Through the near electrocution David's filial anger and anguish are vanquished, or at least quelled, as if by the agency of the East Side itself: a cacophony of ethnic classed voices of both genders that turns into a concatenation of adult-concern, stranger-love, and communal hope. The melancholia, litanized in a minor key as it were, sounds the pain on the way to embracing hope – David's body partially martyred not to redemption (as Christians might posit it) of father or soul or self, but to the reclamation of Judaic resolve.

Roth wore on his sleeve his affiliation with the great modernist experimenters, whom he knew in part through the tutelage of an older WASP lover Eda Lou Walton. Pietro di Donato, an unemployed bricklayer who proclaimed himself untutored in order to wear his worker's credentials on his sleeve, was in fact an autodidact of great stylistic ambition and lyric inventiveness. Both *Call It Sleep*, with its pronounced Joycean and Eliotic experimentation, and *Christ in Concrete* (1939), a novel in tune with Faulkner, Hurston, and Roth himself, are primarily stream-of-consciousness.[5] In both novels boys face huge social forces beyond fathoming, never mind control, which they experience as animate. Each of the boys shows acute sensitivity to surroundings, especially sense perception, which heightens self-consciousness, at times to a fever pitch of nascent mystical understanding. And both novels play out in Oedipal terms as a crisis of belief and, indeed, of formal religious allegiance. There the influences and convergences end, however. In terms of prospective manhood, precocious David Schearl is boxed in: he has a father who watched his own father be gored, a mother with a dubious sexual history (at least to his father), all-too-curious Jewish girls, a Catholic buddy with a penchant for such Jewish girls, an uncle figure (his father's best friend) who is on the make for his mother, even an earthy aunt with disturbing plans for the dentist: our poor boy can't catch a break until he takes his fate in his own hands. Young Paul's world is also vastly peopled, but the adults (Mediterranean peasants though they be, *because* Mediterranean peasants they still are) know what they are about sexually, even when taking risks, and the young people have much to give each other, however dangerous *that* territory is, youth being youth. Whereas the moral *gravitas* of *Call It Sleep* leads to letting eight-year-old David Schearl just be a boy, that he may rally his family around him and escape for just a little longer the big questions, the weight of *Christ in Concrete* is to make young Paul a man before his time, in tempered triumph; to enfold into his education the increasing stakes of the process of Americanization; and to secure his distance from his beloved yet alienating mother, in the time-honored manner of *mammissimo*.

In the first chapter, which was taken from a prize-winning story, Paul's father Geremio, a bricklayer turned site foreman, is killed horrifically – that is, horribly but also in horrific relentless detail – in a construction accident; others too, through certain fault of Geremio's own. It is Good Friday, and a father-on-earth has been buried alive, crushed to dust, sacrificed to capitalist greed and twenty years of immigrant dreaming. Annunziata, Paul's mother, is left with a half-dozen children, pregnant, too, and after a series of further frustrations and tragedies, ten-year-old Paul must become a brick-layer, a process less fatal but almost as brutal as what his father went through. Abandoned by the Compensation Bureau and the well-fed Irish priests in the local parish and *fortuna* itself, Paul comes to doubt Christ's provenance, God's mercy, slipping down a chain from intercessory appeal to enlightened rage to agnostic disgust, increasingly refusing claims to transcendence. Yet the novel itself insists, Paul's growing-pains notwithstanding, on the divine pulse of the senses, the beauty and wisdom and especially sacred force of the body, an extracatechetical immanence if not a sacramental materiality – and it does so even under conditions of the most intense labor exploitation (the "Great dangerous Job," the violent spell of which we hear about at exquisite length).

In no other novel, not Faulkner not Hurston not Roth, is the sensorium more in overdrive, than it is in *Christ in Concrete*. Bodily experience and consciousness of the body are always at stake: at work and at play, along tenement halls and out on the streets, in festive celebration on the rarest of days and in talk every waking moment. The opening pages before Geremio's accident introduce the work culture of the immigrants and set the tone for the novel to come, as men talk sexual shop with both an earthiness and a lyricism utterly unprecedented in American literature. The gender of a newborn is invoked as a matter of a bell rather than a rose bud, "seafruits" are recommended for aphrodisiacal recuperation (leaving unspoken the issue of why), and bragging rights go to fertility not virility, as an easy homosociality is created from and circuits back into deeply felt (and gorgeously rendered) heterosexuality. Soon into the novel proper, Annunziata gives birth in a wildly blunt (the women are more vulgar than the men), darkly comic, downright knowing cry against male-seeded pain and for female-delivered life.

There is, once again, no scene in the entire canon to rival it. Throughout the novel, Paul himself is exposed to a combination of adult refulgence, working-class men's virile drift (including a trip to the whorehouse), and, most directly – this is a coming-of-age-novel after all – the temptations of tenement opportunity. For there is this neighbor girl, Gloria, whose "broad and shapely" invitation is real (even her mother plays along) and whose invitingness is as haloed as it is enfleshed, Paul's fear of heresy *to the contrary*. Wherever one turns, *Christ in Concrete* presses against the hold of official Christianity (callous hierarchy, an abstract jealous vindictive God, doctrinal sexual suspicion) in favor of a reasserted, industrialized and thus modernized though not quite Americanized, Mariolatric paganism, in which Mary is on the altar with her saints, the body is vessel to the spirit, and Mary's boy Christ, to the extent he is still to be supposed, is the redeeming intercessor of *all* humanity: "Did they not all live [in tenements] atop the other and feel and taste and smell each other? ... They, like me, are children of Christ" (100). Blasphemous as it sounds, perhaps Geremio did not die in vain after all.

Nathanael West's *Day of the Locust* (1939) is best known as a parodic rendering of Hollywood wanna-bes and hangers-on in the 1930s, with a truly prophetic – that is, culturally predictive – imaginative force, since its ending riot captures the frustration of the misdirected disenfranchised: an effort to explain, before its time, why Americans go ballistic, whether individually, collectively, or – just beyond the frame of its narrative – as part of a reactive militarized police force (which began of course in Los Angeles).[6] For West, the Hollywood fantasy machine inculcates forms of desire – economic, physical, semiotic – that morph into psychological and social violence, with emphasis everywhere on the material betrayal, spiritual vacuity, and psychological self-immolation of the industry of "pretend." Accomplished young scholars have offered us fascinating accounts of the meaning of its characters' unprovoked, seemingly inscrutable laughter (Frances McDonald), of West's conservative Judaic knowing (Lisa Naomi Mulman), of its resistance against human commodification (Robert Seguin) – not to mention this volume's own William Solomon, who has implicated the novel's grotesque aesthetic of deformity in fascism.[7] And it is hard for any reader today, teacher or student, not to be aware of the conflation that West insists upon between male frustration and female manipulation – the sexist, indeed misogynistic scapegoating of women that concentrates West's critique and around which the story turns.

The novel is focalized primarily over a male observer-participant, Tod Hackett, though it drifts elsewhere, too. It is narrated throughout in a nasty comic dead-pan, in which it is often difficult to tell where unwitting self-indictments end and West's saddened, frightened condemnation begins – though Tod is given, in his dialogue at least, a few West-like zingers. Hackett is a Yale MFA grad who has been invited by a movie studio to learn set design. Hackett is hit by a thunderbolt of erotic infatuation for an aspiring seventeen-year-old actress, Faye Greener, who is as practical and narcissistic as they come – and the plot consists primarily of Hackett and several other men circling around Faye, in ways that directly invoke (once again) *The Sun Also Rises*. Again we see the heightening of formal experiment in the 1930s by means of a self-conscious revision of this novel from the 1920s: West restages Hemingway at almost every turn, including that of plot – wounded men fighting over a self-indulgent female, with elegant bullfights turned, literally, into pathetic cockfights, and incidental death becoming a riot of destruction – in order to undercut, viciously, the moral complexity, alternative intimacies, and varied (including anticapitalist) pooling of resources that Hemingway imagined.

On the one hand, West is a unique talent, arguably our first postmodernist several decades ahead of his time, indebted on his father's German-Jewish side to high-end education (think Benjamin and the Western Marxists), more Elias Canetti (a direct influence) than not. On the other hand, the central trajectory of his critique is utterly American – that is, West operates in lock step with our Pauline Puritan heritage, with (for all his eurosophistication) an under pull of Victorian shock. He insists on reading the corruption of mass-culture almost entirely in terms of a violently wayward sexuality generated by the California dream that anything and everything is possible. Not only does Faye's manipulative promiscuity include schoolgirl outfits and antics – "her invitation wasn't to pleasure, but to struggle, hard and sharp," the lure of actual *and* statutory rape – but a Hollywood mom instructs her six-year-old white boy in the blues-expressed mimicry of the sexual pain of mid-life black women and a drag queen's uncanny comfort on stage gives way off stage to the Brechtian alienation effect – when the queen is supposed to be a man for real, instigating gender-panic around the room. Most telling for West's ferocious dismissal of Hollywood's seductive impulse is its play within a play: a "stag film," at a high-end brothel, featuring a maid whose eye is on the girl of the family (lesbian pedophilia!), but first, in a version of vaudevillian Marx Bros routine, she must submit to the advances on a ladder of increasing titillation and inappropriateness. The film breaks right before the molestation of the girl, which the audience assumes – reasonably enough! – is a rigged game, and howls in anger. Clever and damning, West's reflexivity is nonetheless as ferociously manipulative as the film itself, for even brothel porn – never mind mainstream Hollywood (including pre-Censorship Hollywood) – was not always that way.

In short, *Day of the Locust* is all transgression, no redemption – Hollywood at the moment, all of America soon to come. Given the assurance of

West's moral indignation and the assuredness of his political anger (in which an Orthodox Jewish conservatism and an anti-capitalist radicalism of one order or another warp into each other), there would appear, to my ears, not a Christian impulse in this story beyond the patristic misogyny and sexual conservatism – he is that far from the masterful secularizations of Christian impulse produced by Jewish (and Irish) (and even, in the case of Frank Capra, Sicilian) Hollywood. The transgression is the culture's doing, and an entire migrant people, those California-seekers, guilty one and all, are condemned to hell on earth, as there is no heaven. *The Day of the Locust* is American dark comedy born out of and sending forth Jewish male cynicism – and all the more astonishing for that. It is *the* nadir, by which I mean the obscene climax, of the obsessive American interrogation of beset sexuality. And, as such, it is the novel of the 1930s, looking back to *Billy Budd* and forward to *Blue Velvet*, that I most love to hate.

NOTES

1 Nina Baym, "Melodramas of Beset Manhood: How Theories of American Fiction Exclude Women Authors," *American Quarterly* 33 (Summer 1981): 123–139; Leslie A. Fiedler, *Love & Death in the American Novel* (New York: Criterion Books, 1960).

2 Parenthetical page references are to the following commonly available editions: Nella Larsen, *Passing* (New York: Modern Library, 2002), ed. Mae Henderson, with forward by Ntozake Shange; Claude McKay, *Banjo* (New York: HBJ, 1957); George S. Schuyler, *Black No More* (New York: Modern Library, 1999), with forward by Ishmael Reed.

3 Parenthetical page references are to the following editions: William Faulkner, *Absalom, Absalom!* (New York: Vintage, 1990); Zora Neale Hurston, *Their Eyes Were Watching God* (New York: Harper & Row, 1990), with forward by Mary Helen Washington.

4 Henry Roth, *Call It Sleep* (New York: Farrar, Straus and Giroux, 1991), with forward by Alfred Kazin.

5 Pietro di Donato, *Christ in Concrete* (New York: New American Library, 1993), with forward by Studs Terkel.

6 Nathanael West, *Miss Lonelyhearts and Day of the Locust* (New York: New Directions, 1969).

7 Frances McDonald, "Ha-Ha and Again Ha-Ha: Laughter, Affect, and Emotion in Nathanael West's *Day of the Locust*," *American Literature* 88: 3 (2016): 541–568; Lisa Naomi Mulman, *Modern Orthodoxies: Judaic Imaginative Journeys of the Twentieth Century* (New York: Routledge, 2012), pp. 32–38; Robert Seguin, "New Frontiers in Hollywood," *Around Quitting Time: Work and Middle-Class Fantasy in American Fiction* (Durham, NC: Duke University Press, 2001), pp. 83–120; William Solomon, *Literature, Amusement, and Technology in the Great Depression* (New York: Cambridge University Press, 2002), pp. 156–177.

9

CHRISTOPHER VIALS

The "Race Radical" Thrust of Ethnic Proletarian Literature in the 1930s

The year 1941 saw the publication of Thomas Bell's *Out of this Furnace*, a novel covering the experiences of several generations of Slovakians and Slovakian American steel workers in Braddock, Pennsylvania. The Slovakian American author, born Adalbert Thomas Belejcak to immigrant parents in that industrial town, certainly followed the dictum "write what you know." Like so many novels of the 1930s and 1940s, its political bite comes from its simultaneous emphasis on workplace exploitation and multilayered, ethno-racial conflict. For instance, in his snapshot of Braddock steel mill neighborhoods of the 1900–1910 period, Bell sketches a pattern in which class status is ethnically marked, defining not only one's position in the factory but also one's location in the city. He writes, "When the Irish came the Americans and English, to whom sheer precedence as much as anything else now gave a near monopoly of the skilled jobs and best wages, moved to the streets above Main and into North Braddock ... New mills and furnaces were built, new supplies of labor found. The Slovaks came; and once more there was a general displacement."[1] He adds that for English-speaking peoples, "it was a disgrace to work on a level with the Hunkies," referencing an ethnic slur often leveled at Eastern European immigrants.

Had Bell been animated by different politics, he might have shown a virtuous people who rose through perseverance and hard work to claim their rightful place in the American ethnic quilt. But *Out of this Furnace* is a novel of the Popular Front generation. Its working-class Slovakian characters are perpetrators as well as victims. In the final chapter, Kracha, the first immigrant character to arrive in Braddock in the 1880s, disparages new arrivals to the neighborhood in language characteristic of the ethnic literature of the period. Kracha, now an old man, laments, "It's too bad the niggers had to come. They never bother me, but some of my neighbors have moved, especially the ones with daughters ... They all live together like so many animals." Dorta, his interlocutor and generational peer, contradicts him in equally blunt language, "The very things the Irish used to say about the Hunkies the Hunkies now say about the niggers. And for no better reason" (330). As the final chapter suggests, if Braddock's Slovakians rise, it is not through racially-coded virtue nor assimilation into American racial norms, but through the cross-ethnic, cross-racial labor alliance embodied by the newly formed Congress of Industrial Organizations (CIO), the organizational and political rebuke to the long-standing pattern of oppression and assimilation embodied by Kracha. The novel ends with a victorious strike that brings legally-protected union membership to the mills for the first time and extends that membership to all workers, regardless of their ethnoracial status or skill level. Yet the ending is nonetheless ambiguous. The final scene finds the younger protagonist Dobie content yet troubled: he worries about the future given the concentrations of corporate power that still remain and, more profoundly, about the inherently alienating nature of factory work.

In key regards, *Out of this Furnace* is indicative of the ethnic literature of the period, literature which could just as easily be classed as working class or "proletarian" literature. What one quickly notices about a reading list of proletarian novels and memoirs in the 1930s and 1940s is how many of its titles could also figure as ethnic literature. As this chapter argues, this convergence speaks to more than literary history: it also indicates a crucial historical rupture. This body of work foregrounded the ethnoracial hierarchies upon which American capitalism depended, and even its authors' limitations open up generative discussions on the dynamics of capital accumulation and racial formation in the United States. As David Roediger noted of *Out of this Furnace*, for instance, the white ethnic characters, while exploited, were not in the same position as African Americans, as Dorta suggests. While exposed to the whims of Irish American foremen, their probationary whiteness and common Catholicism gave them social access to those foremen, who ensured that they entered the factory on a higher tier than workers of color.[2]

Be that as it may, much of the ethnic literature of the 1930s and 1940s possesses what Jodi Melamed calls a "race radical" quality.

> Race radicalism originated in the forceful anticolonial and leftist antiracist movements of the 1930s and 1940s, which generated crises in the radical break period and beyond that US Cold War racial liberalism could not fully manage. Race radical antiracisms have made visible the continued racialized historical development of capitalism and have persistently foregrounded antiracist visions incompatible with liberal political solutions to destructively uneven global social-material relations.[3]

Race radical texts, she continues, differ from "liberal multicultural" ones in that they cannot be easily assimilated into dominant rubrics of diversity management. Refusing to simply "celebrate diversity" or to merely affirm cultural difference, race radical politics expose interracial conflict as structural, showing its material relationship to capitalist accumulation.

This chapter is devoted to outlining the historical and cultural sites from which mid-century ethnic/proletarian literature emerged. After mapping US racial formation in the 1930s, it locates Depression-era politics within a wider historical arc of racial capitalism, then shows how the cultural production of the period intervened to shape the contours of a historic rupture. Writers of color in this period frequently demonstrated that American capitalism depended on the super-exploitation of nonwhites. Following Manning Marable, they showed that black and brown people were not simply "excluded," but rather, that their labor and the racial ideologies directed against them generated the wealth of the system as a whole.[4] These decades were also a time when working class, white ethnic writers often strove to reject their "probationary white" status and their function as a buffer class in favor of cross-racial class solidarity. In highlighting these narrative strategies, this chapter sheds light on the noncoincidental convergence of ethnic literature and proletarian literature in the middle decades of the twentieth century.

American Racial Formation and Ethnic American Literature in the 1930s

Like Bell, the authors of proletarian/ethnic literature almost always emerged from the very communities they represented in their work, and their biographies remind us of the ways in which the American working class has been disproportionally immigrant and nonwhite in its composition.

Many writers of the 1930s were sons and daughters of the so-called second wave of European immigration in the 1890–1910 period. To date, this immigration wave was the largest in US history (as a proportion of the US population); its members hailed primarily from southern and eastern Europe and included a sizable number of east European Jews. These immigrants were what Matthew Frye Jacobson termed "probationary whites." That is to say, they were legally classified as white, which made them eligible to immigrate, vote, and own property, but they lacked social acceptance by the dominant members of civil society, which tended to block their admission into the professional middle class.[5] By the Depression, however, the number of these new immigrant arrivals considerably thinned due to a fierce nativist backlash in the 1920s. This backlash found legislative expression in the passage of two landmark immigration-restriction bills, the Quota Act of 1921 and the Johnson Reed Act of 1924, both directed primarily at southern and eastern Europeans.[6] This legislation, combined with the ravages of the economic crisis, caused a net loss in emigration during the 1930s as many migrants returned home. Thus, European ethnic enclaves of that decade contained a higher than usual number of second generation Americans who were increasingly moving out of their immigrant neighborhoods. As Michael Denning notes, they were a largely English-speaking generation, many of whom had passed through public high schools instituted in most states through Progressive-era reform.[7] Out of this ethnic matrix came 1930s Christian Eastern European writers such as Louis Adamic and Thomas Bell; Italian American writers John Fante, Pietro di Donato, and Jerre Mangione; and a host of Jewish American writers including Mike Gold, Nelson Algren, Tillie Olsen, Henry Roth, Kenneth Fearing, Lillian Hellman, Albert Halper, Joseph Freedman, Guy Endore, Jo Sinclair, Meyer Levin, Beatrice Bisno, Daniel Fuchs, Edward Dahlberg, Clifford Odets, and Arthur Miller.

At the same time, American cities and industrial towns in the Midwest and Northeast saw the arrival of significant numbers of African American migrants from the South. Successive waves of the Great Migration in the 1910s and 1920s, fueled by industrial expansion and job openings during World War I, had led to a critical mass of African Americans in urban centers in the North. With a firm foothold outside of the Jim Crow South, they created a vibrant, black public sphere of newspapers, radio programs, and magazines, all tailored to African American experience; this black public sphere formed an "imagined community" that facilitated the rise of civil rights.[8] In the 1930s and 1940s, the work of writers, poets, and playwrights such as Richard Wright, Gwendolyn Brooks, Claude McKay, Shirley Graham, Arna Bontemps, Countee Cullen, William Attaway, Langston Hughes, Ann Petry, Alice Childress, Dorothy West, and Chester Himes contributed to this new black public sphere, one that extended geographically and temporally well beyond the confines of the so-called Harlem Renaissance of the previous decade.

Restrictive immigration legislation of the 1920s also impacted the contours of two other ethnoracial groups during the Depression: Asian Americans and Mexican Americans. It is important to remember that before the Quota Act (1921) and the Johnson Reed Act (1924), there were no limits to the number of immigrants admitted to the United States. The Naturalization Law of 1790 restricted citizenship to "any alien, being a free white person," ensuring an immigrant flow overwhelmingly European in origin that lasted from the beginning of the republic up until the passage of the Immigration and Nationality Act of 1965. As Mae Ngai reminds us, this legislation created the very category of the illegal alien, along with the institution of the Border Patrol and the legal apparatus of detention.[9]

Be that as it may, Mexicans and people of Mexican descent living in the United States were considered "white" by law; as a result, they freely crossed the border before the 1920s and had a sizeable presence in the Southwest dating back to before US annexation and the Treaty of Guadalupe Hidalgo (1848). Though Mexicans were exempt from quota restrictions of the 1920s legislation, their border crossings were subject to increased scrutiny along the newly militarized border. The Mexican Revolution created a refugee exodus from Mexico, causing the number of Mexicans living in the United States to jump from 224,000 in 1910 to 651,000 in 1920. While this influx was welcomed by large landowners in need of labor, it incensed white small farmers; with the onset of the Depression, it also angered poor whites desperate for the kinds of agricultural jobs they had previously scorned. As nativist tempers flared across the southwest, immigration authorities put into motion a complex administrative apparatus that "repatriated" four hundred thousand persons of Mexican descent in the early 1930s, one-half of whom were US citizens (52. 64–75).

By and large, English-speaking readers would have to wait beyond the 1930s for a Mexican American prose that could index such experiences. Josefina Niggli's collection *Mexican Village* appeared in 1945 and was one of the first literary works to introduce the lives of Mexican and Mexican American border-crossing protagonists to a national US audience. Other Mexican American writers who translated their generational experience of the 1930s would have to wait decades to find an audience for their stories. Américo Paredes wrote *George Washington Gomez: A Mexico-Texan Novel* in 1940, yet it did not find a publisher until 1990. Similarly, *Barrio Boy*, Ernesto Galarza's story of his migration from a small Mexican village to Sacramento, California, set partly in the 1920–1940 period, did not appear until 1971. In both cases, it took the Chicano movement of the late 1960s and early 1970s to make their stories legible to publishers.

Asian American writers of the period were only nominally more fortunate in their dealings with the publishing industry, though they also faced brutal racialization in the United States. In the 1930s, most people of Asian descent in the United States lived in Hawaii or the West Coast and had roots in either China, Japan, or the Philippines. Due to the colonial relationship, Filipinos were considered "US Nationals" with the ability to travel and seek work in the United States, albeit without the possibility of citizenship. Their numbers on the US mainland swelled in the late 1920s as large Western landowners sought new sources of labor to replace those kept out by the new border controls;[10] by the 1930s, Filipinos formed a larger share of the agricultural proletariat on the West Coast, often working in the fields alongside Mexican, Chinese, and Japanese laborers. As Bulosan's *America is in the Heart* illustrates, Chinese and Japanese communities on the West Coast during that decade were more established than the newer Filipino enclaves. New arrivals from China and Japan were ineligible for citizenship, as they were not legally classed as "free, white, persons," yet many Chinese and Japanese with deeper roots in the country had gained a foothold as United States citizens thanks to an unintended consequence of the Fourteenth Amendment. Aimed at emancipating former slaves, this constitutional amendment granted citizenship to anyone born in the United States, thus even children born to aliens ineligible for citizenship could gain legal status in the country.

Be that as it may, all of these Asian groups suffered under nativist legislation that grew in intensity during the 1920s and 1930s. Chinese workers were still barred from entering the country under the Chinese Exclusion Act of 1882 – the first immigrant act to bar a specific nationality – which was not repealed until 1943. Western states passed various alien land laws, tacitly aimed at Chinese and Japanese immigrants, that prohibited "aliens ineligible for citizenship" from purchasing land. The 1930s saw a wave of state and federal legislation aimed at Filipinos, who were more recent arrivals to the United States. Driven by nativists on the West Coast, the most consequential of these laws were the federal Tydings-McDuffie Act (1934), which limited Filipino immigration to a mere fifty people per year and the Filipino Repatriation Act (1935) under which any Filipino who left the country was not allowed re-entry.[11]

Despite this oppressive domestic atmosphere, international events gave Asian American writers a few openings for their work. The Pacific War (1937–1945) put Asia in the international headlines: images of Chinese bodies and cities eviscerated by Japanese bombs during Japan's invasion of the mainland in 1937, combined with the wartime alliance with China and the Philippines after December 1941, gave Chinese and Filipino authors a small window of access to a sympathetic US audience.[12] Chinese-born H. T. Tsiang took advantage of this window to publish his novel about a laundryman in New York, *And China Has Hands* (1937). His earlier and more surreal novel *The Hanging in Union Square* (1935) was self-published. Filipino American poet José Garcia Villa published the short story collection *Footnote to Youth: Tales of the Philippines and Others* in 1933, yet Filipino American literature only came into its own after the US entrance into World War II. The 1940s saw the publication of Villa's poetry collection *Have Come, Am Here* (1942) as well as Carlos Bulosan's many essays and works, including the short story collection *Laughter of My Father* (1944) and the auto-ethnographic *America is in the Heart* (1946). Japanese American writers, infamously incarcerated as "enemies from within" during the war, had to wait until after hostilities ceased to find publishers for their work: the list of such authors includes Sadakichi Hartmann, Toyo Suyemoto, Toshio Mori, Hisaye Yamamoto, Miné Okubo, and John Okada.[13] Toshio Mori's collection *Yokohama, California* (1949), which documented Japanese American life in California before the incarceration, was largely composed in the late 1930s and early 1940s. The work of Bulosan, Tsiang, and Mori in particular form a distinctly Asian American working-class prose literature of the Popular Front era.

Challenging Deep Structures of Racial Capitalism

While the United States entered the Depression with deep racial structures, some of which intensified over the course of the decade, this is not the whole story. As indicated by the proliferation of new ethnic American literary works in the 1930s, there was also widespread resistance against those structures that took a distinctly intersectional hue. They challenged class exploitation and ethnoracial hierarchy at the same time, and they did so because they seemed to recognize a deeply rooted historical truth: that racial consciousness lay at the very origins of capitalism.

According to Theodore Allen, modern conceptions of race were forged in the early capitalist English settlements in the New World in the late seventeenth century. In the Chesapeake Bay in North America and in the West Indies, the English bourgeoisie found that it could not ensure social control in an environment where all laborers were equally immiserated. The system of bond labor they devised in the early seventeenth century, which bound Europeans and Africans alike, broke down with the multiracial revolt of Bacon's Rebellion in 1676. Thereafter, slave codes would introduce divisions among laborers by establishing the black body as a marker of the most degraded forms of labor, thus spawning a system in which people classed as nonwhite were to be relegated to lowest tiers of the workforce. The corollary to this system of racial capitalism was the creation of a buffer class – what Allen terms the "intermediate stratum" – whose members would be given police roles and relative privileges, and thus would ally with the bourgeoisie on the basis of race and help them enforce the system of accumulation. In the West Indies, the creoles formed this buffer class; in Spanish America, it was the *caciques;* in North America, it was poor and middle-class whites. Thus was the white race created in the English New World.[14]

Racial hierarchy is thus the creation of modern capitalism. Moreover, because race has been essential to the political and cultural hegemony of the ruling class, it is a material force that facilitates the accumulation of wealth. This system of social control – what Cedric Robinson called "racial capitalism"[15] – persists to this day and has proven remarkably difficult to challenge. But the challenge has come at various points of US history during periods of multiracial organizing: with abolition in the antebellum period, with civil rights and the radical movements of the late 1960s, and with the Popular Front of the 1930s and 1940s. In each case, not only do marginalized groups attempt to secure "rights," but a whole system of accumulation is compromised as the class alliance between elite and nonelite whites breaks down. Culture, as we will see, plays an important role in this rupture.

Left-wing movements organized around worker power, antiracism, and antifascism – retroactively labeled "the Popular Front" by Michael Denning – were on the rise in the 1930s, and their successes, in part, were built upon questioning the racial and ethnic hierarchies upon which American capitalism was built. This movement made a tremendous political impact by acting as a force from below that enabled New Deal and pro-labor legislation. Indeed, in terms of political influence, Denning sees the 1930s as the historical high-water mark of the American left (xvii). During the Cold War, the movements of the period were frequently dismissed as a Moscow-driven plot: liberal and conservative Cold Warriors quickly rescripted the Popular Front as a coalition of naïve, fellow-travelling "pinks" deceptively led by a hidden "red" core of communist cadres (4–6). While the term Popular Front indeed came from the Communist International, the organizations that carried left and liberal politics in the period were diverse in ideology and membership, and they frequently disagreed over priorities and ideas. They included labor unions like the American Federation of Labor and the new Congress of Industrial Organizations (CIO), founded in 1935; racial justice groups like the National Negro Congress (NNC), the National Association for the Advancement of Colored People (NAACP), and El Congreso del Pueblo de Habla Española (Congress of Spanish Speaking Peoples); and political parties like the Socialist Party, the American Labor Party, the Socialist Workers Party, and the Communist Party of the United States (CPUSA).

In the 1930s, labor union and socialist organizing was attuned to race in ways that the country had not seen since the onset of its industrial revolution. The organizing campaigns of the CIO and the CPUSA in particular called attention to racial divisions among the working class in ways that previous class-based organizations like the AFL and the American Socialist Party had typically ignored or even widened. In the late nineteenth century, for example, the AFL actively participated in Chinese and Japanese exclusion campaigns, and as part of this effort, its President Samuel Gompers published the infamous 1902 pamphlet: "Meat vs. Rice: American Manhood against Asiatic Coolieism. Which Shall Survive?" By contrast, the CIO, founded in 1935, fought against the very use of race and ethnicity to mark class position, a long-standing shopfloor reality that Bell highlighted in his novel. With some exceptions, the older AFL had organized its locals by trade, not workplace. This practice ensured that the organization represented only skilled laborers and thus reinforced the ethnic and gender divisions on the shopfloor. The AFL tended to use union power, in other words, to widen the gap in pay between male German, Irish, and Anglo workers and everyone else. The CIO, by contrast, organized workers of all skill-levels into the same bargaining unit based on where they worked, a practice that brought skilled machinists, unskilled assembly line workers, and even janitors – and hence men and women, black and white, new immigrant and native – into a common organization.

Meanwhile, the CPUSA, unlike the older American Socialist Party, became a genuinely multiracial organization by highlighting colonialism and white supremacy as tools of the bourgeoisie that ultimately degraded all workers. The CPUSA even endorsed a form of black nationalism with its "Black Belt Thesis." In 1928, the Sixth World Congress of the Comintern passed a resolution stating that African Americans in "black belt" counties of the US South were an oppressed nation and thus had a right to self-determination.[16] This thesis is sometimes remembered for its unrealistic advocacy of a black-led republic in the US South, which did little to attract black working-class support. But its importance goes far beyond its spatial politics, for the thesis and the Party's broader program contradicted decades of white socialist practice that deemed race epiphenomenal to questions of class. This position was expressed in detail in the CP publication, *Negro Liberation* (1938), written by Jewish American communist James Allen (born Sol Auerbach):

> It is a misconception still too common in the labor movement that the solution of the Negro question differs in no essential respects from the solution of the labor problem as such, and if the demands of the white workers are met, those of the Negro workers will also be satisfied at the same time ... When applied in practice this view unavoidably leads to deserting the fight of the Negroes for equal rights and to capitulating to white chauvinism. For such a placing of the question ignores those extra demands, *over and above those of the white workers*, which arise from the super-exploited conditions of the Negro masses.[17]

While Allen was clear that "sections of white workers indirectly benefited from the super-exploitation of the Negroes," he also argued that addressing the specifics of black racial exploitation would benefit the working class as a whole. Prior black liberation struggles of the Reconstruction era, he stressed, had extended democracy to poor whites as well (9, 42).

Such emphasis on cross-racial and pan-ethnic class alliance was facilitated by two main factors: the formation of sizable black communities in northern cities along with their emergent, politicized public sphere, and the anticolonial bent of the Communist International in the early 1930s and its impact on class radicals in the United States, even outside the Party (for instance, communists not only influenced the CIO's organizing strategy but also had a hand in the federation's establishment).[18] Combined with the general left turn in American politics during the Depression, a turn that tends to make people look up the social ladder rather than down for the source of their problems, these politics gave the multitude of new immigrants and their children a politics of collective advancement that challenged the simple assimilation to racial norms evidenced by Kracha in *Out of this Furnace*.

Ultimately, however, the limitations of the New Deal ensured that southern and east European mobility would be in the form of whiteness. As has been abundantly documented, signature New Deal reforms like the Fair Labor Standards Act (1938) and the Social Security Act (1935) excluded domestic and farm workers, who were overwhelmingly people of color. And the benefits of the Aid to Dependent Children program (established in 1935) and the National Housing Act (1934) were distributed very unevenly by discriminatory program administrators.[19] Overall, while most working-class people benefited from the labor and social democratic reforms of the 1930s and 1940s, racial divisions of work and income remained. Most nonwhite workers also benefited from the reforms of the era – their incomes and material standing indeed rose, especially as more and more African Americans left the South for newly accessible union jobs in the North. By one estimate, black wages were rising twice as fast as those of their white coworkers by the end of the war, mainly because of the democratization of unions and the extension of labor protections beyond high wage industries like steel and auto.[20] Widespread formal and informal segregation in housing and employment remained, however.

Yet the meaning of the cross-racial class alliances of the 1930s and 1940s cannot be reduced to how the New Deal state responded to their demands. What these coalitions represented was a challenge to the racial foundations of capitalism; they opened a breach that would be widened by black freedom and people of color movements in the decades that followed.

A Cultural Front

Many of the artists and writers of the decade yoked themselves to these movements. They devoted their work to the long-term project of creating new cultural values that would accompany the Popular Front's more immediate legislative and organizational goals, forming what Denning called "the cultural front" of the movement. In the literary realm, each novel or memoir typically told the working-class stories of a particular place, a specific trade, or a particular ethnic group; in so doing, each author aimed to make experiential connections beyond the boundaries of their own factories, towns, and neighborhoods, creating a new class-conscious, national fabric from the ravages of the Depression.

Ever since the generation of scholars publishing in the 1980s and 1990s opened the canon of twentieth century American literature beyond a handful of high modernists praised by New Critics, one is likely to encounter the term "proletarian literature" when discussing literary output in the 1930s.

In contemporary Soviet writings, the purpose of "proletarian literature" was to document the experiences of oppressed workers in capitalist countries and to identify emergent dynamics leading to their liberation; by contrast, "socialist literature," aligned with socialist realism, was to monumentalize the worker in socialist countries while also identifying his/her ongoing struggles. In the first half of the 1930s, writers aligned with the communist currents, inspired by the Proletkult literary movement of the Communist International, tended to take the term "proletarian literature" quite literally to mean working class writers telling their stories, and telling them in a way that would help accelerate the demise of capitalism. In the middle of the decade, this subject position-based definition of "proletarian" was revised through a lively debate in left-wing literary circles. In the pages of cultural journals such as *The New Masses, Partisan Review*, and *Anvil*, some argued that the term "proletarian" should be reserved for writers from working class backgrounds who wrote from their own experiences, albeit with a political, anticapitalist edge. Others argued that "proletarian" was defined less by the author's class background and more by their politics: in this view, the term would apply to most writers who devoted their work to the anticapitalist struggle, regardless of their subject matter or class position. By 1935, the latter definition held more sway, which opened the way for middle class writers such as John Steinbeck or socialist writers on middle-class life such as Josephine Herbst and James T. Farrell to be classed as "proletarian writers," even in communist circles. Yet, ironically, as political perspective became the crucial determinant, the term "proletarian literature" appeared with less and less frequency, even in communist cultural journals like *The New Masses*.[21]

While the Communist Party of the United States (CPUSA) enjoyed an unprecedented influence in the 1930s and 1940s, many on the left were unaffiliated with it, and anticapitalist and antiracist writers of the period typically published their work and received critical praise or scorn regardless of what the Party thought of their work. Indeed, the idea that writers submitted themselves and their literary content to Party discipline is a Cold War cliché that has long been debunked by scholars of the period.[22] Nonetheless, for those in the orbit of the CPUSA press, the consciously intersectional rubric of the Black Belt Thesis and slogans such as "Black and White Unite and Fight" proved quite influential, especially as they intersected with the rise of an emergent black public sphere and the organizational culture of the CIO.

African American writers in the 1930s and 1940s took pains to show, as Allen wrote, "those extra demands, *over and above those of the white workers*, which arise from the super-exploited conditions of the Negro masses." While contributing to a class-conscious, proletarian literature, they in no way minimized conditions of racial oppression; moreover, they subjected white and black leftists who did so to ruthless critique. For example, Richard Wright's collection *Uncle Tom's Children* (1938) focuses almost entirely on the mechanisms and brutality of Jim Crow racism in the South. Its final stories "Fire and Cloud" and "Bright and Morning Star" point to cross-racial organizing amongst the working class as the way forward. Yet, at the same time, it demonstrates that a 'class only' approach that minimizes racial struggle is naïve. In "Bright and Morning Star," for instance, African American communist organizer Johnny Boy castigates his mother Sue for referring to black people as "our folks." He tells her, "Ma, Ah done tol yuh a hundred times. Ah cant see white n Ah cant see black ... Ah sees rich men n Ah sees po men."[23] Yet it is Johnny Boy's colorblind faith that proves naive. He ignores Sue's caution about trusting unfamiliar whites and unwittingly lets a white informant know the location of a communist meeting; this blind trust ultimately leads vigilantes to their location, where the mob kills mother and son alike. Viewed in the context of fleeting moments of successful cross-racial collaboration and black militancy at earlier moments in the collection, this final plot turn of *Uncle Tom's Children* manages to avoid a strict black nationalism and a colorblind socialism; it suggests instead a pragmatic class politics that attends to the realities of racial hierarchy and racial abjection.

Wright was a member of the CPUSA at the time he wrote the collection, and his attention to racialized class oppression and his emphasis on African Americans as the vanguard of the revolution in the South was fully in line with the Black Belt Thesis. He would extend such politics in his more famous *Native Son* (1940), which castigates white leftists and liberals for their naïve and paternalistic racial attitudes. Through the character Henry Dalton, a white philanthropist and landlord, the novel also suggests that Chicago's elites owe their wealth directly to the extraction of inflated rents from the city's black working class. The racial ordering of urban space, which forces

African Americans to live in only a few select areas, drives up the rent for black tenants and concentrates wealth in the hands of a white, rentier class.

The drive to show the "extra demands" and "super-exploited conditions" of people of color was not limited to African American writers. H. T. Tsiang's *And China Has Hands* (1937) continues this impulse as well. Born into poverty in the Jiangsu Province of China, Tsiang immigrated to the United States as a young man, where he continued his education at Stanford and Columbia and lived the rest of his life, working as a Hollywood actor frequently cast in stereotypical Asian roles.[24] His novel *And China Has Hands* follows the life of a Chinese laundryman in New York, Wong Wan-Lee, and describes in detail his daily routine of never-ending labor from dawn to dusk. Tsiang writes that every evening, Wan-Lee "retired to the back room [of his laundry], washed cooked, ate, and slept. Day in and day out, year in and year out, that is the life of a Chinese laundryman, and Wong Wan-Lee was one of them."[25] At the same time, the author makes clear that white supremacy is what keeps Wan-Lee in his super-exploited, proletarian position. His desire to save money is repeatedly thwarted by the machinations of whites: namely, a building inspector who demands exorbitant bribes and the white laundrymen who spread vicious rumors about their Chinese competitors. There is not a single positive white character in the entire book; more than this, apart from the building inspector and a waiter named "Butcher Face," mentioned only in passing, there are no white characters in the novel at all. Tsiang does not see racial supremacy as a uniquely American problem, however: white racists in *And China Has Hands* join forces with Japanese and Chinese fascists who share their racial theories. In the end, the novel ends, like so many of its generation, with a strike: but here, it is a multiracial strike against a Chinese American cafeteria owner who had fired Wan-Lee's Afro Asian girlfriend because she was an affront to "national race purity" (102). In this literary instance, Tsiang thus uses antifascism as a way to articulate the racialized nature of capitalism not simply within the United States but on a global scale.

Emerging from a more advantaged position, white ethnic authors of the Popular Front often challenged racial capitalism by symbolically rejecting their historic function as members of a buffer class. By embracing working class solidarity and striving (although not always successfully) to overcome their own racial training vis-à-vis people of color, they rejected the road to assimilation traditionally available to probationary whites, one premised on possessive individualism and the acquisition of unequivocal white status. It is important to note here the prevalence of titles by Jewish Americans in the list of proletarian/ethnic literature of the 1930s. Alan M. Wald estimates that nearly 50 percent of the authors in the Communist-led literary movement in the United States were Jewish Americans, a surprising number given that Jews comprised only 2–3 percent of the US population at that time. He attributes this strong Jewish participation to a number of factors, including the historical ties to socialist movements in Europe that Jewish immigrants brought over with them; the appeal of pan-ethnic, communist universalism to young men and women trying to break free from ghetto isolation and orthodox elders; the threat of fascism in Europe and the militant role of the communist movement in opposing it; and finally, the fact that the publishing industry and the largest Jewish population in the United States were located in the same place: New York City.[26]

Out of this metropolis came what is probably the most distinctive Jewish American proletarian prose piece of the period: Mike Gold's autobiographical *Jews without Money* (1930). Its author, born Itzok Isaac Granich, was an early editor of *The New Masses* and regular writer for *The Daily Worker*, where he regularly commented on literary matters and opined on "proletarian literature." His status as a popular speaker and debater cemented his national reputation, prompting Wald to write: "no single individual contributed more to forging the tradition of proletarian literature as a genre in the United States after the 1920s. All who came after Gold would stand on the shoulders of his legacy."[27] Published at the very beginning of the decade, *Jews without Money* established the tone for the many ethnic/proletarian novels to follow. Set at the turn of the century, it follows the struggles of young "Mikey," his family, and his peers in the immigrant ghettoes of the Lower East Side of Manhattan. Like so other ethnic works of the period, its message is a paradoxical amalgam: it seeks to elevate and preserve what is best of the author's ethnic culture, yet at the same time, it rejects ethnic nationalism in favor of cross-ethnoracial, working class unity in opposition to the ruling class.

Prefiguring multiculturalism, the book wistfully celebrates elements of East European Jewish immigrant culture, particularly its speaking and storytelling modes. "Talk has ever been the joy of the Jewish race," he writes, "great torrents of boundless exalted talk. Talk does not exhaust Jews as it does other people, nor give them brain fag; it refreshes them. Talk is the baseball, the golf, the poker, the love and the war of the Jewish race."[28] Yet Gold is quite critical of other practices within the community: particularly orthodox religion and the Zionism it offers as a solution to Jewish American alienation and misery. Clearly, Gold was drawn more to secular Jewish culture and the storytelling modes it offered him as a writer than the extant practices of Jewish religion (although, as we will see, Judaic notions of the Messiah structure his revolutionary solution).

Thus, for Gold, Jewish culture is not something simply to be negated on the path to revolutionary transformation. Yet at the same time, he is quite clear that the solution to the poverty and misery of the ghetto is not to be found solely within his own community, nor, of course, can it be achieved through assimilation to the dominant American culture and its narrative of immigrant success. His father Herman's failed interpolation within these latter ideological fantasies structures much of the book. Herman, a struggling painter and naïve optimist, dismisses socialist talk in the neighborhood and instead tries to emulate wealthy Jews that he knows: Baruch Goldfarb, "a Zionist leader and the owner of a big dry goods store" (207), and his boss, Zechariah Cohen. When Herman falls sick with "the painter's nausea," a common affliction of the trade, neither of his heroes come to his aid. The final chapters of the book find Herman still struggling from his afflictions, afflictions directly attributable to his exploitation at the hands of those he admired. Struggling to make ends meet as a lowly banana peddler, he becomes the embodiment of the pitfalls of Zionism and American immigrant success narratives; his story is the tragedy of a misguided political alliance with any bourgeoisie, be it Jewish or Christian.

As a narrative of the left turn in American literature, Gold's book advocates lateral alliances amongst the exploited. Interethnic strife between East European Jews and other white ethnic groups permeates the story. We are told from an early point that Mikey and his "little gang of Yids" could not enter Irish or Italian neighbors without fear of a beating; they, in turn, beat any outsiders who entered their neighborhood as well. Mikey's mother, far more practical than his father, suggests a way out of such parochialism: she not only rebukes Herman's blind faith in the rich but also his blanket rejection of Christians. She overcomes his contempt of an Irish family in their tenement once she recognizes that they too were dispossessed in their countries of origin: "And Herman," she says, "that woman used to gather mushrooms in the forest in Ireland. Just the way I gathered them in Hungary" (171).

But the gestures of alliance do not end with the other white ethnic groups in his immediate environment. More complex and coded are the ways that *Jews without Money* rejects the racial path to assimilation afforded to probationary white immigrants. A key character in Mikey's gang is a boy named "Nigger": his very name is admission of the racism within the Lower East Side. Yet Nigger paradoxically functions as a rebuke of antiblack racism through the way Gold renders his symbolic blackness. The gang gives him this name because of his dark complexion and because of his utterly abject poverty: his family is the poorest and most exploited in the neighborhood (261). Yet, as in the Party's writings on negro liberation, this symbolic figuration of blackness becomes the vanguard of the resistance. "Nigger" becomes the defender of the neighborhood as he punishes its oppressors both within and without. Far from functioning as a traditional minstrel, he punches an anti-Semitic school teacher on the nose for calling Mikey "a little kike," and as an adult, he kills the Jewish gangster Louis One Eye who had plagued the neighborhood.

On a more fundamental level, however, Gold's protagonist rejects the settler colonial logic that interpolates white immigrants by refusing to play the game of cowboy and Indian. The narrator reveals that Buffalo Bill "was my hero then; I was reading the gaudy little paper books that described his adventures." His American pop cultural education teaches him to read ethnoracial conflict in the terms of this settler colonial fantasy. He explains his decision to return home by way of Mulberry Street one day as a brave one because "That was the land of the hereditary enemy – the Italians lived there. I might be killed. But Buffalo Bill would have gone by way of Mulberry Street." He imagines himself rescuing "a beautiful white maiden" from their clutches, and when the Italians do eventually attack him, he writes that "they surrounded me, whooping like Indians." He ends the chapter by writing "I needed a Messiah who would look like Buffalo Bill, and who could annihilate our enemies" (186–190).

The final lines of the book return to the Messiah, a figure he learned about through his mother's religious instruction. Gold writes, "O workers' Revolution ... You are the true Messiah. You will destroy the East Side when you come, and build there a garden for the human spirit" (309). Gold can be faulted for failing to concretely figure nonwhiteness in sympathetic nonwhite characters. But the resolution of the book rejects the buffer class role for probationary whites using a less conventional tact. It suggests that the "way out" is through the destruction of the very grammar of division amongst the marginalized afforded by US popular culture, a grammar structured by the false messiahs of bourgeoisie emulation and by the settler colonial imaginary of Buffalo Bill. Rather than enforcing the nation's hierarchical structure by playing the role of cowboy – which gives one the right to render one's ethnoracial rivals as "Indians" and destroy them – Mikey's story and its conclusion promotes a revolution in which the best of one's ethnoreligious culture can be preserved through a socialist synthesis that will eliminate hierarchies among peoples.

Perhaps what is most striking about the proletarian/ethnic novels of the period, their most race radical feature, is their long historical memory. Bell references the immigrant waves of the English, the Irish, and the east Europeans, each serving as cheap labor in their day. Of his neighborhood, Gold writes "The red Indians once inhabited the East Side; then came the Dutch, the English, the Irish, then the Germans, Italians, and Jews. Each group left its deposits, as in geology" (180). More than a decade later, Carlos Bulosan would write, "We are all Americans that have toiled and suffered and known oppression and defeat, from the first Indian that offered peace in Manhattan to the last Filipino pea pickers."[29] These authors were aware that their stories, and the ethnoracial conflict that figured so prominently in them, entered a long history of migration and exploitation that developed its patterns long before they were born. Beyond merely advancing the antifascist campaigns and labor organizing drives of their day, they labored to break a hellishly repetitive cycle, a cycle that would turn the immigrant of today into the oppressor of tomorrow, and that would extend the violence against black and brown bodies and souls into perpetuity. They did so, in part, by directing attention up the social ladder, to those who profited from the system and set it in motion, not across or down at the person next door whose labor created the wealth and security that so few people, of any race, seemed to truly enjoy. Since race continues to be a marker of class – and thus of a socio-political logic that enables each cycle of accumulation to complete its grisly circuit – the proletarian/ethnic novel of the Popular Front has become another geological layer that we would do well to excavate.

NOTES

1 Thomas Bell, *Out of This Furnace* (Pittsburgh: University of Pittsburgh Press, 1976), 122.
2 David Roediger, *Working toward Whiteness: How America's Immigrants became White* (New York: Basic Books, 2005), 123–124.
3 Jodi Melamed, *Represent and Destroy: Rationalizing Violence in the New Racial Capitalism* (Minneapolis: University of Minnesota Press, 2011), xvii.
4 Manning Marable, *How Capitalism Underdeveloped Black America: Problems in Race, Political Economy and Society*, 1983 (Boston, MA: South End Press, 1999), 2, 7.
5 Matthew Frye Jacobson, *Whiteness of a Different Color: European Immigrants and the Alchemy of Race* (Cambridge, MA: Harvard University Press, 1999).
6 Mae Ngai, *Impossible Subjects: Illegal Aliens and the Making of Modern America* (Princeton: Princeton University Press, 2004), ch. 1.
7 Michael Denning's *Cultural Front: The Laboring of American Culture in the Twentieth Century* (London: Verso, 1997), 7, 60–61, n. 485.
8 Bill Mullen, *Black Popular Fronts: Chicago and African-American Cultural Politics, 1935–46* (Urbana-Champaign: University of Illinois Press, 1999), ch. 2. The term "imagined communities" is taken here from Benedict Anderson's *Imagined Communities: Reflection on the Origin and Spread of Nationalism* (London: Verso, 1983).
9 Ngai, *Impossible Subjects*, chs. 1–2.
10 Mae Ngai, "From Colonial Subject to Undesirable Alien: Filipino Migration, Exclusion, and Repatriation, 1920–1940, *Re-collecting Early Asian America*,

ed. Josephine Lee and Imogene Lim, et al. (Philadelphia: Temple University Press, 2002), 114.

11 On restrictive legislation aimed at Filipinos, see Ngai (2002).

12 Chris Vials, *Realism for the Masses: Aesthetics, Popular Front Pluralism, and U.S. Culture, 1935–1947* (Jackson: University of Mississippi Press, 2009) 111–113.

13 See Floyd Cheung, "Good Asian/Bad Asian: Asian American Racial Formation," *American Literature in Transition: 1940–1950*, ed. Christopher Vials (Cambridge: Cambridge University Press, 2018).

14 Theodore Allen, *The Invention of the White Race, Volume II: The Origin of Racial Oppression in Anglo-America* [1997] (London: Verso, 2012).

15 Cedric Robinson, *Black Marxism: The Making of the Black Radical Tradition*. 1983 (Chapel Hill: University of North Carolina Press, 2000), 2.

16 Robin D. G. Kelley, *Race Rebels: Culture, Politics, and the Black Working Class* (New York: The Free Press, 1996), 109, 115.

17 James Allen, *Negro Liberation* (New York, International Publishers, 1938), 27.

18 Fraser Ottanelli, *The Communist Party of the United States: From the Depression to World War II* (New Brunswick, NJ: Rutgers University Press, 1991), 47–48.

19 Roediger, *Working toward Whiteness*, 206, 210, 224–234.

20 On overall progress for the US working class from the Depression to World War II, see Lizbeth Cohen, *A Consumers' Republic: The Politics of Mass Consumption on Postwar America* (New York: Alfred Knopf, 2003), 69–71. On black and white wage comparisons, see Nelson Lichtenstein, "Class Politics and the State during World War II," *International Labor and Working-Class History* 58 (Fall 2000), 264.

21 This account is wholly indebted to Barbara Foley, *Radical Representations: Politics and Form in US Proletarian Fiction, 1929–1941* (Durham, NC: Duke University Press, 1993), ch. 3.

22 Denning, *Cultural Front*, 4–21; Foley, *Radical Representations*, 44–85; Vials, *Realism for the Masses*, xxvii–xxviii. On a similar dynamic within political organizing, see Robin D. G. Kelley, *Hammer and Hoe: Alabama Communists During the Great Depression* (Chapel Hill: University of North Carolina Press, 1990), 119–151.

23 Richard Wright, *Uncle Tom's Children*, 1938 (New York: HarperPerennial, 1993), 234.

24 Floyd Cheung, introduction to *And China Has Hands* (Forest Hills, NY: Iron Weed Press, 2003), and Alan M. Wald, "Introduction to H.T. Tsiang," *Into the Fire: Asian American Prose*, ed. Sylvia Watanabe and Carol Bruhac (New York: Greenfield Review Press, 1996).

25 H. T. Tsiang, *And China Has Hands* (Forest Hills, NY: Iron Weed Press, 2003), 27.

26 Alan M. Wald, "Jewish American Writers on the Left," *The Cambridge Companion to Jewish American Literature*, ed. Hana Wirth-Nesher and Michael Kramer (Cambridge: Cambridge University Press, 2003), 171–172.

27 Alan M. Wald, *Exiles from a Future Time: The Forging of the Mid-Twentieth-Century Literary Left* (Chapel Hill: University of North Carolina Press, 2002), 39.

28 Mike Gold, *Jews without Money*, 1930 (New York: Carroll and Graf, 1998), 112–113.

29 Carlos Bulosan, *America is in the Heart*, 1946 (Seattle: University of Washington Press, 189).

10

NATHANIEL MILLS

African American Historical Writing in the Depression

As Ralph Ellison's protagonist navigates Depression-era New York in *Invisible Man* (1952), he comes across the eviction of an elderly African American couple, the Provos. Their possessions, piled on the sidewalk, include "a small Ethiopian flag, a faded tintype of Abraham Lincoln," a headline about Marcus Garvey's deportation, and, finally, Primus Provo's manumission papers, dated 1859. The protagonist is startled by how these items suggest that the arc of modern black history is uncannily telescoped into the span of one lifetime. *"It has been longer than that, further removed in time,"* the protagonist thinks of slavery, "yet I knew that it hadn't been."[1] If Provo, a former slave, is still living in 1930s New York where he is still subject to racial and economic marginalization, then the history of African Americans is one long period of contemporaneity, and the past is not past but alive, visible, and continuous with the present. This scene reads as Ellison's own recollection of the Great Depression, when black writers, critics (including Ellison himself), and historians were preoccupied with the representation of a history whose role in conditioning the present, and ability to offer usable epistemological and political resources, was undeniable. *Invisible Man*'s protagonist is conscious of the immediacy of the historical, and as the setting of the novel suggests, such consciousness was a major influence on black thought and expression during the Depression.

That consciousness resembles what Georg Lukács called "the feeling for history, the awareness of historical development" that arose in Napoleonic-era Europe. In his analysis of the originating contexts of this sociocultural "feeling," Lukács identifies "the concrete possibilities for men to comprehend their own existence as something historically conditioned, for them to see in history something which deeply affects their daily lives and immediately concerns them." As a result, historical fiction of the early nineteenth century no longer invoked the past as "mere costumery" superficially distinct from the present. Instead, novelists like Walter Scott depicted "the specifically historical," the way in which socioeconomic arrangements of past moments shaped the psychology, culture, and political consciousness of individuals and classes in those moments.[2] For Lukács, the modern historical novel renders the past in terms of Marxism's materialist understanding of history, whose engine of development is not great individuals or national destinies but the actions of the masses, whose agency is determined by and responds to conditions that define both the particularity of past periods as well as the emergence of the present from out of those periods.

During the 1930s, a cognate of Lukács's "specifically historical" consciousness emerged in the works of prominent black critics, writers, and historians who engaged in representing the history of people of African descent in the United States and the Caribbean. These writers grasped that history as a narrative of the movement of the black masses through moments of social and economic struggle linked by developing material conditions. For these writers this history both illuminates the origins of the present and suggests possible paths of future development. At the same time, writers often engaged in historiographical struggle against the racist agendas of hegemonic white-authored histories and historical fictions. Ellison's Depression-era protagonist is struck with a certain "feeling for history" arising from his recognition of the particular arc and present implications of black history. Black writers and historians of the 1930s were similarly motivated and sought to illuminate the historical origins of the present and suggest resources for plotting history's way out of the racial and economic oppressions of the Depression.

Many African American writers during the Depression were connected with the literary organs and associations of the Communist left.[3] As a result, their literary and historical sensibilities were influenced by Marxism's law of history as a progression, animated by class struggle, from feudalism to capitalism to socialism; and by Marxism's more general conviction that history is the source of revolutionary possibilities and perspectives. In addition, Depression-era African American writers were often eager to distance themselves from the Harlem Renaissance. In the 1930s an analytical engagement with history, informed by Marxism and by the political culture of the black masses, seemed a modern and scientific alternative to what was widely seen as the bourgeois limitations of the writers of the preceding decade. In 1941, Ellison voiced his generation's consensus when he wrote that "American Negro fiction of the 1920's was timid of theme, and for the most part technically backward, ... apologetic in tone and narrowly confined to the expression of Negro middle class ideals."[4] Richard Wright, in "Blueprint for Negro Writing" (1937), wrote that "a Marxist analysis of society" that sees reality as conflictual and subject to historical change can ground a modern mode of black writing in touch with the radical intuitions of the folk and surpassing the "humble" works of previous black writers.[5] Finally, in this turn to history, black writers were participating in a wider cultural trend: historical fiction was a bestselling genre during the 1930s, a decade whose unique sociopolitical challenges – how did we get to this point, and how do we move beyond it? – brought historical representation to the forefront of US culture.

This essay examines how Depression-era black literary criticism and historical discourse approached the past in order to undermine racist distortions of black history as well as to enable revolutionary thought and practice in the present. It concludes with a reading of the representational strategies of two prominent African American historical novels by Arna Bontemps: *Black Thunder* (1936), about the attempted 1800 Virginia slave revolt led by Gabriel, and *Drums at Dusk* (1939), set in the opening stages of the Haitian Revolution in 1791. Identifying this "feeling for history" extends disciplinary periodizations of the 1930s in African American letters beyond narrower generic lenses of naturalism or social protest, and invites other considerations of the operations of historical consciousness in twentieth-century African American writing.

Capturing "The Historical Process as a Whole": History in Depression-Era African American Literary Discourse

Informing many discussions of African American writing in the Depression was the general expectation, explicit or implicit, that Marxist historical theory enabled a text to rectify racist historical distortions, fashion a narrative of the past that could explain the development of present conditions and possible futures, and craft portraits of characters that are both aesthetically complex and historically representative. Scott, Lukács's model of the historical novelist, depicts the past by "[giving] living embodiment to historical-social types," to the extent that the reader can "re-experience the social and human motives which led men to think, feel and act just as they did in historical reality." Thus, "the human-moral conception of his characters" expresses various social, economic, and cultural forces animating historical development (35, 42, 60). African American literary production of the 1930s advanced similar objectives, and one critic points out that Bontemps's *Black Thunder* is "Scottian" because it uses fictional techniques to recover the "spirit of the times" as manifested in the lives and consciousness of its characters.[6]

African American literary critics held similar expectations about the way historical representations should be crafted. Ralph Ellison's first publication, published in the black left journal *New Challenge*, was a review of African

American writer Waters Edward Turpin's *These Low Grounds* (1937), a novel tracing the fortunes of an African American family from slavery to the onset of the Depression. Ellison faulted Turpin for not creating characters shaped by historical events and processes. As a result, his characters "are carried through the period of Reconstruction with no mention of the fact"; "[t]hey transverse [sic] the distance from birth to death with but the most superficial motivation"; and they "all seem to possess ... the same psychology." This aesthetic failing stemmed, Ellison argued, from Turpin's "lack of historical and political consciousness" and failure to situate the events and characters of his novel within "the historic process as a whole."[7] As William Maxwell clarifies, by this latter phrase Ellison means "the materialist conception of history hammered out by Marx, which held that the advance of productive forces in the economy set the course of class conflict and, in turn, the fundamental trajectory of human history."[8]

Richard Wright also thought that Turpin's novel failed to capture the particular consciousnesses of his characters within history. In a 1937 *New Masses* review essay – well-known today because, alongside his discussion of *These Low Grounds*, it offers Wright's notorious critical evaluation of Zora Neale Hurston's *Their Eyes Were Watching God* (1937) – Wright acknowledges the significance of Turpin's project, calling *These Low Grounds* "the first attempt of a Negro writer to encompass in fiction the rise of the Negro from slavery to the present." However, Wright finds Turpin's characters not to be fully fleshed-out "human beings" as Turpin fails "to make us feel the living quality of their experiences."[9] In reading Turpin, both Wright and Ellison work with the same compositional criteria as Lukács: an effective historical novel must capture how historical transitions were lived by and reflected in the consciousness of individuals of the period.

Ellison often assumed that historical fiction, because it represents a past that is materially connected to the present, should be able to provide resources for present struggles. In 1940, he reviewed Conrad Richter's *The Trees*, a novel of the colonial-era Ohio frontier. It doesn't deal with black history, but Ellison praised *The Trees* for rendering the shift from "the life of hunters" to "farming and the civilization of the pioneer settlement," a Marxist economic shift from one mode of production to another. Richter illustrates that shift by showing how it conditions his characters. The novel also locates anti-imperialist sentiments in its historical period, which Ellison finds helpfully inform the Communist left's contingent political objectives in 1940, when Communists were opposed to US entry in World War II as an imperialist venture.[10]

Ellison praised the black left writer William Attaway's historical novel of the Great Migration, *Blood on the Forge* (1941), for illustrating twentieth-century

African American experience in Marxist historical terms as a transition from the feudal South to the capitalist North. Unlike Turpin's characters, who seem to exist outside of history, Attaway's are clearly shaped by being "swept out of the center of gravity of one world, blindly into that of another." Through their individual development, Attaway depicts "the clash of two modes of economic production" in a "world of changing values." However, Ellison found that Attaway failed to show the emergence of new forms of proletarian consciousness in the black masses under capitalism.[11] In a later essay on *Blood on the Forge*, Ellison emphasized that a gesture toward the *future* direction of materialist historical development is needed to make the novel not merely "a summation of phases of the Negro people's aching past," but "a guide and discipline for the future."[12]

Ellison allegorized his critical requirements for historical representation in his 1941 *New Masses* short story "Mister Toussan." Here, two African American youths, Buster and Riley, are frustrated that Rogan, a white man, refuses to let them pick cherries from a tree in his yard. The racial and economic motives of Rogan's prohibition make clear that their desire for cherries, although they aren't conscious of this, is an antiracist and anticapitalist one. The Edenic allusion of the setup suggests that Buster and Riley's desire is, like myth, outside history – not that it's fantasy, but that it's a desire that persists across historical periods, so long as racial and economic exploitation persist. Buster and Riley are faced with the manifestation, in their own present, of a historically shaped and consistent mode of oppression, but they can't access a politically-useful understanding of it. Instead, they channel their frustration into a story they've heard about "Toussan," a black man from "Hayti," who once "whipped Napoleon!" Their narrative, however, is ahistorical: they believe "Hayti" is in Africa, and one remarks on the similarity of "Toussan" to "Tarzan," indicating the story's status as escapism. Their revelry ends when Riley's mother scolds them for acting in an unseemly manner where whites can see them, and this return of real, historical racial and economic prohibitions deflates them.[13] Buster and Riley are excited by the story of Toussan, but it can do nothing to empower them because it relegates the past to the remote realm of fantasy: they are thus unable to chart historical and material connections between slavery in Haiti and Jim Crow in the present, between Rogan's racism in Depression America and Napoleon's attempt to resubjugate revolutionary Haiti in 1801. This is, for Ellison, the bad kind of historical representation: depicting characters in the past as being unaffected by specific social and economic conditions. Such an approach severs past conditions from the present moment that emerged from them and that they can illuminate. The boys' story also fails to capture the agency of the black masses within history – an agency whose viability in the Haitian Revolution should speak to its necessity under Jim Crow – by instead romanticizing long-dead "great men" like "Toussan." "Mister Toussan" theorizes, in negative form, Marxist protocols for historical representation.

In contrast, in *12 Million Black Voices* (1941), Richard Wright realized those protocols. Wright recounts a lyrical history of African Americans that establishes the 1930s as a time of collective black empowerment shaped by the recent transition from the feudal South and by struggles against modern forms of racial and economic exploitation. Radicalized by historical material conditions, African Americans are "ready to accept more change" by "moving into the sphere of conscious history."[14] Ellison greatly admired Wright's imaginative retelling of the scope of black history, finding it possessed of future-looking political inspiration and instruction: "When experiences such as ours are organized as you have done it here," he wrote to Wright, "there is nothing left for a man to do but fight."[15] Marxism's influence on black critics and writers like Ellison and Wright in the 1930s meant that a certain Marxist feel for the historical as the basis of political knowledge enabled black writers to understand their people's past as a source of strategies for those committed, in the present, to achieving a better future.

Black Jacobins and Other Revolutionaries: 1930s African American Historical Scholarship

The 1930s was also a watershed moment in black historical scholarship, as two major studies of the decade – W. E. B. Du Bois's *Black Reconstruction* (1935) and C. L. R. James's *The Black Jacobins* (1938) – now stand as authoritative accounts and influential texts of US and Caribbean cultural studies. Like Depression historical fiction, these works use Marxism to re-evaluate black history and produce new accounts of black political agency, to identify sociopolitical examples from the past that can inform present struggles, and to challenge the racist agendas of white historiographies.

In 1931, influenced by a recent trip to the Soviet Union, Du Bois began reading Marx alongside historical scholarship on the Civil War and Reconstruction.[16] The resulting volume, *Black Reconstruction*, refuted historical accounts that abstracted black agency from the Civil War and Reconstruction and that esteemed the latter as a misguided program compromised by the inability and ignorance of ex-slaves. Du Bois reformulated the Civil War as a "general strike" in which slaves secured the Northern victory by deserting the South's plantation economy and lending their labor to the Northern cause. In Du Bois's history, as in Marx's, labor and working-class activism are the engines of historical change from one mode of production (slave-based feudalism) to another (modern capitalism). Du Bois analyzed the strengths and failures of Reconstruction by comparing it to the Marxist concept of the dictatorship of the proletariat, the postrevolutionary rule of the proletariat that builds the social and economic foundations of socialism.[17]

Given its Marxist bent and revisionist ambition, *Black Reconstruction* was criticized in professional history journals, and while comparatively well received in the mainstream press, the study did not sell well. It also was received unevenly on the left by critics skeptical of its applications of Marxism.[18] For instance, Loren Miller, a black left journalist who reviewed the book for *New Masses*, argued, in a debatable reading, that Du Bois mistakenly attributed the triumph of American capitalism in part to the white working class, a move that, for Miller, reflected Du Bois's bourgeois "hostility to working-class movements."[19] As did African American fiction, African American history inspired discussion and debate within the black left over procedures for rewriting the past in Marxist terms. *Black Reconstruction* also provoked struggles over the historical representation of American race relations. Lawrence J. Oliver shows how *Black Reconstruction* so outraged the white racist novelist Thomas Dixon that he crafted his last work, *The Flaming Sword* (1939), a historical novel spanning the first three decades of the twentieth century, as a "dramatic counterstatement not only to *Black Reconstruction* but to Du Bois's ideas in general." Dixon's title came from *Black Reconstruction*'s characterization of the white South as a "flaming sword" blocking the possibility of social and economic justice; by revaluing this image, Dixon positioned his novel as what he called an "authoritative record" of race in America.[20]

Black Reconstruction inspired the African American writer Margaret Walker in the other direction. Walker began writing her historical novel of slavery and Reconstruction that would eventually be published as *Jubilee* (1966) in the 1930s, when she was a member of the left. Walker didn't consult *Black Reconstruction* until after the 1930s, but Du Bois's Marxist narrative influenced her novel's representational choices.[21] Hazel Carby describes Walker's project as "rooted in her response to the thirties and proletarian literature," and *Jubilee* thus offers "her philosophy of history, which is to be understood as the necessary prehistory of contemporary society."[22]

Du Bois's work demonstrated the utility of Marxism for organizing revolutionary historical representations against reactionary distortions. For example, the white Communist historian Herbert Aptheker echoed some of Du Bois's arguments in *The Negro in the Civil War* (1938) and *Negro*

Slave Revolts in the United States (1939). Understanding slavery as a mode of production in Marxist terms, Aptheker recovers the role played by slaves in effecting the South's defeat during the Civil War, and the longer history of slaves' class struggles against slavery. His longer work *American Negro Slave Revolts* (1943) would become an authoritative historical account of black resistance.

The Trinidadian historian C. L. R. James similarly employed Marxist theory in his retelling of the Haitian Revolution in *The Black Jacobins*. Masterfully implementing Marxism's dialectic of historical change, in which revolution is determined and conditioned by structural economic forces yet must be enacted through the calculations of individuals, James characterizes the Revolution in Marxist terms. Benjamin Balthaser points out how, in *Black Jacobins*, "the Caribbean slave plantation ... is the site of modern production" and, accordingly, slaves are "modern subject[s]" empowered with the political agency and skill of the proletariat.[23] James writes that the Haitian Revolution thus demonstrates the global, transhistorical validity of Marxist theory: "the half-savage slaves of San Domingo were showing themselves subject to the same historical laws as the advanced workers of revolutionary Paris; and over a century later the Russian masses were to prove once more that this innate power will display itself in all populations when deeply stirred and given a clear perspective by a strong and trusted leadership."[24] James inserts black popular resistance and individual leadership into history; recovers a past moment of class struggle and democratic experimentation that can instruct such struggles in the present; and vindicates, against the claims of hegemonic historical traditions, the revolutionary acumen of people of African descent.

James's interventions parallel a major 1930s US cultural tendency: the appropriation of the Haitian Revolution by the left. Michael Denning notes that "the story of Haiti's 'black Jacobins'" functioned as "an allegory of anti-colonialism" in the decade.[25] Balthaser argues that "more than any other historical event, it was the image of black colonial revolt in the global South that gripped the radical imaginary of the 1930s," as the Haitian Revolution became a politically-productive setting for a range of novels and theatrical productions, including *Drums at Dusk*, white proletarian writer Guy Endore's historical novel *Babouk* (1934), and the Federal Theatre Project's "voodoo *Macbeth*" (1936) and *Haiti* (1938) (Balthaser 118). Marxist theory and interracial working-class political discourse influenced many of these works. For instance, in *Babouk*, as Barbara Foley writes, Endore "stressed the economic basis of slavery," representing the Revolution "from a Marxist standpoint."[26] Stephanie Batiste describes the well-known "voodoo *Macbeth*" production as "proletarian and activist," and suggests that *Haiti* enacts a historical teleology that is clearly inflected by Marxism: "The expressionistic aspects of the play that render the interiority and actions of characters beyond their control position the developments in the play as almost inevitable, as society itself strives toward balance, justice, and nobility."[27] *Black Jacobins* theorizes explicitly the implications of the Haitian Revolution as it was often represented in US and African American radical culture: namely, as an illustration of Marxist historical laws and an instance of black revolutionary agency.

The Problem of Popularity: Black Historical Writing and Bestselling Historical Fiction

Beyond the influence of Marxism, another reason for the historical consciousness of black writing in the Depression is that, simply put, historical fiction was massively popular during the period. Gordon Hutner writes that the number of historical novels published during the decade was "unprecedented," as works like *Anthony Adverse* (1933), *Gone with the Wind* (1936), and others dominated bestseller lists. Hutner argues that the crisis of the Depression led the middle class to "see the fragility of its purchase on the so-called American Way of Life," and popular historical fiction reflected a "historical consciousness," a turning to the past to offer consolations or resources for a newly unsettled middle class. Hutner shows how authors of 1930s bestselling middle-class fiction aimed "to suggest how the present came into being and thus to see the formation of social, economic, regional, familial, and psychological pressures on the current moment."[28] Hazel Carby argues that Margaret Mitchell's *Gone with the Wind* takes the measure of social and economic changes accompanying the post–Civil War transition to capitalism. Scarlett O'Hara typifies a new generation of white women navigating gender norms as well as a new class contending with changing historical forces: "Scarlett is in many ways the new capitalist woman who literally builds the new Atlanta." Yet Mitchell also identifies what she sees as a danger in capitalism: namely, the threat of "mass democracy" to "civilization," a threat Mitchell diagnoses by representing African Americans as bestial and uncivilized (130–131). Just like black writers on the left were doing for very different social and political reasons, Margaret Mitchell was seeking the historical origins of a present defined by change and struggle. As Molly Haskell notes, *Gone with the Wind* was received as a "Depression fable."[29]

African American historical writing tended to be pitted against such popular fictional and historical works. When Ralph Ellison criticized *Drums at Dusk* in 1941, he compared it to *Anthony Adverse*, the best-selling historical romance, implying that the former too offers only a superficial engagement with the past as décor ("Recent" 24). The challenge of *Gone with the Wind* particularly hovered over African American historical writing. Eugene Holmes saw it as both a "poorly constructed novel" and a political and ideological threat that popularized "all of the old stereotypes" of African Americans.[30] Walker's *Jubilee* was in part, Carby writes, "a direct response" to the "mythology" of history *Gone with the Wind* helped cement in the popular imagination (133).

In contrast to *Black Reconstruction*, not only was Dixon's rebuke *The Flaming Sword* a commercial success, but so was historian Claude Bowers's *The Tragic Era: The Revolution after Lincoln* (1929), a hegemonic account of Reconstruction as a corrupt and misguided program. Claire Parfait argues that Bowers's book succeeded because it offered a history of Reconstruction that conformed to white expectations (286–287). Writing African Americans into Southern history, and thus turning that history from a narrative of white tragedy to one of black agency, was a priority of Depression-era black writers and historians who conducted it in large part against popular historical misconceptions.

The Futures of Our Past and Present: Representations of Revolution in Arna Bontemps's 1930s Historical Novels

Arna Bontemps is the writer who best demonstrates Depression-era black historical sensibilities, at length, in two novels: *Black Thunder* and *Drums at Dusk*. Both novels exhume connections between past historical moments and the present in order to speak to Depression-era sociopolitical concerns of the left. They accomplish this through sophisticated literary techniques that illustrate the aesthetic complexity politically instrumental representations of history often require. *Black Thunder*, for example, was enthusiastically praised by African American critics on the left for both its aesthetic richness and its use of the historical novel genre to oppose racist historical distortions. Dorothy Peterson called it "the writing of a poet" that departs from "other stories of slave days" by showing "the power and daring of the slaves and the real fear that such a display of power inspired in their masters."[31] Ralph Ellison noted its formal complexity and "high seriousness" ("Recent" 24), while Eugene Holmes argued it both "enriched the field of the Negro novel" and "has shown Negroes themselves that they were worthy subjects for depiction rather than for ... purply romancing" (71–72).

Black Thunder opens with "Old Ben," a household slave on a Richmond-area plantation. We see him carefully wind a "tall clock" in the plantation manor.[32] He here exemplifies what Christine Levecq calls his "[association] with regular, repetitive movements" that illustrate "the compulsions of passivity and routine that restrain his will to freedom" (117). Ben's act allegorizes history as stasis rather than narrative: nothing changes for African Americans, as bondage is continually reinscribed just as Ben winds the clock night after night. Since Gabriel's revolt will fail to disrupt this cycle of servitude and Ben will be the one to betray Gabriel's plans to the whites, this opening foreshadows Gabriel's defeat. The fear that will drive Ben's betrayal is precisely the fear of change, of narrative motion: when he thinks about Gabriel's uprising, he envisions "filthy black slaves" and a "crowd of mad savages" breaking into his master's fine house (61, 73). This vision of slaves literally entering the manor and figuratively violating the recursive stability of white rule gestures toward the Marxist nature of the rebels' ambition – they seek to jumpstart temporal progress, to push history out of a present in which oppression is rewound regularly. Opening the novel with Ben winding the clock, then, foreshadows Gabriel's failure to accomplish this progress, but also highlights the necessity of continuing to seek resources through which historical cycles of oppression might be broken. For as Eric Sundquist writes, from Bontemps' perspective in the 1930s "little had changed through the Civil War, Reconstruction, and the rise of Jim Crow," so that "the need for African-American resistance to white racism had hardly lessened since Gabriel himself stood trial."[33]

Bontemps not only seeks, like Du Bois or Aptheker, to document and recover Gabriel's efforts in the face of historiographical erasures of slaves' agency. He also seeks to extract, from this failed uprising, lessons for subsequent black revolutionary strategy. In this way, he redefines Gabriel's revolt as not a failed and finished past episode, but as an effort that, because of the persistence of the conditions against which it was taken, remains informative in the 1930s. On the night of Gabriel's planned uprising, a storm prevents his march on Richmond. Gabriel hopes to try again, but in the meantime his plot is betrayed and he and his fellow rebels are hunted down. When the storm comes on, some of Gabriel's followers see it as a conjure "sign," a "bad hand against" their uprising (84). Later, an elderly slave woman tells Juba, Gabriel's lover and fellow revolutionary, that Gabriel erred in disregarding conjure practices: "They ain't paid attention to the signs." Instead, he relied solely on the authority of the Bible – "a white man's book" – to ensure victory. The woman claims that the success of the Haitian Revolution, by contrast, was due to the fact that the revolutionaries performed a ritual before their uprising. Alluding to reports of a Vodou ceremony performed by rebels in the initial stages of the Revolution, she explains that they "kilt a hog in the woods. Drank the blood." If a black revolutionary aims to be successful in struggle, "he ... is obliged to fight the way he know," with his particular cultural resources (166).[34]

Black Thunder both underscores and complicates this lesson. Early in the novel, the slaves are inspired by a message from Toussaint Louverture, addressed to "Brothers and Friends," that urges its readers to spread the example of the Haitian Revolution (66). The note doesn't specify the race or nation of its addressees, and it seems to come to Gabriel's circle from a Haitian trading vessel docked in Richmond. It thus references Marx's narrative of modern world history in *The Communist Manifesto*, in which the proletariat communicates and constitutes itself, across international and cultural lines, as a dialectical consequence of the spread of capitalism and trade. Gabriel plans to write a similar proclamation, "soon's we get our power," addressed "to all the black folks in all the States" (67, 116). This shift from an open-ended address that is potentially international and interracial, to a racially-exclusive one conceived apropos of an *unsuccessful* revolution, suggests that when it comes to revolution, black cultural solidarity and practices should not be entirely separated from Western cultural resources and interracial tactics. C. L. R. James writes that Toussaint Louverture was, like Gabriel, inspired in part by a white man's book, the Abbé Raynal's *A History of the Two Indies*, as well as by Enlightenment ideals more broadly. Moreover, the postrevolutionary society he ruled before his downfall was, while not free from the racial tensions of the old order, marked by cooperation between blacks and revolutionary whites, by a "policy of reconciliation with the whites" (16–17, 214). As Michaela Keck argues, the influence of the French and Haitian Revolutions in the novel means "Gabriel's revolt provides the vision of a democracy that includes men and women of all social ranks and skin colors."[35]

The novel also features, as major characters, a circle of white radicals in Richmond referred to as Jacobins, who espouse both French Revolutionary and quasi-Marxist positions. One, Alexander Biddenhurst, refers to slaves as the "American proletariat" (76), and envisions an interracial alliance of white and black workers that resembles the "Black and White, Unite and Fight!" slogan of the 1930s left. The Jacobins are depicted sympathetically, but they fail to foresee fully the uprising and take no part in it. However, their inaction doesn't imply a critique of white radicalism or Western revolutionary traditions. As Sundquist notes, their role in the text is to provide "ideological context" for the uprising (107), and Keck contrasts their progressivism to "the racism of the white working class instrumentalized by the planter elite" (41–42). In keeping with Marx's emphasis, in *The Communist Manifesto*, that revolution arises from the organic lived experience of the masses rather than from conspiratorial radicals, the Jacobins are necessarily relegated to the sidelines of the main action.[36]

As out-of-time 1930s leftists, the Jacobins allow Bontemps to analyze Gabriel's uprising from the perspective of the present. Biddenhurst attributes Gabriel's failure to the contingency inherent in class struggle: "barring the storm," he thinks, Gabriel would have replicated the Haitian Revolution. He sees this contingency as irreducible – "life was like that" – and, by its very nature, enjoining continued revolutionary practice. He vows to keep working in secret against slavery, to "keep the spark alive by agitating" (152). Biddenhurst's lesson complements that of the slave woman: Gabriel's failure stems from the chance nature of struggle, from the fact that while historical conditions inspire mass revolutionary movements, they do not guarantee or foreordain their success, and a failure in one instance necessitates organizing and trying again.

Gabriel's error can thus be interpreted in two equally-valid ways: as a failure to make use of black cultural practices, but also as a failure to recognize that there are no objective assurances of revolutionary progress. At an early meeting of the conspirators, they read the Bible and find justification in a passage from Ezekiel, in which God declares: "The people of the land have used oppression, and exercised robbery, and have vexed the poor and needy. . . . And I sought for a man among them that should make up the hedge, and stand in the gap before me in the land, that I should not destroy it: but I found none. Therefore have I poured out mine indignation upon them." Gabriel declares that he is the "man" who will "stand in the gap" and ensure God's destruction of the oppressors (46–47). William Scott observes that Gabriel reverses the sense of the text: "Gabriel hears the passage as promising the deliverance of divine justice precisely *not* because the man in the middle is missing, but *by means of* one who will be able to stand in the gap." Scott reads this passage as signaling the novel's thematic interest in mediations between "language and discursive concepts" and "a material realization of justice,"[37] but from a Marxist perspective it raises the familiar problem of whether revolutions occur through the subjective agency of individual leaders or through structural, "divine" processes of determination. Gabriel misreads the Bible to position himself as the agent of an objectively ensured transformation. This misreading of one "white man's book" suggests a misreading of another: the text of Marx and its familiar misinterpretation as assuring linear historical progress. Gabriel assumes his uprising is divinely authorized and neglects the importance of tactical planning: he doesn't consider black folk culture and he underestimates logistical issues thrown up by the sheer contingency of events, here figured by the weather. However, the subtle diagnosis of Gabriel's revolt in *Black Thunder* mitigates its failure by preserving it as instructional and inspirational for future revolutionaries.

Drums at Dusk – for which Bontemps used *Black Jacobins* as a source[38] – similarly endeavors to establish the present significance of a past moment of revolutionary struggle.[39] The novel is set before and during the onset of the Haitian Revolution in August 1791, when slaves and maroons rose up and destroyed plantations in the area surrounding the French colonial city of Cap-Français. Toussaint Louverture is a minor figure, waiting in the background until the moment is right for him to assume leadership and turn the revolt into a proper revolution. "We must take time and keep our wits about us," he tells Mars, an elderly slave anxious to join the insurrection. Toussaint waits to see how the French will organize their defense, and what position the colony's mulatto class will take. "It gives us time to think," he reminds Mars, presenting himself as a shrewd political tactician: he demonstrates the patience and planning Gabriel overlooks.[40]

The novel's protagonist, the Frenchman Diron Desautels, misrecognizes Toussaint as a "god-like authority" who can "weld miserable, ignorant and disunited savages into a fighting force" (162). Unlike the Jacobins in *Black Thunder*, Diron is unreliable despite professing radical sentiments. As Michael P. Bibler and Jessica Adams point out, "Diron is an idealist who comes close to patronizing the slaves he wants to help" (xxv). His opposition to slavery stems primarily from an idealist, Rousseauian concern that it violates Nature, and one Frenchwoman describes Diron's radicalism as his "mistress," suggesting a superficial set of political motives (105). When the uprising occurs, it appears to Diron as mere chaos: "He had always thought of the struggle for liberty as something intensely real. Now it was hard to accept what his eyes saw" (182). One can only see revolution as an intolerable destabilizing of order itself by the "ignorant and disunited," and Toussaint as a god rather than a human tactician, if one's sympathies are ultimately invested in the ruling class. Diron perceives the Revolution in much the same way Ben imagined Gabriel's planned revolt.

Throughout *Drums at Dusk*, the reader is challenged to see past Diron's misconceptions to the actual dynamics of revolutionary struggle. The reader must learn to see revolution and historical change as material processes driven by the exploited masses and their leaders rather than by the idealism of intellectuals, and to recognize change as an objective fact of historical development rather than a fearful shattering of a static reality. Diron and the other French characters are the main focus of the novel, and because the Revolution develops mostly in the background of what is otherwise a middlebrow historical romance, the reader must read the novel as a Marxist might read the historical record, learning to recognize the stirrings of the masses and to reconstruct the tactical decisions made by revolutionaries at key junctures that might offer political resources in the present.

Drums at Dusk instructs the reader through two formal strategies: its use of spectral imagery and its suspension of resolution at the novel's conclusion. As Jacques Derrida argues, the figure of the ghost in Marx signifies the transhistorical nature of Marxism's ethical call for justice, a call that, like the ghost, requires our commitment and cannot be consigned to a no-longer relevant past.[41] Ian Baucom similarly argues that the prevalence of ghosts and themes of haunting in postmodern representations of slavery works to "reconceive our basic notions of temporality, periodicity, and contemporaneity."[42] The ghost suggests the continuity of the present and the past as one elongated moment of oppression. Ghosts' out-of-time existence indexes what black writers and historians emphasized in the 1930s: consciousness of the past's shaping influence on the present, and the future-looking obligation to justice that flows from that consciousness.

Drums at Dusk opens with a description of the road between Cap-Français and the plantation where much of the novel will take place: "Only ghosts walked on that pathway now. Ghosts – and people so old they were about to become ghosts" (1). This opening sentence purports to locate the reader in a fixed historical time and place through its reference to *"that* pathway," but it proceeds instead to blur the boundaries between the novel's setting and other times and places. We are located not in a discrete time and place, but on a "pathway," a conduit of movement and transition. Bontemps's sentence construction brings the "ghosts" of the past to the "now" of the present, where they travel among those who are defined by their future status of being "about to become ghosts." The repetition of "ghosts" at the beginning, middle, and end of the sentence further underscores this use of the ghost to reconfigure past, present, and future. The opening sentence introduces the novel's concern not simply with 1791 Haiti, but with the movement of history itself, the connections or "pathways" from 1791 to 1939 and beyond. The "pathway" also organizes a geographic figure of time, connecting the past historical mode of production of slavery (the plantation) with the geopolitical order of imperialist capitalism (Cap-Français) emergent in 1791 and still operative in the present. The reader is set down in a past in which the political desires of exploited persons for a better future express the same revolutionary hopes of those who are oppressed in her own present.

The novel ends when the political situation is still uncertain. The initial uprising has passed, Toussaint has yet to assume command, French troops are preparing for an attack, and "[t]he blacks ... had no idea what to do next" (219). Bontemps thus recreates the potential of this historical juncture, this window of time when the course of events have not yet been determined, and when the present is still open to a range of possible futures achievable through human action. If no revolution has yet ended in an exploitation-free society, then one strategy for inspiring revolutionary optimism is to recover past windows of such possibility. *Drums at Dusk* ends in historical suspension for the same reason *Black Thunder* ends with the uprising's defeat: both refuse a formal closure that would relegate the events to a finished past, and thus both novels require the reader to see that the future for which past revolutionaries fought is still waiting and ready to be realized.

Conclusion

A trace of the historical consciousness of the 1930s can be seen in post-modern African American historical fiction. Works like Sherley Anne Williams's *Dessa Rose* (1986), Toni Morrison's *Beloved* (1987), and Edward P. Jones's *The Known World* (2003), to name a few, seek to establish the ethical implications of the past, particularly the trauma of slavery, for black identity in the present. These authors share with 1930s writers the general assumption that historical representations should prioritize the ethical or political goal of highlighting the past's relevance for emancipatory needs in the present. However, Kenneth Warren argues that this later turn to the historical in African American literature is motivated by not-so-radical ambitions: he sees it as an attempt by the African American middle class to represent its own sociopolitical concerns as those of a homogenous black community. In a period when resistance to Jim Crow laws no longer guarantees a set of political needs shared by all African Americans, historical fiction redefines what it means to be black as "memory," a unifying, inherited experience of history that binds African Americans together, thereby licensing the elite to frame its class interests as the interests of all black people.[43] Warren's controversial argument is perhaps a sign of how the revolutionary politics of Depression-era black historical writing are unevenly translated – abandoned in some cases, but in others modified, improved, and rendered more inclusive of identities beyond race and class – in the projects of postmodern black historical fiction. Yet because the representation of the past continues to serve as an important ground for debate in African American literature, the Depression and its historical sensibilities should be recognized as inaugurating this major thematic concern of black literary history.

NOTES

1 Ralph Ellison, *Invisible Man* (New York: Vintage, 1995), 271–272.
2 Georg Lukács, *The Historical Novel* (Lincoln, NE: University of Nebraska Press, 1983), 32, 24, 19.
3 For a judicious account of transactions between African American writers and Communism during the 1930s, see Lawrence P. Jackson, *The Indignant Generation: A Narrative History of African American Writers and Critics, 1934–1960* (Princeton, NJ: Princeton University Press, 2011).
4 Ellison, "Recent Negro Fiction," *New Masses*, August 5, 1941, 22.
5 Richard Wright, "Blueprint for Negro Writing," *New Challenge* 2 (Fall 1937): 59, 53.
6 Christine Levecq, "Philosophies of History in Arna Bontemps' *Black Thunder* (1936)," *Obsidian III: Literature in the African Diaspora* 1, no. 2 (2000): 114.
7 Ellison, "Creative and Cultural Lag," *New Challenge* 2 (1937): 91.
8 William J. Maxwell, "'Creative and Cultural Lag': The Radical Education of Ralph Ellison," in *A Historical Guide to Ralph Ellison* (New York: Oxford University Press, 2004), 72.
9 Richard Wright, "Between Laughter and Tears," *New Masses*, October 5, 1937, 25.
10 Ellison, "Hunters and Pioneers," *New Masses*, March 19, 1940, 26.
11 Ellison, "The Great Migration," *New Masses*, December 2, 1941, 23–24.
12 Ellison, "Transition," *The Negro Quarterly* 1, no. 1 (1942): 92.
13 Ellison, "Mister Toussan," *New Masses*, November 4, 1941, 19–20.
14 Wright, *12 Million Black Voices* (New York: Basic Books, 2008), 145, 147.
15 Quoted in Lawrence Jackson, *Ralph Ellison: Emergence of Genius* (Athens, GA: University of Georgia Press, 2007), 260.
16 Bill V. Mullen, *W. E. B. Du Bois: Revolutionary Across the Color Line* (London: Pluto, 2016), 75–76.
17 W. E. B. Du Bois, *Black Reconstruction in America: 1860–1880* (New York: Free Press, 1998).
18 Claire Parfait, "Rewriting History: The Publication of W. E. B. Du Bois's *Black Reconstruction in America* (1935)," *Book History* 12 (2009): 279–284.
19 Loren Miller, "Let My People Go!" *New Masses*, October 29, 1935, 24.
20 Lawrence J. Oliver, "Writing from the Right during the 'Red Decade': Thomas Dixon's Attack on W. E. B. Du Bois and James Weldon Johnson in *The Flaming Sword*," *American Literature* 70, no. 1 (1998): 135–136, 132.
21 Margaret Walker, "How I Wrote *Jubilee*," in *How I Wrote "Jubilee" and Other Essays on Life and Literature* (New York: Feminist Press, 1990), 51–57.
22 Hazel V. Carby, "Ideologies of Black Folk: The Historical Novel of Slavery," in *Slavery and the Literary Imagination* (Baltimore, MD: Johns Hopkins University Press, 1989), 136.
23 Benjamin Balthaser, *Anti-Imperialist Modernism: Race and Transnational Radical Culture from the Great Depression to the Cold War* (Ann Arbor, MI: University of Michigan Press, 2016), 130–131.
24 C. L. R. James, *The Black Jacobins: Toussaint L'Ouverture and the San Domingo Revolution* (New York: Dial, 1938), 202.
25 Michael Denning, *The Cultural Front: The Laboring of American Culture in the Twentieth Century* (London: Verso, 1997), 396–397.

26 Barbara Foley, *Radical Representations: Politics and Form in U.S. Proletarian Fiction, 1929–1941* (Durham, NC: Duke University Press, 1993), 201.

27 Stephanie Leigh Batiste, *Darkening Mirrors: Imperial Representation in Depression-Era African American Performance* (Durham, NC: Duke University Press, 2011), 85, 107.

28 Gordon Hutner, *What America Read: Taste, Class, and the Novel, 1920–1960* (Chapel Hill, NC: University of North Carolina Press, 2009), 163, 122.

29 Molly Haskell, *Frankly, My Dear: "Gone with the Wind" Revisited* (New Haven, CT: Yale University Press, 2009), 101.

30 Eugene C. Holmes, "Problems Facing the Negro Writer Today," *New Challenge* 2 (1937): 71.

31 Dorothy R. Peterson, Review of *Black Thunder*, by Arna Bontemps, *Challenge* 1, no. 5 (1936): 45–46.

32 Arna Bontemps, *Black Thunder* (Boston: Beacon Press, 1992), 10.

33 Eric J. Sundquist, *The Hammers of Creation: Folk Culture in Modern African-American Fiction* (Athens, GA: University of Georgia Press, 1992), 96.

34 C. L. R. James vividly describes this ceremony (67). Laurent Dubois points out that reports of the ceremony and sacrifice were unreliable, clouded by reactionary bias or poetic license. Dubois argues that the event should be interpreted as "a symbol of the achievement of the slave insurgents of Saint-Domingue, a symbol not of a specific event whose details we can pin down, but rather of the creative spiritual and political epic that both prompted and emerged from the 1791 insurrection." See Dubois, *Avengers of the New World: The Story of the Haitian Revolution* (Cambridge, MA: Harvard University Press, 2004), 99–102. The role of conjure in *Black Thunder* is frequently discussed in scholarship, and is often seen as a privileged vernacular epistemology. For instance, Eric Sundquist argues that Bontemps uses conjure to "recover the meaning of the insurrection from a variegated African-American point of view" (98), and Daniel Reagan counterposes the efficacy of conjure and orality to the ruses of text, linking Gabriel's failure to his favoring of "the scriptural word." See Reagan, "Voices of Silence: The Representation of Orality in Arna Bontemps' *Black Thunder*," *Studies in American Fiction* 19, no. 1 (1991): 78.

35 Michaela Keck, "Marginocentricity and Cosmopolitan Interconnections of Black Radical Thought in Arna Bontemps's *Black Thunder*," *Atlantic Studies* 14, no. 1 (2017), 42.

36 That Bontemps perhaps intended to align the Jacobins with this Marxist position is suggested by the fact that the two main Jacobin characters in the novel are based on historical figures who did in fact take part in Gabriel's planning (Levecq 115).

37 William Scott, "'To Make up the Hedge and Stand in the Gap': Arna Bontemps's *Black Thunder*," *Callaloo* 27, no. 2 (2004): 523.

38 Michael P. Bibler and Jessica Adams, "Race, Romance, and Revolution," in *Drums at Dusk*, by Arna Bontemps (Baton Rouge, LA: Louisiana State University Press, 2009), xvii.

39 As Ellison's dismissive comparison to *Anthony Adverse* suggests, *Drums at Dusk* wasn't received nearly as well as its predecessor. The editors of the Louisiana University Press edition attribute this in part to the fact that the novel focuses on white characters, ends before the Haitian Revolution is properly underway, and

unlike *Black Thunder* doesn't show "a strong black character fighting – in this case, successfully – for the freedom of all people of color" (Bibler and Adams, ix–x). There is also much less scholarship dealing with *Drums at Dusk*. The most sustained critical treatment is Mark Christian Thompson's provocative identification of fascist sensibilities in the novel. See Thompson, "Voodoo Fascism: Fascist Ideology in Arna Bontemps's *Drums at Dusk*," *MELUS* 30, no. 3 (2005): 155–177.

40 Arna Bontemps, *Drums at Dusk* (Baton Rouge, LA: Louisiana State University Press, 2009), 195.

41 See Jacques Derrida, *Spectres of Marx: The State of the Debt, the Work of Mourning, and the New International* (New York: Routledge, 1994).

42 Ian Baucom, *Specters of the Atlantic: Finance Capital, Slavery, and the Philosophy of History* (Durham, NC: Duke University Press, 2005), 324.

43 Kenneth W. Warren, *What Was African American Literature?* (Cambridge, MA: Harvard University Press, 2011), 96.

II

JENNIFER HAYTOCK AND WILLIAM SOLOMON

Popular Fiction in the 1930s

> The standard by which to measure Popular Culture is not the old
> aristocratic High Culture, but rather a potential new, *human* culture, in
> Trotsky's phrase, which for the first time in history has a chance of
> superseding the *class* cultures of the past and present.

The epigraph to this chapter is the final sentence of Dwight Macdonald's "A
Theory of Popular Culture," his contribution to the February 1944 issue of
Politics, a journal he also edited. In this article he stakes out an optimistic
stance on the problem of popular culture that would completely disappear
when he revised the piece nine years later. Politically oriented critics have
paid, he asserts, inadequate attention to the topic. Gilbert Seldes' appreci-
ation of the "seven lively arts" is a notable but insufficient treatment because
he simply expresses his delight in certain cultural phenomena while ignoring
their historical significance. A commentator adhering to socialist ideals
should, on the contrary, scrutinize current incarnations of popular culture
not to endorse them but as a means of analyzing their meaningfulness, their
respective psychological effects on the audience being of particular importance for such an investigation. Though by no means an apologist for popular
culture, Macdonald was initially not as stringent in denouncing commercial
entertainment as were Theodor Adorno and Max Horkheimer in "The
Culture Industry: Enlightenment as Mass Deception," the best-known chapter of their *The Dialectic of Enlightenment*, a critical study published in the
same year as Macdonald's article. The latter's attitude toward "synthetic
folk heroes" like Superman, Tarzan, the Lone Ranger, and Sherlock Holmes
is a case in point. Encouraging intellectuals to reflect on such figures, he finds
that they possess certain virtues in that they "unite power with morals in an
attractive way" and in so doing "give us an important clue to the deepest,
and least satisfied, cravings of our era."[1] Whether in promoting the use of
science for worthwhile endeavors, or in helping men to "break out of the
mechanized rut of modern life" and thus restore to them a lost "faith in their
ability to cope with raw nature," these fictive individuals, according to him,
supply the populace with better role models than the ones leaders in the real
world offer. Notably, MacDonald also remarks on the contrasting fact that
the images of women in circulation in the mass media are almost exclusively

that of victims, and cannot therefore function as the basis for empowering identifications. The star of the early movie serial *Perils of Pauline* was, for instance, not a heroine but an object of pity, as is Helen Trent, one of many contemporaneous radio "weepers" (23). The representational absence in question discloses for him the superficiality of the women's movement to this point in time. When one descends into such "profound cultural depths," one realizes that "emancipation" has not yet been satisfactorily achieved. Further advances in gender equity thus require that female figures worth admiring as well as sympathizing with be produced for mass consumption.

At this stage of his career, then, Macdonald discerned in popular culture a potential to perform beneficial social tasks. Admittedly, this promise had yet to be fulfilled, but he envisioned a future in which the general public would be given what it deserved. In this sense, he had yet to abandon the kind of progressive aspirations that had animated a considerable portion of cultural practice in the preceding decade. In this chapter, we examine two Depression-era narrative phenomena that at least partially justify the (ultimately fleeting) hope of the radicalized critic: (1) the ongoing relevance of bestselling fiction about women, whether in the form of realism, historical novels, or light romances; and (2) the continued generic development of hardboiled crime fiction.

Women's Bestsellers

Jennifer Haytock

In Faith Baldwin's *That Man is Mine* (1937), Valentine Loring explains her strategy for re-designing a bookstore window display:

> [M]ost of the people who read books aren't awfully high-brow. Anyone – just the average sort – passing by wouldn't have given that window another glance. All very dull, you know, books on what-are-we-coming-to and have-you-had-your-morning-psychology? You have to attract everyone. Bookshops should be like gregarious people, open-minded, openhearted, with plenty of room for all sorts of friendships and acquaintances. So I put a book on diet, and three detectives and a couple of romances and some travel books. Now it offers a more varied fare, doesn't it? Something for everyone.[2]

Valentine captures the nature of contemporary readership in that she recognizes that books are consumer goods targeted toward different audiences. She implements advertising strategies by displaying books and acknowledging the variety of products available, each with its own readership. In the 1930s, literary realism – despite the critical inclination toward modernist and proletarian fiction – remained a staple of consumers' attention. As Valentine later demonstrates when she tries to use fiction to guide her romantic choices, realism helped readers navigate a complex American society particularly during a decade of disruption.

In the early part of the twentieth century, a fully established middle class found reading to be one of the key markers, or even creators, of their status. As Amy Blair points out, the volumes of reading manuals published around the turn of the century were targeted toward "literary novices, people whose education had topped the barrier of literacy but who had not been able to breach the barrier of taste."[3] Around this time, the United States economy turned its quite impressive forces to mass production and the creation of a consumer culture. Consumerism required inducing people to spend money, that is, persuading them that they needed the material goods, including books, that industries wanted to sell them. In her foundational study *A Feeling For Books*, Janice A. Radway argues that in the first decades of the twentieth century books "were especially evocative symbolically because they carried a series of semantic entailments that spoke of their association with the learning, gentility, and contemplative leisure of that earlier era when manners, cultivation, and the signs of good breeding were so important."[4] Radway and Joan Shelley Rubin show how tastemakers played a role in explaining to a public interested in cementing their middle-class status which books were the most appropriate for them to read. Gordon Hutner, more recently, explores how realist novels that today are largely forgotten helped shape the communal life of the nation in the middle of the century: they bound people together, he argues, and helped them understand their society and their roles.[5]

With so many books to choose from, consumers looked for guidance to direct how they spent their money and time. Bestseller lists helped readers discern what one ought to read in order to be up to date. In 1895, *Bookman* began publishing bestseller lists, intended as an industrial tool for those in the field, and *Publishers Weekly* followed suit in 1912. In 1931, the *New York Times* began publishing such lists to the general public. As Laura J. Miller explains, while such lists pretend to be objective reports about how many copies sell, data gathering methods have always been unclear and open to dispute. Still, the lists have influenced the marketing of books and consumer decision-making.[6] In the 1930s, such lists became another directive for what people should read in order to keep up with their peers. Readership itself was part of the national conversation: in *Books: Their Place in a Democracy* (1930), R. L. Duffus argued that Americans did not read enough books and laid the blame at the feet of publishers and booksellers who ignored the mass market and general reader. In response, the National Association of Book Publishers asked O. H. Cheney to assess the state of the industry, and in his eponymous Report he blistered publishers for their poor business practices.[7]

Yet in the 1930s, some organizations focused particularly on the general reader: book clubs. The well-known Book-of-the-Month Club, founded in 1926, promised members that they would receive books vetted by prominent literary figures of the day such as Henry Seidel Canby and Dorothy Canfield Fisher, also an established author. An early advertisement for the Club reminded readers that "there are few things more annoying than to *miss* the outstanding books that everybody else of intelligence is reading, discussing, and enjoying."[8] The Club proposed to fix this problem by regularly identifying and providing those "outstanding books" and thus bringing the subscriber into the circle of the "intelligent" and up to date. Similarly, the Literary Guild, founded the following year, announced its existence by calling consumers' attention to the "humiliating realization" that more books are sold in Russia than in the United States and that "every civilized country has a larger audience for good books than exists here." Like the Book-of-the-Month Club, the Literary Guild offered its readers a discriminating Editorial Board that would save them the hassle and expense of sifting through the mass of published novels to find the "best books" to "interest the person of wide culture," providing both "value" and "pleasure."[9] Thus book clubs helped create a national identity that required Americans to keep up both with international rivals in the name of civilization and with friends and neighbors, from whose conversation and company one might be excluded.

Between bestseller lists and book clubs, American readership became part of a powerful consumer industry. Authors whose work we recognize today from college reading lists, such as Willa Cather and Ellen Glasgow, published novels that appeared on the bestseller lists and were chosen as Book-of-the-Month Club selections (*Shadows on the Rock* [1931] and *Vein of Iron* [1935]). Two other well-known novels, however, perhaps best exemplify the merging of consumerism and readership in the 1930s: Pearl S. Buck's *The Good Earth* (1931) and Margaret Mitchell's *Gone with the Wind* (1936). Buck's novel dominated the bestseller lists in 1931 and 1932, became a Book-of-the-Month Club selection, and was adapted for stage and film. Its appeal lay in a combination of an exotic location and relevant domestic themes: set in China, the protagonist Wang Lung works hard as a farmer to create a better future for himself and his family and tries to hold onto his sense of rightness and decency. When a drought forces the family to move to the city, they find themselves in a world to which they don't belong. Caught in a riot, Wang Lung and his wife end up stealing money and jewels from a wealthy man, which they use to reestablish themselves on their land.

But their relationship isn't easy, and they have to contend with challenges from their children who, at the end of the novel, plan to sell the land their father has spent his life acquiring. Thus, the novel reflects hardships that many Americans experienced or saw others facing: the destruction of the belief that hard work and frugal living would result in prosperity and respect; the loss of a home and physical dislocation; and a discontented urban working class threatening rebellion. As David Welky notes, however, the novel shows "how to find happiness, how to appreciate home and stability," lessons that may have comforted its readers.[10]

Mitchell's *Gone with the Wind* became even more successful than *The Good Earth*, though for many of the same reasons. Its publisher timed its release to coincide with its selection for the Book-of-the-Month Club, it swept the bestseller lists, it won the Pulitzer Prize, and it was soon chosen for a film adaption.[11] People gave parties celebrating Mitchell's portrayal of the leisurely plantation life of white members of the Old South, making the novel a phenomenon that continued to spin off in its cultural impact. In this novel, Mitchell wove together key themes of 1930s literature: nostalgia for a lost past; an interest in American history; adversity in the face of economic hardship; heterosexual romance and passion; and a strong, working heroine. Scarlett O'Hara's transformation from an ornamental Southern belle to a hard-headed businesswoman places the text in its contemporary context, yet the novel's creation of a glorified past of leisure offered (presumably white) readers an escape from the realities of the Great Depression. Both *The Good Earth* and *Gone with the Wind* performed ideological tasks while also registering aspects of current existence: the nostalgic past offers utopian escapism while the transformation of the main characters reiterates a present preoccupation with adaptation and survival in a brutal environment.

Whereas Buck and Mitchell offered relief for readers eager to forget about financial pressures, other popular writers addressed the contemporaneous subject of middle-class economic struggles directly. Josephine Lawrence, who was the first writer to have two novels in a row chosen as Book-of-the-Month Club selections, often portrayed middle-class family life under strain in the 1930s, "a picture of American life all too close to home," as Hutner puts it, "a domestic world where readers recognize their familiar worlds of discomfort and apprehensiveness."[12] Her *Years Are So Long* (1934) and *If I Have Four Apples* (1935) focus on difficult questions about what children owe their parents in their old age and how a family can maintain its middle-class identity in the face of a budget that won't stretch to purchase the consumer goods that help fashion that identity. In *If I Have Four Apples*, for example, many characters obsess over the perceived independence and status that owning a car brings them, even though public transportation is better suited to their budgets.

Many of the most popular novels of the 1930s built on the relationship of the individual to American history. Margaret Ayer Barnes, for example, who began her writing career when she was in her forties, won the Pulitzer Prize for her first novel, *Years of Grace* (1930), which also topped the bestseller list that year. Following its heroine from her teenage years in the 1890s to her fifties, this novel focuses on key moments in a woman's life, from her first romance to her marriage, to her experience as a young parent to a woman considering the choices of her adult children. Fidelity and friendship are also prominent themes. Barnes's next bestseller, *Within this Present* (1933), follows several generations of a family with more attentiveness to historical events, such as the Chicago World's Fair, World War I, and the Great Depression. Although the main character's marriage briefly founders due to her husband's infidelity, the novel champions loyalty and endurance as the true paths to happiness and goodness. The family's moral character represents that of the nation, chastened by its excesses into more humbled respect for work and community.

Like Barnes, Jessie Fauset, the first literary editor for W. E. B. Du Bois's journal *The Crisis*, published realist novels about generations of American families. In contrast, Fauset had a narrower audience, as her works focused on African American characters. Still, the two women found themselves facing a similar problem: they both wrote realist novels at a time when the critical field had established a preference for a different type of writing, that is, the new, the experimental, and the jarring and alienating. With a broad audience of white readers who were invested in realist literature, Barnes still did well. Fauset, however, faced a less receptive national audience, and even among black readers found herself challenging a preference for the "folk," provided by Zora Neale Hurston's *Their Eyes Were Watching God* (1937), and Nella Larsen's more genteel modernism in *Quicksand* (1928) and *Passing* (1929). Yet critics now are returning to Fauset's work for her depictions of racial identity as embedded in American history. Her 1931 novel *The Chinaberry Tree*, for example, portrays two generations of mixed race women who have to contend with discrimination, particularly from other African Americans, a prejudice based on color and a legacy of sexual exploitation that produces lighter skinned women. In her next and last novel, *Comedy, American Style* (1933), Fauset again turned to the damage caused by African Americans who prefer lighter skin, as Olivia Cary's denial of her dark-skinned son causes his suicide. More open-minded characters still discover that their happiness rests in romantic pairings with similarly positioned individuals; the light-skinned Phebe Grant loses a darker-skinned suitor when he realizes that he could be lynched because of his connection with a woman who appears to be white. This novel also emphasizes the importance of meaningful work outside the home for women, both for personal fulfillment and to help support their families during the Depression.

Like Barnes and Fauset but with even greater success, Edna Ferber built her reputation by writing about individuals and community in American contexts. She had made her name in the previous decades, publishing her first novel, *Dawn O'Hara*, in 1911. She won the 1925 Pulitzer Prize for her novel *So Big*, which was adapted for film three times, and had winners with her novels *Show Boat* (1926) and *Cimarron* (1929). Her 1931 novel, *American Beauty*, follows an old New England family from their time as settlers in the eighteenth century through their decline over the next 150 years. The family finds a measure of renewal and salvation through marriage into an immigrant family and, in the next generation, into a family of new money, thus raising questions of eugenics and racial purity. Ferber also made the bestseller list in 1935 with the multigenerational *Come and Get It*, about a businessman in the logging industry and its environmental consequences. Ferber's ability to link family stories to social and economic issues helped make her work appeal to readers of her time and offers insight for critics now concerned with the middlebrow and the endurance of literary realism.

Fannie Hurst, another widely successful writer of the decade, was, like Ferber, well established by the 1920s. She began her publishing career with short stories, starting in 1912. Her 1923 novel *Lummox* became a bestseller, as did *Back Street* (1931) and *Imitation of Life* (1933). Although literary critics treated these works as sentimental sops to the working classes – Hurst was one of the writers referred to as the "sob sisters" – readers found these works deeply pleasurable and meaningful, and they have come to the attention of recent scholars for what they can tell us about women's lives and emotional educations in fact and fiction. In *Back Street*, the working woman Ray Schmidt gives up her promising career to become the mistress of a prominent Jewish banker. Opening the novel in the 1890s, Hurst represents the history of working women, as it was at this time that women began moving to cities and into white collar jobs. Though in the vanguard of this movement, Ray seems strikingly regressive in her choice to become so literally a "kept woman." Her willingness to be financially supported by her married lover and physically contained within her apartment is incongruous with her previous independence. The novel inscribes a reckless, excessive, and possibly appealing form of love while simultaneously, but perhaps less obviously, undermining that love through a harsh portrayal of its costs: after Walter's death, Ray cannot support herself and dies of starvation.

Imitation of Life, immensely popular at the time and made into three movie versions, has become fascinating to critics due to its complex portrayal of race relations and the challenges facing professional women. In this novel, Hurst creates a reluctant businesswoman, Bea Pullman, a widow forced to provide for herself and her daughter. Bea claims to want only a home and security, but this very desire drives her out of the home to make more and more money in her restaurant empire, causing her to miss out on her daughter's life and her own chances at romance. When she finally finds a lover, he decides instead to marry her daughter. In this plot, Hurst critiques the materialism of the American Dream as Bea Pullman falls victim to the lure of infinite success: finding security in money, the possibility of making more money seems to mean even more security. Bea's achievement is possible only because she hires a black woman, Delilah Johnson, to manage her domestic obligations. Rendered by Hurst as a stereotypical Mammy figure with no desires of her own but to be joined with her God, Delilah represents a problematically simplified vision of black womanhood. Yet Delilah's light-skinned daughter Peola, raised with Bea's daughter Jessie, is a more complicated character. Delilah repeatedly teaches Peola that Jessie's privileges are not for her, a lesson that ultimately drives Peola away from her family and across the racial line. She ends up passing for white, far from her mother. Thus, *Imitation of Life* depicts two mothers divided from their respective daughters by the complex issues of race, sexuality, and class.

Hurst's sentimental novels and their mixed reception link her to another sort of fictive material, often considered "light fiction" or popular romances. Much of women's popular fiction was regularly dismissed as drivel and even damaging to readers. Katherine Fullerton Gerould most prominently made this claim in her essay "Feminine Fiction,"[13] published in the *Saturday Review of Literature* in 1936, in which she condemns the novels of such writers as Margaret Culkin Banning, Kathleen Norris, Alice Druer Miller, Faith Baldwin, Temple Bailey, and Margaret Widdemer. Their work, Gerould claims, "states no vital problem for the mind to solve, ... lays on us no duty of moral selection." She finds particularly troublesome the failure of "the creation, the accurate delineation, of human character," which encourages the reader to indulge in "narcissism." At the invitation of the editor Henry Canby, Banning responded with a piece titled "The Problem of Popularity," in which she defends the importance of women's fiction in large part because it *is* popular: she sees value in respecting average readers.[14] Banning writes, she explains, because "I would like to find out and tell in fiction why women get in their own way and defeat themselves and why they refuse opportunities." She regrets a national literary criticism that values proletarian and modernist fiction while ignoring "the rest of the people in the United States who also can read and do read incessantly." These people, she argues, deserve a robust literature that reflects and interrogates their experiences, and only a critical establishment that takes popular literature seriously will help improve it. On this point, Banning concurs with Gerould that much popular writing could be better: she writes that she'd like critics to say to popular authors, "You use up a great deal of human time. You are very well paid. Can't you improve your prose and go a little deeper into human life?" Here, Banning shows respect for women's work, including both the writing and reading of popular fiction.

This "light fiction" offers its own insights about the commercial appeal of novels for women in the 1930s. While generally realist, its characters tend to lack the depth of those by Barnes, Fauset, Ferber, and Hurst, yet they sold tremendously well. Faith Baldwin, for example, was a highly prolific writer, publishing about a novel a year from 1921 to 1977. In the 1930s and 1940s, she was at the height of her productivity. Many of her novels focus on working women and their struggles with romance. In her 1931 novel *Sky-scraper*, for example, a young couple who work in the same office building overcome questions of fidelity, discover their true dreams, make decisions about controlling their sexual passion, and face prejudices against working wives. As Banning writes in defense of Baldwin, "she always has some interesting modern situation to analyze."[15] Baldwin's sales record – her *Times* obituary notes that she made over $315,000 from her writing in 1936[16] – suggests that readers valued seeing themselves and their problems in fiction.

Kathleen Norris, too, had a remarkably long career writing romances, publishing from 1911 to 1959. In her 1931 novel *Second-hand Wife*, the main character Alexandra Trumbull falls passionately in love with a married man, who divorces his wife and marries her. Although they're happy, Alexandra feels out of place in her husband's wealthy world, and only when she realizes she can improve her stepdaughter's life by revealing that her husband's divorce was fraudulent does she start to find meaning in her life. As her "husband" begins his divorce proceedings over again, she decides not to worry that she's spent years with a man to whom she's not legally married, casting off custom and social opinion in favor of the personal truth of their relationship. In *Beauty's Daughter* (1934), the nurse Victoria Herrendeen marries a doctor and produces many children quickly. When her husband begins an affair with their neighbor, Victoria rejects the advice of her much-divorced mother and stays silent for three years until her husband chooses to end his illicit relationship. In both of these novels, Norris affirms a

self-sacrificing heterosexual love as central for women's identity while refusing to mold that love consistently in the shape of marriage.

The popular fiction discussed here may best be considered as a vital link in
the genealogy of twentieth-century literature. Its success was built on the
reputations of authors established before the 1930s and distributed by
industrial methods largely developed in the previous decades. Although the
appeal of the familiar – realism, historical novels, light romance – may be
laid at the feet of the upheavals of the Great Depression, it's also important
to recognize that this kind of fiction remains the staple of bestseller lists
today. Readers find both themselves and escape through fiction that helps
them understand the world they live in.

Crime Fiction

William Solomon

> Lately she had taken to reading the detective books; they had god-awful
> pictures and they left you feeling rotten but they did have things in them
> like the things that really happened.
>
> Robert Stone, *A Hall of Mirrors*

In his 1953 revision of "A Theory of Popular Culture" (tellingly retitled "A
Theory of Mass Culture"), Dwight Macdonald made it clear that he found
nothing worthwhile in the proliferating bulk of items designed for mass
consumption. Citing Gresham's law, Macdonald felt that everywhere he
looked the bad stuff had driven out the good. Worst of all was the "sensational style" of the detective story, which he saw as a "rank, noxious
growth" complicit with the rapid decay of previously accepted standards
of behavior.[17] Identifying Dashiell Hammett's *The Glass Key* (1931) as an
especially reprehensible artifact, he condemned the Depression-era narrative
as little more than a "chronicle of epic beatings," further disparaging it on
the grounds that it degraded the "classicists'" concern with tracking down
the criminal culprit to "a mere excuse for the minute description of scenes of
bloodshed, brutality, lust, and alcoholism" (68). Moreover, generic decline
was for him a mirror reflection of the sociological tendency that had reduced
human values to their lowest common denominator. As the level of "morality sinks to that of its most primitive and brutal members," aesthetic taste
too falls "to that of the least sensitive and most ignorant" (68).

To challenge Macdonald's gloomy outlook, one need only look back
roughly a decade to the point of view articulated by one of the most
distinguished practitioners of modern hardboiled fiction. Indeed, in "The
Simple Art of Murder" (1944), Raymond Chandler asserted that respectable

codes of conduct remained intact in the contemporary detective story, which thus retained from his perspective the potential to function as the site of a renewed ethics.

The opening paragraphs of Chandler's celebrated essay seek to situate the detective or mystery story vis-à-vis the commercial book trade. After denouncing the "best sellers" that merely imitate the great works of literary realism, he turns to the genre for which he had by this time become well known. Crime fictions, he argues, tend not to sell that well because their primary topic – murder – is insufficiently conducive to "uplift."[18] Narratives or this sort are customarily focused on "the frustrations of the individual" and are therefore less marketable than materials designed to contribute to the moral elevation of the consumer. What then is the author's rationale for composing tales of violence and cruelty? An answer appears at the end of the critical piece when Chandler describes the detective as a "hero," as "a man of honor." The implication is that the value of the writer's labor comes from his capacity to produce a figure of nobility with whom readers might wish to identify. "He must be a complete man and a common man and yet an unusual man?" And what distinguishes the ideal private eye is his capacity to maintain control over his desires without eliminating them altogether. He must possess an even temperament. He should be "neither a eunuch nor a satyr" and his vocational pride and trustworthiness insure that he "will take no man's money dishonestly" – though when treated insolently he may seek "a due and dispassionate revenge." Equally imperative is that his actions establish him as a reliable guide for others, as someone whose behavior they can model their own on: "[h]e must be the best man in the world and good enough for any world" (18).

In sharp contrast to historically adjacent cultural phenomena like the proletarian novel (a prevalent trend in the first half of the 1930s) and documentary ventures (which were ubiquitous in the second half of the decade), crime fiction in the period neither focused on the industrialized workplace nor affirmed collective solutions to current socioeconomic problems. Nor were the tough-guy novelists explicitly motivated by a progressive or revolutionary political agenda.[19] Moreover, while their radicalized contemporaries aspired to contribute to the realization of a more democratic future, crime writers pessimistically investigated the burdens of the familial past on persons existing in a seemingly dead-end present. The primary concern of this willfully sensationalist form of print entertainment was with the successes and failures of fictive incarnations of the hardboiled individual to act decently in a world of horrific brutality.[20] Thus, the novels of Dashiell Hammett and Chandler show the tortuous struggles of their respective protagonists to renounce erotic and financial temptations, and in complementary fashion the cautionary fables of writers such as James M. Cain and Horace McCoy depict the disastrous consequences of breaking the law. Throughout the Depression era, the genre functioned as an arena for ethical experimentation. In an extension of the Naturalist tradition inaugurated by Emile Zola, crime fiction in the 1930s supplied the setting for a series of tests designed to investigate how a particular subject should or should not react to extreme situations. As we will see later in this chapter, in accordance with the decidedly masculinist paradigm of the genre, feminine sexuality repeatedly constituted the potentially lethal reality the male adventurer was compelled to confront in his ultimately unsatisfied quest for spiritual redemption.

Long praised as one of the finest achievements in the field, Hammett's *The Maltese Falcon* (1930) is exemplary in that its ethically charged conflict revolves around the relationship between a female client (Brigid O'Shaughnessy) and the private eye (Sam Spade) she has asked to help her. The murder of both Spade's partner and the man he (Archer) was tailing lead swiftly to the revelation that Brigid had given a false name and incorrect information when hiring Spade. Her subsequent, well-orchestrated apology is infuriating because it is both seductive and disorienting: "'This is hopeless,' he said savagely. 'I can't do anything for you. I don't know what you want done. I don't even know if you know what you want.'"[21] Of course, it turns out that like everyone else involved in the case, her object of desire is the ornamental black statuette, which she has found and then hidden so that Joel Cairo and Kasper Gutman won't get it. In the ensuing events, the bird and Brigid prove to be metaphorically aligned. That the woman and the prize possession are interchangeable is brought out late in the novel when, after a brawl with her previous associates in a hotel room, Spade insists Brigid accompany him into the bathroom so that he can determine whether she has stolen a thousand-dollar bill during the struggle. In this curious scene, he orders her to disrobe and scrutinizes her naked body to see if she has hidden the money on her person. That he doesn't find what he is looking for temporarily alleviates his concerns about her trustworthiness; yet the search prefigures Spade's discovery late in the novel as he cuts away its black enamel surface, that the falcon is fake, that it is not the fabulously jeweled artifact he had been seeking. The implication is that Brigid, too, is less valuable than she appears.

In the end, the question that remains, since he admits he has probably fallen in love with her, is whether or not he should sacrifice himself for her sake or turn her into the cops for shooting his partner. He resolves not "to play the sap" (581) for Brigid on the grounds that this would constitute a betrayal of his business partnership, would compromise his professional integrity, and worse would lead to his hanging: "when one of your organization gets killed it's bad business to let the killer get away with it. ... I'm a detective and expecting me to run criminals down and let them go free ... [is] not the natural thing ... [and] no matter what I wanted to do now it would be absolutely impossible for me to let you go without having myself dragged to the gallows" (582). Having made a practical and reasonable decision against eros in favor of his vocational duty and his life, Spade is pleased with himself for having adhered to a maxim that at least does not betray his personal code of conduct. Yet in a final twist, his secretary Effie Perine recoils when he happily reports what he has done, her reaction ("Please don't touch me" [584]) suggesting he is as much a morally repugnant monster as a virtuous role model for others.

Hammett's ambiguous thematic treatment of issues pertaining to loyalty and desire was also at the forefront of his next novel, *The Glass Key* (1931). The narrative pivots on the tense friendship between a small-time gambler, Ned Beaumont, and his racketeer boss, Paul Madvig, in the context of electoral shenanigans. The latter believes that, if he swings the local vote Senator Henry's way and thus gets him reelected, as a reward Paul will both solidify his political control over the city and be in position to marry Janet, the Senator's daughter. Ned is dubious the deal will work out and sardonically advises Paul to secure a written guarantee for the "pound of flesh" he is after. Notably, as the dramatic action unfolds, Hammett invests the tale (by way of Freudian psychoanalysis) with a mythic resonance. The perhaps tongue-in-cheek pun generated by the two protagonists' respective given names (Ned and Paul/Oedipal) adds a legendary feel to the volatile familial dynamics structuring the plot (an effect reinforced by the name of Paul's daughter from another marriage: Opal). The conflict between the two men is clearly framed as a sibling rivalry since both refer to Paul's biological parent as Mother. Moreover, the solution to the mystery reveals that Paul's would-be father-in-law, the Senator, has in fact killed his own son in a fit of rage, beating him with a walking stick in the street. Ultimately, the only way to put things right is to allow Henry to be convicted for the crime of filicide, yet in the course of arranging this Ned winds up stealing his best friend's girl. Previously, Ned had shown he was willing to suffer great pain to avoid betraying his pal, allowing himself to be tortured for refusing to supply another local mobster with "the dope on Paul" (667). In the end, however, Ned's actions demonstrate there is honor among hoodlums only until an attractive woman gets involved.[22]

The specificity of James M. Cain's noir fiction in the 1930s is that it depicts just how far its male antiheroes will go under the spell of the femme fatale. In *The Postman Always Rings Twice* (1934) Frank's obsession with

Cora leads him to conspire with her to do away with her husband, Nick Papadakis. The remarkable exhibition of savage lust that occurs after they have successfully staged "the Greek's" death by car crash suggests that their moral and legal transgressions have increased the sexual intensity of their relationship, the possibility of (eternal) punishment for their evil deeds in no way a barrier to their desire:

> I was some kind of animal, and my tongue was all swelled up in my mouth, and blood pounding in it.
>   "Yes! Yes, Frank, yes!"
>   Next thing I knew, I was down there with her, and we were staring in each other's eyes, and locked in each other's arms, and straining to get closer. Hell could have opened for me then, and it wouldn't have made any difference. I had to have her, if I hung for it. (41)

However, as the pressure of the ensuing court case builds, the lovers turn on each other, displaying a cruel indifference that startles them both. After having strained to come up with a scheme to get rid of Cora, Frank inadvertently causes her death in a second automobile accident; and it is for this real repetition of the fake event that he is, ironically enough, tried and convicted. Intriguingly, while in the death house awaiting execution, Frank, inspired by the thoughts of another prisoner, reflects on the possibility that he had wanted to commit the crime for which he has been condemned: "There's a guy in No. 7 that ... says you got two selves, one that you know about and the other that you don't know about, because it's subconscious. It shook me up. Did I really do it, and not know it?" (105). Frank emphatically rejects this suggestion, but it remains a disconcerting idea for the reader as well, for it serves as a reminder that we too are not entirely aware of our sometimes reprehensible motivations. The significance of the down-and-out drifter's fate, then, is that it brings to light a subjective propensity for evil that ethical speculation ignores at the risk of rendering itself innocuous.

Similarly, Cain's next novel, *Double Indemnity* (1936), confronts its readers with the possibility that seemingly normal individuals may be manipulated into breaking the law in the vain hope of satisfying their erotic and monetary lusts. An agent for General Fidelity of California, Walter Huff tells us he is not sure "how good" his explanation of "the high ethics of the insurance business" is "going to sound" given how attractive his client (Phyllis Nirdlinger) is: ("[u]nder those blue pajamas was a shape to set a man nuts").[23] And excited by her willingness to do away with her husband, he finds himself fascinated with the abyss of evil into which he is about to plunge: "I was standing right on the deep end, looking over the edge ... I was trying to pull away from it, there was something in me that kept me edging a little closer" (119). Unable to resist the impulse toward transgression, he is not deterred by the fact that his partner in crime somewhat insanely considers herself to be the embodiment of the death drive: "Maybe I'm crazy. But there is something in me that loves Death. I think of myself as Death, sometimes" (124). Only after the pair have murdered her husband and staged his demise as a suicide does Walter grasp the gravity of the mistake he has made. "I had killed a man to get a woman. I had put myself in her power . . . and I would have to die" (158). Worse, he is horrified to learn later on that Phyllis is genuinely mad, a "pathological case" (206), who has killed many times before, even using her position as head nurse in a sanatorium run by her father to eliminate children by somehow infecting them with pneumonia. It is at this instant that he realizes, or admits, as had Horace Benbow under different circumstances a few years earlier, in Faulkner's *Sanctuary* (1931), "that there is a logical pattern to evil."[24] Walter's solution is a suicide pact with Phyllis, and the writing of the narrative breaks off shortly thereafter as the two drown themselves by jumping overboard while traveling on a ship to Mexico.

Horace McCoy's equally gloomy tale of poverty and woe, *They Shoot Horses Don't They* (1935), also features a speaker who is all but dead at the time of narration; yet he is a more sympathetic character than any of Cain's male protagonists. What Robert Syverton has done is shoot Gladys – his bitter, world-weary partner in a dance marathon – in the head to put her out of her misery. But he has done so at her request, he explains, and is in truth just a nice guy with good intentions put in an impossible position. In the eyes of the law, of course, he is guilty. The only thing left for him to do is give us the background to the incident, a task he carries out under the imminent imposition of his death sentence in both senses of the term. In the narrative present, the myriad clauses constituting the judge's pronouncement of Robert's punishment (execution) extend in broken fashion across the entirety of the text, intermittently interrupting the prisoner's account of why he chose to act as he did in the past. The critical burden of the book, then, is to denounce an inhumanely rigid legal system in need of reform on the grounds that "the individual is punished for sins that are the responsibility of society."[25] Yet McCoy adds a modern twist to a protest motif that derives from ancient tragedy in that the montage structure of the book establishes a clear analogy between the court proceedings and the dance marathon: both are spectacles designed to entertain the masses, to satisfy the public's craving for images of corporeal suffering and emotional anguish. Just as the contestants are kicked out of the derby for any infraction of the rules, Robert is disqualified from a highly competitive existence. Moreover, the crowd observing the trial derives as much pleasure from this loser's fate as do those watching the marathon's fallen participants as they prove unable to keep moving and collapse from exhaustion. Both scenarios require that one "bring in the undertaker" and this is precisely the point: it is exciting to see others in effect kill themselves in the struggle to remain among the living.[26] McCoy underscores the comparison by having dance officials solicit audience members to participate in the endurance event as "judges" (to keep track of the number of laps a given couple completes) much as jury duty offers persons the opportunity to be involved in a potentially thrilling trial. Although the legitimacy of the Law rests on its commitment to maintaining order, it surreptitiously offers to its adherents an excess, an enjoyment they should be ashamed to attain.

Appearing shortly after the end of the Golden Age of the detective story, the world-weary resilience of Chandler's Philip Marlowe would seem to offer a moral counterweight to Cain's despicable protagonists as well as to McCoy's forlorn victim. Yet the courageous character's series of disappointing non-exploits indicates otherwise, the futile aspects of his adventures marking the historical obsolescence rather than perpetuation of the paradigm of the heroic individual as deserving of emulation. Marlowe's status as a knight in tarnished armor has been duly noted by most of his commentators, but the degree to which his frustrating failures signal the decline of the romance lineage has been less frequently underscored.[27] Not only do his clients rarely want him to complete his assignments, forcing him to carry out his task against their wishes, but the ladies he nobly strives to help are hardly worthy of his devotion. For instance, in *The Big Sleep* (1939), he is hired by General Sternwood to extract one of his daughters (Carmen) from a blackmail scheme, only to discover that she is a nymphomaniac who in an epileptic fit shot her brother-in-law and that her older sister (Vivian) subsequently covered up the killing. Worse, in Chandler's 1940 masterpiece, *Farewell My Lovely*, Marlowe is eventually employed by a Mrs. Grayle who predictably turns out to be both the unholy object of his quest (a missing nightclub singer named Velma Valento) and the guilty party responsible for several murders. And Mrs. Murdock in *The High Window* (1942) is not much better. A drunkard and bully, she has been manipulating her traumatized secretary, Merle Davis, for decades to hide the fact that she (Murdock) was the one who pushed her husband out the titular window to his death. That the always chivalric Marlowe protects the chastity of the vulnerable Merle is admittedly admirable; but his myriad erotic renunciations may be viewed less charitably as evasive maneuvers rather than as manifestations of his exemplary integrity. For one gets the impression that he must ward off all emotional intensity lest he fall to pieces like Jake Barnes in *The Sun Also Rises* when the latter lets his defenses down at night. Not surprisingly, Marlowe, like his predecessor, often has to reach for the bottle to calm his frazzled nerves.

That there is a humorous dimension to Chandler's highly stylized portrait of stoic manliness has not gone unnoticed, and it is in this register that his artistry prefigures post-1930s literary appropriations of the ostensibly melancholic genre. Erstwhile Marx Brothers collaborator S. J. Perelman's *New Yorker* parody "Farewell My Lovely Appetizer" (1944) amusingly draws attention to among other distinguishing aesthetic traits the detective writer's penchant for descriptive precision, but in so doing Perelman merely hyperbolized what was already hiding in plain sight in the original. For as Geoffrey Hartman put it: Chandler's "is a clownish world: grotesque, manic ... hilariously sad. Chandleresque is not far from Chaplinesque."[28] From this perspective, it was Chandler who in truth set the stage for Chester Himes's trademark blend in the 1950s and 1960s of "slapstick action and populist sentiment" to produce from France "a vision of American society as a violent absurd racial carnival" (McCann 54–56).[29] Meanwhile, Flannery O'Connor was giving a theological spin to noirish material in her *Wise Blood* (1952), a bizarrely funny drama of brutal aggression; Vladimir Nabokov was busy reinventing Cain's confessional approach as modernist black humor in *Lolita* (1955); and William Burroughs was combining hardboiled diction and carnival-grotesque imagery in *Naked Lunch* (1959) – the latter two first published in Paris by Olympia Press. Such work in turn paved the way for Terry Southern's "I Am Mike Hammer" (1963), as well as the quintessentially postmodern, ironic texts of Thomas Pynchon (*The Crying of Lot 49* [1964]) and Ishmael Reed (*Mumbo Jumbo* [1972]) – not to mention the The Firesign Theatre's "The Further Adventures of Nick Danger," which fills the entire second side of their 1969 LP *How Can You Be In Two Places At Once When You're Not Anywhere At All?* Significantly, Hammett's lighthearted final novel, *The Thin Man* (1934) presaged all these comic repetitions of a predominantly tragic mode, which leads one to wonder in retrospect whether the actual legacy of the Depression-era cultural phenomenon that has been under investigation here was its contribution to an ethics of seriocomic laughter.[30]

NOTES

1 Dwight Macdonald, "A Theory of Popular Culture," *Politics* February 1944: 22–23.
2 Faith Baldwin, *That Man Is Mine* (New York: Farrar & Rinehart, 1937), 42.
3 Amy L. Blair, *Reading Up: Middle-Class Readers and the Culture of Success in the Early Twentieth-Century United States* (Syracuse, NY: Syracuse University Press, 2012), 4–5.

4 Janice A. Radway, *A Feeling for Books: The Book-of-the-Month Club, Literary Taste, and Middle-Class Desire* (Chapel Hill: University of North Carolina Press, 1997), 162.

5 Gordon Hutner, *What America Read: Taste, Class, and the Novel, 1920–1960* (Chapel Hill: University of North Carolina Press, 2009).

6 Laura J. Miller, "The Best-Seller List as Marketing Tool and Historical Fiction," *Book History*, Vol 3. (2000), 286–304.

7 For more on the state of the industry, see David Welky, *Everything Was Better in America: Print Culture in the Great Depression* (Urbana: University of Illinois Press, 2008).

8 Display Ad, *New York Times* (16 May 1926), BR32.

9 "Why Has No One Thought of this Before"? Literary Guild of America Circular. (W. E. B. Du Bois Papers, University of Massachusetts Amherst Special Collections & University Archives, 1927) http://oubliette.library.umass.edu/view/pageturn/mums312-b039-i354/#page/1/mode/1up

10 Welky, 165.

11 See Welky, 197–214, for more about the appeal of the novel and the publicity strategies for the book and film.

12 Hutner, 192.

13 Katharine Fullerton Gerould, "Feminine Fiction," *Saturday Review of Literature* (11 April 1936), 3–4, 15.

14 Margaret Culkin Banning, "The Problem of Popularity," *Saturday Review of Literature* (2 May 1936), 3–4, 16–17. See also Hutner, 137–141, for a full account of the debate between Gerould and Banning and the response from Canby.

15 Banning, 4.

16 "Faith Baldwin, Author of 85 Books and Many Stories, Is Dead at 84," *New York Times* (19 March 1978): 38.

17 Dwight Macdonald, "A Theory of Mass Culture," *Mass Culture: The Popular Arts in America*, eds. Bernard Rosenberg and David Manning White (Glencoe, IL: Free Press, 1957), 68.

18 Raymond Chandler, "The Simple Art of Murder," *The Simple Art of Murder* (New York: Vintage Books, 1988), 1–2.

19 For a compelling account of the genre as "a symbolic theater" where the ideological tensions of the era were played out, see Sean McCann, *Hard-Boiled Crime Fiction and the Rise and Fall of New Deal Liberalism: Gumshoe America* (2000).

20 In *Love and Death in the American Novel*, Leslie Fiedler ingeniously conflates the proletarian and detective novel by classifying both as manifestations of a gothic impulse obsessed with the terrors of urbanized violence (New York: Dell, 1966), 481–485, 498–500. Alfred Kazin had made a similar argument at the beginning of the 1940s in *On Native Ground*: "The violence of the left-wing writing all through the Thirties, its need of demonstrative terror and brutality, relates that writing to the slick, hard-boiled novel." Quoted in *Tough Guy Writers of the Thirties*, ed. David Madden (Carbondale: Southern Illinois University Press, 1968), xxxii. Representative texts from this perspective include Edward Anderson's novel *Thieves Like Us* (1937) and Daniel Manwaring's short story "Fruit Tramp" (1934). The latter is collected in *Hard-Boiled: An Anthology of*

American Crime Stories, eds. Bill Pronzini and Jack Adrian (New York: Oxford University Press, 1995).

21 Dashiell Hammett, *Complete Novels* (New York: Library of America, 1999), 419.

22 On Ned as a masochist, see Greg Forter *Murdering Masculinities: Fantasies of Gender and Violence in the American Crime Novel* (New York: New York University Press, 2000), 11–45.

23 James M. Cain, *Double Indemnity* (New York: Alfred A. Knopf, 2003), 112.

24 William Faulkner, *Sanctuary* (New York: Vintage, 1985), 221.

25 Lee Horsely, *Twentieth-Century Crime Fiction* (Oxford: Oxford University Press, 2005), 171.

26 Horace McCoy, *They Shoot Horses Don't They?* (New York: Serpent's Tale, 1995), 23.

27 See however George Grilla, "The Hard-Boiled Detective Novel," *Detective Fiction: A Collection of Essays*, ed. Robin W. Winks (Woodstock, VT: Countryman Press, 1988), 108–110. Replacement figures had already started popping up elsewhere in the Depression-era cultural field. Coming from the same pulp milieu as the Black Mask Boys, Kenneth Robeson's (Lester Dent) Doc Savage and Maxwell Grant's (Walter Gibson) the Shadow would serve at decade's end as touchstones for the comic book superheroes Superman and Batman, who debuted in print in 1938 in Action Comics # 1 and 1939 in Detective Comics # 27 respectively. On the magazine that created "a medium which became a vehicle for the 'hard-boiled' writers, those writers whose heroes acted as rugged individualists while they brought justice to the deserving," see Philip Durham, "The *Black Mask* School," *Tough-Guy Writers*, 51–79; and William F. Nolan, *The Black Mask Boys: Masters of the Hard-Boiled School of Detective Fiction* (New York: Mysterious Press, 1985), 19–32.

28 Geoffrey T. Hartman, "Literature High and Low: The Case of the Mystery Story," *The Poetics of Murder: Detective Fiction and Literary Theory*, eds. Glenn W. Most and William W. Stowe (New York: Harcourt Brace and Jovanovich, 1983), 223. See also Ross Macdonald, "The Writer as Detective Hero," *Detective Fiction*, 183–184.

29 Or was it Hammett? With regard to his convoluted plots, Margaret Atwood proposes, "in their carnage: they resemble multiple car crashes. This was the age of the Keystone Kops, when mayhem was first portrayed on the screen, and surely some of the brawls and corpse-fests in Hammett were intended to be funny in this quasi-slapstick way." www.theguardian.com/books/2002/feb/16/crime.margaretatwood. See also Ross Macdonald: "I think *The Maltese Falcon* ... is tragedy of a new kind, dead-pan tragedy." *Self-Portrait: Ceaselessly into the Past* (Santa Barbara, CA: Capra Press, 1981), 112. Perelman, on the other hand, gave credit to Chandler, declaring in a 1969 interview that "He took the private-eye legend, which had been invented by Dashiell Hammett, and refined it and added an element that was not very obvious, and that was humor." *Conversations with S. J. Perelman* (Jackson: University Press of Mississippi, 1995), 53.

30 One might add to the list above two late countercultural mutilations of the codes of the detective novel: Thomas Berger's *Who Is Teddy Villanova?* and Richard Brautigan's *Dreaming of Babylon*, both published in 1977, though the latter is set in 1942.

12

WILLIAM SOLOMON

Performance and Politics in the 1930s

Like the burlesk comedian, I am abnormally fond of that precision which
creates movement.

E. E. Cummings, *Is 5*

What if I write circuses? No one says a novel has to be one thing. It can
be anything it wants to be, a vaudeville show . . .

Ishmael Reed, *Yellow Back Radio Broke-Down*

T. S. Eliot's name has long been synonymous with high modernism in part
because his monumental accomplishment, *The Waste Land* (1922), is a
notoriously difficult work of art that makes great demands on the reader.
But critical declarations he voiced in the 1930s counter the impression that
he was an elitist snob who loathed "low" cultural materials. In the Norton
lectures he delivered at Harvard, and which were published shortly thereafter as *The Use of Poetry & The Use of Criticism* (1933), Eliot turned on
several occasions to the realm of popular entertainment to evoke an idealized
model of the artist's relationship to the public. In concluding his first talk, he
argued that poets wish mainly to provide pleasure and divert their audience,
and they logically hope they will reach as large a number of people as
possible. Thus, from "one point of view, the poet aspires to the condition
of the music-hall comedian."[1] Correlatively, in bringing the next lecture to a
close he affirmed the widespread fondness in Elizabethan England for "beer
and bawdry," and therefore for the sort of people whom one might encounter "in the local outlying theatres to-day" and who legitimately crave "cheap
amusement to thrill their emotions, arouse their mirth and satisfy their
curiosity" (44). Dullness (then and now) is the only real crime dramatists
might commit, as in order to survive one must delight prospective ticket
purchasers. Finally, in the last lecture he revisits this topic, declaring again
that many who write poetry "would like to be something of a popular
entertainer" and are therefore likely to find "fulfilment in exciting . . . communal pleasure," the satisfaction of accomplishing such a task serving as a
reward for the strain of literary labor, as "compensation for the pains of
turning blood into ink" (147).

The desire on the part of experimental writers to match the cultural
achievement of popular entertainers remains an insufficiently appreciated

aspect of Depression-era literary practice. Indeed, through the decade inventive American writers sought to renegotiate their position in the overall field of cultural production by aligning themselves with (rather than repudiating) various forms of commercial revelry. Henry Miller remains the most telling case in point, his embrace of burlesque and vaudeville routines and fond memory of Coney Island attractions and silent screen comedians animating his quasi-autobiographical endeavors at this initial stage of his career. But such predominantly though not exclusively urban amusements (the circus is an important exception to this rule) also helped shape Djuna Barnes's compositional strategy in *Nightwood* (1936); impacted shorter materials by Thomas Wolfe, William Saroyan, and Eudora Welty; and even played a subtle role in James Agee's documentary labors. Although the specificity of the disparate literary projects listed earlier requires individual analysis, taken together they indicate the emergence of a new ambition to incorporate into literary ventures the affective force and corporeal excitement associated with residual modes of collective fun or leisure. Moreover, as they developed the appeal of theatrical spectacle at the expense of illusionary narration, the authors in question increasingly tended to invoke the prospective reader's presence, taking the latter into consideration as a performer on stage might a member of the actual audience in attendance at an enjoyable show.

In so doing, they were bringing to creative fruition a critical revaluation of aesthetic priorities that had its origins in this country in the mid-1920s. Key essays by two major figures in modernist prose and poetry respectively helped initiate this transition: John Dos Passos's "Is the 'Realistic' Theatre Obsolete?" and E. E. Cummings's "The Adult, the Artist and the Circus" and "Coney Island." The first two of these appeared in print in 1925 in *Vanity Fair*, whereas the third was published in the same magazine the following year. These three pieces helped lay the groundwork for the subsequent emergence in the 1930s of a performance-based approach to literary composition.

The occasion for Dos Passos's critical intervention was the Theatre Guild's recent production of his friend John Howard Lawson's *Processional*, a play Dos Passos admired, on the one hand, because it had shattered "many theatrical conventions" and, on the other hand, because it augured a solution to the dangers threatening to render the stage extinct. As one of the last survivors of "the arts of direct contact," the theater, to avoid following "the bison and the dodo," must discover a way to respond to the challenge the rise of the technical media – "the movies and radio and subsequent mechanical means of broadcasting entertainment and propaganda" – currently pose to it.[2] Although it has outlasted religion as "the focus of mass emotion," the imperiled theater has lost over time the communal centrality it had in antiquity when plays "had their real being [and] where they were acted and applauded and hissed by the populace as spectacular and emotional entertainment" (76). The mistake the present-day theater continually makes is to try and satisfy the jaded tastes of its well-heeled clientele while ignoring the desires of an (prospective) audience composed of "unsophisticated hot-blooded people." In adhering to "the idiotic schism between Highbrow and Lowbrow," contemporary playwrights have wasted their energy on dated and insufficiently invigorating fare that repeatedly fails to wring "people's minds and senses and hearts" (76).

It is therefore to be expected that Lawson's avant-garde enterprise, which abandoned drama's traditional reliance on the invisible fourth wall, shocked those in attendance on opening night. Long accustomed to being given the impression that they are looking into "a room, one side of which is imagined to be transparent," the spectators were startled to learn that *Processional* dispensed with "the power of illusion" and did not seek to maintain the pretense that what one sees "going on on the stage really exists in the world of actuality." Whereas the "great triumph of the realistic theatre" may be sarcastically summarized via the claim that "people put their umbrellas up coming out of *Rain*," Lawson's antithetical aim was "to put on a show," to construct a performance that would "invade the audience's feelings," that would "move and excite" rather than fool or perceptually hoodwink them. Long before the dissemination in the United States of the notion of proletarian realism, Lawson resisted the temptation to "convince the audience that by some extraordinary series of coincidences they have strayed into a West Virginia mining town in the middle of an industrial war" (77). Predictably, the innovative playwright's effort to begin the process of climbing "out of the blind alley of realism" was received by those ill-equipped to handle it as an unpleasant experience; "horror and consternation" were the reaction of the intellectuals who had come to see "real life honestly set down." However, there are many who are not "afraid of being moved either in space or time or in their feelings." These are the kind of people who when "coaxed . . . to take a ride on a roller coaster" will not get "sick" and hold "on desperately" praying it will stop. Kinetic fun neither frightens nor makes the urban masses nauseous, and the target audience of a non-verisimilitudinous theater should therefore be those "who genuinely desire motion," especially since "a trip to Coney Island on a Sunday afternoon" demonstrates that "there are great many people . . . in New York . . . crazy to ride on roller coasters" (77).

Cummings's even more enthusiastic, hyperbolic endorsement of a popular recreation in "The Adult, the Artist, and the Circus" furnishes him with the context to explain his understanding of the existential virtues of modernist aesthetics. In the essay, he implores his reader not to be tricked into accepting the "perfectly superficial distinction" the vulgar draw "between the circus show and 'art' or 'the arts,'" lest one overlook the vital contribution all such cultural practices make to the general wellbeing of society.[3] The circus and art must, however, be considered independent of what Cummings ironically terms the "lofty amusements" – the legitimate theater, movies, and radio – and disparages as "powerful anaesthetic[s] known as Pretend," the pernicious effect of which is to deaden sensation (252). Whereas the only thing these artificial palliatives are good for is to help neurotic grown-ups repress their childhood memories of overwhelming enjoyment, the circus is a genuinely "curative institution," the "outrageous intensity" of which has the potential to bring mental illness, physical disability, and criminal behavior to an end. Out of concern for the future health of the nation, the legislative branch of the government should therefore declare regular exposure to the delights of "the menagerie" mandatory. "Were Congress to pass a bill compelling every adult inhabitant of the United States of America to visit the circus at least twice a year … I believe that, throughout the entire country, four out of five hospitals, jails, and insane asylums would close down … [and] hundreds of cripples – lame, halt, or blind – would toss their infirmities to the winds" (253). Not only would such a "highly concentrated dose of wild animals" prove "indispensable to the happiness of all mature civilized human beings" but its cathartic effect would in addition leave "millions of psychoanalysts" out of a job. If the active ingredient of the remedy in question is a chaotic "*kind of mobility*," optically absorbed movement functions in this desirable fashion to the degree that it constitutes an authentic encounter with the generally overlooked cause of collective sickness: human finitude (254; emphasis in the original): "At positively every performance Death himself lurks, glides, struts, breathes, is" (255).

Significantly, Cummings goes on to define the death defying feats of human daredevils as great artistic achievements in their own right. One memorable risk taker can be compared to Cézanne because, like the painter, the skilled performer died "in the execution [in both senses of the word] of his art" (255). Such a death is "illustrious" in that it amounts to a sacrificial gesture that supplies the spectator with one of those "thrilling experiences of a life-or-death order" required to jolt one into an awareness of one's own mortality (255). The essay's final paragraph then confirms that the motivation behind Cummings's exaggerated praise of the circus was to upend commonplace attitudes toward artistry. Of the four analogies he offers in conclusion, all of which provocatively conflate the two spheres, the last one is the most indicative in that it aligns a figural mode of linguistic expression with the bodily behavior of living (marine) creatures on display: "the fluent technique of seals and of sea lions comprises certain untranslatable idioms, certain innate flexions, which astonishingly resemble the spiritual essence of poetry" (256).

Cummings's tribute to Coney Island extends this line of argumentation, asserting that the amusement park is superior to the theater (defined here as a site of deception) and the circus (the realm of the "hair-raising, breath-taking, and pore-raising") in that it is a fusion of the two that combines their respective elements to constitute an "incredible temple of pity and terror, mirth and amazement."[4] The singular achievement of this "miracle mesh," however, is that its mechanized attractions dissolve the distinction between embodied spectator and fabricated spectacle: "the essence of Coney Island's 'circus-theatre' consists in its *homogeneity*. THE AUDIENCE IS THE PEFORMANCE" (259; emphasis in the original). In soaring through the air on a roller coaster, the park's patrons become acrobats, actively involved in the kinetic experience rather than passive observers of the movement of others. The pertinence of the recreational phenomenon for the enthralled commentator is that it augurs the future of art in general and literature in particular. Riding figures what writing and reading alike hope to achieve someday: the status of an act taking place in the present and that in the process overcomes all spatial and temporal difference. In the following decade, Henry Miller would seek to realize this perhaps impossible goal via an autobiographical project that, in bold defiance of traditional expect-ations, shifted the focus away from representation toward comic performance.[5]

Banned in the United States until the 1960s, *Tropic of Cancer* appeared in print in Paris in 1934 by virtue of Jack Kahane's Obelisk Press, one of the last of the small, privately owned and operated presses that had served in the preceding decade as a primary condition of possibility of literary modernism. Gaining access to this nonindustrialized mode of cultural production enabled Miller to abandon a key generic convention and invest his autobio-graphical discourse with the force of an event taking place at the moment of composition. Finding an alternative to the large publishing firms granted Miller a degree of freedom from the pressure to conform to the demands of the commercial marketplace, which in turn allowed him to adopt an unusual approach to narrative temporality; by getting "off the gold standard of literature" he could make the grammatical decision to emphasize the first-person present tense.[6] Rejecting the assumption that the speaker can only report what has previously happened to him, Miller's work situates the reader as someone hearing about occurrences instantaneously, as if they are in the process of unfolding. This striking appeal to the here and now is evident in the first line – "I am living at the Villa Borghese" (1) – and continues as the speaker/writer declares that he can barely keep up with the frenetic pace of his existence. "So fast and furiously am I compelled to live now that there is scarcely time to record even these fragmentary notes" (12). The temporal entanglement rather than separation of life and art, of spontaneous action and interpretive reflection, makes the unpredictable contingencies of everyday life part of both the story and its telling. Thus, when a ringing telephone suddenly "interrupts" a nascent commentary on the state of contemporary society, it is just as well for he would "never have been able to complete" the thought anyway (12).

The partially feigned rapidity with which Miller claims to be writing complements the formal organization of the book as a kind of vaudeville or burlesque show. Rather than a causally motivated narrative, *Cancer* treats the page as a stage where a discontinuous series of scattershot routines, all of which feature the same nonstop monologuist striving to convey his feelings, take place. It is the dramatically shifting moods of the clownishly eccentric performer with regard to his situation, relation to others, and future prospects – his often abrupt transitions from exuberant delight to bitter vengefulness, compassion to disdain, optimism to despair – that constitute the focal point of the funny bits he has concocted to capture his audience's interest. Consequently, the value of the text derives less from its status as an epistemologically valid documentary account of the joys and sorrows of the expatriate lifestyle than from its capacity to transfix and excite the reader via the construction of a "caricature of a man." Although the phrase comes from a description of his friend, Moldorf, what is said about the latter holds for the ludicrous speaker as well ("We have so many points in common that it is like looking at myself in a cracked mirror" [9]). Both possess a mind that "is an amphitheater, in which the actor gives a protean performance," the myriad roles he plays including "clown, juggler, contortionist, priest, lecher, mountebank." Whether or not *Cancer's* subject matter is referentially grounded or not is therefore of minimal consequence. Miller's strolls through Paris, his encounters with prostitutes, his sexual escapades, and adventures with his pals, probably all happened; but these are offered not as a means of furnishing accurate knowledge about the way he inhabits an unfamiliar milieu but instead as material for humorously oriented, if frequently obscene verbal performances. The typical expectation of cognitive gain may be denied, yet in compensation one is given the opportunity to hear about or watch surprisingly aberrant or transgressive behaviors that may either disgust or titillate but are always intended to produce a strong emotional reaction of some sort. Whether the scene involves Miller prematurely ejaculating in the midst of a nightclub hookup and vomiting in a drunken frenzy in a hotel room afterward; or arranging a disastrous brothel visit for a licentious friend who mistakenly defecates in a bidet; or imagining a bloodbath during a classical concert, the primary goal remains to entertain in as stimulatingly provocative a manner as possible. In sum, the effect Moldorf has on his wife Fanny when he manages to make her squirm as if there "is something inside her, tickling" her, and that she'll "die laughing if she doesn't find" (36), is analogous to the impact Miller aspires to have on his reader.

In a significant passage late in the text Miller figures the affective dimension of his semi-improvisational humorous undertaking in electrical and erotic terms as the putting of "the live wire of sex between the legs" in order to hit the reader "below the belt" and scorch "the very gizzards" (249). The trope makes apparent that his aim was to incorporate what Henry Jenkins has called the vaudeville aesthetic into an avant-garde project, the pressing goal of which was to go beyond the provision of pleasure and generate states of painful ecstasy.[7] Cognate with contemporaneous formulations such as Antonin Artaud's idea of a "Theatre of Cruelty," George Bataille's theory of laughter, Walter Benjamin's views on shock (as articulated in "The Work of Art in the Age of Mechanical Reproduction" [1936] and "On Some Motifs in Baudelaire [1939], as well as the motivation underlying Louis-Ferdinand Céline's novelistic practice in *Journey to the End of the Night* (1932) and *Death on the Installment Program* (1936), Miller's anarchic social imperative was to revitalize the perceptual faculties and resurrect the emotional sensibility of the enfeebled inhabitants of urban-industrial modernity.[8] "Behind the gray walls there are human sparks, and yet never a conflagration" (245). Bodies and minds must be violently assaulted in the desperate hope of the writer that the suffering he causes will serve as a stimulus that will restore to others the energy they require to live with proper intensity. "If now and then we encounter pages that explode, pages that wound and sear, that wring groans and tears and curses, know that they come from a man with his back up, a man whose only defenses left are his words" (249). Forceful writing (as wiring) is the only way to blast through "the hard carapace of indifference" and make people attentive to the awfulness of civilized existence. The "obscene horror" must be confronted by creative beings who desire to bring something out of the abyss, the "yawning gulf of nothingness" from which others turn away in fear. Bringing his uncritically gendered metaphor to a close, he therefore proclaims that the admirable artist must hitch "his dynamo to the tenderest parts; if only blood and pus gush forth" (250). And to accomplish this task the writer as performer must be willing to make a "frightening spectacle" of himself, to exhibit himself like a monstrous concatenation of a stand-up comedian and burlesque stripper. Those who wish in carnivalesque manner to turn "everything upside down," must "bellow like crazed beasts," must "rip out" their

"entrails;" "anything less shuddering, less terrifying, less mad, less intoxicated, less contaminating, is not art" (255).

As the decade wore on, Miller would clarify in subsequent works the
degree to which his investment in a range of popular amusements served
as a touchstone for his aesthetic intervention in the world. For example,
"The Fourteenth Ward," an autobiographical reminiscence that opens *Black
Spring* (1936), concludes with a grotesque reverie that conflates his youthful
literary heroes (Dostoevski and Swift) with a Coney Island attraction, the
Dragon's Gorge, as if his first experience of reading these authors was
analogous to taking a ride on this scenic railway. Equally pertinent is "Into
the Night Life …" contained in the same collection and which has as its
epigraph "A Coney Island of the Mind." Framed as the reproduction of a
sleeping subject's passage through a series of hallucinatory dreamscapes, he
eventually arrives at a destabilized version of the recreational site where
everything "slides, rolls, tumbles, spins, shoots, teeters, sways and
crumbles."[9] Allusions to the dime museum display of human oddities also
occur throughout his oeuvre, most notably in "An Open Letter to Surrealists
Everywhere" in the context of a viewing of a Salvador Dali painting at an art
exhibition. ("And what was it I witnessed in the festival of the
Unconscious? … the organs of the human body, the parts we look at
without shuddering only in the butcher's shop") – a sight that brings to
mind the "incongruous and anomalous" corporeality of Bowery freak
shows.[10] Lastly there is his expression in "The Golden Age," a tribute to
the avant-garde film director Luis Bunuel, of his past adoration of the silent
screen generation of slapstick comedians, "each with his own special brand
of monkey shines," a trend that culminated in Laurel and Hardy's *Battle of
the Century* insofar as this film brought "pie-throwing to apotheosis"
(*Cosmological Eye* 54).

However, without question the most revealing of Miller's numerous references to popular entertainment occurs in his 1939 sequel to *Cancer*: *Tropic
of Capricorn*. Late in the book he recalls a moment in the 1920s when
commercial preoccupations had ruined the fun of amateur modes of play,
talented individuals henceforth hired by "the radio and movies" where their
skills were wasted. But one "wonderful nut" escaped this fate, "an anonymous performer on the Keith circuit who was probably the craziest man in
America." He could hold an "audience spellbound," "just improvised,"
"never repeated his jokes or his stunts," and "gave himself prodigally."
His "energy and joy" were "so fierce nothing could contain it." This is of
course a portrait of Miller's primary role model as a writer, and as such
retroactively confirms the comic dimensions of his autobiographical enterprise. Crucially, as the passage unfolds, the cathartic intentions animating

his project, as well as its collective thrust and correlative status as an act of protest, also become apparent. The following quotation is a lengthy yet indispensable summary of the emancipatory effects Miller envisioned his personal brand of literary lunacy having on the country:

> He was the whole show and it was a show that contained more therapy than the whole arsenal of modern science. They ought to have paid a man like this the wages which the President of the United States receives. They ought to sack the President of the United States and the whole Supreme Court and set up a man like this as ruler. This man could cure any disease on the calendar. ... This is the type of man which empties the insane asylums. He doesn't propose a cure – he makes everybody crazy ... when you laugh until the tears flow and your belly aches. ... Nobody can persuade you at that moment to take a gun and kill your enemy; neither can anyone persuade you to open a fat tome containing metaphysical truths of the world and read it. If you know what freedom means, absolute and not a relative freedom, then you must recognize that this is the nearest to it you will ever get. If I am against the condition of the world it is not because I am a moralist – it is because I want to laugh more.[11]

At first glance, Djuna Barnes would seem not to have felt the same sort of affinity with popular amusements that Miller repeatedly expressed in cele-bratory fashion throughout the Depression era. In the series of articles she composed for assorted newspapers between 1913 and 1919, she frequently adopted a reserved stance when commenting on recreational phenomena. "If Noise Were Forbidden at Coney Island, a lot of People Would Lose Their Jobs" (1914) is exemplary in this respect, a skeptical tone and impression of disgust evident in her account of a day spent observing how the crowd of people indulge themselves at the amusement park. Barnes's disdain for collective leisure pursuits would in turn appear to be reflected in the formal recalcitrance of her most important literary achievement, *Nightwood* (1936). An extraordinarily difficult work of art, the recourse the novel takes to methods of writing associated with the early modern period helped ensure that only those with the proper training and educational background would find it immediately accessible. Indeed, the contrived, oratorical manner in which many of the characters and the narrator speak, combined with the densely figurative nature of the language of the text, confirm that Barnes did not care to make the reading process a gratifyingly easy one. With this in mind, it is revealing that Robin Vote, the frustratingly elusive object of desire for her three successive lovers – Felix Volkbein, Nora Flood, and Jenny Petherbridge – is compared to a monstrously lonely Coney Island attraction, "the paralysed man," a performer narcissistically unwilling to "take his eyes off a sky-blue mounted mirror" that reflected his own "'difference'" back to himself for his personal enjoyment.[12] The allusion both situates those wishing to possess the enigmatic woman as spectators of a sideshow phenomenon and suggests they deserve the sorrow they endure as punishment for their inability to break free of the spell a freakishly self-absorbed being, an exotic thing "outside the 'human type,'" has cast over them. The quintessentially modernist text thematically denigrates in this fashion the compelling hold its cultural antagonist exerts over the pathetically yearning masses.[13]

This is, however, only half the story, for the ubiquity of the circus in *Nightwood* encourages a diametrically opposed interpretive perspective. Two decades before, in one of her journalistic pieces, Barnes had characterized the "three-ringed circus" as "a system of joy" that remained valuable to her insofar as it remained a place where one might acquire secret wisdom about a condition of existence before the derived distinction between humans and animals took hold. At the circus the self might recognize her lost counterpart in the form of a wild beast in a cage.[14] That this autobiographical experience has been transferred in *Nightwood* to Robin is evident when Nora (who does advance publicity for the Denckman circus) draws her away from a lioness that has transfixed the younger woman. Yet this recurrent motif of a primitive intimacy, of a nostalgia for a lost bond with a savage other, is less telling for my purposes than the explanation provided earlier in the text as to why Felix "insinuated himself into the pageantry of the circus" (10).

What draws him to the "amiable actresses," the acrobats, swordswallowers, and lion tamers of the European circus, is that he discerns in "their splendid and reeking falsification" a mirror image of his own social masquerade (10–11). Like the costumed performers, he has garbed himself in accordance with an artificial identity; as his father did before him, he pretends to possess an aristocratic lineage, a claim to "nobility, royalty" that is fabricated rather than authentic. Despite what they have in common, there is a crucial difference between Felix and the performers in that his constructed disguise, the title of Baron he has given himself, is designed to hide the humble Jewish background of which he is ashamed. In sharp contrast, the members of the circus troupe have no desire to mislead; they misrepresent who they are to dazzle rather than dupe the public, to add an aura of the "mysterious and perplexing" to the way they appear in front of an audience. This is the source of "that great disquiet called entertainment" (11): the open avowal of one's status as a simulacrum, a copy with no original, a produced effect.

The point is that this articulation, by way of a popular amusement, of a Nietzschean aesthetic of appearance that acknowledges itself as appearance, supplies the modernist writer with the basis for her own art of rhetorical performance. The latter manifests itself in *Nightwood* in the form of Matthew O'Connor, part charlatan, part physician, whose marvelous monologues, filled with stunning displays of linguistic virtuosity, also reek with falsehood. Yet as Felix eventually realizes, the reprobate doctor's fictive speech has its redeeming qualities. He is "undoubtedly ... a great liar, but a valuable liar" (31). Or, as the doctor himself explains to a despairing Nora after Robin has abandoned her, his speech is motivated as an antidote to anguish: "Do you know what has made me the greatest liar this side of the moon? Telling my stories to people like you, to take the mortal agony out of their guts, and to stop them from rolling about, and drawing up their feet, and screaming, with their eyes staring over their knuckles with misery which they are trying to keep off" (114). Perpetually in need of money, he talks "away like mad" for the same reason Miller's anonymous vaudeville performer did: to succor (and sucker) the sorrowful.

It was not only American writers abroad whose work was in the Depression era determined positively by recreational practices. A considerable number of authors working in the United States in the 1930s also looked to popular amusements for formal guidance or functional inspiration. Admittedly, Katherine Anne Porter's organization of "Circus" (1935) as an analysis of the anxiety-inducing aspects of a young girl's first trip to the circus does not rise above the thematic. Nor does Thomas Wolfe's affectionate treatment of this topic in "Circus at Dawn," also appearing in print in 1935, render the phenomenon as more than a romantic memory of an idealized communal existence.[15] His "Gulliver" (1935) is a bit more significant in that the autobiographical speaker turns to the carnival world of freaks as a means of expressing his feelings about his own extreme tallness, although here, too, it is difference rather than similarity that is stressed. When not subject to a gaze that feeds "its fascinated eye on their deformities," the performers occupy a communal realm "he cannot enter."[16] Lastly, William Saroyan's "The Daring Young Man on the Flying Trapeze" utilizes the physical gracefulness in risky circumstances of a circus aerialist as an analogy for its impoverished and starving protagonist's precarious situation in the world; but the fact that the same title encompasses the writer's 1934 collection of stories as a whole suggests that for him the image of the acrobatic performer also served as a reflexive metaphor for the literary daring of the innovative young artist seeking to break into print.

Even more relevant are several of Eudora Welty's oft-anthologized stories dating back to the late 1930s. The title of her first collection, *A Curtain of Green* (1941) hints at the theatrical paradigm structuring her early work; but it is pieces like "Petrified Man" and "Keela, the Outcast Indian Maiden" that demonstrate her enduring concern with sideshow phenomena. The latter is particularly important because it interrogates critically the capacity of the voice, in the form of the barker's pitch, to direct vision toward a cognitively inaccurate understanding of the human oddity on display. Thus Steve, an ex-barker in a traveling circus, cannot overcome the guilt plaguing him now that he has come to understand that his oratory reinforced the false impression that a disabled African American man was a Native American wild woman, a geek, who enjoyed consuming the heads of live chickens. But Welty's relationship as a writer to such attractions is not simply that of a skeptical commentator, for in an equally famous short fiction, "Why I Live at the P.O," her untrustworthy narrator behaves in a comparable manner, striving to persuade her interlocutor that she is providing a truthful rendering of the events leading up to her decision to leave home. Similarly, in "Powerhouse," Welty tests the reader's ability to resist the coercive power of an unreliable speaker. The rhetorical trap "Powerhouse" (the titular figure is based on the jazz band leader Fats Waller) sets for the "listener" is meant to reveal the racist assumptions habitually framing the white spectator's attitude toward black musicians. "When you have him there performing for you, that's what you feel" the narrator as master of cere-monies cajoles us into believing. "You know people on a stage – and people of a darker race – so likely to be marvelous, frightening."[17] Here Welty borrows the verbal dynamics employed in a popular cultural practice in order to undermine the biological essentialism it encourages; yet in so doing she offers no reassuring position outside what she indirectly discloses to be an epistemologically unreliable and ideologically pernicious means of delud-ing gullible persons into having faith in what is not true.[18]

Whereas Welty's engagement in the latter half of the 1930s with public amusements draws critical attention to the way in them speech acts tend to masquerade as statements of fact, James Agee, in *Let Us Now Praise Famous Men* (1942), posits joke telling as a promising, because affective-charged, mode of relieving the tensions and sense of isolation his documentary labors entailed. The first of only two allusions in the book to comic performance occurs in the section titled "On the Porch: 2." During this speculative pause in the action, the author admits the virtual impossibility of completing his designated task of reproducing actuality, of providing a referentially accur-ate depiction of the conditions of existence determining the suffering of the three impoverished Alabama tenant farmer families with whom he is staying. So great are the limitations of the "language of 'reality' ... the heaviest of all languages," that only someone with "incredible strength and trained skill" could handle words in a way that would "impart the deftness, keenness, immediacy, speed and subtlety" of the world.[19] The only viable alternative that might alleviate the cognitive burden in question is the jesting method employed by the stand-up comedian. Wit opens a communicative path that would reach its destination in a more economically efficient manner than the reflexive documentarian expects his project will. The other missing pre-requisite would be a reader or prospective reader sufficiently prepared to catch "what is thrown," a reader as responsive as "an audience to whom the complex joke can simply be told, without the necessity for a preceding explanation fifteen times the length of the joke" (208). Unfortunately, no one (including Agee) in the current literary scene can write in this way; still it remains an admirable aspiration.

This passing evocation in the middle of the book of the virtues of theatrical humor is innocuous enough, but it acquires additional significance when the topic is broached again at the end of the lengthy text. There it surprisingly acquires the status of the absent center of the project as a whole. While listening in the company of Walker Evans to two animals (perhaps foxes) call back and forth to one another, Agee is reminded of "an old, not specially funny vaudeville act in which the whole troupe builds up and burlesques a dramatic situation simply by different vocal and gesticulative colorations of the word 'you'" (411). The effect of this natural variant of a comic call-and-response routine is in the end a redemptive one for its auditors. Figuring the impact of the verbal gag in corporeal terms as an enjoyably shattering one, Agee (who in 1939 had collaborated with Robert Fitzgerald on a favorable review for *Time* of Miller's two *Tropics*) claims that "our whole bodies broke into a laughter that destroyed and restored us more even than the most absolute weeping can" (413). The vaudeville aesthetic does not solve the epistemological predicament in which the author finds himself caught, nor does it eliminate the ethical tension disturbing him; it nevertheless turns "out to have been the most significant, but most unfathomable, number in the show" (415). In conclusion, the mysterious profundity of comic performance grants it an importance that exceeds the descriptive mania, the exhaustive cataloguing of the real that constitutes the bulk of the text.

In the first sentence of his 1939 essay, "Avant-Garde and Kitsch," which would become one of the most influential critical codifications in the United States of the priorities of high modernism, Clement Greenberg insisted upon the necessity of distinguishing between two historically adjacent cultural phenomena: an Eliot poem and a Tin Pan Alley song. Although products of the same civilization, the lyric work of art and the popular tune must be separated, and it is the burden of his ensuing discussion to establish the conceptual basis for maintaining this essential opposition. He therefore endorses "aesthetic purification" as the only way to keep industrially manu-factured culture, the disturbingly "ersatz" other of a properly "esoteric" art, at a distance. From Greenberg's gloomy perspective, the socioeconomically determined "interval" between the avant-garde and kitsch had become by this point in time "too great to be closed by all the infinite gradations of a popularized 'modernism.'" [20]

The concern of the present essay has been to contest this viewpoint by excavating examples of Depression-era literature that successfully ventured across this cultural divide. What escaped Greenberg was that fact that in this period significant contributions were made to the ongoing attempt to modify the heritage of modernism, to derive artistic inspiration from popular forms of entertainment without necessarily sacrificing a commitment to social progress. The end result of this enterprise was the emergence of a performance-based aesthetic that combined sensationalist excitement, artistic innovation, and utopian longing. On the other side of World War II, the achievement of the Beats furnishes a glimpse of subsequent manifestations of the tendency in question. Lawrence Ferlinghetti's aptly-titled poetry collection *A Coney Island of the Mind* (1958) is worth mentioning in this context. So too is Jack Kerouac's "Seattle Burlesque," an excerpt from *Desolation Angels* (1965) originally printed in a 1957 issue of the *Evergreen Review*. This piece was also selected by Leroi Jones for inclusion in *The Moderns*, a 1963 anthology focused, as he put it in the introduction, on an enduring "tradition of populist modernism that has characterized the best of twentieth-century American writing."[21] Also contained in the anthology was William Burroughs's "Vaudeville Voices," which featured material from *The Ticket that Exploded* (1962), the second installment in *The Nova* or *Cut-Up* trilogy. I want to close with the familiar term that Burroughs devised for his montage/collage method of rearranging preexisting texts, since cut-ups semantically condenses the two interrelated topics of this discussion: an investment in avant-garde techniques and interest in practical jokers.[22] In sum, the mixed desire on the part of writers in the 1930s to experiment and to amuse, and correlatively to generate painful and pleasurable effects, set the stage for what we have subsequently learned to conceptualize as the impure aesthetics of postmodernism.

NOTES

1 T. S. Eliot, *The Use of Poetry & The Use of Criticism* (Cambridge, MA: Harvard University Press, 1961), 22. Similarly, in the preceding decade, in his well-known "London Letter" (1922), he stated that the popular music-hall artist Marie Lloyd fully deserved the public affection she had received during her lifetime because her performances both made people "happy" and constituted a communal experience, one in which those in attendance joined the chorus and in so doing "engaged in that collaboration of the audience with the artist which is necessary

in all art." T. S. Eliot, *Selected Essays* (New York: Harcourt, Brace and Company, 1975), 172–174.

2 John Dos Passos, "Is the 'Realistic' Theatre Obsolete?" Many Theatrical Conventions Have Been Shattered by Lawson's *Processional, The Major Nonfictional Prose*, ed. Donald Pizer (Detroit, MI: Wayne State University Press, 1988), 75.

3 E. E. . Cummings, "The Adult, the Artist, and the Circus," *Another E. E. Cummings* (New York: Liveright, 1998), 256.

4 E. E. Cummings, "Coney Island," *Another E. E. Cummings*, 258.

5 For a recent discussion of the repercussions of Cummings's critical repurposing of popular entertainment on his literary prose, see Justus Nieland, *Feeling Modern: The Eccentricities of Public Life* (Urbana: University of Illinois Press, 2008), 109–132.

6 Henry Miller, *Tropic of Cancer* (New York: Grove Press, 1961), 243. To my knowledge, the only other Depression-era text to employ the first-person present tense in this hyperbolic fashion is Tom Kromer's minor yet fascinating "down-and-out" novel, *Waiting for Nothing* (1935).

7 Henry Jenkins, *What Made Pistachio Nuts? Early Sound Comedy and the Vaudeville Aesthetic* (New York: Columbia University Press, 1992), esp. 59–95.

8 In "Sacrifice," an essay dated 1939–1940, Bataille proposed that laughter is a communicative activity in which "a live current" circulates from one individual to another. *October* 36 (Spring 1986): 62. In *Conversations with Professor Y* (1955), Céline explains his "emotive" style in the Depression era as having been an effort to plug "right into the nervous system" (Normal, IL: Dalkey Archive Press, 2006), esp. 93, 107. Sergei Eisenstein's critical formulation in the mid-1920s of a "Montage of Attractions" is a crucial precursor to all of the aesthetic theories mentioned above. He made his debt to the circus and other popular entertainments explicit in the essays he devoted to this topic.

9 Henry Miller, *Black Spring* (New York: Grove Press, 1963), 160.

10 Henry Miller, *The Cosmological Eye* (1939; New York: New Directions, 1961), 172–73.

11 Henry Miller, *Tropic of Capricorn* (New York: Grove Press, 1961), 303–305. An early version of the ideas articulated in this passage can be found in "Burlesk," the penultimate piece in *Black Spring*.

12 Djuna Barnes, *Nightwood* (Normal, IL: Dalkey Archive Press, 1995), 121.

13 In this regard, T. S. Eliot's advice to the reader in his 1937 introduction to *Nightwood* is justified. "To regard," he states, " this group of people as a horrid sideshow of freaks is not only to miss the point, but to confirm our wills and harden our hearts in an inveterate sin of pride" (New York: New Directions, 1961), xvi. The pernicious function of such spectacles is to supply viewers with the pleasure of feeling they are superior to the suffering objects put on display, which is for Eliot not Barnes's intent as a novelist.

14 Djuna Barnes, "Djuna Barnes Probes the Souls of Jungle Folk at the Hippodrome Circus," *New York*, ed. Alyce Barry (Los Angeles, CA: Sun and Moon Press, 1989), 190–197.

15 For more on these two pieces and related materials, see Patricia L. Bradley, *Robert Penn Warren's Circus Aesthetic and the Southern Renaissance* (Knoxville: University of Tennessee Press, 2004).

16 Thomas Wolfe, "Gulliver," *Thomas Wolfe Short Stories* (New York: Penguin Books, 1947), 95.

17 Eudora Welty, "Powerhouse," *A Curtain of Green* (New York: Harvest, 1979), 254–255.

18 I explore this matter in greater detail in "The Rhetoric of the Freak Show in Welty's *A Curtain of Green*," *Mississippi Quarterly* 68: 1–2 (Winter-Spring 2015): 167–188.

19 James Agee, *Let Us Now Praise Famous Men* (New York: Mariner, 2001), 208.

20 Clement Greenberg, "Avant-Garde and Kitsch," *Art and Culture: Critical Essays* (Boston: Beacon Press, 1989), 16. The essay was first published in *Partisan Review*.

21 Leroi Jones, "Introduction," *The Moderns: An Anthology of New Writing in America* (New York: Corinth Books, 1963), xvi.

22 Two recommendations for further investigation in this area: (1) the underground filmmaker Jonas Mekas' autobiographical masterpiece, *Walden* (1969), especially the portion titled "Notes on the Circus," where the images of the dazzling performers on their respective apparatuses functions as a series of reflexive figurations for the cinematic artist's skillful handling of his camera during the shooting process. (2) Clancy Sigal's classic road novel, *Going Away* (1962), a meditation on the fading of the legacy of Depression-era radicalism in Cold War America. Of particular interest in the present context is the narrator's discovery while working for a distributor of old Hollywood films of the subversive potential of sabotaging the prints (by snipping away crucial frames) before they are sent out to television stations for consumption by late night viewers (Boston: Houghton Mifflin, 1962), 472–492.

13

CAREN IRR

Remembering the 1930s in Contemporary Historical Fiction

"I ain't no FOP, goddammit! I'm a Dapper Dan Man!" Everett Ulysses McGill indignantly declares in the Coen Brothers' *O Brother Where Art Thou?* (2000). Satirizing the Depression-era classic *Sullivan's Travels*, the Coens exaggerate the brand name fixations of their loquacious hero, milking laughs from the manic grooming habits he follows even when on the run from a chain gang. The fact that McGill is played by the famously handsome George Clooney only underscores the irony of this characterization. Clooney's own arguably foppish star power advances the Coens' project of relentlessly overturning the documentary sincerity and social purpose associated with the 1930s; the filmmakers archly comment on what they see as the racist motives underlying period representations of folk authenticity whether this ethic is applied to hair, regional songmaking, or marital union. In *O, Brother*, in other words, the Coens remade the 1930s in the style and for the concerns of their own millennial moment – one painfully aware of the grooming of the image.

The Coens are not alone in adapting their accounts of the Great Depression to the needs of a later period. Novelists, filmmakers, historians, social scientists, and politicians obsessively return to the decade that economists Thomas E. Hall and J. David Ferguson have called "the seminal macroeconomic event of the twentieth century," sifting through the historical record for a useable past.[1] Such efforts frequently engage with shifts in economic thought, retelling the story of the thirties in order to stake a claim in a contemporaneous debate over political economy. In rethinking economic history, narratives of the Depression invert, condense, negate, distend, or displace existing narratives about poverty, family, ethnicity, and childhood. Examining the various ways writers have remembered the 1930s thus reveals not only the logic of fictional responses to conflicts within economic thinking but also how literature imagines (or blocks) resolutions to the social contradictions exposed during periods of capitalist crisis.

While the social disruptions triggered by the Great Depression have inspired fictional responses in every subsequent decade, these responses have become less autobiographical and more pointedly interpretive (and thus literary) with the passing of the generation of Americans that came to adulthood during the 1930s. By the 1980s, both the most ardent advocates for the New Deal social welfare project and its immediate beneficiaries had made way for a later group. This later group's initiatives faced powerful opposition from Ronald Reagan's neoliberal economic agenda, and US policy shifted away from redistribution schemes and toward the financialization of capital. Concomitantly, novelists describing the 1930s during the 1980s largely turned away from questions of political struggle to consider the predatory violence and potential for criminality latent within finance capital. During the 1990s, the expansion of the financial and technology bubbles led to a related shift, as a number of writers demonstrated a fascination with the suburban prosperity of the 1950s – a period set in opposition to the purportedly exceptional deprivation of the 1930s. When the 1990s bubble burst, too, in a series of escalating crises leading to the 2008 recession, fictional treatments of life during the Depression returned in force in a group of writings that scoured the 1930s for lessons in enduring low growth, deep inequality, and political polarization.

In none of these phases, however, did historical fiction depicting the 1930s seek the documentary accuracy of a chronicle. Instead, novelists selectively revived motifs from the 1930s to explore contemporaneous anxieties about the stability of the capitalist system. In many cases, they downplayed both the cross-class solidarity and racial tensions of the Depression era while disregarding the restorative potential of state action. Post-1980s historical novelists tended to focus instead on local, voluntaristic activities in a domestic context. This narrative foreclosure of internationalism and the positive potential of the political sphere in contemporary historical fiction devoted to the 1930s might be understood as an anticipation of the protectionist impulses of the Trump presidency, or it might suggest an in-gathering of resources necessary for survival in difficult times. No matter how one explains their reinterpretation, though, the events of the 1930s remain vital to the imaginary of twenty-first-century American fiction.

Accounting for the Depression

Since the 1980s, US fiction set during the 1930s has relied on themes developed by economic historians. Among centrist economists, the Depression prompted two enduring debates. The first asks which policy errors were responsible for the deep double-dip depression for which the 1930s are famous. Those scholars following John Maynard Keynes, one of the most influential economists of the twentieth century and an open advocate of the New Deal, blame problems with fiscal policy – that is, a lack of or poor direction for spending. In contrast, anti-Keynesians associated with the Chicago school of economics attribute the Depression to failures of monetary policy – especially rules governing the supply of money, interest and credit, and the gold standard. Anti-Keynesian positions have been central to the neoliberal dismantling of the New Deal since the 1980s. Both Keynesians and anti-Keynesians, however, blame so-called secular stagnation (or periods of very low growth and increasing inequality) on policy errors rather than the logic of capitalism itself.

The second centrist debate shifts the question away from the causes of the Depression and toward the means of its resolution, asking whether and how World War II can be understood to have ended the Depression. Post-Keynesian economists such as Josef Steindl assert that warfare spending triggered a wave of technological innovations, productivity increases, and market expansions that restored vitality to US enterprises, in so doing ensuring a potentially worrying dependence on militarization and massive energy consumption.[2] This position articulated many of the concerns of the energy-conscious 1970s. In the 1990s, however, Robert Higgs and Paul Romer argued that wartime expenditures did not end the Depression, as a full-blown recovery did not begin until after the eradication of the rationed consumption practices of the early 1940s. Higgs and Romer's disavowal of a concern with militarization demonstrates the neoliberal naturalization of disembodied market forces so characteristic of the Reagan era.[3]

Both of these debates among mainstream economists concentrate on domestic issues. By contrast, radical economists have tended to place the Depression in a longer historical and more global framework. Following Joseph Schumpeter, Paul Sweezy and more recently Michael Roberts have explained the crisis of the Great Depression as the result of a periodic alignment of several well-documented waves – the falling rate of profit that follows periods of technological saturation, migration and demographic patterns, and inventory cycles.[4] The world-systems theorist and economic historian Giovanni Arrighi adds an important element of social analysis to this approach, defining the longer period of 1898–1948 as a period of "fatal crisis" for market capitalism, a crisis triggered in part by the system's difficulty meeting the political and material demands of workers. Arrighi draws on the language of "polarization" developed by Samir Amin to describe the late phases of the British-dominated imperial system as one dependent on a sharp opposition between the resources of the highly developed core and its underdeveloped peripheries.[5] The Depression of the

1930s, on this account, occurred because that polarized structure collapsed under the weight of increased immiseration and the lack of purchasing power in the colonies, forcing a new class compromise to emerge in the metropole after 1945 when the liberation struggles in the newly postcolonial nations released new demands.

Radical economists, in other words, have interpreted the social changes of the 1930s as political rather than economic in origin. They see crises of capitalism as either predictable or at least unsurprising and treat the downturn of the 1930s as a sign of regime change or shifting hegemony rather than as a unique event in need of explanation. Many of these perspectives have been reinvigorated since the financial crisis of 2008 – an experience that has triggered some discussion of the prospects for a leaderless or decentered global economy. That is, attention to the waning of American hegemony since the late 1990s has revived attention to the 1930s as a period of transition. If twenty-first-century conditions suggest a polycentric geopolitical situation may be emerging – or at least one characterized by an unstable situation that Arrighi calls "domination without hegemony" by the United States – then these concerns anchor recent treatments of the 1930s in economic history and the reconsideration of working people's needs during that period in particular.[6]

The theses and concepts economic historians have employed usually make only indirect appearances in historical fiction set during the 1930s, but they permeate the figures, mood, and events of these narratives nonetheless. Every novelistic representation of the Depression takes for granted certain explanations for the events it depicts, often for reasons that have a good deal to do with the concerns of the moment when it was written. These reasons, of course, change over time, and they differ considerably from the explanatory accounts of the Depression offered during the 1930s. The figures of heroic proletarian resistance that were important in the period disappear almost entirely from contemporary historical fiction, for instance; they are largely obscured by a preoccupation with middle-class nostalgia and state bureaucracy. Also, as the Coen Brothers example reminds us, the discourse of folk authenticity lost much of its charm sometime after the 1970s, supplanted by a concern with an ever-expanding consumer culture. Historical distance, in other words, does not necessarily make later accounts of the Depression more objective or credible than those offered during the period, but it does demonstrate how magnetic the raw materials of the Great Depression continue to be. The events of the 1930s remain central to visions of American history, because they pose as-yet unanswered questions about the viability of capitalism. For this reason, they need to be interpreted anew with each passing decade.

Caren Irr

Remembering the Thirties in the Age of Reagan

Scholarly discussions of American literature of the 1980s are shifting away from a celebration of the aesthetic outliers and would-be rebels of the period – whether those are understood as being embodied by edgy experimentation (Pynchon, DeLillo, Gass, Barthelme) or important voices in the identity politics/culture wars (Morrison, Alexie, Roth, et al.). These are the groupings that Mark McGurl calls techno-modernism and high cultural pluralism in *The Program Era*. McGurl understands both of these strains of 1980s writings as expressions of developments in the American university.[7] He identifies these moments with the professionalization of creative labor and the transformation of universities from spaces of relative social mobility and uplift into managerial training grounds. In line with this effort to rethink the 1980s in terms of its sociological rather than aesthetic significance (a task always easier to accomplish in retrospect), other critics have turned their attention to arguably more mainstream writing that captures central developments of the decade. Leigh Claire La Berge's insightful *Scandals and Abstractions: Financial Fictions of the Long 1980s*, for instance, describes the parallel rise of financialization and a genre of financial fiction or "fi-fi" that depicts and advances that process. La Berge analyzes Brett Easton Ellis's scandalous *American Psycho* in relation to its setting in the milieu of Wall Street investment bankers, arguing that the novel's aesthetic complexity creates ideological and material investments in the mystificatory processes of the stock market.[8] Thinking of the literature of the 1980s in this way – as manifesting the dynamics of contemporaneous capitalism – is of course not entirely new. This is also the premise of Fredric Jameson's enormously influential reading of postmodernism as the cultural logic of late capitalism. Jameson mapped out a group of aesthetic effects (such as blank parody and the waning of affect) in would-be experimental art forms that he traces back to the ultra-rapid temporality and disconcerting placelessness of finance capital.[9] Pulling this analysis from the experimental edges into the popular, realist, and genre narratives of the same decade helps us read this cultural logic as more than an esoteric or anticipatory phenomenon. The effects of late (or, as other debates want to call it, neoliberal) capitalist initiatives were felt far and wide in the 1980s. These effects include the placement of a particular filter on pictures of the 1930s. The filter blocks antiquarian nostalgia and selects features of the historical narrative that resonate with 1980s-era concerns. It accentuates the instability of financial speculation and the violence of predatory mergers. That is, the 1980s-era portrait of the 1930s locates the origins of Ellis's murderous investment banker in the gangsterism of the earlier decade.

At least, this is the hypothesis that animates E. L. Doctorow's *Billy Bathgate* (1989). The third of Doctorow's novels to be set in the Depression-era Bronx milieu where the author was born, *Billy Bathgate* is also the least autobiographical. The novel observes the notorious Jewish gangster Dutch Schultz during his decline. As his organization devolves into excessive brutality, Schultz evades prosecution by moving to upstate New York and operating under pseudonyms. While hiding out, Schultz and his henchmen purchase the good will of the locals and even accept baptism into a Christian church. Much of the novel's comedy derives from the mismatch between the gangsters' motives and their efforts at small-town gentility, but this is not ultimately a book that heroizes the gangster as entrepreneur – a tactic we might associate with, say, Mario Puzo. Unlike *The Godfather (1969), Billy Bathgate* stresses the damage inflicted by the illicit businessmen.

For example, Doctorow's novel begins with several shocking killings observed by the titular Billy, a young initiate into the gang. Billy is both terrified and impressed by the gangsters. A child of an insane single mother and a playmate of orphans in a neighboring asylum, Billy is drawn into the hyper-masculine, hyper-paternal world of the gang quite easily. However, the writerly energy of the novel displaces Billy's visceral reactions to the surplus brutality of the killings with spirals of anachronistically mature reflection on their meaning. Billy explains that he "knew from [his] own career with him that Mr. Schultz liked to be pursued, he was vulnerable to people who were attracted to him, followers, admirers, acolytes, and the otherwise dependent, whether show-off kids, or women whose men he killed."[10] These close observations of Schultz and Billy's impregnation of Schultz's high society girlfriend at a rural swimming hole pull the concerns of this book toward problems of social reproduction and the intergenerational legacies of brutality. Billy learns and then applies codes of masculinity from Schultz – albeit not from a high-energy young gangster founding a new organization but rather from the decadent, off-the-hook killer his mentor has become. During the 1930s, gangster films such as Howard Hawks's 1932 film *Scarface* often focused on police pursuit, establishing conventions for action scenes. Indirectly affirming the state's containment and neutralization of populist uprisings, this motif appropriately responded to the statist needs of the New Deal. In the 1980s, however, Doctorow shifts the focus to the exaggeratedly successful replication of gangsterism in legitimate business. At the end of the novel, readers learn that Billy's exaggeratedly erudite narration results from his use of mob resources to procure an Ivy League education and a job in an elite financial institution. For Doctorow, these presentist concerns motivate the narrative. As he told Terry Gross on the National Public Radio show "Fresh Air," the novel points out the differences between the relative clarity of 1930s-era distinctions between business and criminality and 80s-era intermingling of the categories: "It's not quite as clear today in the 1980s who is exactly criminal and who isn't. We've had occasions of public officials who have been supposed or sworn to uphold the law who have, in fact, broken it. And all that kind of thing just leeches it away, gives you almost a wish for the good old days when a crook was a crook and everyone else wasn't."[11] Although he imagines the 1930s through the nostalgic lens of the "good old days," Doctorow also counters this impression by stressing the economic violence that decade set in motion. His conclusion is not the magical rescue criticized by some reviewers, then; it is one of the novel's most cynical passages, as it finds in the 1930s the seeds of the insider trading and investment banker scandals of the later decade. The denouement of the novel makes this concern very clear. Recalling the betrayal that allowed his own survival and rise, Billy mourns the effects on Irving Berman, the mathematical genius of the operation. A ventriloquist for Schultz who uses the vocabulary of numbers on his death bed, "Abbadabba" Berman gives Billy the combination to the safe containing the key to his future wealth: "Three three. Left twice. Two seven. Right twice. Three three" (304). This succinct code provides a marked contrast to Schultz's self-glamorizing deathbed speeches. Billy concludes that Schultz died of "the gangsterism of his mind" (308), while Berman lives on through his trans-formation into numbers and currency. Although morally ambiguous, Berman still ultimately proves a better father figure than the incoherent Schultz, since he provides for Billy's welfare. Berman's patrimony allows his surrogate son to leave behind his mother's madness and the orphan asylum; he becomes a father himself and the head of a legitimate business funded by dirty money.

In the end, Doctorow links physical and financial survival – emphasizing speculative risks and criminality. In a moment when New Deal regulation of finance was under direct assault, Doctorow developed a story of the 1930s that prompts reflection on the origins of the assets that are being deregu-lated. His Dutch Schultz fathers the Jason Bateman of *American Psycho*.

Interregnum of the 1990s

In *A Life Between Two Deaths*, Phillip Wegner designates the period between the fall of the Berlin Wall and the events of September 11, 2001 "the long nineties." Wegner identifies a set of distinctive concerns in American narra-tives of the long decade – many of which are worked out in historical fiction and alternate histories. He asserts that the questions of periodization that lie at the heart of both of these genres respond to a perceived need to rethink the history of the twentieth century in the wake of the "death" of Soviet Communism and the associated ideologies of the Cold War. Wegner argues that the effects of this crisis became manifest in American narratives only after September 11 replayed that crisis, dramatizing a sense of endings and a new arrangement of the world system.[12] The narratives appearing before September 11 demonstrate an unsettled, incomplete affect, as they cast about for means with which to recognize a collective trauma. Wegner's thesis suggests reasons why so many celebrated historical novels of the 1990s return to the 1950s and early 1960s. Certainly, this occurs in Don DeLillo's *Underworld* (1997), David Guterson's *Snow Falling on Cedars* (1994), Dorothy Allison's *Bastard Out of Carolina* (1992), Philip Roth's *American Pastoral* (1997), and Toni Morrison's *Paradise* (1997), for example. Many 1990s-era authors turned to the past for analogies that might anchor an uncertain present. At the crest of major wave of speculation, writers of the 1990s felt an affinity for the localized affluence of the 1950s.[13] But, as John Kenneth Galbraith cautions in his 1994 introduction to *The Great Crash, 1929*, bubbles have a tendency to burst, and the reputed peace and affluence of the 1950s had a conflicted origin in the Great Depression.[14]

Similarly, 1950s-focused novels that proliferated during the 1990s reveal a dependence on stories of the 1930s. They typically revert at key moments to the decade of the mature author's childhood, grounding their sensibilities in a reaction to the norms of the Depression and measuring the imagined economic zenith of the 1950s against the nadir of the 1930s. The Depression appears fleetingly in these novels as an origin point for a version of American modernity that was cresting in the 1950s – a version premised on technocracy and hyperbolic militarism. From the point of view of these narratives, during the 1930s, these forms were not yet firmly set in place. The 1930s serve as a "moment of danger" in the Benjaminian phrase that Wegner so nicely rescues – that is, as a period of risk when many options remain open.

Roth's hero Swede Levov, for instance, compresses these sentiments into a single sentence, describing a party taking place "in a ballroom just at the edge of the country club's golf course for a group of elderly adults who, as Weequahic kids of the thirties and forties, would have thought a niblick (which was what in those days they called the nine iron) was a hunk of schmaltz herring."[15] The process of overcoming the Weequahic kids' former economic and social exclusion is never complete; they – and Swede on their behalf – inhabit their country club grandeur with the wounds of the 1930s embedded deep within their psyches. Having survived the dangers of the Depression, these former ghetto kids remain alive to the contingency of their situation and critical of the latest crop of youngsters who take affluence for granted.

While Roth presents the 1930s as a repressed moment of origin – a repression that briefly leaks into the present by means of the pseudo-Yiddishism "niblick" – other narratives more frontally present the break from the 1930s. Shirley Ann Grau, for instance, is a white southern writer whose family sagas often turn, like Roth's on historical memory. In her Pulitzer-winning 1964 novel, *A Keeper of the House*, she examines inter-racial romance, racist ideology, and the political fall-out of secrets in Civil Rights–era Alabama. Developing a passage from *Keeper of the House* on "left-over children" who "went about in little bands, like stray dogs,"[16] Grau's 1994 companion text *Roadwalkers* opens with African American siblings sleeping in the rough, begging for food, hiding from adult author-ities, and struggling to survive. Initially a group of three, they lose a sister along the way, before brutal kidnappers separate the remaining brother from his nameless younger sister, leaving her stranded in a Catholic orphanage. These opening passages recall Steinbeck, Caldwell, and other 1930s writers who depicted the south in mythic terms, but the novel most directly associates them with Margaret Bourke White's photos of share-croppers – namechecking the FSA photographer later in the novel when the orphan's daughter begins to study art history. She inherits her artistic interests from her mother; at the orphanage, the roadwalking child refuses speech and conversion, preferring to channel her passion into drawings and dressmaking.

It is, in other words, the cultural effects of the deprivation of the 1930s that provides the real subject of *Roadwalkers*. The last two-thirds of the novel recount an integration struggle, when the orphan's daughter becomes one of the first African American students at an elite boarding school. The daughter lives out her taciturn parent's quest for social acceptance and walks the halls of the boarding school gorgeously attired in her mother's creations. These extravagant dresses replicate the imagery of her mother's years as a feral child, and they make the daughter both an emblem and antithesis of those years of wandering.

This treatment of the thirties as a primal scene of deprivation, declawed but still dangerous, also energizes some memoirs of the period – perhaps most notably Frank McCourt's account of a gritty Limerick upbringing in *Angela's Ashes* (1996). McCourt, Grau, and Roth's narratives are survivors' stories, though, and they insist – sometimes just a bit too firmly – on the path from poverty to plenty. The fantasy of the 1990s, after all, was that the technology bubble would endure indefinitely, staving off future economic crises. This is the story that came to an end not so much in 2001 but rather in 2008.

Reimagining the Depression in the Age of Financial Crisis

The financial crisis of 2008 triggered a major revival of crash narratives in American culture. Innumerable journalistic descriptions of the rapid decline in stock market prices, along with the cascading closures of major financial institutions, echoed the firmly entrenched stories of the Great Depression. In Wegner's terms, we might think of the 2008 crisis as a second "death" forcing reflection on the crash of 1929 and the use of crisis rhetoric more generally. It is, however, a death with a difference. After all, while the centrality of financial capital to the American economy since the 1980s might suggest that a crash in the credit market would have had a more deleterious effect in 2008 than it did during the 1930s, the social impact was not identical. Unemployment rates reached 25 percent in 1933, but during the twenty-first-century crisis, the peak of unemployment in the United States was 10 percent, and production did not collapse to the degree it did during the 1930s (see Roberts). Although xenophobic and racist movements certainly took on momentum after 2008 – often in forms directly modeled on the right-wing populism and fascism of the Depression years – those political echoes should not prevent recognition of the fact that no matter how weakened they have been by decades of neoliberal assault, the instruments of social security and wealth redistribution developed during the New Deal buffered the American populace from the worst effects of the 2008 recession. While sacrificing the interests of homeowners to those of the owners of banks deemed too big to fail, the Obama administration nonetheless contained the worst damage inflicted by the neoliberal consensus.[17]

Rather than a massive depression on the scale of the 1930s, then, the aftermath of 2008 more closely resembled a secular stagnation. Michael Roberts in *The Long Depression* describes this stagnation as resembling a squashed square root symbol (i.e., a sharp decline followed by a partial recovery and a plateau at a level below that recorded at the beginning of the cycle). In contrast, the events of the 1930s looked more like a flying W (i.e., two deep troughs followed by a recovery at higher levels). The post-2008 plateau exacerbated inequality domestically, while suggesting to scholars such as Temin and Vines the erosion of US hegemony on the world stage and the emergence of a "leaderless" global economy.[18] Although Panitch and Gindin disagree, arguing that the recession demonstrates the continued centrality of the United States to the global economy, they also see the deep saturation of the national economy by digital communications technologies and automation as promising long periods of low growth in the first decades of the twenty-first century.[19]

In short, in comparison to the Great Depression of the 1930s, the 2008 crisis had a different structure and character. It revealed the instability of a debt-driven financial model rather than the vulnerability of industrial production to financial markets. Also, rather than triggering a forceful correction from the state, the political aftermath of the 2008 crisis amounted to a paralysis on the left and the revival of austerity measures and accelerated privatization measures on the right. Pointing out the ideological continuities that obscure a structural difference, economic historian Philip Mirowski called 2008 "the crisis that didn't change much of anything" (1). The slogan "2008," then, names a project of ideological containment rather than a single moment or event. This project extends from the first years of the twenty-first century through the mid-2010s. Although a group of 2008 novels has already begun to emerge (see Adam Haslett's *Union Atlantic* [2009], Paul Auster's *Sunset Park* [2010], Imbole Mbue's *Behold the Dreamers* [2016], and Mischa Berlinski's *Peacekeeping* [2016]), substantial reflections on the 2008 crisis period have also taken place indirectly through contemporaneous stories of the 1930s.

Twenty-first-century novelistic accounts of the 1930s emphasize ways of living with low growth, problems of social reproduction, and precarious employment in a consumerist rather than producerist economy. These are distinctly anachronistic concerns, although they have some basis in the culture of the Depression. They also lead to revisions of some of the major narratives produced during the Depression – such as the strike novel and the bottom dogs or drifter narrative. However, for a reconsideration of the main themes of the Great Depression from the point of view of the racial and ethnic subjects socially marginalized throughout the twentieth century, one might do no better than to turn to young adult literature such as Christopher Paul Curtis's *Bud, Not Buddy* (1999) or Pam Muñoz Ryan's *Esperanza Rising* (2000), both prize-winning contributions to their genre that respectively interpret African American and Chicana experiences of the 1930s for younger readers.

Among novels for adults, Anita Shreve's *Sea Glass* (2002) offers a particularly clear example of the way that classic themes of 1930s fiction are being rewritten in the twenty-first century. Set in a New Hampshire milltown, *Sea Glass* takes the preparation for a strike as its central action, and its violent climax hinges on an exchange of fire initiated by an untrustworthy would-be supporter of the strike. The concluding author's note mentions the influence of strike novels set in Gastonia – the kind of novels that often feature political conversion or middle-class discovery of conditions in the mills. In place of these more didactic themes, *Sea Glass* focuses on the emotional, romantic, and sexual motives of its several characters. In the midnight conversations of the strike committee, for instance, warm interpersonal relationships overcome any class or political hostility: "'Once you see the world the way [the wealthy Jewish Communist] Louis does – once you *allow* yourself to see it – it's very hard to see it again the way you used to. My sort, I mean. We seem, well, despicable, really'," a wealthy heiress reflects; "'I don't think you're despicable'," the union advocate reassuringly responds before the conversation turns to his love life.[20] Easy communication between classes and political persuasions occurs along emotional lines in this novel, and ultimately the real malfeasance in the novel centers on that staple of the domestic novel, the cheating husband. Shreve's earlier novel *The Pilot's Wife* (1998) was selected for the Oprah Book Club, and here she seems to be aspiring to an unusual synthesis of the domestic melodrama and the political novel. Shreve's reformulation of the latter modifies the prismatic collectivity that was so important for 1930s writers such as John Dos Passos in *U.S.A.* Her title refers to the beachcombing that unites the two women at the center of the novel – the socialite and the cheated-on wife. The bits and pieces of glass they collect become metaphors for their beautiful individuality, and the final sentence of the novel reinforces this association. The middle-class wife appears in a beatific form appreciated by the boy she has altruistically taken responsibility for raising: "Mrs. Beecher ... standing in the doorway with a white platter in her arms, and even from the beach wagon Alphonse can see how beautiful all the glass is in the sunlight" (376). These gorgeous pieces are cemented together in a memento platter, and an alternate family forms when the two female friends informally adopt Alphonse. This domestic stability resolves the masculine struggles in the workplace. Shreve's emphasis on beauty and perception thus shifts the concerns of the strike novel from action to reflection (literally) from a distance; the beautiful fragments suggest an adaptive response to living with less rather than a struggle for justice. This compensatory aestheticism is a crucial ideological marker of secular stagnation.

The figure of the non-nuclear family as a unit of survival also anchors Pete Hammill's *North River* (2007). Panned in the *New York Times* for its supposed sentimentality about the misery of Irish immigrants, this tenth novel by an acclaimed journalist and longtime New York resident makes more sense if read in relation to other representations of the Depression. Hammill's central concern is actually not ethnicity. The novel's protagonist is a public-spirited doctor who takes charge of a grandson suddenly placed in his care; he hires and falls in love with a tough Sicilian nanny. The novel maps the new routes through the city that the doctor discovers as he shields his household from the FBI and gangsters reminiscent of those populating Billy Bathgate's world. As in other 1930s narratives, this unconventional family provides emotional and material sustenance to persons enduring inexplicable social violence; learning how to cope with reduced expectations of security and how to nurture the young with limited resources are the hero's primary tasks. As a doctor, he is driven toward cure but has to settle for amelioration – a "healthy fatalism," Hammill calls this attitude.[21]

In *North River*, Hammill updates Depression-era ethnic novels such as Pietro di Donato's *Christ in Concrete* (1939) or Henry Roth's *Call It Sleep* (1934). He begins with an ethnic enclave whose immigrant aspirations are dampened by the Depression, but rather than emphasizing interethnic rivalries, he stresses multicultural coexistence and the shared fabrication of the urban tapestry. The Irish Dr. Delaney takes his Spanish-speaking grandson and the Sicilian nanny whom they both come to love to enjoy spaghetti and gelato at his neighborhood restaurant; the Depression is here rethought as the opening up of a panethnic social space organized around shared needs. Unlike Shreve's radiant non-nuclear family, though, Hammill's lacks cash. No wealthy socialite rescues the doctor; his only recourse is the dirty money of mobsters, and his practice flounders because he treats the indigent. Profitability does not promise to rebound in *North River*, and the doctor's lingering wartime injuries suggest militarism will not guarantee recovery. Hammill's novel might not reek of immigrant misery, then, but it does not promise uplift either. The novel pits local solidarity against a stalled recovery.

Contemporary historical fiction set during the Depression most closely approaches the optimism of an uplift narrative when exploring popular consumer culture. Sarah Gruen's *Water for Elephants* (2006) examines this theme in a circus story, and Paulette Jiles's *Stormy Weather* (2007) tackles North Texas horse-racing. In the same vein, Alan Brennert's *Palisades Park* (2013) imagines the transformations of a New Jersey amusement park. At the center of the story is the maturation of young Toni. She idolizes high divers and trains to become one herself, an activity that parallels her post-1945 embrace of civil rights. Far from suggesting vulnerability, Toni's precarious partial employment as french fry vendor, lifeguard, and ultimately diver at the park energizes her – making her an advocate for the inclusion of all Americans in the big tent of consumerism. A similar theme undergirds Brennert's description of the tiki bar that Toni's father lovingly reconstructs from his memories of the war in the Pacific. Personal liberation, social integration, and class mobility all result from a hard-working commitment to consumer pleasures in this novel. The family is driven by a desire to secure access, for instance, to a "kitchen separate from the landlord's downstairs, a back entrance of their own so they could enter and exit with some degree of privacy, and a living room whose windows at night framed the lights of Manhattan, glittering like sequins on an evening dress."[22] Rhapsodizing about domestic comforts, Brennert's novelistic rewrite of the story of mid-century economic life expresses a nostalgia for Keynesian consumerism rather than fear of a crisis and collapse of production. This thinking allows the figuring of the Depression as a thrilling high dive – that is, as a risk rendered pleasurable by the rapidly fulfilled expectation of the diver's rise to the comfortable middle-class surface.

If *Palisades Park* presents one of the most magical imagined solutions to the crisis of the 1930s, then Marilynne Robinson's *Lila* (2014) offers a tough-minded complement to that romance. The third volume of Robinson's Gilead trilogy, *Lila* is narrated from the point of view of the titular orphan. Her sensibility provides a crucial counterpoint to the settled masculine perspectives of other volumes. While *Gilead* (2004) and *Home* (2008) focus on town history and the religious scruples of Lila's eventual husband, the elderly Reverend Ames and his dissatisfied son, *Lila* is a novel of feminine wandering. It begins with Lila's barely comprehended memories of being rescued from neglect and joining a band of migrant laborers. This informal collective eventually disintegrates, and Lila reinvents herself as shopgirl, prostitute, cleaner, drifter, wife, and ultimately mother. The episodes in this tour of women's low-wage labor coalesce around a Biblical passage. Lila ruminates repeatedly on Ezekiel 16:6, "*I passed by thee, and saw thee weltering in thy blood,*" twisting and turning the phrase as she opens herself up from a preoccupation with suffering to a recognition of the care evidenced by the fact of her survival. Acknowledging that she has been the object of care in the past – however dimly recalled – allows Lila to accept herself as beloved and well housed in the present; she also comes to believe herself capable of surviving the imminent death of her child's father. This transformation of the heroine's spiritual life allows her to enter an eschatological time that fortifies her during a period characterized by deprivation.

Despite her provisional acceptance of material shelter, though, Lila always remains a drifter at heart. She nearly leaves Gilead in the company of a boy who has taken refuge in one of her own former hide-aways, and even when she gives birth, she detaches almost immediately – describing her own newborn son as "that orphan he was first he always would be, no matter how they loved him. He'd be no child of hers, otherwise."[23] Robinson's version of the unconventional family, then, does not magically resolve the social crises of the 1930s. The members of her trio of orphans remain crucially alienated from one another, and that is the sign of their belonging to one another. Each of them may privately achieve some grace on the basis of "weltering" in their blood, but their fundamental condition is suffering, drifting, and rumination. In this manner, Robinson develops a downbeat parable for living with the lowered expectations of secular stagnation. While not refusing the allure of beauty, companionship, or domestic consumerism, her heroine sidesteps a narrative teleology that ends in a happy version of the 1950s. As in *Home* (set in 1956), Robinson treats the affluence of the United States at midcentury as the exception to a longer – perhaps cosmic – period of wandering in the Iowa desert, a wandering relieved only by the shared recognition of a profound and existential indebtedness.

Having sifted quite seriously in her two preceding volumes through the moral scruples of white liberals when confronted with the legacies of slavery and the unfinished project of civil rights, Robinson shifts the ground in *Lila* to conditions of existence that she presents as underlying those deeply felt ethical concerns – scenes of extreme economic deprivation. The salvation narrative that civil rights struggles have provided to white Americans is no more sufficient for addressing the economic problems in her trilogy than household comforts are. As a whole Robinson's trilogy closely examines the interlinked problems of racial and economic inequality, but its final volume provides no particular exit strategy. The New Deal feels as distant from its Iowa perspective as do European and Pacific theaters of battle, and she presents altruistic sacrifice for the poor or the enslaved as an intensely conflicted project. Rather than resolving the story of the Depression, then, in an overly easy story of social progress, Robinson strands her readers in an unsparing scene where the survivors of the patriarch's death are themselves already superfluous because they have been orphaned at birth and in perpetuity.

Reflections on the Depression Anti-Epic

As the generation of writers who were adults during the 1930s faded away, the narratives describing this indisputably important decade shifted. The active and personal struggle to survive and high-stakes efforts to combat capitalism or fascism lost their centrality in the story of the Great Depression. Instead, looking back at the 1930s, many later authors find in that period a more quotidian story of social reproduction. They replace the grand struggle to found a modern civilization – that is, the conventional struggle of the epic – with a minor-key accommodation, mitigation, and adaptation to reduced circumstances. Post-1980s stories focused on the intergenerational legacy of the Depression frequently turn, in other words, on the question of how to live with the decay of the institutions forged during the 1930s. They are social novels of the echo and the aftermath, rather than political novels of the struggle.

These retrospective sequels center on motifs that many considered peripheral during the 1930s – mass culture, criminality, and the perspectives of women and children, for instance. Few post-1980s stories of the Depression address the rise of heroic leaders, and social movements are often depicted in the phases of their dissolution or decay. Late-twentieth- and early-twenty-first-century Depression narratives concentrate instead on the small hero who finds a niche in which to ride out a storm. To the extent that these novels do describe a heroic rise to affluence (as, say, in *Billy Bathgate*) this occurs largely outside of the frame of the narrative; contemporary historical novels focused on the 1930s far more often concentrate on the figure of the second-generation heir – using the weak concept of "generation" to draw attention to processes that perpetuate the effects of the crisis in a different register. Geographically, the unconventional families described in these novels generally inhabit small towns or unglamorous peripheries. Their turning points avoid macrocosmic systemic change or climactic battles; they hinge on moments of shifting sensation or drift. These novels thus collectively counsel adjustment to a future that promises the waning – or perhaps implosion – of US political and economic hegemony, and that adjustment looks a lot like keeping one's head down.

In his introduction to the 2008 edition of *The Sublime Object of Ideology*, Slavoj Zizek describes a process of "Ptolemization."[24] When faced with Copernicus's discovery that the planets revolved around the sun, the Ptolemaic astronomers who had advocated a terracentric theory resisted a change to their conceptual system, preferring to create elaborate defenses and supplements rather than moving toward the bolder, simpler, but more shattering Copernican explanation of new data. In like manner, historical novelists since the 1980s tend to look back to the 1930s and Ptolemaically extrapolate from its concerns. In so doing, they sidestep the more disturbing possibility that the world-system has entered a new phase of regime change – one that bids farewell to pax Americana, with all of its flaws, and welcomes in a chaotic interregnum (to borrow Wolfgang Streeck's term[25]). The minor-key historical novels describing the 1930s provide, then, both an analogy for the present crisis and a means of misrecognizing the depth of that crisis. Of course, it remains to be seen whether a new Copernican economic history will ever appear. Until such a moment, though, the story of the 1930s remains a vital resource for exploring the moral, political, and social risks associated with the history of capitalism.

NOTES

1 Thomas E. Hall and J. David Ferguson, "It's Finally Over," *The Great Depression: An International Disaster of Perverse Economic Policies* (Ann Arbor: University of Michigan Press, 1998), 160.

2 Frank G. Steindl, "What Ended the Great Depression? It Was Not World War II," *The Independent Review* 12: 2 (Fall 2007): 179–197.

3 Robert Higgs, "Regime Uncertainty: Why the Great Depression Lasted So Long and Why Prosperity Resumed after the War," *Depression, War, and Cold War: Studies in Political Economy*, Independent Institute (2006): 3–29; Christina D. Romer, "What Ended the Great Depression?" *The Journal of Economic History* 52: 4 (1992): 757–784.

4 Michael Roberts, *The Long Depression: How It Happened, Why It Happened, and What Happens Next* (Chicago: Haymarket, 2016). See also Michael A. Bernstein, "The Great Depression as Historical Problem," *OAH Magazine of History*, 16: 1 (2001): 3–10.

5 Samir Amin, *Re-Reading the Postwar Period: An Intellectual Itinerary* (New York: Monthly Review Press, 1994).

6 Giovanni Arrighi, "American Century: The Making and Remaking of the World Labor Movement," *Transforming the Revolution: Social Movements and the World-System*, ed. Samir Amin (New York: Monthly Review Press, 1990), 55–95.

7 Mark McGurl, *The Program Era: Postwar Fiction and the Rise of Creative Writing* (Cambridge, MA: Harvard University Press, 2011).

8 Leigh Claire La Berge, *Scandals and Abstractions: Financial Fiction of the Long 1980s* (New York: Oxford University Press, 2015).

9 Fredric Jameson, *Postmodernism, or the Cultural Logic of Late Capitalism* (Durham, NC: Duke University Press, 1991).

10 E. L. Doctorow, *Billy Bathgate* (New York: Random House, 1989), 125.

11 www.npr.org/2015/07/24/425892294/fresh-air-remembers-billy-bathgate-author-e-l-doctorow

12 Philip Wegner, *Life Between Two Deaths, 1989–2001: U.S. Culture in the Long 1990s* (Durham, NC: Duke University Press, 2009).

13 Sam Cohen, *After the End of History: American Fiction in the 1990s* (Iowa City: University of Iowa Press, 2009).

14 John Kenneth Galbraith, *The Great Crash, 1929* (1955; New York: Mariner, 2009).

15 Philip Roth, *American Pastoral* (New York: Houghton Mifflin, 1997), 45.

16 Shirley Ann Grau, *The Keepers of the House* (New York: Alfred A. Knopf, 1964), 158.

17 Philip Mirowski, *Never Let a Serious Crisis go to Waste: How Neoliberalism Survived the Financial Meltdown* (New York: Verso, 2013), 173–175.

18 Peter Temin and David Vines, *The Leaderless Economy* (Princeton, NJ: Princeton University Press, 2013).

19 Leo Panitch and Sam Gindin, *The Making of Global Capitalism: The Political Economy of American Empire* (New York: Verso, 213).

20 Anita Shreve, *Sea Glass* (Boston: Little, Brown, 2002), 323.

21 www.independent.com/news/2007/oct/11/pete-hamills-new-novel-emnorth-riverem/; Pete Hammill, *North River* (Boston: Back Bay Books, 2007).

22 Alan Brennert, *Palisades Park* (New York: St. Martins, 2013), 59.

23 Marilynne Robinson, *Lila* (New York: Farrar, Strauss, Giroux, 2014), 256.

24 Slavoj Zizek, *The Sublime Object of Ideology* (1989; New York: Verso, 2008), vii.

25 Wolfgang Streeck, *How Will Capitalism End?: Essays on a Failing System* (New York: Verso, 2016).

FURTHER READING

Anthologies

Aaron, Daniel and Robert Bendiner. Eds. *The Strenuous Decade: A Social and Intellectual Record of the Nineteen-Thirties*. New York: Anchor Books, 1970.

Banks, Ann. Ed. *First-Person America*. New York: Random House, 1980.

Clurman, Harold. Ed. *Famous American Plays of the 1930's*. New York: Laurel, 1980.

Conroy, Jack and Curt Johnson. Eds. *Writers in Revolt: The Anvil Anthology 1933–1940*. New York: Lawrence Hill and Co., 1973.

Filler, Louis. Ed. *The Anxious Years: America in the Nineteen Thirties; a Collection of Contemporary Writings*. New York: Putnam, 1963.

Gregory, Horace. Ed. *New Letters in America*. New York: Norton, 1937.

Hart, Henry. Ed. *American Writers' Congress*. New York: International Publishers, 1935.

Hicks, Granville. Ed. *Proletarian Literature in the United States: An Anthology*. New York: International Publishers, 1935.

Nekola, Charlotte and Paula Rabinowitz. Eds. *Writing Red: An Anthology of American Women Writers, 1930–1940*. New York: Feminist Press, 1987.

North, Joseph. *New Masses: An Anthology of the Rebel Thirties*. New York: International Publishers, 1969.

Phillips, William and Philip Rahv. Eds. *The Partisan Reader: Ten Years of Partisan Review 1934–1944*. New York: Dial Press, 1946.

Salzman, Jack and Barry Wallenstein. Eds. *Years of Protest: A Collection of American Writings of the 1930s*. New York: Pegasus, 1967.

Shannon, David. A. Ed. *The Great Depression*. Upper Saddle River, NJ: Prentice Hall Trade, 1960.

Swados, Harvey. Ed. *The American Writer and the Great Depression*. New York: Macmillan, 1966.

WPA. *American Stuff: An Anthology of Prose and Verse by Members of the Federal Writers' Projects*. New York: Viking, 1936.

Secondary Materials General

Aaron, Daniel. *Writers on the Left: Episodes in American Literary Communism*. New York: Columbia University Press, 1992.

Further Reading

Balthaser, Benjamin. *Anti-Imperalist Modernism: Race and Transnational Culture from the Great Depression to the Cold War*. Ann Arbor: University of Michigan Press, 2015.

Browder, Laura. *Rousing the Nation: Radical Culture in Depression America*. Amherst: University of Massachusetts Press, 2011.

Carpetti, Carla. *Writing Chicago: Modernism, Ethnography and the Novel*. New York: Columbia University Press, 1993.

Cowley, Malcom. *Think Back on Us: A Contemporary Chronicle of the 1930's*. Carbondale: Southern Illinois University Press, 1967.

Denning, Michael. *The Cultural Front: The Laboring of American Culture in the Twentieth Century*. New York: Verso, 1996.

Dickstein, Morris. *Dancing in the Dark: A Cultural History of the Great Depression*. New York: Norton, 2010.

Fiedler, Leslie. "The Beginning of the Thirties: Depression, Return, and Rebirth." *Waiting for the End*. New York: Dell: 1964, 32–50.

"The End of the Thirties: Artificial Paradises and Real Hells." *Waiting for the End*. New York: Dell: 1964, 51–64.

"The Search for the Thirties." *No! in Thunder*. Boston, MA: Beacon, 1960, 161–168.

Irr, Caren. *The Suburbs of Dissent: Cultural Politics in the United States and Canada During the 1930s*. Durham, NC: Duke University Press, 1998.

Kaladjian, Walter. *American Culture between the Wars: Revisionary Modernism and Postmodern Critique*. New York: Columbia University Press, 1994.

Maxwell, William J. *New Negro, Old Left: African American Writing and Communism between the Wars*. New York: Columbia University Press, 1999.

Mullen, Bill V. *Popular Fronts: Chicago and African-American Cultural Politics, 1935–46*. Urbana: University of Illinois Press, 1999.

Mullen, Bill V. and Sherry Linkon. Eds. *Radical Revisions: Rereading 1930s Culture*. Urbana: University of Illinois Press, 1996.

Pells, Richard. *Radical Visions and American Dreams: Culture and Social thought in the Depression Years*. Urbana: University of Illinois Press, 1998.

Phillips, William. "What Happened in the 30's." *Commentary* 34 (1962): 204–212.

Rahv, Philip. "Proletarian Literature: A Political Autopsy." *Southern Review* 4: 3 (Winter 1939): 616–628.

Scandura, Jani. *Down in the Dumps: Place, Modernity, American Depression*. Durham, NC: Duke University Press, 2008.

Shulman, Robert. *The Power of Political Art: The 1930s Literary Left Reconsidered*. Chapel Hill: University of North Carolina Press, 2000.

Staub, Michael. *Voices of Persuasion: Politics of Representation in 1930s America*. New York: Cambridge University Press, 1994.

Stratton, Matthew. *The Politics of Irony in American Modernism*. New York: Fordham University Press, 2013.

Suarez, Juan. *Pop Modernism: Noise and the Reinvention of the Everyday*. Urbana: University of Illinois Press, 2007.

Sussman, Warren. "The Culture of the Thirties." *The Development of an American Culture*. Eds. Stanley Coben and Lorman Ratner. New York: St. Martin's Press, 1983.

Vials, Christopher. *Realism for the Masses: Aesthetics, Popular Front Pluralism, and U.S. Culture, 1935–1947*. Jackson: University Press of Mississippi, 2009.

Wald, Wald. *Writing from the Left: New Essays on Radical Culture and Politics*. New York: Verso, 1994.

Fiction and Poetry

Barnard, Rita. *The Great Depression and the Culture of Abundance: Kenneth Fearing, Nathanael West, and Mass Culture in the 1930s*. New York: Cambridge University Press, 1995.

Bogardus, Ralph F. and Fred Hobson. Eds. *Literature at the Barricades: The American Writer in the 1930s*. Tuscaloosa: University of Alabama Press, 1982.

Bone, Robert. *The Negro Novel in America*. New Haven, CT: Yale University Press, 1970.

Casey, Janet Galligani. Ed. *The Novel and the American Left: Critical Essays on Depression-Era Fiction*. Iowa City: University of Iowa Press, 2004.

Coiner, Constance. *Better Red: The Writing and Resistance of Tillie Olsen and Meridel Le Sueur*. New York: Oxford University Press, 1995.

Cook, Sylvia Jenkins. *From Tobacco Road to Route 66: The Southern Poor White in Fiction*. Chapel Hill: University of North Carolina Press, 1976.

Edmunds, Susan: *Grotesque Relations: Modernist Domestic Fiction and the U.S. Welfare State*. New York: Oxford University Press, 2008.

Entin, Joseph. *Sensational Modernism: Experimental Fiction and Photography in Thirties America*. Chapel Hill: University of North Carolina Press, 2007

Filreis, Alan. *Modernism from Right to Left: Wallace Stevens, the Thirties, and Literary Radicalism*. New York: Cambridge University Press, 1995.

Foley, Barbara. *Radical Representations: Politics and Form in U.S. Proletarian Fiction, 1929–1941*. Durham, NC: Duke University Press, 1993.

French, Warren. *The Social Novel at the End of an Era*. Carbondale, IL: Southern Illinois University Press, 1966.

Gregory, Horace and Marya Zaturenska. *A History of American Poetry 1900–1940*. Harcourt Brace, 1946.

Hapke, Laura. *Daughters of the Great Depression: Women, Work, and Fiction in the 1930s*. Athens: University of Georgia Press, 1995.

Jennison, Ruth. *The Zukofsky Era: Modernism, Margins, and the Avant-Garde*. Baltimore, MD: Johns Hopkins University Press, 2012.

Kazin, Alfred. *On Native Grounds: An Interpretation of Modern American Prose Literature*. 1942. New York: Doubleday & Company, 1956.

McCann, Sean. *Gumshoe America: Hard-Boiled Fiction and the Rise and Fall of New Deal Liberalism*. Durham, NC: Duke University Press, 2000.

Millgate, Michael. *American Social Fiction: James to Cozzens*. Edinburgh, Scotland: Oliver & Boyd, 1964.

Mills, Nathaniel. *Ragged Revolutionaries: The Lumpenproletariat and African-American Marxism in Depression-Era Literature*. Amherst: University of Massachusetts Press, 2017.

Moglen, Seth. *Mourning Modernity: Literary Modernism and the Injuries of American Capitalism*. Palo Alto, CA: Stanford University Press, 2007.

Further Reading

Nelson, Cary Nelson. *Repression and Recovery: Modern American Poetry and Politics of Cultural Memory*. Madison: University of Wisconsin Press, 1991.

Rabinowitz, Paula. *Labor and Desire: Women's Revolutionary Fiction in Depression America*. Chapel Hill: University of North Carolina Press, 1991.

Rideout, Walter. *The Radical Novel in the United States, 1900–1954: Some Interrelations of Literature and Society*. Cambridge, MA: Harvard University Press, 1956.

Scott, William. *Troublemakers: Power, Representation, and the Fiction of the Mass Worker*. New Brunswick, NJ: Rutgers University Press, 2012.

Smethurst, James Edward. *The New Red Negro: The Literary Left and African-American Poetry, 1930–1946*. New York: Oxford University Press, 1999.

Solomon, Eric. "Fiction and the New Deal." *The New Deal*. Eds. John Braeman, Robert H. Bremer and David Brody. Columbus: Ohio State University Press, 1975, 310–327.

Solomon, William. *Literature, Amusement, and Technology in the Great Depression*. New York: Cambridge University Press, 2003.

Steiner, Michael C. Ed. *Regionalists on the Left: Radical Voices from the American Left*. Norman: University of Oklahoma Press, 2013.

Szalay, Michael. *New Deal Modernism: American Literature and the Invention of the Welfare State*. Durham, NC: Duke University Press, 2000.

Takayoshi, Ichiro. *American Writers and the Approach of World War II: A Literary History*. New York: Cambridge University Press, 2015.

Thurston, Michael. *Making Something Happen: American Poetry Between the World Wars*. Chapel Hill: University of North Carolina Press, 2001.

Wixson, Douglas. *Worker-Writer in America: Jack Conroy and the Tradition of Mid-Western Literary Radicalism, 1898–1990*. Urbana: University of Illinois Press, 1994.

Yerkes, Andrew C, *"Twentieth-Century Americanism:" Identity and Ideology in Depression-Era Leftist Fiction*. New York: Routledge, 2013.

Documentary

Allred, Jeff. *American Modernism and Depression Documentary*. New York: Oxford University Press 2009.

Magione, Jerre. *The Dream and the Deal: The Federal Writers' Project 1935–1943*. New York: Syracuse University Press, 1996.

Rabinowitz, Paula. *They Must Be Represented: The Politics of Documentary*. New York: Verso, 1994.

Stott, William. *Documentary Expression and Thirties America*. New York: Oxford University Press, 1976.

Drama and Performance

Batiste, Stephanie. *Darkening Mirrors: Imperial Representation in Depression-Era African American Performance*. Durham, NC: Duke University Press, 2012.

Clurman, Harold. *The Fervent Years: The Group Theatre and the Thirties*. New York: Harcourt Brace, 1975.

Further Reading

Dinerstein, Joel. *Swinging the Machine: Modernity, Technology, and African American Culture Between the World Wars.* Amherst: University of Massachusetts Press, 2007.

Fearnow, Mark. *The American Stage and the Great Depression: A Cultural History of the Grotesque.* New York: Cambridge University Press, 1997.

Hilmelstein, Morgan Yale. *Drama Was a Weapon: The Left-Wing Theatre In New York, 1929–1941.* New Brunswick, NJ: Rutgers University Press, 1963.

Rabkin, Gerald. *Drama and Commitment: Politics in the American Theatre of the Thirties.* Bloomington: Indiana University Press, 1964.

Saal, Ilka. *New Deal Theatre: The Vernacular Tradition in American Political Theatre.* New York: Palgrave Macmillan, 2007.

Sporn, Paul. *Against Itself: The Federal Theater and Writers' Projects in the Midwest.* Detroit, MI: Wayne State University Press, 1995.

Journals and Literary Criticism

Bloom, James. *Left Letters: The Culture Wars of Mike Gold and Joseph Freeman.* New York: Columbia University Press, 1992.

Gilbert, James Burkhart. *Writers and Partisans: A History of Literary Radicalism in America.* New York: John Wiley & Sons, 1968.

Hyman, Stanley Edgar. *The Armed Vision: A Study in the Methods of Literary Criticism.* New York: Vintage, 1961.

Murphy, James. *The Proletarian Moment: The Controversy Over Leftism in Literature.* Urbana: University of Illinois Press, 1991.

Selected Historical Studies

Allen, Frederick Lewis. *Since Yesterday: The 1930s in America.* New York: Harper and Row, 1940.

Bendiner, Robert. *Just Around the Corner.* New York: Harper and Row, 1967.

Fraser, Steve and Gary Gerstle. Eds. *The Rise and Fall of the New Deal Order.* Princeton, NJ: Princeton University Press, 1989.

Galbraith, John Kenneth, *The Great Crash of 1929.* New York: Mariner, 2009.

Kempton, Murray. *Part of Our Time: Some Ruins and Monuments of the Thirties.* New York: New York Review of Books, 1998.

McElvaine, Robert S. *The Great Depression: American 1929–1941.* New York: Random House, 2009.

Parrish, Michael E. *Anxious Decades: America in Prosperity and Depression 1920–1941.* New York: W. W. Norton & Company, 1994.

Schlesinger, Arthur. *The Age of Roosevelt, 3 vols.* New York: Mariner Books, 2003.

Wecter, Dixon. *The Age of the Great Depression 1929–1941.* New York: Prentice Hall, 1948.

Primary Materials
Autobiography

Eastman, Max. *Love and Revolution: My Journey Through an Epoch.* New York: Random House, 1964.

Herbst, Josephine. "The Starched Blue Sky of Spain." *The Noble Savage* 1 (March 1960).

Hicks, Granville. *Part of the Truth: An Autobiography*. New York: Harcourt Brace & World, 1965.

Howe, Irving. "A Memoir of the Thirties." *Steady Work: Essays in the Politics of Democratic Revolution*. New York: Harvest, 1967.

Hughes, Langston. *I Wonder as I Wander: An Autobiographical Journey. 1956*. New York: Hill and Wang, 1993.

Josephson, Matthew. *Infidel in the Temple: A Memoir of the Nineteen Thirties*. New York: Knopf, 1967.

Kazin, Alfred. *Starting out in the Thirties*. New York: Little Brown, 1965.

MacDonald, Dwight. "Politics Past." *Memoirs of a Revolutionist*. New York: Farrar, Straus Cudahy, 1957.

McCarthy, Mary. "My Confession." *Encounter* (February 1954): 43–56.

Wright, Richard. *The God that Failed*. Ed. Richard H. Crossman. New York: Columbia University Press, 2001, 115–162.

Literary Reportage and Photographic Journalism

Adamic, Louis. *My America, 1928–1938*. New York: Harper and Brothers, 1938.

Agee, James and Walker Evans. *Let Us Now Praise Famous Men. 1942*. New York: Mariner Books, 2001.

Anderson, Sherwood. *Puzzled America*. New York: Charles Scribner's Sons, 1935.

Appel, Benjamin. *The People Talk: Voices from the Great Depression*. New York: E. P. Dutton, 1940.

Asch, Nathan. *The Road: In Search of America*. New York: W. W. Norton, 1937.

Caldwell, Erskine and Margaret Bourke-White. *You Have Seen Their Faces*. Athens: University of Georgia Press, 1995.

Dreiser, Theodore. *Tragic America*. New York: Horace Liveright, .

Evans, Walker. *American Photographs*. New York: Museum of Modern Art, 2012.

Gellhorn, Martha. *The Trouble I've Seen*. London: Eland Books, 2013.

Lange, Dorothea and Paul Taylor. *An American Exodus*. Paris, France: Jean-Michel Place, 1999.

Lynd Robert and Helen. *Middletown in Transition: A Study in Cultural Conflicts*. New York: Harcourt Brace, 1937.

MacLeish, Archibald. *Land of the Free*. Cambridge, MA: Da Capo Press, 1977.

McKenney, Ruth. *Industrial Valley*. New York: Harcourt Brace, 1939.

Rorty, James. *Where Life is Better: An Unsentimental American Journey*. London: Forgotten Books, 2017.

Seldes, Gilbert. *The Years of the Locust*. New York: Little Brown & Co., 1933.

Wilson, Edmund. *The American Earthquake: A Documentary of the Twenties and Thirties*. New York: Farrar, Straus and Giroux, 1958.

Wright, Richard and Edwin Rosskam. *Twelve Million Black Voices*. New York: Basic Books, 2008.

Literary Criticism of the 1930s

Burke, Kenneth. *Counter-Statement. 1931*. Berkeley: University of California Press, 1968.

Calverton, V.F. *The Liberation of American Literature*. New York: Charles Scribner's Sons, 1932.

Dahlberg, Edward. *Can These Bones Live*. Ann Arbor: University of Michigan Press, 1967.

Gold, Michael. *The Hollow Men*. New York: International Publishers, 1941.

Hicks, Granville. *The Great Tradition: An Interpretation of American Literature Since the Civil War*. New York: Macmillan, 1933.

Farrell, James T. *A Note on Literary Criticism*. New York: Columbia University Press, 1993.

Matthiessen, F. O. *American Renaissance: Art and Expression in the Age of Emerson and Whitman*.

Ransom, John Crowe et al. *I'll Take My Stand: The South and the Agrarian Tradition*. Baton Rouge: Louisiana State Press, 1978.

The World's Body. Baton Rouge: Louisiana State Press, 1968.

Rourke, Constance. *American Humor: A Study of the National Character*. New York: Harcourt, 1931.

Tate, Allen. *Reactionary Essays on Poetry and Ideas*. New York: Scribner's and Sons, 1936.

Wilson, Edmund. *The Shores of Light: A Literary Chronicle of the Twenties and Thirties*. New York: Farrar Straus and Young, 1952.

Winters, Yvor. *Maule's Curse: Seven Studies in the History of American Obscurantism*. New York: New Directions, 1938.

INDEX

Index

Carby, Hazel, 186, 188–189
Cather, Willa
  The Professor's House, 155
censorship, 101–104, 120, 222
Chandler, Raymond, 214–215
  The Big Sleep, 214
  Farewell My Lovely, 214–215
  The High Window, 214
  parodies of, 215
  style, 215
  "The Simple Art of Murder," 208–209
characterization
  in historical fiction, 182–184
  in theater, 117
Chicago, IL, 136, 138, 173
childbirth, 140, 158
Chinese American writers, 167, 174
Christian Eastern European writers, 165
cinematography, 94
circus, 220–222, 227–229
Civil War (USA), 150–153, 185–188
class status, 130, 162
class struggle. *See also* ethnic-racial solidarity
  in literature, 136–137, 162–163
  in poetry, 77–82, 84, 88–89
  in Sacco-Vanzetti case, 67
  in theater, 113–114, 118–119
  of workers, 72–73
Clurman, Harold, 113, 118
Coles, Robert, 92
collective validity and art, 37–39
comedy
  as communication path, 229–230
  effects on readers, 224–226, 229–230
  jokers, 229–231
  on racism, 149
  seriocomic examples, 149, 215
  theatrical techniques, 112
Communism
  disillusionment with, 115
  dismissal of, 27–28, 32–33, 129
  literary portrayal of, 58–62
  in literary radicalism, 22, 24, 29–30,
    32–33, 45–46
Communist Party (CPUSA)
  African Americans and, 170–171, 173
  disillusionment with, 138
  negative aspects, 28
  nonmembers, 22, 67, 172
  and proletarian writers, 127
  and radical writers, 33, 67, 172
  and Soviet Union, 23, 33
  support by intellectuals, 18, 45

support for workers, 73, 170–171
  in USA election, 45
Coney Island, 222, 225–226
Congress of American Writers, 39
Congress of Industrial Organizations (CIO),
  73, 163, 169–170
Conn, Peter, 24–25, 27, 29
  American 1930s: A Literary History, The,
    24–25, 27, 29
Conroy, Jack, 127–133, 138
  The Disinherited, 12, 133–135
conservative views. *See* Right views
consumerism, 2, 200–202, 244, 246–247
contemporary fiction on 1930s, 15–16,
  234–235, 237, 241–242
Cowley, Malcolm, 138, 142
crash narratives, 243
crime fiction, 14
  controversy about, 208–209
  detective characterization in, 209–211,
    214–215
  evil conduct, question of, 14, 212–213
  femme fatale in, 210–212
  1930s examples, 210–214
  post-1930s examples, 214–215
  seriocomedy in, 215
  victim narratives, 211–214
criminality, and business, 239–240
critique methods and issues, 85, 102–103
cultural commitment, 23–25
cultural front, 32, 45, 115, 127, 171
cultural workers, 22–23, 27, 31, 115, 142
Culture and the Crisis (pamphlet-manifesto),
  18, 45
Cummings, E. E., 220–222
  "The Adult, the Artist, and the Circus,"
    219–222
  "Coney Island," 219, 222
Cunard, Nancy
  Negro Anthology Made By Nancy Cunard, 82

Daily Worker, The, 175
Davidson, Donald, 42
death-defiance, 221
deception of masses, 2–3, 37, 199
Denning, Michael, 6, 31–32, 115, 121, 136,
  169, 187
  *Cultural Front: The Laboring of American
    Culture in the Twentieth Century, The*, 6,
    31–32
detective fiction. *See* crime fiction
Dewey, John, 49–51
  Art as Experience, 49–51

Index

dialogue, 117, 148–149
Dickstein, Morris, 6, 24–29
  Dancing in the Dark: A Cultural History of the Great Depression, 6, 24–29
di Donato, Pietro, 157
  Christ in Concrete, 9, 59–62, 157–159, 246
direct address, 84–85
direct citation, 80–82
disciplines in scholarship, 20, 34
Dixon, Thomas
  The Flaming Sword, 186, 189
Döblin, Alfred
  Berlin Alexanderplatz, 97, 102, 104–105
Doctorow, E. L.
  Billy Bathgate, 15, 239–240
  The Book of Daniel, 8–9
documentaries, 5–7, 10–11
  boundary shifting in, 100, 102
  challenges, 93
  description and motivation, 92–94, 96, 107
  vs. entertainment, 103
  as fictional constructions, 105–107
  power of images in, 95–96, 106–107
  as radical intervention, 101
  Steinbeck, John and, 10–11, 56, 94–100, 105–106
  as witness, 106–107
documentary materials, 67–69, 76–83, 97–98, 104–105, 141–142
domestic themes, 202–204, 244–245
Dos Passos, John, 9, 18, 55, 57, 67–69
  The 42nd Parallel, 4, 55, 98, 104, 135
  Facing the Chair: Story of the Americanization of Two Foreign-born Workmen, 67
  "Is the 'Realistic' Theatre Obsolete?," 219–220
  U.S.A., 57, 67–69
Du Bois, W. E. B.
  Black Reconstruction, 185–187, 189
Duffus, R. L.
  Books: Their Place in a Democracy, 201

Eastern European writers, 165
economic debates on Great Depression
  centrist, 235–236
  radical, 236–237
economic history and historical fiction, 15–16, 234–235
  connection between, 237
  minor-key response, 248–249
  in 1980s, 235, 238–240
  in 1990s and beyond, 235, 240–242

post-1980s, 235, 248–249
after 2008 crisis, 244–248
Eldridge, David, 24–25, 27, 29
  American Culture in the 1930s, 24–25, 27, 29
Eliot, T. S., 42, 230
  The Use of Poetry & The Use of Criticism, 218
  The Waste Land, 45, 83, 218
Ellis, Brett Easton
  American Psycho, 238
Ellison, Ralph, 33, 181
  Invisible Man, 180–181
  as literary critic, 182–185, 188–189
  "Mister Toussan," 184–185
Endore, Guy
  Babouk, 187–188
entertainment, 199, 213–214, 218. *See also* amusements, public; popular fiction
  circus, 220–222
  experimental writers for, 14–15, 218–219, 223–226
  mass media, 2, 219
  theater, 11, 111–112, 115, 120–121, 219
episodic literature, 7, 12, 133–134, 147–149
escapism, 14, 26, 184, 203. *See also* popular fiction
ethical questions, 6, 14, 195, 210, 212, 230
ethnic-racial literature, 13, 162–163. *See also* minority literature and sexuality
  African American (*see* African Americans)
  Asian American, 165–166, 174
  capitalism in, 168–171
  contemporary, 244–246
  cultural front for, 171–178
  Eastern European American, 165
  Italian American, 59–62, 165
  Jewish American, 165, 174–177
  Mexican American, 166
  as proletarian, 162–164, 177–178
  race radicalism in, 13, 163–164, 177–178
  Slovakian American, 162–163
  writers of, 164–168, 174–175
ethnic-racial solidarity, 13, 118–119, 164, 168–171, 173, 175–177, 191, 246
ethnic slurs, 162–163
European aesthetic influences, 64, 72, 97, 113
Evans, Walker, 92, 101
  Let Us Now Praise Famous Men, 95
evil conduct, propensity for, 14, 212–213
experience
  as goal for audience, 219–220, 222
  as literary material, 8, 13, 42–43, 75–76, 133–134, 138, 166, 172

Index

Index

Index

Index

realist fiction. *See* popular fiction
Reconstruction, 185–187, 189
"Red Decade," 29
Regionalism, 43
regional literature, 62, 64
religion, 86
  effect on characters, 60, 147, 151, 155,
    158–160
  Jewish, 155–158, 175
  Puritan heritage, 160
reportage, 98
revolution, 27
  Bolshevik, 34
  Dewey's aesthetic theory, 51
  failure of, 192
  future, 192, 194
  Haitian, 184–185, 187, 190–191, 193–194
  justification for, 192
  in literature, 58–59, 96, 177, 189–194
  Marxism on, 191–193
  in poetry, 85–87
  strategies for, 190–191
  as tricky goal, 103
Reznikoff, Charles, 77–78
  Testimony, 10, 77–78
  *Testimony: The United States (1885-1915)
    Recitative*, 77
rhymes, 87
Rice, Elmer, 102
  We, the People, 122
Richter, Conrad
  The Trees, 183
Rideout, Walter, 29–31, 134
  *Radical Novel in the U.S., 1900-1954:
    Some Interrelations of Literature and
    Society, The*, 29–31
Right views
  of New Deal artistic programs, 50
  of political aesthetics, 7, 39–44
Rivera, Diego, 103–104
Roberts, Michael
  The Long Depression, 243
Robinson, Marilynne
  Lila, 16, 247–248
Rockefeller Center, 103–104
romances. *See* popular romance
Romer, Paul, 236
Roosevelt, Franklin Delano, 48, 93–94, 119
Roth, Henry
  Call It Sleep, 19, 155–158, 246
Roth, Philip
  American Pastoral, 241–242
Rubin, Joan Shelley, 201

Rukeyser, Muriel, 78–82
  "George Robinson: Blues," 80–82
  "The Book of the Dead," 10, 78–82
  U.S. 1, 78

Saal, Ilka, 11, 111
Sacco and Vanzetti case, 6, 18, 59, 67–68, 80
San Francisco News, 97
Saroyan, William
  "Aspirin is a Member of the N.R.A.," 3–4
  "The Daring Young Man on the Flying
    Trapeze," 228
satire, 119–120, 141, 146, 234
Saturday Review of Literature, 206
Schiller, Friedrich, 37, 49–50
Schuyler, George
  Black No More, 146, 149
Scott, Sir Walter, 180, 182
Scott, William, 192
"Scottsboro boys" case, 80, 82–83, 114
secular stagnation, 236, 243, 245, 247
Seldes, Gilbert, 199
September 11, 2001 events, 240–241
sexuality in minority literature, 12–13
  in 1920s upper class, 155
  sex-race entanglements, 146–147, 149–155
  sexual Freudian tale, 155–158
  sexual violence, 160–161
  temptations in, 158–159
Shreve, Anita
  Sea Glass, 15, 244–245
Sifton, Claire and Paul
  1931, 112–113
signage, 101
Sklar, George
  Stevedore, 118–119
Slade, Caroline
  Sterile Sun, 98
slave revolts, 186–187, 189–190
slavery, 151–153, 168, 180, 185
Slovakians, 162–163
Smedley, Agnes
  Daughter of Earth, 138
social democracy, 6, 32
social function
  of art, 46
  of literature, 59, 96
  of performance-based literature, 15,
    224–226, 230
socialism, 19, 172
social justice. *See* activism, leftist; literary
    radicalism, debates
social realism, 93

269

Cambridge Companions to...

AUTHORS

TOPICS